Modern Panama

Few have a complete understanding of the recent history of Panama, markedly since the signing of the Carter-Torrijos Treaty in 1977. Although the treaty set the stage for the country to finally control all of its territory, little is known about how Panama has fared, both as a manager of a major waterway and as a sovereign nation in a unique region. Authors Michael L. Conniff and Gene E. Bigler seek to fill this major gap in Latin American history with *Modern Panama*, a thorough account of the recent political and economic developments in Panama. Despite the country's continued struggle with political corruption, Conniff and Bigler argue that changes since the turnover of the Canal have been largely positive, and Panama has emerged into the twenty-first century as a stable, functioning democracy with a growing economy, improved Canal management, and a higher standard of living.

Michael L. Conniff is Professor Emeritus of History at San José State University. His recent publications include *A New History of Modern Latin America* (2017, with Lawrence Clayton and Susan Gauss), *Panama and the United States*, 3rd ed. (2012), *Populism in Latin America* (2012), and *Black Labor on a White Canal* (1985).

Gene E. Bigler is a retired US Foreign Service Officer who worked on the final transition of the Panama Canal from the US to Panamanian ownership. He has also taught political science and public policy analysis at The Johns Hopkins University, Nitze School of Advanced International Studies, the Instituto de Estudios Superiores de Administracion (IESA) in Caracas, Venezuela, and at other institutions in the USA and Latin America.

Modern Panama

From Occupation to Crossroads of the Americas

MICHAEL L. CONNIFF
San José State University, California

GENE E. BIGLER
Independent Scholar, Stockton, California

CAMBRIDGE
UNIVERSITY PRESS

CAMBRIDGE
UNIVERSITY PRESS

University Printing House, Cambridge CB2 8BS, United Kingdom

One Liberty Plaza, 20th Floor, New York, NY 10006, USA

477 Williamstown Road, Port Melbourne, VIC 3207, Australia

314–321, 3rd Floor, Plot 3, Splendor Forum, Jasola District Centre, New Delhi – 110025, India

79 Anson Road, #06–04/06, Singapore 079906

Cambridge University Press is part of the University of Cambridge.

It furthers the University's mission by disseminating knowledge in the pursuit of education, learning, and research at the highest international levels of excellence.

www.cambridge.org
Information on this title: www.cambridge.org/9781108476669
DOI: 10.1017/9781108612449

First published 2019

Printed in the United Kingdom by TJ International Ltd. Padstow Cornwall

A catalogue record for this publication is available from the British Library.

ISBN 978-1-108-47666-9 Hardback
ISBN 978-1-108-70119-8 Paperback

Dedicated to Mike's wife Anne and son Miguel
and to Gene's wife Karoline and son Kenneth

Contents

List of Figures and Tables — *page* xi
Prologue — xiii
Acknowledgments — xviii

1 Introduction to Modern Panama — 1
Signing Ceremony for the 1977 Carter-Torrijos Treaties — 1
Early Twentieth Century — 3
Postwar Development — 7
Troubles and Treaties — 9
Danse Macabre: The Military in Power — 13
The Carter-Torrijos Treaties and the Panama Canal Act — 19
Panamanian National Identity — 21
Panama and the Zonians — 25

PART I

Introduction to Part I — 29

2 The 1980s: A Halting Transition toward Democracy — 31
Funeral for General Omar Torrijos — 31
Premature Transition to Democracy — 32
Resurgence of the Guard — 37
1984 Presidential Election and Ardito Barletta Administration — 41
The Noriega Crisis of 1987–89 and the National Civic Crusade — 48
Assessing Blame — 51
Canal Transition — 54
Reversion — 59

Panamanianizing the Canal 62
Panama's Economy in the 1980s 68
The Christmas Invasion and Aftermath 71

3 The Endara Administration: Civilians Learned to Prevail 72
Secret US Pre-Invasion Swearing-In of Endara 72
The Endara Administration, Year One 73
Postmortem on 1989 Invasion 78
Endara on His Own, 1991–94 80
Electoral Reforms and Outcomes 85
Panama's Role in Canal Management 89
Panama Rebounded 95

4 The Pérez Balladares Administration: Return of the PRD 98
The Pérez Balladares Inauguration 98
The Pérez Balladares Administration 99
Reversion Continued 106
Final Year of ARI under Ardito Barletta 112
Canal Management 114
Final Years of the Panama Canal Commission 121
Multinational Counter-Narcotics Center 123
1999 Election 125

PART II

Introduction to Part II 129

5 The Moscoso Administration: Millennial Transitions 133
Turnover of Panama Canal 133
Tough Start for the First Woman in Charge 136
Backroom Politics and Overcoming a Troubled Start 140
Not Quite the End of the "Special Relationship" 144
The Special Relationship Became a Security Partnership 147
Getting the Economy Rolling and the Free Trade Route to Globalization 151
A Maritime Strategy Finally Emerged 156
Adjusting the Social Development Agenda 159
A Scandal-Strewn Path to the 2004 Election 162
2004 Election 166

6 The Torrijos Administration: Uneven Progress Spread Discontent 170
Martín Torrijos's Inaugural Address 170
A Torrijos Rode Again 172
Construction Drove the Boom 176

Reform Aftershocks Ended the Honeymoon 177
Panama Strove for Global Stature 180
Bush's Refuge in Latin America 184
Poisoned Drugs and More Storm Clouds 186
More Uneven Progress on Human Development 189
The Boom Became More Maritime 190
More Spillover from the Dangerous Neighborhood 192
Politics in the Mud: the 2009 Election 194

7 Panama's Canal: Better than Ever 200
Kick-Off of New Locks Project 200
Panamanianizing the Asset 202
Safer Transits and Getting Noticed 204
Market Responsiveness and Canal Revenue 207
Continuous Modernization 209
Making the Canal More than a Passageway 212
Putting Planning on Steroids 216
A Right-Size Expansion Plan 219
A Really Big Ditch 222
From Engineering Wonder to Business Juggernaut 229

8 The Martinelli Administration: Trouble in Boom Times 232
A "Fast and Furious" President Took the Reins 232
A Different Kind of Leadership? 236
Doing Business in a Tough Neighborhood 241
The Administration Took a Hard Right Turn 245
The People Pushed Back, Again and Again 249
Rivalries and Ambitions Shook Up the Government 252
Lopsided Economic Growth Continued 256
Corruption Undermined the Plans 260
The 2014 Election: Voters Insisted on Alternation 264

9 The Varela Administration: Toward a More Humane Society 272
Inauguration of Canal Expansion, June 2016 272
Varela Turned the Tables on His Predecessor 273
The Seventh Summit of the Americas and Adjusting Global Roles 279
Unfinished Business: Holding Martinelli & Co. Responsible 281
Building Out the Centerport: Spokes of the Hub of the Americas 286

Colon in the Spotlight at Last 294
Corruption Drew Unwanted Attention 297
The Challenges of Achieving Social Progress 302
Political Disarray on the Road to the 2019 Elections 305

10 Conclusions 311
A Fourteen-Day Tour of Panama 311
Looking Back, 1980–2018 314
Restoring Democracy and Human Rights, Dismantling the Army 315
Managing the Canal and Its Expansion 317
Growing the Economy toward the Hub, Boosting Standards of Living 319
Forging Broader International Roles, Attracting Foreigners 322
Vouchsafing Nationhood 325

Interviews by Authors 328
Unpublished Documentary Sources 330
Bibliography 332
Index 340

Figures and Tables

FIGURES

0.1 Map of Panama *page* xv
1.1 1977 Carter-Torrijos Treaties signing 2
1.2 Presidents Harmodio Arias and Franklin Delano Roosevelt 6
1.3 Map of Canal Zone 10
1.4 Students with flag in 1964 11
1.5 Torrijos with crowds 17
2.1 Ardito Barletta in 1984 42
3.1 1994 sample ballot 88
4.1 Pérez Balladares and Jacques Santer 100
5.1 Canal turnover in 1999 135
5.2 Mireya Moscoso at Summit of the Americas 136
5.3 Centennial Bridge 163
6.1 Presidents Torrijos and Bush 172
6.2 Presidents Torrijos and Carter inaugurate Canal expansion 181
7.1 Annual transits and tonnage 205
7.2 Locks diagrams 224
8.1 Martinellis and Obamas 234
8.2 Diablo Rojo Bus 240
8.3 José Domingo Arias at Superior Electoral Tribunal 265
9.1 Varela, St. Malo, and Obama 276
10.1 Illustrated map 312
10.2 Crossroads of the Americas 319

TABLES

2.1 Panamanianization of the Canal Work Force, 1979–90 page 63
2.2 Gross Income to Panama 1987 66
5.1 Access to Sewage and Refuse Services in Panama by Poverty Level 160
7.1 Major Modernization Projects, 1997 to 2010 211

Prologue

On the eve of the transfer of the Panama Canal from US to Panamanian ownership, political scientist Mark Falcoff published a pessimistic book, with the subtitle, *What Happens When the United State Gives a Small Country What It Wants?*[1] In it he argued that Panamanians would mismanage the Canal and fall to fighting among themselves over the spoils of the former Canal Zone. Democracy, the economy, social well-being, and even national harmony would be lost because of the misguided 1977 treaties. Many of his informants were prominent Panamanians worried over the historic events about to occur. Meanwhile, the United States would give up a valuable asset for naught, a lose-lose outcome.

Our book looks back over the period preceding Falcoff's to assess the quality of his evidence and then at the next twenty years of Panama's history, allowing us to judge whether his predictions came true. In brief, we find that his reading of the pre-turnover years overlooked positive developments in the political, economic, and social realms that should have forecast a more positive future, for the Canal and the nation itself. Then, our account of the post-turnover years shows consolidation of democratic government, a booming economy, technological prowess by elites in the public and private sectors, and, most surprising of all, improved Canal management that resulted in Panama becoming a hemispheric crossroads. The United States reaped applause for ending a colonialist enclave and shedding a strategic vulnerability. In other words, a win-win outcome.

[1] Mark Falcoff, *Panama's Canal: What Happens When the United States Gives a Small Country What It Wants*. Washington, DC: AEI Press, 1998.

Had Panama not remained a liberal democracy, these achievements may not have occurred and Falcoff's predictions might have materialized. But in fact, the nation continued constitutional traditions laid down in the previous century, interrupted only by the 1968–89 military dictatorship. A recent study of 178 governments around the world found Panama ranked forty-seventh on a range of measures of "liberal democracy." Its strong showing owed much to the quality of its elections.[2] This book attempts to explain how Panama achieved these improvements over the last generation. Our concluding chapter takes up these matters again.

According to recent global surveys, respondents in Panama ranked quite high, 27th out of 156 nations, on five measures of perceived well-being, or the "happiness index." Among Latin American countries, Panama came in behind only Costa Rica, Mexico, and Chile. Panama's rankings were especially high for purpose (satisfaction in employment) and physical well-being (good health). These outcomes seem to reflect the fact that Panama's job market has been robust due to economic growth rates of between 5 and 10 percent annually during the past decade and a half. People feel good about their work. Also, Panamanians enjoy a benign tropical climate and efficient public health care. Compared with results of a 1980 survey, revealing that 67 percent of rural and 43 percent of urban Panamanians did not earn enough to satisfy their nutritional needs, the recent findings show an extraordinary advance in people's standards of living.[3]

Panamanians express optimism over having gained control over their territory and destiny. It was not always so. For three centuries Panama formed part of the Spanish empire and was subject to close supervision because of the huge amount of Peruvian silver transported across the Isthmus, from the Pacific to the Atlantic, en route to Spain. Then, during most of the nineteenth century, Panama was a province of Colombia, governed by politicians in distant Bogota. On several occasions, they

[2] V-Dem Institute, "Democracy for All? V-Dem Annual Report," (Gothenburg: University of Gothenburg, 2018).

[3] J. Helliwell, R. Layard, and J. Sachs, *World Happiness Report* (New York: Sustainable Development Solutions Network, 2018). For the 1980 study, see Andrew Zimbalist and John Weeks, *Panama at the Crossroads: Economic Development and Political Change in the Twentieth Century* (Berkeley & Los Angeles, 1991), 124–27. Cf. also the United Nations Development Program, *U.N. Human Development Report for 2015* (New York: United Nations, 2015).

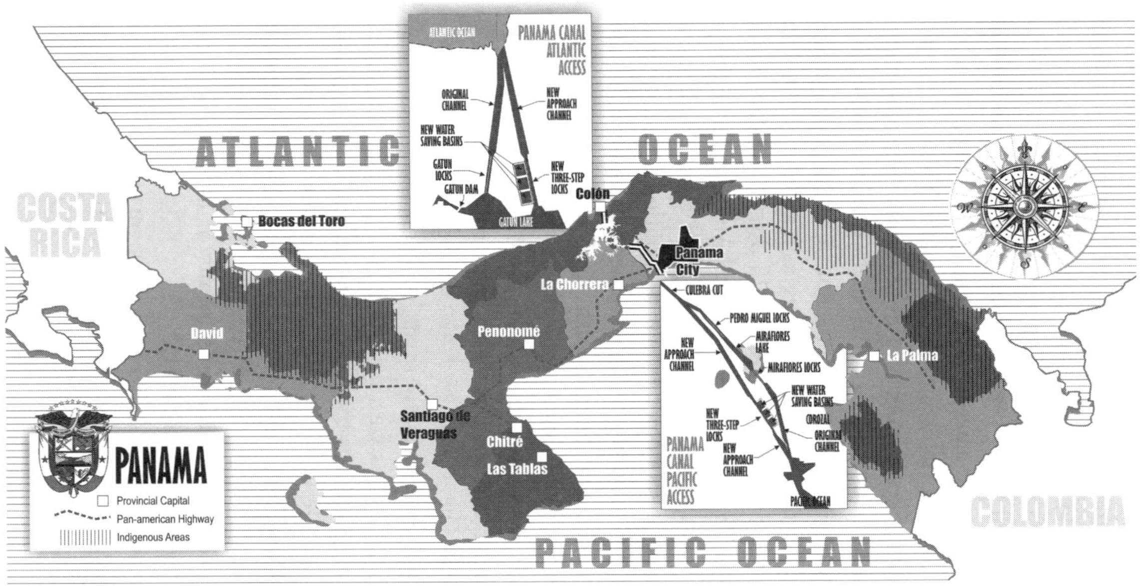

FIGURE 0.1 Map of Panama. Courtesy of Roberto Radrigan.

attempted to break away but failed, the latest during the War of a Thousand Days (1899–1902).

Finally, the United States, which abetted Panama's separation from Colombia in 1903, took choice lands in the country's midsection to build and operate the Panama Canal. Ensconced in a 500+ square-mile zone entirely controlled by the United States, the Canal split Panama in half and made integrated development impossible.[4]

The 1977 Panama Canal Treaty began a process of turning the Canal over to Panama by 1999, setting the stage for the country to finally control all its territory and benefit fully from its geographical location. This book portrays just how Panamanians took advantage of this newfound independence.

Panamanians gained a deeper sense of their own nationhood and identity after the transfer of the Canal. For most of the twentieth century, they struggled to assert themselves as "a nation, not just a Canal." While this was true, the outside world usually treated Panama as simply the place the US Canal crossed Central America. Since the year 2000, Panamanians have managed the Canal with great efficiency and turned it into an engine of economic growth and national integration.

Even before the Canal turnover, the government inaugurated a superb museum, the Museo del Canal Interoceánico de Panamá, to portray the evolution of the Isthmus as a transit route, first by mule trains, then by steam railroad, and finally by the Canal itself. This signaled that Panamanians embraced and took pride in their role as a vital link in global supply chains. The Canal had always been a key feature of Panama's self-identity, as expressed in its coat of arms: "Pro mundi beneficio." They did not feel as warmly toward the surrounding military bases – indeed, on two occasions the legislature rejected base expansion.

This book recounts how in a brief period Panamanians have transformed their nation from a simple maritime path between two seas to a complex hub for the movement of people, goods, knowledge, and services in many directions via multiple means of exchange. Nobody today claims that Panama is just a canal.

Despite these positive assertions, this book does not claim that Panama is a totally happy place, a kind of Shangri-la or paradise on earth.[5] As a

[4] This story is told succinctly in Michael L. Conniff, *Panama and the United States*, 3rd ed. (Athens: University of Georgia Press, 2012).

[5] Despite this disclaimer, Panama ranked at or near the top of recent studies of happiness. See the Gallup-Healthways Global Well-Being Index, www.healthways.com/blog/topic/global-report

relatively young nation, with at least three moments of independence (from Spain in 1821, from Colombia in 1903, and from the United States in 1999), it has serious challenges of many sorts and must make its way through global affairs without the protection of a superpower. This book also examines those problems and the many risks Panamanians face in coming years. We remain optimistic that they will surmount them, but the means to do so are not always obvious nor are the results guaranteed. We return to these questions in the concluding chapter.

Acknowledgments

Many colleagues in Panama, the United States, and elsewhere helped us research and write this book. We gratefully thank the following persons in Panama: Nicolás Ardito Barletta, Alberto Aleman Zubieta, Eloy Alfaro, Samuel Lewis Navarro, Juan David Morgan, Jorge Luis Quijano, Omar Jaén Suárez, Eduardo Vallarino, Alfredo Castillero Calvo, Berta Thayer, Ana Elena Porras, Rodolfo Sabonge, colleagues in the Club Rotario de Panamá, and the persons listed as interviewees in "sources."

In the United States, we thank Frederick Becker, Ambler Moss, Richard Millett, David McCullough, Orlando Pérez, Peggy Scranton, Richard Wainio, Joseph Reeder, Linda Watt, Michael Donoghue, and two anonymous manuscript reviewers.

Special thanks to Paul Losch, Head Librarian for the Latin American and Caribbean Collection, for his help accessing rare materials in the Panama Canal Museum Collection, Department of Special and Area Studies Collections, George A. Smathers Libraries, University of Florida. We also thank Philip Williams, Director of the University of Florida Center for Latin American Studies, for invitations to the 2014 Panama Considered Conference, that began the process of writing this book. And our warm acknowledgement of Adrienne Samos, who managed the Spanish edition of our book in Panama, including its translation.

Besides those who contributed to this book, we thank the many friends, colleagues, and mentors who have educated us about Panama for more than a half century. Conniff studied at the University of Panama and began his professional career as an employee of USAID in 1965. He lived there for over three years as a Fulbright professor and visiting researcher, and is author of books, articles, and chapters on Panama. In

1968, Bigler decided to top off his Fulbright studies in Ecuador by taking his bride on a honeymoon in Panama, plus to compare Velasco Ibarra and Arnulfo Arias. He returned briefly in the 1970s and 1980s as a visiting lecturer and researcher, served there three years as a diplomat at the turn of the century, and resumed visits in 2006 as a researcher and consultant. We are grateful for the generosity and insights that Panamanians shared with us, and we hope that we do justice to what we were taught about a country and its people who have become so close to us.

We accept full responsibility for errors and omissions in this book.

1

Introduction to Modern Panama

I return to my country convinced that the future of our relations rests in the hands of excellent statesmen.

Brig. General Omar Torrijos, upon signing the 1977 Treaties.

SIGNING CEREMONY FOR THE 1977 CARTER-TORRIJOS TREATIES

On September 7, 1977, Panamanian dictator Omar Torrijos and US president Jimmy Carter signed the historic Panama Canal treaties that bear their names, thereby setting up intense drives to win ratification in both countries.[1] The US Senate, which needed a two-thirds majority to ratify, clearly posed the biggest challenge, because many senators opposed giving the Canal to Panama in 1999. Opinion polls showed the public solidly against the action. Still, Carter emphasized that ending the 1903 treaty, that allowed the United States to build and operate the Canal in the first place, satisfied larger moral and strategic goals. He noted that his predecessors, from Kennedy to Ford, had contemplated abrogation of the 1903 treaty, and that it had taken fourteen years of mutually aggravating relations to negotiate a deal satisfactory to both nations.

The signing ceremony, broadcast on NBC television, took place in the Hall of the Americas, in the historic Pan American Union building in Washington, DC, down the street from the White House. OAS Secretary

[1] Graham Hovey, "Carter, Torrijos Sign Canal Pacts in the Presence of Latin Leaders," *New York Times*, Sept. 8, 1977.

FIGURE 1.1 President Jimmy Carter and General Omar Torrijos signing the historic 1977 Panama Canal Treaties. US National Archives.

General Alejandro Orfila hosted the event, which was attended by representatives from twenty-six nations in the hemisphere. The setting, meant to convey the support Latin Americans gave to the deal, also hinted at the opprobrium that would greet its rejection. The ratification struggle became the most contentious since that for the 1919 Versailles Treaty that ended World War I – an effort that failed. Career diplomat Ambler Moss, who coordinated the US push, later remarked, "the Carter Administration realized it had a much worse Congressional problem in the Senate than it ever anticipated getting the treaties through." The campaign lasted seven months before succeeding.[2] These were truly dramatic developments.

* * * *

Although this book focuses on Panama's history since 1980, Chapter 1 provides background for the momentous events to come: Canal treaty implementation, the Noriega crisis, the Christmas invasion of 1989, the restoration of democracy, the turnover of the Canal, and Panama's

[2] Quote from "Interview with Ambler Moss," Library of Congress, 1988. See Michael L. Conniff, *Panama and the United States: The End of the Alliance*, 3rd ed. (Athens, GA: University of Georgia Press, 2012), ch. 7.

amazing blossoming since that event, including construction of a new set of canal locks. Footnotes and references cannot begin to account for the huge historical literature about Panama, built up over more than a century. Thus, we keep such documentation to the essential, emphasizing key authors, unpublished sources, and personal observations. Because of the close relationship Panama had with the United States, what one of us called the "forced alliance," this introduction narrates US actions more than later chapters will. After the turnover of the Canal in 1999, portrayed in Chapter 5, US influence faded considerably. Likewise, as it progresses, the story increasingly reflects Panamanian voices, sources, viewpoints, and data. They deserve a clear and honest telling of their recent history.

EARLY TWENTIETH CENTURY

Panama's existence as an independent country began on November 3, 1903, when its leaders ended eighty-two years as a province of the Republic of Colombia to the east.[3] Their act of separation remains tangled in controversy, because of the role the United States played in fomenting it and then obliging the new nation to sign a highly disadvantageous treaty that gave away rights to build and operate a ship canal. Under it, the US government appropriated over 500 square miles of territory in the middle of the country, to build, operate, and defend the future canal. Panamanians had to sort out their political, economic, and social destinies under the watchful eye of its US big brother, whose main local concern was to avoid disruption of its business of moving ships from one ocean to the other. The United States increasingly expanded its strategic interest there with military bases to advance its growing power on the world stage. By law, Panamanians allowed and sometimes invited military intervention by US forces to impose order and monitor elections. They adopted the US dollar as their currency to facilitate commerce and financial cooperation. They agreed to eschew an army and instead created a police force and tolerated US supervision of its ranks. Panamanians in the early twentieth century found their independence very much circumscribed by US influences, public and private.[4]

[3] Panama became the first (and only) Colombian province to achieve both the status of independent republic (1840–41) and federal state (1855–86). Panama never returned to provincial status after 1886, when it became a regional authority with jurisdiction over what is today its sovereign territory.

[4] The best place to begin is Alfredo Castillero Calvo's edited *Historia general de Panamá*, 5 vols. (Panama: Consejo Nacional del Centenario, 2004). The last two volumes cover the twentieth century. An update by the same historian is *Panamá: Historia contemporanea*

Panamanians wrote a constitution and elected leaders, passed laws and codes, and set up government agencies to accomplish the people's business. On paper the government looked a lot like that of the United States: a four-year presidential term, a national legislature, an independent judiciary headed by a supreme court, and elected provincial and municipal administrations. In fact, a sui generis regime evolved in which wealthy families prevailed in politics and used their influence to secure economic and status benefits at all levels of government. Foreigners, having settled in Panama since the sixteenth century, often enjoyed special privileges and standing, usually in the private sector. A few big companies, foremost among them United Fruit, also figured prominently in public affairs. And the Interoceanic Canal Commission, which oversaw the waterway, exercised the ultimate authority on the Isthmus, that of the US government.[5] As the British minister wrote to the Foreign Office about the pre-WWI era, "It is really farcical to talk of Panama as an independent state. It is really simply an annex of the Canal Zone."[6]

At the time of the 1911 census, Panama had just 432,000 inhabitants, mostly rural, with few high schools and no universities. The new nation lacked public health facilities, and most of its infrastructure of roads, bridges, electricity, sewage, and communications dated back to the previous century. The capital had 55,000 inhabitants, more than 10 percent of the national total, recently swelled by migration and immigration to work on Canal construction. Jamaicans and Barbadians made up the great majority of newcomers, eventually numbering tens of thousands. Panama appeared a nation struggling to establish itself.[7] The only overland route across the Isthmus besides the railroad and the Canal until the 1930s was the mule trail built to connect Spain to its colonies in the Pacific. An east-west Pan-American Highway remained a distant dream.

(Madrid: Fundación MAPFRE, 2014). Political coverage dominates in Patricia Pizzurno Gelos and Celestino Andrés Araúz, *Panamá republicano (1903–1989)* (Panama: Manfer, 1996). Foreign relations feature in Conniff, *Panama.*

[5] A glossy 411-page publication in 1917 provided a snapshot of political, social, economic, and cultural leaders: *El Libro Azul de Panamá/The Blue Book of Panama*, compiler and editor William T. Scoullar (Panamá: Imprenta Nacional, 1916–1917).

[6] Michael L. Conniff, "Panama Since 1903," *The Cambridge History of Latin America*, ed. Leslie Bethell (Cambridge: Cambridge University Press, 1990), vol. 7, 610.

[7] Omar Jaén Suárez, *La población del Istmo de Panamá*, 4th ed. (Panama: Editorial Universitaria, 2013), 50–53, 678–80; Marco A. Gandásegui, hijo, "Población y sociedad en el siglo xx," Castillero Calvo, *Panamá*, 505–62, passim.

An especially energetic president between 1912 and 1924, Belisario Porras, put a positive stamp on national affairs. He stabilized relations with the United States and celebrated the opening of the Panama Canal in 1916 (it opened in 1914 but to international traffic only in 1920, due to the war and construction difficulties). Porras built schools, hospitals, asylums, highways and bridges, a national archive, and other critical infrastructure. He also gave scholarships to scores of promising young men to study abroad and bring home their new professional talents. His influence proved so pervasive, one biographer called him a king without a crown and another the father of his country. To be sure, Porras and every president after him pressed the United States to amend the exploitative terms of the 1903 treaty, and they achieved small improvements over the years. But gradually the contradictions between the promise of being a global maritime center and the reality of virtual exclusion from Canal operations hardened into anger and anti-American sentiment as the century wore on.[8]

The 1930s brought marked change to Panama, much of it caused by the Great Depression and US economic retrenchment. On the positive side, however, the accession of Franklin D. Roosevelt to the White House in early 1933 brought hope of better relations throughout the hemisphere, with the unveiling of his Good Neighbor Policy. Panama underwent a coup in January 1931, led by the nationalist and patriotic group Acción Comunal, that brought to power more forceful figures, especially the brothers Harmodio and Arnulfo Arias. Both had risen from small-town obscurity by studying abroad on Porras's scholarships, Harmodio in law at Cambridge and University of London and Arnulfo at University of Chicago and Harvard medical school. Harmodio won election to the 1932–36 presidential term and attempted to protect the economy from sharp layoffs and reduced demand in the Canal and elsewhere.[9]

After Roosevelt's inauguration, Arias traveled to Washington to present Canal grievances that Acción Comunal had formulated in the mid

[8] Peter Szok, "Rey sin corona: Belisario Porras y la formación del estado nacional, 1903–1931," in *Historia General*, ed. Castillero Calvo, III:I, ch. 4; Pizzurno and Araúz, *Panamá republicano*, ch. 3; Michael L. Conniff, "Promoting Global Trade: The Panama-Pacific Expositions," in *Panamá cosmopolita: la Exposición de 1916 y su legado*, ed. Adrienne Samos (Panama: Biblioteca 500/Municipio de Panamá, 2017), 18–77.

[9] William Francis Robinson, "The Arias Madrid Brothers: Nationalist Politics in Panama," PhD diss., Auburn University, 1999, ch. 1; Michael L. Conniff, "Turning Point: Anglo-American Assessments of Panama in 1929–1932," in *Historia y globalización: Ensayos en homenaje a Alfredo Castillero Calvo*, Comp. Ángeles Ramos Baquero. (Panama: Editora Novo Art, 2017), 199–212.

FIGURE 1.2 Presidents Harmodio Arias and Franklin Delano Roosevelt during visit to Panama in 1934. Franklin Delano Roosevelt Library.

1920s: equal pay and benefits for Panamanian employees, repatriation of laid-off foreign workers, ending eminent domain land annexations, and barring commissary and restaurant sales to non-employees. These and other issues proved serious enough to require treaty negotiations, which Roosevelt assigned to the State Department.[10] The following year Roosevelt reciprocated with a visit to Panama.

Panama's crack diplomat Ricardo Alfaro traveled to Washington and worked with Secretary of State Cordell Hull on revisions to the 1903 Treaty, which, when signed in 1936, took its authors' names. Most important, it ended the protectorate status of Panama that had led to dozens of interventions. It also raised the annuity to $430,000 to compensate for the 1932 devaluation of the dollar, ended the US right of eminent domain, curbed commissary and PX sales to non-employees, lifted the ban on radio stations, allowed Panama to operate customs houses on Canal docks, and pledged to equalize employment terms for Panamanian workers. These meaty issues promised to improve life in Panama during the hard times.

[10] Conniff, *Panama*, 88–91.

Unfortunately, the US Senate neglected to act on it until 1939, when it was forced to ratify it to pave the way for a crucial meeting in Panama of Latin American foreign ministers to plan for hemispheric defenses during the war in Europe.[11]

In 1940, Arnulfo Arias won the presidency and instituted a nationalist regime that, among other things, resisted US defense preparations for the Panama Canal. A new constitution took away citizenship from many immigrants and banned others, centralized government, and created a social security agency, among other provisions.[12] The regime proved short-lived, however, because Arias's justice minister overthrew him, with US encouragement. For the next several years the new president, Ricardo Adolfo de la Guardia, cooperated closely with US authorities. Once the United States entered the war, military spending in Panama skyrocketed. Congress had appropriated funds in 1939 for a third set of locks to accommodate the navy's capital ships, infusing more money and immigrants into Panama, but the work was cancelled in 1943. Still, World War II proved a major turning point for Panama.[13]

The economic boom of the war years, a proverbial dance of the millions, plus the overwhelming weight of US presence, brought demographic and economic change to Panama. The Canal Zone itself housed some 100,000 people, including workers, military personnel, and dependents, approximately 15 percent of the national population. Labor demand and urban opportunities (schools, a university, hospitals, service jobs, a decent standard of living, etc.) caused robust cityward migration.[14]

POSTWAR DEVELOPMENT

After the war, Panama's population expanded, and its society grew more complex, so that by mid century its nearly one million inhabitants sorted into upper, middle, and lower classes, with striking urban and rural differences remaining. People increasingly gravitated to Panama City,

[11] Pizzurno and Araúz, *Panamá republicano*, ch. 7.

[12] Article 61 of the 1941 Constitution denied women the status of citizens. An electoral law issued that same year allowed women to vote in municipal elections provided they had high school or vocational diplomas. Women obtained the full right to participate as candidates and voters under the 1946 Constitution. For a brief history of the suffragist movement in Panama, see Yolanda Marco and Ángela Alvarado, *Mujeres que cambiaron nuestra historia* (Panama: UNICEF/Universidad de Panamá/Fondo Canadá-Panamá, 1997).

[13] Pizzurno and Araúz, *Panamá republicano*, chs. 8–9.

[14] Gandásegui, "Población," 514–16.

location of most government jobs and services, Canal operations, industry, educational and cultural institutions, and businesses. By 1980, the capital swelled to 874,000 inhabitants, a third of the national population. Still, by international comparison, Panama remained a small and sparsely settled nation.

The wealthy made money from agribusiness, industries, and banking services. Members of the middle class earned livings working in private business, government (including education), the media, and self-employment, especially in the professions. The lower classes subsisted on wages in myriad kinds of jobs, often outside the formal economy. People at the bottom of the pyramid suffered from underemployment, hunger, irregular housing, and poor health. In many ways Panama's society resembled those of many underdeveloped nations in the region. Remarkably, few Panamanians benefitted from employment at or transfers from the Panama Canal.[15]

Social mobility expanded with the spread of elementary schools, the opening of new high schools, and the founding of the University of Panama (1935). A professional class began to form, drawn by rapid growth in medical, dental, and legal services. Postwar years saw rising expectations for persons aspiring to middle-class status, and government employment also formed a path to achieve it. Well-to-do families sent their male children abroad for college, usually in the United States, an almost sure ticket to a better life. Still, Canal employment remained largely beyond their reach, due to endogamous hiring practices there.

Panama's economy would have been more prosperous were it not for US policies that limited benefits from the Canal flowing to it. National leaders dreamed of tapping into global trade and services attracted by the Canal, and, by the 1960s, they planned steps to realize that dream. By that time, Panama offered ship registry for a growing share of the world's merchant marines. Its admiralty courts and specialized law firms settled a significant portion of maritime disputes. Its Colon Free Zone, established in 1952 as a bonded warehouse, assembly, manufacturing, and re-export center, utilized Canal traffic for receiving and shipping goods. By the late 1960s, it was the second largest free zone in the world, after Hong Kong. In 1970, Panama created the International Banking Center to service offshore financial needs from around the world. Yet despite these initiatives, Panamanians believed that true prosperity would only come

[15] Ibid., 533–50. A classic from the period is John and Mavis Biesanz, *The People of Panama* (New York: Greenwood Press, 1955).

with greater integration of Canal operations into its national economy, something the United States resisted.[16]

TROUBLES AND TREATIES

After 1945, Panama's treaty negotiators took up the so-called bases question: whether the United States could extend its occupation of scores of bases where it had set up air defense positions during the war. Arnulfo's successor, President de la Guardia, had traded use of these bases, supposed to expire at the end of hostilities, for twelve key concessions by the United States, most of which had been postponed until after the war. By various dilatory means, the Pentagon held off evacuating the bases until December 1947, and, instead, convinced the government to sign an agreement to lease bases for five more years and the major airfield at Rio Hato for ten years. Panama would receive some $25,000 annual rent plus a $137,000 subsidy for maintaining roads to the bases. Panamanian nationalists vehemently objected to the treaty terms, in huge street demonstrations led by students, and the Assembly unanimously rejected the deal less than two weeks after its signing. Termed the *rechazo* (rejection), this act surprised both governments and signaled a new nationalist fervor on the part of Panamanians.[17]

The 1950s saw more concerted efforts to channel business, employment, and income from the Canal to the nation, to raise standards of living. President José Antonio Remón (1952–55) campaigned to pressure his US counterpart, Dwight D. Eisenhower, to revise the terms of the 1903 treaty and to alter the way the Canal did business. He traveled to Washington with deep backing from opinion polls and giant rallies, and Eisenhower instructed the State Department to negotiate improvements, in what became the 1955 Treaty. Remón's personal triumph ended, however, when assassins killed him just a few months later.[18]

[16] Through much of this period, economists from US and international agencies urged Panama to expand into areas like agriculture, mining, and industry. See Conniff, *Panama*, 102–07; and Andrew S. Zimbalist and John Weeks, *Panama at the Crossroads: Economic Development and Political Change in the Twentieth Century* (Berkeley & Los Angeles: University of California Press, 1991), chs. 2–4.

[17] Pizzurno and Araúz, *Panamá republicano,* 332–40. The Rio Hato airfield had been a key logistics center for US air operations in the entire Pacific Basin during WWII.

[18] Ibid., ch. 12; Conniff, *Panama,* 105–10. Cf. Larry LaRae Pippin, *The Remón Era: An Analysis of a Decade of Events in Panama, 1947–1957* (Stanford: Institute of Hispanic American and Luso-Brazilian Studies, 1964).

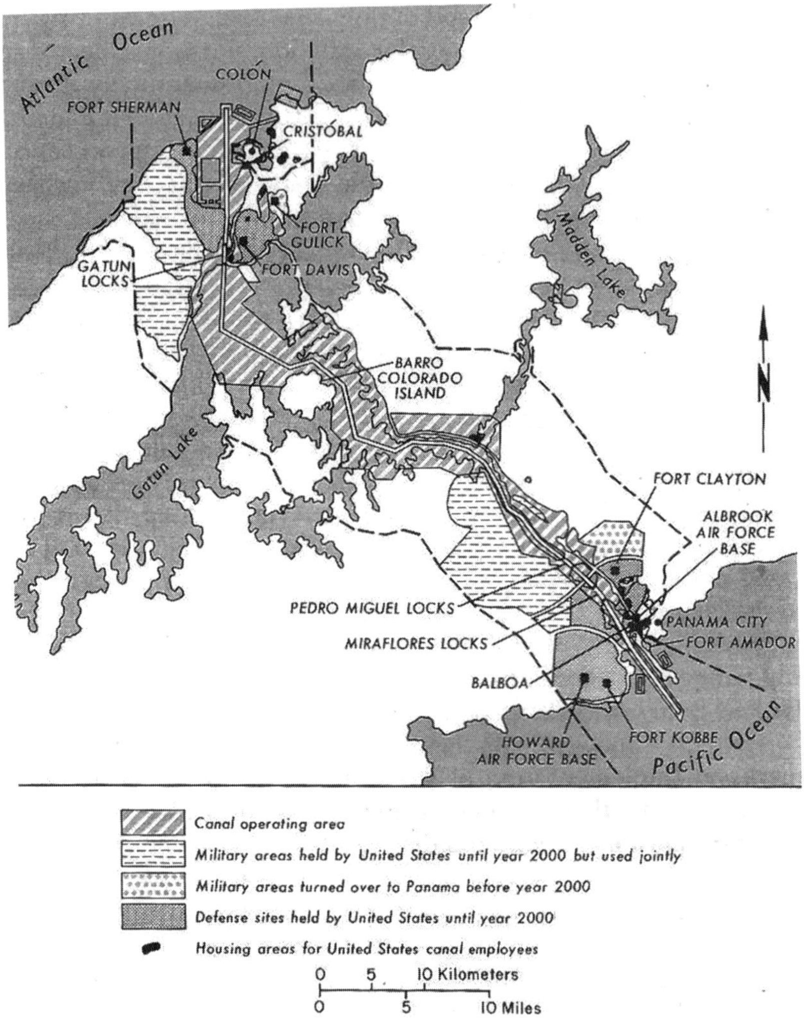

FIGURE 1.3 Panama Canal and US bases in 1980s. Sandra W. Meditz, and Dennis Michael Hanratty, eds. *Panama: A Country Study*. Washington, DC: Federal Research Division, Library of Congress, 1989, 54.

The concessions Remón won in 1955 paled when compared with the benefits Egypt gained by its seizure of the Suez Canal the following year, action acquiesced to by Eisenhower. Discontent mounted in the late 1950s, among Panamanian students, politicians, intellectuals, and workers. Violent protests broke out, and tensions rose further with the 1959

FIGURE 1.4 Panamanian students carrying national flag to raise in the Canal Zone, January 1964. Hoover Institution and Archives, Stanford University.

overthrow of Fulgencio Batista in Cuba. Business as usual became hard to sustain in Panama without changing its relationship to the United States. Panama's elite worried that they could lose control over events.[19]

On January 9th, 1964, the worst public protests since the 1925 renters' strike erupted, bringing the nation to a standstill and throwing relations with the United States into turmoil. A delegation of formally dressed students from the nearby National Institute entered the Canal Zone to protest the improper display of the US flag without its Panamanian counterpart, which they took with them. Their flag was damaged, and students were roughed up during a tense confrontation, and police ejected the protesters. Crowds formed outside the Zone, and word spread that the Zonians had defiled their flag, a powerful symbol of national sovereignty and Panama's residual rights to the area. Soon rock- and Molotov bomb-throwing and shouting degenerated into sniper fire, from without and within the Zone. Three days of protests followed, leaving two dozen dead (including four Zone soldiers), fire-gutted buildings, and ruptured diplomacy between the two countries as

[19] Pizzurno and Araúz, *Panamá republicano*, ch. 13; Conniff, *Panama*, 110–15.

the Panamanians mourned the dead, whom they celebrate even today as martyrs. Tensions had never been more severe.[20]

Throughout the remainder of 1964, presidential elections in both countries prevented major progress toward solving problems in Panama, yet a number of study groups looked into ways to ameliorate the still-volatile Canal situation. President Lyndon Johnson appointed as his new ambassador economist and former boxer Jack Vaughn, a Spanish-speaker who sympathized with Latin Americans. As various proposals surfaced, including for a sea-level canal, Johnson warmed to the idea of a major initiative in Panama. After his November landslide election victory, he and his Panamanian counterpart, newly elected Marco Aurelio Robles (1964–68), began to negotiate a replacement to the hated 1903 treaty. Panamanians hoped that a new Canal regime would pull their country out of the economic doldrums it had floundered in for nearly two decades.

Mid-1960s negotiations for a replacement Panama Canal treaty proved complex and fraught with peril. Robles had won an election tainted by claims of fraud from runner-up candidate Arnulfo Arias, and his public image suffered from his stern law-and-order actions while serving previously as minister of government and justice. Labor and student strikes punctuated his presidency and detracted from an otherwise productive period of economic growth. Colon and interior provinces also experienced unrest and strikes. Robles lacked the skills for public relations, compromise, and back-room deals that might have headed off his growing unpopularity, with the public as well as other politicians.[21]

In this unstable environment, the secret negotiations for new canal treaties raised further doubts about Robles's tenure. When the "three-in-one" treaties (canal administration, sea-level project, and defense) were initialed and leaked to the press in mid 1967, public opinion had already

[20] Ibid., 116–21. Cf. Alan McPherson, "Courts of World Opinion: Trying the Panama Flag Riots of 1964," *Diplomatic History*, 28:1 (Jan. 2004): 83–112; Pizzurno and Araúz, *Panamá republicano*, ch. 14; Jonathan C. Brown, *Cuba's Revolutionary World* (Cambridge: Harvard University Press, 2017), ch. 12; and Michael E. Donoghue, *Borderland on the Isthmus: Race, Culture, and the Struggle for the Canal Zone* (Durham, NC: Duke University Press, 2014), 82–87. Panama has been the only Latin American country to break diplomatic relations with the United States. President Roberto F. Chiari accused the great power of aggression and only restored relations after Johnson formally undertook to negotiate a new Canal treaty. See Pizzurno and Araúz, *Panamá republicano*, 464–75.

[21] Ibid., ch. 15.

mounted against them. In December, the National Assembly voted against ratification. Meanwhile, Robles nominated David Samudio for the May 1968 presidential election. The latter's tax hike proposals alienated a good part of the oligarchy, whose representatives in the Assembly split off to join Arias's opposition Panameñista Party. In early 1968, the Assembly impeached Robles and promoted the first vice president into the palace. Had the National Guard not intervened to block this action and disband the Assembly, Robles would have fallen. As it was, he had lost any chance of ratifying the treaties or leaving office with dignity.

Arnulfo Arias won the 1968 election, his third such victory since 1940. And the National Guard lost no time in overthrowing him a third time, after only eleven days. The coup of October 11, 1968, enacted by a group of mid-ranking officers, ushered in a twenty-one-year period of military government. These officers formed an interim junta and, like some of their South American counterparts, began to contemplate a longer period in power. The treaties definitively came off the table, following Lyndon Johnson's decision not to submit them to the US Senate.

DANSE MACABRE: THE MILITARY IN POWER

Many good studies chart the rise of militarism in Panamanian politics, often with US support. For starters, President Remón converted the National Police into the National Guard in 1953. Panamanians already recognized the former police chief as a king-maker in politics, a role he played masterfully during the troubles of 1948–50. The US government, meanwhile, overhauled its Canal operations and its stance in the rest of the hemisphere, reflecting strategic changes brought by the Cold War and the Korean conflict. In 1951, Congress, recognizing the downgraded position of the Canal and its attendant bases, put the Canal administration on a self-support basis and curtailed many of the generous benefits its US employees enjoyed. In that situation, Panama could be expected to increase its part in keeping order on the Isthmus using the more advanced military capability of a national guard. As a US ally and participant in military assistance programs, Panama's new Guard qualified for heavier armaments and more officer training at the recently formed School of the Americas in Fort Gulick. These moves coincided with efforts to stem the spread of communism in the hemisphere. As long as the Guard did the bidding of civilian officials, and cooperated with the

Pentagon, democracy would be protected. It did, however, have an antagonistic relationship with Arnulfo Arias stemming from earlier confrontations.[22]

Between Remón's 1955 death and the 1968 coup, the Guard remained behind the scenes. That changed when it overthrew Arnulfo Arias days after his inauguration. The immediate cause of the coup was Arias's intention to rotate some ranking officers away from the capital or even outside the country to neutralize them, something he had vowed not to do before the election. (He had already given Commandant Col. Bolívar Vallarino a lucrative retirement package.) When rumors of the reassignments surfaced, the Guard easily overthrew Arias, who took refuge in the Canal Zone. The US embassy, caught by surprise, acted coolly toward the new junta.[23]

Once in power, Guard leaders developed a taste for the perquisites and rewards that come with high office. Real authority migrated from the initial junta (called the Combo) to two officers, Major Boris Martínez and Lt. Colonel Omar Torrijos. These two worked together uneasily until the latter shouldered the former out four and a half months later. For the next decade, Panama lived under a military dictatorship headed up by Torrijos and staffed by Guard officers close to him.

The new regime encountered vocal opposition from politicians, labor leaders, intellectuals, and students, many of whose offices and schools shut down, and from sporadic guerrilla fighters. In December 1969, some disgruntled Guard officers tried to overthrow Torrijos but failed. The commander of the Chiriqui Guard headquarters, Manuel Antonio Noriega, proved crucial in thwarting the coup and rose in rank quickly afterward, as a "loyalist." Torrijos settled in for the long haul and promoted himself to Brigadier General, despite his sagging popularity. Neither the US government, now headed by President Richard Nixon,

[22] Among the many excellent studies, see Carlos Guevara Mann, *Panamanian Militarism: A Historical Interpretation* (Athens: Ohio University Center for International Studies, 1996); Steve C. Ropp, *Panamanian Politics: from Guarded Nation to National Guard* (New York: Praeger/Stanford: Hoover Institution, 1982); Robert C. Harding II, *Military Foundations of Panamanian Politics* (New Brunswick, NJ: Transaction Publishers, 2001); Thomas L. Pearcy, *We Answer Only to God: Politics and the Military in Panama, 1903–1947* (Albuquerque: University of New Mexico Press, 1998). Other sources appear in later chapters. Author Bigler recalls foreign aid official Jack Vaughn, later ambassador to Panama, stating that he resigned when his budget was raided to buy arms for the new Guard.

[23] In addition to the foregoing sources, see also Pizzurno and Araúz, *Panamá republicano*, ch. 16.

nor the OAS felt any desire to intervene in Panama's turn toward militarism and even less to resurrect treaty talks.[24]

Having survived the coup attempt, Torrijos broadened his bases of support by appointing technocrats, disgruntled politicians, businessmen, and personal friends to key government positions. One of the latter, Demetrio "Jimmy" Lakas, a Colon-born engineer from the business community, headed up the provisional junta and later served as civilian president from 1972 to 1978.[25] Another early collaborator, University of Chicago-trained economist Nicolás Ardito Barletta, who had worked on national planning in the president's office, became planning minister in the 1970s, president in the 1980s, and head of Canal Zone reversion efforts in the 1990s. Fernando Manfredo Jr. served on the new Electoral Tribunal and later in the cabinet, and he eventually played a major role in Canal management under the treaties. Other key civilians from these early days took part in 1970s treaty negotiations, covered later in this chapter. This early generation of "Torrijistas" swung the ship of state considerably to the left of its previous course.

Torrijos also began calling his regime "revolutionary," resembling more that of Peruvian general Juan Velasco Alvarado than the Cuban Fidel Castro. His core slogan, "Nuevo Panamá," found echoes in other promotional phrases, like "a caring dictatorship" and "a different revolution." Some programs derived from earlier efforts around the hemisphere, like land reform, economic development (with help from international banks), an offshore financial center, agriculture and fishing, and a 1972 Labor Code favorable to workers. Other reforms sought to bolster Torrijos's political legitimacy through new representative institutions, especially the 505-member Assembly of Representatives of Municipalities (so-called "people's power," replacing the earlier National Assembly, dissolved in 1968) and a new constitution promulgated in 1972. These initiatives took place under dictatorial conditions of censorship, intimidation, arbitrary imprisonment and exile, and favoritism for supporters. Once the subservient Assembly approved the draft constitution, it designated Torrijos the "maximum leader of the

[24] By 1969, the governments of Brazil, Argentina, and Peru were also run by the military. Thirty years later, in Panama, a National Truth Commission documented over a hundred cases of disappearances and deaths of opponents attributable to the Guard.

[25] Eric Pace, "Demetrio Lakas, 74, Panama Leader Who Had Role in Shaping Canal Pacts," *New York Times*, Nov. 7, 1999; Conniff, *Panama*, 125–28.

Panamanian revolution," i.e. head of state. No one was fooled by a few trappings of democracy.[26]

These programmatic efforts found complements in generous subsidies to businessmen who allied with the new government. A coterie of owners, anxious to take advantage of the regime's need for friends, stepped forward to receive contracts, concessions, grants, and special treatment of all sorts. A spate of highway projects begun in 1969 stretched into the mid 1970s and enriched numerous contractors. Torrijos also nationalized some utilities, like the electricity, telephone, and gas provider Boise Cascade, allowing the government to subsidize rates to consumers and build new hydroelectric dams and distribution grids. He invested in projects designed to stimulate production of sugar, farm-raised fish and shrimp, ocean trawling, and agricultural goods. Finally, in 1970, he authorized Panama's International Banking Center to host and regulate off-shore banks and contribute to capitalization of the economy.[27]

Minister of Planning Ardito Barletta worked up a comprehensive plan for development, called *Estrategia para el desarrollo nacional, 1970–1980*, that sought to guide efforts across the regime. Although he could not guarantee the return of the Canal Zone, Ardito Barletta created a blueprint that could be followed if and when the Canal became Panamanian. Eschewing traditional autochthonous approaches, he envisioned an economy fully integrated into global commerce, manufacturing, labor markets, and finance. Commerce obviously had to tap into the thousands of ships transiting the Canal each year, but it would also better utilize the international airport for air cargo. To service the exploding containerization of shipping, he proposed marshalling yards in the nation's ports, where cargoes could be rerouted to final destinations. A revived railroad could handle container transfers between the two oceans. Better roads would abet multi-modal transportation. Manufacturing should follow the Colon Free Zone model, similar to the maquiladoras in Mexico, where firms from around the world located operations in tariff-free bonded areas and where inputs and final products moved

[26] A hard-hitting denunciation of the regime appeared in Richard M. Koster and Guillermo Sánchez Borbón, *In the Time of the Tyrants, Panama: 1968–1990* (New York: W. W. Norton & Co., 1990). Cf. Sharon Phillipps Collazos, *Labor and Politics in Panama: The Torrijos Years* (Boulder, CO: Westview, 1991). An insider's perspective on the regime is provided by the general's cousin and fellow officer, Roberto Díaz Herrera, *Omar: De Cuerpo Entero (Anecdotario biográfico)* (Panama: Editora Sibauste, S.A., 2013).

[27] Nicolás Ardito Barletta, *Huellas: contribuciones públicas nacionales e internacionales, memorias* (Bogota: Panamericana, 2016), 3–4. See also Zimbalist and Weeks, *Panama*, ch. 4.

unrestricted. Employees in these sectors, bringing fresh skills and entrepreneurial talent, should be welcomed from around the world to engage in Panama's growth. Capital should also be fluid once funds began flowing into the International Banking Center. Ardito Barletta's vision proved prescient and also embodied the national identity "hub of the Americas," to be discussed in the section on national identity. Far from laissez-faire, it provided a comprehensive plan tailored to Panama's special circumstances and competitive advantages.

Torrijos, meanwhile, began touring the countryside in a jeep, wearing fatigues and his trademark bush hat, attempting to boost his popularity. He promised poor rural residents land reform, crop subsidies, public health clinics, agrarian assistance, schools, and other local benefits, similar to campaigns by Cuba's Fidel Castro in the early 1960s. While such programs did reach formerly isolated towns and villages, they boosted government expenditures and payrolls markedly. By 1982, Panama would have the highest debt-to-GDP and per capita foreign debt in the hemisphere, a legacy of the military government. Meanwhile, virtually the only news published or broadcast came through government-controlled media.[28]

FIGURE 1.5 Omar Torrijos addressing a crowd supporting his efforts to transfer the Canal. The background sign reads *Hoy la caña, mañana el canal* (Today the sugarcane, tomorrow the canal). © 1977 Tom Zimberoff/Fundación Omar Torrijos.

[28] Zimbalist and Weeks, *Panama*, 127–28.

Torrijos's shift toward institutionalizing his rule in 1972, with a constitution and subservient legislature, also included selection of a civilian president, Demetrio "Jimmy" Lakas, to soften the regime's image. The Assembly rubber-stamped Lakas.[29] The new president took over many of the ceremonial duties that had swamped Torrijos, including legislation, day-to-day diplomacy, press relations, and inaugurating public works. Not exactly a puppet, Lakas played essential parts in the government without wielding full power, exercised behind scenes by Torrijos.

Lakas and his cabinet members launched what can only be called a "shotgun" approach to development, most of whose pellets fell short of their targets. First, they promoted agricultural expansion, focusing on soy, coffee, potatoes, onions, and cattle. Next, they nationalized and operated three sugar mills. Various foreign aid agencies chipped in with funding and expertise. Trying to boost human capital, Lakas wove educational and health initiatives into this largely rural program. They also licensed a major copper mining company to exploit promising ores along the Caribbean coast. Finally, they attempted to stimulate industrial growth through various subsidized firms, including those in the Colon Free Zone. Most of these efforts failed. A few investments, like the ATLAPA convention center and airport expansion, eventually prospered.[30]

In 1974, commerce minister Fernando Manfredo took command of Panama's battles in the first Banana War in Central America. Officials of neighboring countries met in Panama in 1974 to form the Union of Banana Exporting Countries, to demand a uniform tax on exports. The major US companies, United Fruit (UFCO) and Standard Brands, registered vehement objections, defending contracts that sometimes dated back to the nineteenth century. Using divide and conquer tactics, UFCO threatened and sometimes shut down operations to pressure exporting countries. Manfredo, wielding the authority of Torrijos, proposed buying out the UFCO properties in Panama to sell fruit to the shippers. In 1975, UFCO's chief negotiator, Eli Black, discovered to have given bribes to high officials in Honduras, committed suicide, leaving matters up in the air. Several countries backed down on the tax, but Panama did take over the lands, imposed labor contracts, nationalized

[29] Pizzurno and Araúz, *Panamá republicano*, ch. 17.
[30] Ibid., 550–53.

the ports, and forged a mutually beneficial relationship with UFCO (rebranded Chiquita in 1985).[31]

THE CARTER-TORRIJOS TREATIES AND THE PANAMA CANAL ACT

Despite dictatorship and economic missteps, Omar Torrijos's favorable legacy rests mostly on his successful negotiation of new Panama Canal treaties between 1971 and 1977, achieving a long-sought goal of all Panamanians. As one of the most portentous treaty successes by the United States in the twentieth century, the story has been told and documented thoroughly. This brief overview provides background for the history of Panama in the rest of the book.

When the military took power in 1968, its leaders showed no interest in pursuing the discredited and unperfected 1967 treaties. The US government likewise had no stomach for taking them up again. President Richard Nixon, inaugurated in January 1969, turned his attentions to Vietnam and then to China. Panama could not have been farther from his thoughts. From Panama's point of view, however, Canal operations remained unfinished business. The new president, Lakas, met with Nixon, who agreed that they should take up the issues again. For a variety of reasons, little progress occurred.

Panama's new foreign minister, Juan Antonio Tack, sought to revive Canal discussions directly with the State Department and to solicit support from the OAS and the UN.[32] By good luck, Panama rotated into a two-year, non-permanent seat on the UN Security Council in January 1972, which Tack used expertly to advance his country's position vis-à-vis the United States. Tack and his UN ambassador, Aquilino Boyd, convinced a majority on the Council to hold its March 1973 meeting in Panama City, arguing that their nation had a legitimate interest in presenting its case. When the time came, Torrijos himself made the pitch, which found

[31] Fernando Manfredo, *La transición del Canal a Panamá 1979–1990: Memorias* (Mexico: By author, 2014), ch. 6; Pizzurno and Araúz, *Panamá republicano*: 555–56. For the company history, see Thomas McCann, *An American Company: The Tragedy of United Fruit* (New York: Crown Publishers, 1976), ch. 12.

[32] Pizzurno and Araúz, *Panamá republicano*, 560–72; Conniff, *Panama*, 128–34. Cf. the quasi-official Panamanian chronicle by Omar Jaén Suárez, *Las negociaciones de los Tratados Torrijos-Carter, 1970–1979*, 2 vols. (Panama: Autoridad del Canal de Panamá, 2005). Panama had used the same tactic, applying international pressure to force the United States into negotiations, in 1964: see McPherson, "Courts."

sympathy among the members. Several pertinent resolutions circulated, and Tack cleverly sought backing for the most strident, which would certainly evoke a US veto, which it did, for only the third time in UN history. The adverse attention this generated obliged the White House to move back into negotiation mode. Tack and National Security Advisor Henry Kissinger signed a list of principles in February 1974 that would guide new talks.

Panamanians pushed hard to make progress in these negotiations, but too many powerful obstacles stood in their way. President Gerald Ford, replacing Nixon the following August, had limited authority and experience in foreign affairs. He relied on Kissinger (now Secretary of State), who evinced little interest in Latin America. The Pentagon famously resisted giving up any strategic asset it possessed. US public opinion opposed any reduction of rights in Panama, and Congress shared that sentiment. And a powerful lobby arose in the United States to prevent any concessions regarding the Canal or its associated bases.[33] The odds against any progress seemed insurmountable.

The accession of Jimmy Carter to the White House in January 1977 finally put the Panama negotiations back on the front burner. Carter believed the United States had a moral and ethical obligation to forge a new relationship with Panama and that doing so would create a more positive climate throughout the hemisphere. Calculating that unpopular treaties would have little chance of ratification in an election year, the Carter team pushed hard to conclude the work, which it did in September. The treaties closely resembled those of 1967, with the addition of careful bargaining with the Pentagon to win its acceptance.

Agreements reached throughout 1974–75 on the potential shape of new treaties, plus the antecedents of 1967 and the Tack-Kissinger Principles, formed a foundation on which to build the new structure. The final product consisted of two treaties, one governing the waterway until December 31, 1999, at which time the Canal would be given to Panama free and clear. The second pledged to guarantee the neutrality of the Canal beyond the turnover, by means of a multilateral convention. (The main treaty addressed the sea-level option, without requiring a separate convention.) The canal operations treaty abolished existing management structures and replaced them with a binational board on

[33] California governor Ronald Reagan stirred the pot considerably during the primary elections, making retention of the Panama Canal a major plank of his campaign against President Ford. Conniff, *Panama*, 131–35 passim.

which US members held a 5–4 majority. Panama would take over nearly 60 percent of the former Zone and over several years would assume responsibility for most public services there. Military bases, now operating under a new Status of Forces Agreement (SOFA), would be consolidated, included in the reduced Canal Area, and gradually turned over to Panama by 1999. Annual payments to Panama from Canal revenues and for services would immediately rise to around $80 million dollars. The treaties themselves proved short, some twenty-two pages, but the accompanying annexes, maps, exchanges of notes, and other documents took up sixty pages, reflecting the complex US installations that had grown up since the canal opened in 1914.

Pushback to the signed treaties from myriad sectors convinced the negotiators that the heaviest work still lay ahead, that of convincing the US Senate to ratify them. The following seven months saw concerted efforts by the administration and its supporters to win over Senate votes for the treaties and equally strenuous efforts by opponents to defeat them. Meanwhile, Panama ratified them by referendum on October 23, 1977. The final Senate vote of 68 for and 32 against, on April 18, 1978, met the two-thirds required for approval. The administration had several more pro votes pledged by senators who preferred not to vote yes to avoid negative backlash in their states. Advocates of the new relationship celebrated, prematurely as it turned out.

The US House of Representatives, kept at arm's length during treaty negotiations, reserved a nasty surprise for the administration and Panama. It had to pass a major enabling bill to implement the treaties, to be called the Panama Canal Act of 1979. Led by treaty opponents John Murphy (D-NY), Robert Bauman (R-MD), Daniel J. Flood (D-PA), and Charlie Wilson (D-TX), with coaching by Senate treaty foes Jesse Helms (R-NC) and others, the House rejected the draft sent over from the White House and wrote its own version, which amounted to a booby trap. The resulting Act subverted the treaty promise of shared management and autonomous operations, giving Congress close oversight powers and hamstringing implementation. Details of the Act and implementation appear in Chapter 2.

PANAMANIAN NATIONAL IDENTITY

Thousands of years of human life on the Isthmus of Panama deposited layers of national identity, as if in archeological strata. Thus, perhaps, an anthropologist needs to wield her tools to dig through the historical sediment and sort out its meanings. Dr. Ana Elena Porras, a multidisciplinary researcher at the University of Panama, has made a very creditable effort to do just this, in her book *Cultura de la interoceanidad*, which might be translated as "culture of interoceanality." She found that people who live sandwiched between two oceans, as Panamanians do, see themselves as different. They forged their identity from seminal moments having to do with the two oceans, such as the day in 1513 when Vasco Núñez de Balboa crossed to the Pacific side of the isthmus and claimed the new body of water for Spain. Thousands of similar moments occurred in the subsequent five centuries. Together, such moments merge into feelings and beliefs held by the people who experience them, giving rise to national identities.[34]

By examining a broad range of historical artifacts, Porras perceived several discrete Panamanian identities derived from living between two oceans for a long time. She presented them as metaphors or intellectual constructs of how Panamanians see themselves and sometimes as how outsiders see them. Some identities pertain to special periods, but most apply to the entire sweep of modern history.

Porras's first interpretive metaphor cast Panama as a *banana republic*, a conception that could be positive (tropical production) and negative, the assumption that a small country which depends on a single export product cannot be a serious, complex nation. This view, more often held by foreign observers, nonetheless rubbed off on Panamanians themselves, in the form of self-doubt about their national worth. It belonged to the twentieth century, the era when US-based UFCO managed most of the country's plantations.[35]

[34] Ana Elena Porras, *Cultura de la interoceanidad*, 2nd ed. (Panama: University of Panama, 2009), 38–41. The construction of the Panamanian official identity can be traced to the second and third decades of the twentieth century. As in other young Latin American republics, the educated elite resorted to an almost mythical celebration of the "heroic miscegenation" produced by the union of subdued female natives and their Spanish colonizers. In other words, the "true" Panamanian was the *mestizo*, excluding other existing ethnic groups from the equation. This notion was famously embodied in the romance between Balboa and the beautiful (and fictional) indigenous princess Anayansi, protagonists of Octavio Méndez Pereira's 1934 biographical novel. See *Vasco Núñez de Balboa. El tesoro del Dabaibe*, 2nd ed. (Madrid: Nuestra Raza, 1936).

On Balboa, see Alfredo Castillero Calvo, *El descubrimiento del Pacífico y los orígenes de la globalización* (Panama: Comité Nacional para la Conmemoración del Quinto Centenario del Descubrimiento del Océano Pacífico, 2013). Peter A. Szok explores early twentieth-century national identity in *La última gaviota: Liberalism and Nostalgia in Early Twentieth-Century Panamá* (Westport, CN: Greenwood, 2001).

[35] Porras, *Cultura*, 200–06.

The second metaphor, *país profundo*, or "deep country," held that core *panameñidad* (Panamanian-ness) emerged from the land and the rural folk who worked it. This comprised those descended from Spanish settlers who farmed, raised livestock, and cultivated for a living. *Interior*, that is, everywhere not within the transit zone, served as a synonym for *país profundo*. This view coincided with traditional social analysis asserting that Panama had two elites, the commercial one in the terminal cities and the rural and agrarian one descended from colonial times. The first was liberal and cosmopolitan, the second conservative and Catholic.[36]

Interiorano (of the interior) identity did not embrace the several major indigenous communities, however, who formed a "marginal" or economically and socially neglected sector, in Porras's view. To this day, the major native peoples – Guna Yala, Ngäbe-Buglé, and Emberá-Wounaan – retain their languages and self-government.

Porras's third perceived identity, commercial emporium, has deep historical roots as well. From the time Panama began transferring shipments of silver from Peru and merchandise from Europe in what some memorialize as the world's first trade fairs, it joined global trade routes, never to disengage from them.[37] Although this commerce languished in the eighteenth century, it sprang up again during the heyday of the Panama Railroad (1855–69), one of the most lucrative ventures in the world at the time. The Canal, of course, cemented this view of Panama as the "crossroads of the world." Some compared it to the Hanseatic States on the Baltic Sea, devoted solely to international exchange. Today one often sees phrases like "Singapore of the Americas" and "hub of the Americas." At heart, this metaphor depicted Panama as a place where the world comes to do business and where Panamanians enjoy a good life participating in it.[38]

Porras took pains to deemphasize geographical determinism, which had suffused so much writing about who Panamanians are. To be sure, geography played a role in the nation's destiny, but the interaction of the transit mentality, the *pais profundo* culture, and the marginalized certainly mediated in the emergence of national identity.

[36] Ibid., 206–10. For a sampling of social class essays, see Marco A. Gandásegui, hijo, compiler, *Las clases sociales en Panamá: Grupos humanos, clases medias, élites y oligarquía*, 3rd ed. (Panama: CELA, 2008). On rural society, see Marcela Camargo, "La historia rural del siglo XX," in *Historia general*, ed. Castillero Calvo, III:I, 110–29.

[37] Alfredo Castillero Calvo, *Los metales preciosos y la primera globalización* (Panama: Editora Novo Arte, 2008).

[38] Porras, *Cultura*, 210–14.

Yet another core element of *panameñidad* found expression in the nation's motto, *pro mundi beneficio,* for the benefit of the world. Here, Panamanians offered up their unique geography (narrow isthmus between two oceans) to facilitate world commerce. Of course, leaders expected that Panamanians would benefit too, yet the US operation of the Canal for most of the twentieth century frustrated them and prevented greater profits, employment, and world status from accruing to their country. For some critics, the motto signified involuntary submission to US wishes and interests. A few asked why not pro Panama beneficio?[39]

"Bridge of the world" conveyed another element of Panamanian national identity. Its geography facilitated transit across the Isthmus, first by mule teams and canoes, later by trains, eventually by Canal, and augmented today by fiber optic cable and airplanes. Few places in the world offer such convenient ways to bypass geographical obstacles as Panama does. The metaphor was easy to visualize.[40]

Porras's list includes "heart of the universe," a broader and perhaps overblown conception compared with earlier ones. None other than Simón Bolívar, in his famous 1815 letter from Jamaica, declared Panama to be a global intersection like the Isthmus of Corinth, Greece, that separated the Gulf of Corinth from the Saronic Gulf, where Greece built a canal in the late nineteenth century. Bolívar's convocation of the 1826 Panama Congress of newly independent American republics reiterated this view of Panama as a potential capital of the Americas.[41]

Yet another metaphor for national identity called attention to its cosmopolitanism, expressing both its historic openness to immigrants and its ties to the rest of the world. People of all origins, races, faiths, politics, and ethnicities were welcomed in Panama, as a necessary condition for its role as a crossroads of the world. This is not to say that some, especially those of European background, didn't achieve greater success than others, but generally everyone found the means to reside, work, form families, and express themselves. An even more explicit metaphor for such openness asserted that Panama served as a crucible of races where all could meet, interact, and prosper.[42]

[39] Ibid., 214–18.

[40] Ibid., 218–24. This does not include the isthmian role in movement of flora and fauna between South and Central America before the arrival of humans.

[41] Ibid., 225–29. The pertinent phrase from Bolívar's letter is quoted at the beginning of Chapter 10. He also referred to Panama as an emporium for the world.

[42] Ibid., 229–38.

The metaphor *Panamá soberana* declared the nation to possess sovereignty, in the face of outside influences like the United States and UFCO. As a slogan, this sentiment often ended up on billboards and walls in times of public unrest and international pressures. It was favored by Torrijos during 1970s treaty negotiations and continued to be invoked during Noriega's rule. It also counteracted, to some extent, the notion of openness to the world, emphasizing instead self-sufficiency and wholeness.[43]

Finally, *Panamá 2000* held out hopes for better times in the new millennium, especially after the turnover of the Canal. The nation would be free of US tutelage and able to chart its own destiny. This utopian vision seemed to come to pass, not immediately after reversion as hoped, but when the nation's economy boomed a few years later. Panama gained greater respect in international organizations, global companies increasingly chose it for regional headquarters, and it succeeded in building new Canal locks that in some ways rivaled the original construction feat.[44]

Porras concluded her analysis by noting how the different metaphors for national identity, some mutually incompatible, all found a conceptual home in the nation-state. As the centuries wore on, more peoples and cultures became layered into the sediment of national identity, so that a broad entity was needed to encompass them all. The Republic of Panama provided such an embrace, especially after 1903. By taking over and successfully managing the Panama Canal after 2000, Panamanians are completing the task of defining themselves.

PANAMA AND THE ZONIANS

A unique US subculture arose in the Canal Zone during the twentieth century, one comprised of American citizens who went to work in Canal construction, as well as their descendants, many of whom chose to take jobs and remain on the Isthmus. Others immigrated from other places and stayed, closely linked to the operations of the Canal. By the time of the 1977 Treaties, some fourth generation Zonians worked for the Canal and exerted inordinate influence on the negotiations and on US public opinion. Many factors bonded the Zonians to the Canal: family heritage, excellent employment conditions, a sense of historic mission, and a subculture shared with thousands of other Zonians.[45]

[43] Ibid., 238–42.
[44] Ibid., 242–45.
[45] The most comprehensive study is Donoghue's *Borderland*. Other basic sources include John Major, "The Panama Canal Zone, 1904–1979," in *Cambridge History of Latin*

These US citizens residing in the Zone had ambiguous relationships with Panamanians, ostensibly their hosts. First, they themselves were not Panamanians. Since the 1903 Treaty ceded the Zone to the United States in perpetuity, they lived in US territory. Persons born there of US parents automatically became citizens. Some bragged about never setting foot on Panamanian soil and others about not speaking Spanish.[46] Second, the storied excellence of the Canal and its operations made its employees and residents feel superior to Panamanians, on whom they looked down as inferiors. They saw the latter suffering from poverty, political upheavals, crime, graft, and general underdevelopment. Third, they viscerally opposed intrusions of Panamanians into Canal matters, except as low-level employees supervised by Zonians. They fought especially against any assertion of Panamanian rights over the lands and the Canal itself. This attitude helped to set up the flag confrontation of January 1964 that led to riots and the eventual abrogation of the 1903 Treaty.[47]

Fourth, as US employees, they enjoyed and protected special perks vis-à-vis Panamanian or third-country nationals. For over forty years, these differences were embodied in a Jim Crow-like discrimination-cum-segregation system known as the Gold and Silver Rolls. When segregation (illegal in US government agencies) became untenable in the Zone in the 1950s, managers shifted to a "US rate/local rate" system that preserved many aspects of its predecessor, mostly by changing terminology.[48]

Finally, later generations of Zonians proclaimed their love of Panama as the Canal's "host nation," even while looking down on its people. They purported to love certain elements of Panamanian culture, like the music of organist Lucho Azcárraga, Carnival celebrations, the folk dance *el tamborito* and its colorful *pollera* skirts, gold *huacas* (indigenous burial artifacts), colorful Guna Yala *molas* (embroidered panels), *ceviche* (cocktail made with local seafood), *Panamá* brand beer, and white *guayaberas* (loose dress shirts). They

America, vol. 7, ed. Leslie Bethell (Cambridge, UK: Cambridge University Press, 1990, 643–70; Harry A. Franck, *Zone Policeman 88*, 2nd ed. (New York: Arno, 1970); John and Mavis Beisanz, *The People of Panama* (New York: Columbia University Press, 1955); and Herbert and Mary Knapp, *Red, White, and Blue Paradise: The American Canal Zone in Panama* (San Diego: Harcourt, Brace, Jovanovich, 1984), an apologia for the Zonians.

[46] One born there, Senator John McCain, ran for US president. Oddly, in 1972, Torrijos had the Assembly extend citizenship to Americans born in the Zone, forcing them to present Panamanian passports at immigration. After the turnover, some used this citizenship to argue for hiring preference in the new Canal agency.

[47] Donoghue, *Borderland*, sketches out a stereotype, 25–26, and a longer portrait on 54–58.

[48] Conniff, *Panama*, 78, 100.

frequented iconic places, like the orchid farms of El Valle, the historic fortress at Portobello, the Pacific beaches, and the western Alpine forest cities of Boquete and Volcan. In the 1950s, Canal employees invented a race in which they paddled *cayucos* (canoes) across the Isthmus. The race persisted for generations, one of the few Zonian traditions embraced by Panamanians and carried on today. Still, most Zonians at the time had only a passing acquaintance with the nation's history and culture.

Zonians kept their territory as well organized and manicured as any on earth. They conserved it spic and span, making sure buildings got painted, lawns mowed, roads repaired, and facilities maintained in working order, almost entirely with local workers. The contrast with run-down tenements and red light districts just outside the Zone seemed to give residents satisfaction. Zone police appeared to have been recruited for their size and brawn, for they evoked awe and fear in visitors. Law and order was to crime prevention what spic and span was to general neatness, a highly valued quality of Zone life. By the same token, authorities kept out riff-raff by stopping cars without Zone plates and questioning non-whites who happened by on foot. Legal infractions they encountered fell under the jurisdiction of the US District court set up there in the 1920s and 30s, that operated with its own code yet under the purview of federal courts in New Orleans.[49] The Zone appeared so well run that a resident couple could title their book about it, *Red, White, and Blue Paradise.*[50]

Panamanians often felt resentful, excluded, angry, and intimidated by Zonians when they happened to interact. Few Zonians spoke Spanish well, so conversations had to be conducted in English. They seldom went to Panama, so encounters usually occurred on foreign, not to say hostile, terrain. Zonians often exuded airs of superiority due to their nationality, jobs in a major maritime facility, advanced education, higher standard of living, and possession of a supposedly more advanced culture. And racism usually lay slightly below the surface of any dealings they might have. To be sure, lots of contacts took place between Panamanians and Zonians, some of them deep and satisfying, especially among youngsters allowed to study in the Zone schools. Yet unhealthy Panamanian–Zonian relations had built up over generations, suggesting that the latter would respond negatively to the possibility that the Canal treaties might be overhauled and end their privileged lifestyle.[51]

[49] Donoghue, *Borderland*, 37–40.
[50] Knapp and Knapp, *Red, White, and Blue.*
[51] Donoghue, *Borderland*, 58–65. On the experiences of two former presidents who had studied in the Zone, see Knapp and Knapp, *Red, White, and Blue*, 187–88.

When presidents Johnson and Robles announced negotiations to replace the 1903 treaty with one addressing Panama's grievances, Zonians mobilized their considerable influence to block the effort. Political party leaders lobbied their Democratic and Republican representatives, unions pressured their national officers, spokespeople testified before congressional hearings, and Zonians sent an avalanche of "personalized" letters to members of Congress opposing any change in Canal status. They argued that the Panama Canal was a wholly owned and operated maritime facility crucial for US trade and prosperity. Its military bases formed a forward defense bulwark in the Southern Hemisphere. Simultaneously, they contended that Panamanians could never operate and defend the Canal adequately and that any diminution of control would harm US standing in the eyes of the world. Such arguments set Zonians irretrievably against Panamanians and their interests, exacerbating relations between them.[52] The same confrontations arose during the mid-1970s treaty negotiations.

During the months that 1977 treaty ratification and enabling legislation went forward, Zonians high in the Canal administration mobilized to undermine the processes. Their rallying points in Washington, DC, included the US Army's Senate Legislative Liaison chief Michael Rhode Jr, the House offices of representatives Bauman, Wilson, Flood, and Murphy, as well as that of Senator Helms, and the law offices of former legal counsel for the Canal, W. Merryl Whitman. (See Chapter 2 for a fuller discussion of these activities.)

* * * *

The 1977 Treaties and the 1979 Panama Canal Act closed out over seventy-five years of sole operation of the Canal, military bases, and accompanying facilities by the US government. They set off a period of awkward implementation in which US and Panamanian authorities struggled to transfer the legal intentions of the treaty framers and congressional leaders into an acceptable reality. These struggles will be covered in the following three chapters.

[52] Knapp and Knapp, *Red, White, and Blue*, 258–63.

PART I

INTRODUCTION TO PART I

The remainder of this book recounts the history of Panama to present days. It begins in Chapter 2, with failed attempts to restore civilian government in the early days of treaty implementation, cut short by the death of Omar Torrijos in an airplane crash and by the rise of Manuel Antonio Noriega as strongman. Panama's relations with the United States deteriorated in the mid 1980s, and treaty implementation ground to a halt, as the latter exacted punishing but insufficient sanctions on the Noriega regime to force his resignation. The economy deteriorated severely, and few families were spared hardship. Civilian opponents of the regime rallied bravely but futilely against goon-squad repression and stolen elections. Even military rivals with hopes of assistance from US forces failed to bring down Noriega. In the end, President George H. W. Bush decided to mount an invasion of Panama just before Christmas 1989 to capture and imprison Noriega and to attempt to normalize frayed relations between the two countries.

Chapter 3 traces the rough road to restoring civilian democratic government in the wake of the devastating 1989 invasion. Promises of aid to rebuild the country fell short, and the interim government of President Guillermo Endara (1990–94) soon lost its authority and effectiveness to lead the recovery. The country drifted uneasily toward a presidential election in 1994, while an influx of capital, backed-up canal transfer payments and foreign corporations, helped revive the economy. The first Panamanian administrator of the Panama Canal Commission (PCC), Fernando Manfredo, took office in early 1990, but was soon replaced by Alberto Alemán. Gradually, treaty implementation got back on track, especially when the US government sent a high official to make sure it happened. As representative government reorganized itself and a strong-willed Electoral Tribunal improved the voting system, the PRD party founded by Torrijos and run by Noriega made a surprising return, winning the 1994 election by a plurality. The new president, Ernesto Pérez Balladares (1994–99), took firm control of the helm of state.

As narrated in Chapter 4, the new administration innovated in many areas at once: economic, political, diplomatic, and social, while stoking the business sector with more investment and freedom. Pérez Balladares's assertive leadership embraced free market capitalism and privatization, while accelerating the process of taking over lands and facilities from the former Zone, a process called *reversión*, usually translated as reversion. Meanwhile, the Canal shifted increasingly to Panamanian management, as executives trained in preceding years took hold of its future, and former military bases were transformed into research centers, new ports, and other facilities. Their goal in running the Canal, as well as that of the out-going US chiefs, was for a seamless transfer of operations on December 31, 1999.

Despite generally good relations with the Clinton administration in Washington and solid economic growth, neither side was pleased in the end. The United States was unable to keep Howard Air Force Base or renew a status-of-forces agreement to support counter-narcotics operations and military cooperation. Pérez Balladares struggled to guarantee his reforms through re-election or to gain any concessions from the United States, and his party lost the presidency in 1999. Mireya Moscoso (1999–2004), head of the Arnulfista (soon to be renamed Panameñista) Party, won a solid victory and stood poised to receive the Canal transfer at the end of the year. The turnover ended an era in Panama's history and began another, coinciding with the start of the new millennium.

2

The 1980s: A Halting Transition Toward Democracy

I have established the republic. But today it is not clear whether the form of government is a republic, a dictatorship or personal rule.

Mustafa Kemal Ataturk

FUNERAL OF GENERAL OMAR TORRIJOS

The huge funeral procession for Omar Torrijos, with perhaps a quarter of a million mourners, wound its way down Avenue of the Martyrs (formerly Fourth of July Avenue), along a border that previously separated Panama City from the Canal Zone. Days earlier, on July 31, 1981, Torrijos had perished when his light plane crashed into a mountainside jungle during a storm. The cortege route traced a line of repeated confrontations between Panama and the United States over the former's rights. It recalled an earlier definition of the Panama Canal as "a body of water entirely surrounded by controversy."[1]

* * * *

Torrijos's death left a mixed legacy. On one hand, he had ruled the country as dictator for thirteen years, having overthrown duly elected President Arnulfo Arias in 1968. Many elite families had lost influence during the dictatorship, as the general appealed to poor and rural people to support his regime. Elections were held only for the Assembly of County Representatives, a weak body the regime easily

[1] "Torrijos: su Último Patrullaje," *El Istmo, suplemento La Estrella*, Aug. 9, 1981. For an exhaustive study of relations across this contested frontier, see Donoghue, *Borderland on the Isthmus*.

manipulated.[2] On the other hand, Torrijos had persevered in his quest to replace the hated 1903 treaty with the United States that gave the colossus the right to build, operate, and defend the Panama Canal, with little participation by Panama. He was credited with concluding negotiations for the 1977 Carter-Torrijos Treaties that eventually gave Panama the Canal free of encumbrances in 1999. And, in 1978, he began a transition to restore democracy under a civilian president. Politicians and military officers saw his death cast these plans into disarray. For all these reasons, the mourners felt genuine grief and loss the day of his burial.[3]

Credible evidence pointed to pilot error as the cause of Torrijos's plane crash, yet numerous conspiracy theories circulated for years. Torrijos's death left a void at the top of Panama's government and provoked a scramble for power.

PREMATURE TRANSITION TO DEMOCRACY

Attempting to sway US senators reluctant to approve the Panama Canal Treaties in 1978, President Jimmy Carter and other heads of state suggested to General Torrijos that the chances of success would be better if Panama proceeded toward democratic government, and Torrijos agreed. He acted partly because his coalition had failed to form a strong administration, and likely due to fatigue as well.[4] He announced that the country would begin a return to democracy, starting with lifting restrictions on political activity and finding a civilian president. His subservient Assembly duly passed Law 81 to allow the return of political exiles, end censorship, and authorize the formation of parties dormant during most of the decade.[5]

[2] The best study of legislatures between 1984 and 2009 is Carlos Guevara Mann's *Political Careers, Corruption, and Impunity: Panama's Assembly, 1984–2009* (Notre Dame, IN: University of Notre Dame Press, 2011).

[3] On Torrijos's personality, leadership style, and strengths and weaknesses, see the thoughtful writings in Nicolás Ardito Barletta, *Huellas: Contribuciones públicas nacionales e internacionales, memorias* (Bogota: Panamericana, 2016), ch. 7, and Steve C. Ropp, *Panamanian Politics: From Guarded Nation to National Guard* (Stanford: Hoover Institution Press, 1982).

[4] Ibid., 79–81.

[5] Nicolás Ardito Barletta, interviews, Apr. 10, 12, 14, 2015; *Huellas*, passim; and "The Political and Economic Transition of Panama, 1978–1991," in *Democratic Transitions in Central America*, eds. Jorge Dominguez and Marc Lindenberg (Gainesville: University of Florida Press, 1997), 32–66. Cf. Robert C. Harding II, *Military Foundations of Panamanian Politics* (New Brunswick: Transaction Publishers, 2001), ch. 5. Useful chronologies are available in John Weeks and Phil Gunson, *Panama:*

To guide administration officials and supporters, he had his staff create a new party, the Partido Revolucionario Democrático (PRD), inspired loosely on Mexico's Partido Revolucionario Institucional. Torrijos clearly dominated the PRD, whose program would consist of "torrijismo," or the policies and actions he had instituted in preceding years.

Prominent among the returned exiles stood Arnulfo Arias, former president from the 1940s and victim of the 1968 coup, still a formidable vote-getter at the head of his Panameñista Party.[6] Meanwhile businessman Roberto "Bobby" Eisenmann founded the independent newspaper *La Prensa* to publish critical information about these unfolding events.[7]

Select Newspapers and Broadcast Media since the 1970s

La Estrella, in continuous print since its founding in 1853, began as a Spanish version of an English-language paper sold to foreigners crossing during the California Gold Rush. Generally mainstream ideologically, it has changed ownership many times in its long history.

El Panamá América, founded in 1928, was associated with the political interests of the Harmodio Arias family. Shortly after the 1968 coup, the military seized full control of Editora Panamá América (EPASA) and all its newspapers, including *Crítica*, the all-time bestselling local tabloid founded in 1958. After the return of civilian government, EPASA reverted to the Arias family and sought to compete with *La Prensa*. In 2010, EPASA was sold to a consortium whose major shareholder is said to be Ricardo Martinelli.*

La Prensa was founded in 1980 by businessman Roberto Eisenmann to oppose military government. It was shut down by the military from 1986 to 1990. When reopened, with technical support from Winston Robles, it pioneered a modern printing plant, a digital edition, and more in-depth, original reporting often critical of incumbent governments and elected officials.

Made in the USA (London: Latin American Bureau, 1991), xiii–xviii, and Thomas M. Leonard, *Historical Dictionary of Panama* (New York: Rowman and Littlefield, 2015), xxix–xxxvi.

6 For the character of parties and their histories, see Guevara Mann, *Political Careers*, ch. 2.

7 This chapter draws heavily on Orlando Pérez, *Political Culture in Panama: Democracy after Invasion* (New York: Palgrave Macmillan, 2011), ch. 4; William L. Furlong, "The Difficult Transition towards Democracy," *Journal of Interamerican Studies and World Affairs* 35, no. 3 (1993): 19–64; Salvador Sánchez González, "La transición a la democracia en Panamá," in *Historia general de Panamá*, ed. Afredo Castillero Calvo (Panama: Consejo Nacional del Centenario, 2004), III:II, 283–301.

(cont.)

El Siglo, founded in 1985 by businessman Jaime Padilla Véliz, was acquired by business tycoon Abdul Waked in 2001, with strong editorial management by Ebrahim Asvat until 2011. The paper sought to add political content to a tabloid format, and its generally independent stance has intermittently made it a circulation leader. Waked, also the major shareholder of *La Estrella* since 2006, apparently released control of both in 2017.

Radio ownership and broadcasting has varied from highly partisan to non-political and has been the most diverse and locally focused medium in Panama. The Eleta brothers extended their radio empire to start television broadcasting in 1960, when RPC Channel 4 went on the air. Medcom and its increasing number of affiliates remained nominally independent. The Roberto F. Chiari family started TVN Channel 2 in 1962; during the dictatorship it was acquired by a group close to the military, headed by Carlos Duque. In 1990, it was sold to another group, and today the Motta family remains the major shareholder of this more independent network. Both broadcasters have offered original national programming since the 1990s. After the advent of cable television in the new century, viewers were offered many more viewing options.

* In 2012, then-President of Panama Ricardo Martinelli also acquired a large percentage of shares of the RCM Nextv television channel, in apparent violation of Law 24 of 1999, which prohibits radio and television concessionaires from controlling a daily newspaper. See Aminta Bustamante, "Martinelli, los medios y el poder," in *La Prensa*, May 8, 2013.

These and other measures, later called a "democratic transition" in the rest of the continent, promised that the implementation of the new treaty would be accompanied by a freer political climate. In evocative language, Torrijos spoke of the military "returning to the barracks." The process would culminate in the direct election of a new president in May 1984.[8] Freedom of the press would be crucial for the transition to succeed.

8 Margaret E. Scranton, *The Noriega Years: U.S.-Panamanian Relations, 1981–1990* (Boulder, CO: Lynne Rienner, 1991), 55 ff; Harding II, *Military Foundations*, 78–92; Andrew S. Zimbalist and John Weeks, *Panama at the Crossroads: Economic Development*

Torrijos also told his close associate and minister of planning, Nicolás Ardito Barletta, that he intended to retire all current members of the Guardia high command and replace them with younger men loyal to himself. He did not wish to have some ambitious senior officers overthrow a civilian leader the way he himself had done in 1968. Clearly, Torrijos intended to lead a return to democracy yet sensed an inclination on the part of the military to retain autocratic rule.[9]

Torrijos chose to be president the talented, handsome, 38-year-old law professor and current minister of education Aristides Royo (1978–82). Born in the suburbs and educated at the hyper-political National Institute, Royo had gone to Salamanca to earn his law degree. Upon his return, he taught law at the University of Panama, joined the prestigious Morgan & Morgan law firm, and then plunged into the political turmoil of 1968. He helped write the Torrijos "revolutionary" constitution of 1972 and participated in treaty negotiations in the mid 1970s. He became minister of education in 1973 and helped create a more positive, reformist image for the regime.

Torrijos, who had come to rely on Royo's judgment and political skills, nominated him for election by the Assembly of Representatives of Municipalities to a six-year presidential term to oversee the democratic transition. Businessman Ricardo de la Espriella became his vice president, in equally automatic fashion. Royo soon created an economic advisory council made up of prominent businessmen Torrijos had cultivated during the 1970s, called the Frente Empresarial del PRD. Torrijos had cleverly won over economic leaders by offering government subsidies, protection, and concessions, following the broader vision enunciated by Ardito Barletta. Now, Royo garnered their support as well, managing to set up Panama's first Chamber of Commerce in 1979.[10] Finally, he led the festivities at a massive celebration of the Panamanian takeover of the former Panama Canal Zone, held on October 1, 1979, which included

and Political Change in the Twentieth Century (Berkeley & Los Angeles: University of California Press, 1991), 121; Leonard, *Historical Dictionary*, 250–51.

9 Ardito Barletta, *Huellas*, 48; Ropp, *Panamanian Politics*, 82–83.

10 On Torrijos's relations with the economic elite, see Ropp, *Panamanian Politics*, 62–66. See also the thoughtful and candid discussion of Torrijos and this period in "Interview with Ambler H. Moss Jr.," Library of Congress Manuscripts Division, 1988. Moss served as ambassador to Panama from 1978 to 1982. Undoubtedly some narcotics traffickers and money launderers managed to slip into the inner circle as well.

the participation of Mexican President José López Portillo and US Vice President Walter Mondale.

When President Jimmy Carter sought a refuge for the deposed Shah of Iran, Torrijos quickly agreed, but he left it up to President Royo to quell the controversy, until the Shah abandoned his hideaway on Contadora Island for a more tranquil residence in Egypt.[11]

Demilitarization of government lay at the core of the transition in Panama, and Royo gave it a civilian face. He implemented Law 81 that lifted rigid controls on speech and politics and set a timetable for return to full democracy in 1984. Pent-up demands and challenges arose, and vocal discontent that had built up to some of Torrijos's programs suddenly erupted. On October 9, 1979, the National Opposition Front organized what it claimed was the largest political demonstration in Panamanian history, attended by about 300,000 people. This was complemented by a sixty-eight-day, nearly nationwide teachers' strike in the fall of 1979. If transition occurred, many objected to its being led by military-installed newcomers.[12]

In 1980 the PRD civilianization process seemed a little more secure, and Torrijos routinely told favor-seekers to go see the president, that he was now retired. The PRD, meanwhile, gathered enough signatures to qualify as a legal party.[13] Slightly relaxed electoral procedures in September 1980, the first open elections since 1968, chose nineteen members of a legislative council within the Assembly. Had the Panamanian transition succeeded, it would have been a first among the many Latin American military regimes to return to democracy during the 1980s.[14] But it was not to be.

As Panama began the new decade, Royo ran into still stronger cross-winds, fanned by the world recession and ambitions among National Guard colonels to extend the dictatorship. Panama's economy skidded into stagnation that felt more painful because of the high expectations people had for prosperity under the new treaties. A November 1981 article in *The New York Times* claimed that Royo seemed to be prevailing in a struggle for power with the new National Guard Commander, Colonel Florencio Flores Aguilar, but warned that economic conditions were deteriorating badly for the masses:

11 "Interview with Ambler Moss."

12 Miguel Antonio Bernal interviews, July 22–23, 1986. Bernal helped lead this and a repeat strike in 1981.

13 Guevara Mann, *Political Careers*, 41–42.

14 Ropp, *Panamanian Politics*, 82–83; Pérez, *Political Culture*, 51–52.

the economy seems to be booming with new luxury apartments and office blocks rising. Over the last decade, Panama has also been a leading "offshore" financial center for Latin America, its 114 foreign banks, including many from the United States, controlling $38 billion in deposits. But such service functions produce little real economic growth. Unemployment, already high, has gone higher and frustrations, barely held in check by Torrijos, threaten to erupt.[15]

Without the gravitas of Torrijos and with the economy on the skids, Royo faced formidable obstacles to returning to an open political system. In some ways, his presidency was also doomed by the death of Torrijos, after which the colonels in the Guard began maneuvering to hold on to power. Royo, who never accepted the primacy of the military, stood in their way. Suddenly, at the end of July 1982, Royo announced his resignation, allegedly for reasons of health. In fact, Guard officers had decided to roll back civilianization with their own transition – to re-militarization. They were not going quietly back to the barracks.

On the first anniversary of Torrijos's death, veteran journalist Alan Riding described the behavior of yet another new commander, Rubén Darío Paredes, at the swearing in of de la Espriella as President. Paredes seemed to be "trying to look constitutional but behaving as though he had just carried out a coup," when he suspended the publication of all newspapers for seven days and demanded the resignation of all the officials of the outgoing government.[16]

Royo's nearly four years in office stood in sharp contrast to the following period, dominated by military chiefs, especially Manuel Antonio Noriega. Civilian presidents de la Espriella and his successor Jorge Illueca openly acknowledged that their authority flowed from the *Comandancia* (headquarters) and served for short tenures. Others, like Nicolás Ardito Barletta and Eric Arturo Delvalle, who attempted to defy Noriega, ended up about as quickly and surely deposed.[17]

RESURGENCE OF THE GUARD

On the military side, several ranking officers who had resisted Torrijos's democratization plans, to protect their positions, began jockeying to take

[15] "Panama: Troubled Passage for a U.S. Ally," *The New York Times*, Nov. 22, 1981. Cf. the analysis of Ardito Barletta, "The Political and Economic Transition," 32–66.

[16] "Panama Military Close to Direct Rule," *The New York Times*, Aug. 4, 1982. For this episode, see Patricia Pizzurno Gelos and Celestino Andrés Araúz, *Estudios sobre el Panamá Republicano (1903–1989)* (Panama: Manfer, SA: 1996), 591–92.

[17] Ardito Barletta's synthesis appears as "The Political and Economic Transition of Panama, 1978–1991," passim.

power after his death. The Guard had long provided muscle for the regime, and its leaders had become accustomed to the power, money, and stature they enjoyed. The Guard also played important roles in suppressing opposition activities, raising money for illicit purposes, and managing intelligence gathering at home and abroad.[18]

In 1981, ranking Guard officers included Col. Florencio Flores (Commander), Col. Rubén Paredes, Lt. Col. Manuel Antonio Noriega, and Col. Roberto Díaz Herrera, most of whom had experience in a variety of activities besides police work and national defense. In mid 1982, fellow officers dismissed Flores as commandant and replaced him with the more politically ambitious Paredes. The new leader had no intention of allowing civilians to exercise real power and planned to run for president himself in 1984. Still, he pushed an electoral reform package through the legislature. To assuage the ambitions of other Guard officers, he signed a secret agreement allowing them to rotate into the presidency after his term ended.[19]

Paredes also appointed a commission to transform the Assembly of Representatives of Municipalities (*corregimientos*) into the Legislative Assembly, one similar to the body that had existed for most of the twentieth century. It would enjoy more autonomy vis-à-vis the executive branch and participate in a broader range of law-making activities. It also inherited the patronage distribution role of its predecessor, allowing its members to win reelection, enrich themselves, and enjoy immunity from prosecution for wrongdoing. Carlos Guevara Mann, a historian who has studied corruption for decades, argues that the 1983 reforms, rather than encourage democratic government, actually extended a long tradition of careerism, corruption, and impunity in that body. The reform was approved in a referendum and took effect the following year.[20]

Meanwhile Noriega, head of the Guard's intelligence branch (called G-2 after US military usage), became second in command under Paredes. When Paredes had to resign in August 1983 to run for president the following year, Noriega assumed command of the Guard and promoted

[18] On general security of the Canal in the twentieth century, see Charles Morris Brooks, *Guarding the Crossroads: Security and Defense of the Panama Canal* (Panama: P & P Group, 2003). Chs. 19–22 cover the period since the 1977 treaties.

[19] Pizzurno and Araúz, *Panamá republicano*, 594–96; Scranton, *Noriega Years*, 67–68.

[20] Guevara Mann, *Political Careers*, 79–81. On the reforms, see Miguel Antonio Bernal, "Evolución constitucional desde la separación de Panamá," in *Historia General de Panama*, ed. Alfredo Castillero Calvo (Panama: Consejo Nacional del Centenario, 2004), III:I, 42–44.

himself to general. He had encouraged Paredes to step down and run but soon double-crossed him; instead he sought a civilian to head the military-backed PRD ticket.[21] First, he offered the candidacy to Fernando Manfredo, a longtime Torrijos friend and collaborator who at the time served as deputy administrator of the Panama Canal Commission (PCC). Manfredo declined, so Noriega's representative invited Nicolás Ardito Barletta to run.[22] He had served in numerous capacities with Torrijos during the 1970s, ending up as minister of planning and economic policy (MIPPE) from 1973 to 1978. From there he went on to be vice president for Latin America in the World Bank.

When Ardito Barletta asked Noriega if the Guard would defer to his presidential authority, in the event he was elected, Noriega assured him it would. Later events proved that Noriega really intended to maintain authority behind the scenes. He needed Ardito Barletta to give legitimacy to the regime and to solve the country's economic problems. Despite the appearance of a return to democracy, then, some suspected that the balance of power still resided in the Guard headquarters in Chorillo, rather than the *Las Garzas* presidential palace, in the Casco Viejo district.[23]

Noriega carried out an even more audacious power grab shortly after becoming commander. With support from the joint committee for defense of the Canal, he pressured the legislature to pass Law 20 to reorganize, strengthen, and convert the Guard (created in 1953 by previous strongman José Antonio Remón) into the Panama Defense Forces (PDF). The Assembly dutifully complied. The new unit was a rapid response force along the lines of the Israeli Defense Force – well-armed, superbly informed, highly trained, and capable of lightning action to thwart potential threats. It also took over other police functions and enjoyed enhanced autonomy from civilian oversight. US authorities went along, since, until 1999, the US military's Southern Command (Southcom), with headquarters in the Canal Area, would backstop the force, and, in the long run, the

[21] Fernando Berguido, *Una vida póstuma* (Panama: Círculo Editorial y de Lectura, 2013), 83.

[22] Fernando Manfredo Jr., *La transición del Canal a Panamá, 1979–1990: Memorias* (Panama: by author, 2014), 173–75. On Ardito Barletta's role in economic planning under Torrijos, see *Huellas*, chs. 3–4. Cf. also Zimbalist and Weeks, *Panama at the Crossroads*, 32–33, 68–74, and passim.

[23] On Noriega's style, personality, relations with US agencies, and scope of power, see "Interview with Ambler Moss."

Treaty for Permanent Neutrality would help to shield the Canal from threats.[24]

At the time, Noriega enjoyed good relations with the national defense establishment in Washington, which included the Pentagon, CIA, DEA, NSC, and other agencies. He had worked with Vice President George H. W. Bush, who "handled" him when he was CIA director. These agencies approved of the beefed-up force, on the grounds that, under the new treaties, Panama would have to shoulder increasing responsibility for defending the Canal. The move also benefitted the escalating US war against the Sandinistas in Nicaragua, where Noriega later served the Iran-Contra operation in multiple ways.[25] The reinforced PDF also fit nicely with the national security doctrines adopted by the US-backed military regimes in the Southern Cone, which stressed fighting domestic communism over external threats. Finally, Law 20 created a buffer between the Panamanian executive branch and the armed services and gave the PDF broad authority to intervene in many aspects of national life.[26]

US support for Panama in 1984–85 was authorized at the highest levels. The 1983–84 Kissinger Commission on Central America recommended major increases in economic and military aid to the region, to block the spread of communism from Cuba there. It spoke of an extra $800 million in the 1984 fiscal year as a down payment on a long-term commitment of $24 billion in economic assistance by 1990.[27] Although Panama received little specific attention in the report, it was clear the State Department intended to help Ardito Barletta's government succeed in returning the country to democracy and adopting austerity measures following the profligate Torrijos years. And the DOD foresaw an accelerated hand-off of Canal protection to the PDF. Economic aid

[24] Pizzurno and Araúz, *Panamá republicano*, 599–600; Scranton, *Noriega Years*, 52–53; Harding, *Military Foundations*, 161–62; Berguido, *Vida póstuma*, 84–85. The text of Law 20 and a constitutional critique appear in the pamphlet by Carlos Bolívar Pedreschi, *De la protección del Canal a la militarización del pais* (San José, Costa Rica: Litografía LIL, 1987), 63–69, 91–111.

[25] "Interview with John A. Bushnell," Library of Congress Manuscripts Division, 1997, 766. Having served in the State Department in 1981–82, he recalled trying to dissuade these agencies from giving inordinate power to Noriega. The CIA pushed for Noriega, however, to help advance the Contra War in Nicaragua.

[26] Carlos Guevara Mann, *Panamanian Militarism: A Historical Interpretation* (Athens: Ohio University Center for International Studies, 1996), 161–65. See also his "La Vida Política en el siglo XX," in *Panamá: historia contemporánea*, ed. Alfredo Castillero Calvo (Madrid: Fundación Mafre, 2014), 163–248.

[27] Henry Kissinger, ed., *Report of the President's National Bipartisan Commission on Central America* (New York: Macmillan, 1984), 57, 78, and 121.

mushroomed from an average $9 million between 1980 and 1984 to $74 million in 1985, and military aid from $15 million to $93 million in the same years. The following year, Congress left Panama out of the AID budget due to the Noriega crisis, but by then the damage had been done. The lopsided emphasis on defense gave credence to the later observation that Noriega was a strongman, nurtured by the United States, who could only be toppled by his creator.[28]

1984 PRESIDENTIAL ELECTION AND ARDITO BARLETTA ADMINISTRATION

The 1984 election could have been a turning point in Panama's destiny, but it was not to be. Ricardo de la Espriella had succeeded to the presidency when the Guard jettisoned Royo in 1982. Later, when Manfredo turned down the PRD presidential nomination, de la Espriella offered it to Ardito Barletta, who, in late 1983, accepted to run based on Noriega's commitment to obey his administration. Ardito Barletta's close collaboration with Torrijos, plus his experience in international finance, made him an excellent choice to address the country's economic malaise. His approval by the PRD sealed his nomination.[29] He lined up backing from David Samudio, the unsuccessful candidate against Arnulfo Arias in 1968, as well as from parties like PALA, the Liberals, and the Republicanos. Haltingly, the country's parties began to evolve from personalistic vehicles toward broader organizations representing diverse elements and interests.

Ardito Barletta's decision to run for president ended the pleasant job he held at the World Bank, but it reflected his earlier work with Torrijos and promised professional rewards. In 1968–70, as director of planning under Torrijos, he had overseen the creation of an ambitious plan for national development, *Estrategia para el desarrollo nacional,* which had guided the Torrijos administration.[30] Later, as minister of planning and economic policy, he had the opportunity to put many of his ideas to work. Ardito Barletta now hoped that as president he could resurrect that plan while also solving short-term difficulties.

[28] Interview with AID desk officer Gary Adams, June 27, 1986, and agency fact sheet.

[29] The rising PRD star, Ernesto Pérez Balladares, resisted, in the belief that his service to the regime and business experience should have led to his nomination. This tended to distance him from Noriega, who made the final decision. Rubén Paredes, also denied the PRD nomination, ran nonetheless on the ticket of an obscure party and came in third.

[30] Ardito Barletta, *Estrategia para el desarrollo nacional* (Panama: Editorial Exedra, 2012), ch. 3.

Ardito Barletta had never run a political campaign before, but he returned home in January 1984 and threw himself into the race with gusto and considerable backing from the government. The coalition he assembled, called the Unión Democrática Nacional, augmented his core PRD support. His platform called for democracy, strong and honest government, economic and national development, and foreign policies favorable to Panama. President Carter's former chief of staff, Hamilton Jordan, provided strategic advice for his campaign.[31] Ardito Barletta focused on winning votes from civil servants and teachers, from whom he expected warm support, and played to large crowds in all regions of the country, including indigenous and ethnic communities. In his wife's province of Los Santos, he wore guayaberas and posed as a man with rural roots. His final rally in the capital mobilized 180,000 supporters, whom he addressed with confidence and vigor.

Ardito Barletta's program drew on the planning he had done since the late 1960s and emphasized utilization of the Canal properties and assets becoming available under the 1977 treaty. It contained fulsome promises

FIGURE 2.1 Nicolás Ardito Barletta with wife and son during 1984 presidential campaign. Courtesy of Nicolás Ardito Barletta.

[31] This account is based largely on Ardito Barletta's interviews of Apr. 10, 12, and 14, 2015; *Huellas*, ch. 6; and his book, *Estrategia para el desarrollo*. The use of either foreign or domestic political experts and advisers for political campaigns would not become common until the mid 1990s.

to working and middle-class citizens. He also addressed the need for governability, that is, stronger public institutions and enhanced government effectiveness. As for eventual ownership of the Canal, he spoke of Panama finally benefitting fully from its superb geographical location and expanding beyond the simple business of ship transits.[32]

Arnulfo Arias, showing his 82 years, threw his hat in the ring as well. Ardito Barletta had met with him the preceding November to argue that he desist from running and choose his own designee as Ardito Barletta's vice president. Arnulfo declined and instead ran a low-key, traditional campaign as the "patriarch of democracy." He declined invitations to debate Ardito Barletta, trying to appear above the fray. Meanwhile, President de la Espriella, hoping to undermine Ardito Barletta and end up extending his own tenure, consulted with Arias, the military's arch-enemy. After failing to convince Arias, de la Espriella was himself deposed for disloyalty. Second vice president Jorge Illueca assumed the presidency in January 1984, three months before the election.

The outcome of the 1984 contest remains controversial, due in part to Arnulfo's vociferous complaints of fraud and reporting by foreign reporters. Ardito Barletta's campaign no doubt received abundant government support, and open favoritism toward him by the US government raised suspicions of meddling. Finally, the fact that Noriega's PDF stood firmly behind Ardito Barletta convinced most that it had rigged the election. After the electoral tribunal annulled some 23,000 of his votes (along with 19,000 of Arnulfo's), Ardito Barletta emerged as the winner, with a margin of less than two thousand votes.[33] He was inaugurated on October 11, 1984, along with a PRD majority in the legislature. Former president Jimmy Carter and US Secretary of State George Schultz flew to Panama to congratulate him, and numerous Latin American heads of state attended. Potential investors began visiting too.

The revamped Legislative Assembly, elected in 1984 and expected to work with the new president, contained a mixed bag of former members and newcomers, totaling sixty-seven. The PRD and its allies won a quarter of the overall votes and just over half the seats. The Panameñistas won a fifth of the votes and a fifth of the seats. Several smaller parties divided up the remaining twenty seats. The PRD majority suggested a continuation of subservient relations with the executive branch, much stronger than the

[32] See his platform statement in *Estrategia para el desarrollo*, ch. 7.

[33] Scranton, *Noriega Years*, 75–7; Berguido, *Vida póstuma*, 85–6; Berta Thayer interviews, Apr. 16, 1993 and Aug. 16, 2014.

Assembly.[34] Subservience did not mean honesty and transparency, however, because corruption continued unabated. Guevara Mann concluded:

> By encouraging bribery, embezzlement, and related corrupt activities, exempting certain individuals from justice (impunity); and manipulating voters through the particularistic assignment of public goods (clientelism), all three traits contradict the notions of political equality and universalism that are central to the idea of democracy.[35]

Clearly, under these circumstances, the Assembly accomplished little of the people's business.

Corruption looms large in Panama's politics, if not always explicitly. Guevara Mann specified three of the dimensions (economic, impunity/prosecution, and political culture) that surface most commonly. A fourth is its institutional impact, as we will observe. Systematic analysis of corruption such as Guevara Mann developed for the Assembly lies beyond the scope of this study. Instead, we will cover episodes as they arise and register contemporaries' judgments about them.

Ardito Barletta first toured friendly nations to show off Panama's newly restored democracy, while at home he enjoyed high approval ratings and support from the two major TV stations. He appointed more technocrats than politicians to his cabinet, intending to run an effective administration. The economy proved most challenging, so he invited prominent US planner Marc Lindenberg to consult with his team. They built on earlier visions of Panama as a hub for global services and trade, comparing it to Singapore, which had enjoyed success as a small nation using its position for strategic advantage. They propagated the concept of Panama as a "Centerport," a place for container marshalling, bonded manufacturing like in the Colon Free Zone, air transport, maritime services, and offshore banking. The president invited Asian investors to support these developments.[36]

In a short time Ardito Barletta posted impressive accomplishments. He overhauled the national budget agency, the Contraloría, and its watchdog twin, the Tribunal de Cuentas, and he won Assembly approval for a new judicial code. He inaugurated the Parque Metropolitano, which incorporated a large part of the forested lands transferred from the former Canal Zone. He had several investment incentives approved. He arranged for the Smithsonian Tropical Research Institute (STRI), long housed in the Zone,

[34] Guevara Mann, *Political Careers*, 50–63, 86–89.
[35] Ibid., 113–14.
[36] Ardito Barletta, *Huellas*, ch. 4; Pizzurno and Araúz, *Panamá republicano*, 608–14.

to become a US-Panamanian entity, and he designated new coastal lands for it to expand its marine research facilities.[37] He empaneled the Tripartite Canal Alternatives Study group, by which Panamanian, Japanese, and US specialists weighed the possibilities of a sea-level Canal, a land bridge, or expansion of the existing facility. Other initiatives also won approval by the legislature.[38]

Ardito Barletta focused most of his presidential powers, however, on achieving economic development. His goal of unleashing the productive energy of the nation faced severe shortages of financing and investment, due to the general depression that overlay the region. The first order of business, then, had to be raising capital from the international banks, which he was fully acquainted with from his World Bank days. To accomplish this, he had to carry out austerity measures to encourage domestic growth and also to qualify for new international credits. The public debt, run up during the preceding fifteen years, stood at an unhealthy 85 percent of the GNP, and spending still ran 7 percent over revenues. His remedy was to trim government payrolls, cut subsidies for public services, assess new taxes, promulgate a less protective labor code, and support industry so it could expand the economy. The opposition, meanwhile, denounced these measures as harmful to the poor and working class, but Ardito Barletta remained steadfast; Noriega and most union leaders, aligned with the PRD, agreed with him.

At first, Noriega seemed to embrace the bitter medicine prescribed by the president. His chief of staff, Col. Díaz Herrera, did not like it, however, calling it imperialist punishment.[39] The reforms, in fact, had the effect of laying off government employees and increasing taxes. Opponents focused their ire on proposed Law 46, submitted to the legislature in November 1984. In hindsight, the president admitted that he may have failed to promote enough public discussion and gather cosponsors to win support. Within a month, huge demonstrations organized by the opposition erupted in the capital, and Ardito Barletta had to retreat on raising taxes.[40]

[37] After conducting a biological inventory of the Canal Zone, the Smithsonian Institution reached an agreement with Panama to make the recently formed Barro Colorado island in Lake Gatun into a biological preserve. The field research station gradually evolved into STRI in 1966, one of the world's foremost tropical research facilities hosting hundreds of visiting researchers from all over the world. The bilateral cooperation established during the 1977 treaty negotiations was later extended by a 1985 agreement.

[38] Ardito Barletta, *Huellas*, ch. 5. See also the discussion on Canal planning below.

[39] Scranton, *Noriega Years*, 78–9.

[40] Miguel Antonio Bernal interviews, July 22–23, 1986.

The following February, Ardito Barletta submitted to the Assembly a milder version of the law, to assuage critics and regain the initiative. This time it passed, and he complemented its rollout with well-targeted pork-barrel projects. Yet by spring 1985, military commanders, especially Díaz Herrera, began to doubt Ardito Barletta's ability to lead the country, and some spoke of "shared governance," i.e. more PDF participation in decision-making. They imposed some cabinet changes in May to enforce their opinions and perhaps pave the way for a military coup. Some US observers also viewed the president as ineffectual. Meanwhile, Ardito Barletta paid a friendly visit to Mexican President Miguel de la Madrid, himself a veteran of economic hard times, and hired a new political consultant to help explain his reforms to the public.

In mid 1985 Ardito Barletta readied his proposal for a World Bank credit to refinance the foreign debt, based on the structural changes he had instituted, such as competitiveness, financial probity, and opening the economy to trade and investment. He shared the draft letter with businessmen, politicians, and labor leaders in hopes of gaining support. Sensing the fragility of the moment, the State Department requested that General John Vessey, Chairman of the US Joint Chiefs of Staff, pay a visit to the president and to General Noriega to urge them to continue on the democratic path.[41]

In late August, the president invited Noriega and other commanders to meet and discuss the World Bank proposal, which Díaz Herrera opposed. As a result, Ardito Barletta agreed to phase in the reforms to dampen their negative impact. They would be implemented over seven months: agricultural to revive farming; labor to raise worker productivity; industrial for factory expansion. Schools would be on vacation during those months, cushioning the potential for public protest. The president informed the legislature that his policies had already produced GDP growth of 5 percent and reduced the fiscal deficit. His assurances would prove to be insufficient.

Within days of launching his economic plan, the president learned of a brutal murder that shocked the nation. On September 13, the charismatic physician Hugo Spadafora, member of a prominent family, had been decapitated and dumped just across the Costa Rican border. Having fought in the civil wars in Central America, Spadafora enjoyed widespread public adulation. He had recently denounced Noriega for various crimes, including drug trafficking, and he announced his intention to enter politics

[41] Ardito Barletta, *Huellas*, 287–301.

in Panama. Critics of the government immediately attributed his horrific murder to PDF agents, and Noriega, although out of the country when it occurred, seemed likely to be behind the act.[42] Public outrage over the Spadafora murder engulfed the nation, and Ardito Barletta promised the family he would appoint a commission to determine responsibility for the crime, which he did.

Vice President Delvalle used the Spadafora crisis to urge Díaz Herrera to push Ardito Barletta out, rather than allow the investigation to proceed, so that he could succeed to the presidency. Díaz Herrera did not need much convincing. Shortly after the president's return from a speech at the United Nations, he was summoned to PDF headquarters. There top officers detained and badgered him for fourteen hours, until he agreed to take leave or step down as president, which the military portrayed to the public as his resignation. At the end of the ordeal, he looked Noriega in the eyes and said, "Remember my words, you are going to regret what you are doing here." And four years later the general went to jail in the United States, later suffered prison in France, and ended up in Panama's penitentiary, released to house arrest just two months before his death in March 2017.[43]

During the coup against him, Ardito Barletta received encouragement from Assistant Secretary of State for Inter-American Affairs Elliot Abrams to "hang tough," despite no concrete support. He later learned that Pentagon operative Nestor Sanchez had apparently condoned the coup. Ardito Barletta believed that the situation had become hyper-polarized, and he mistakenly thought that the military would back down. He received condolences and job offers from colleagues in Washington but declined them. The *Washington Post* denounced the coup as the "beheading of Panama," alluding to the Spadafora murder. The new regime, meanwhile, condemned many of the president's allies as traitors of the

[42] Among the many accounts available, the most vivid is Guillermo Sánchez Borbón, "Hugo Spadafora's Last Day," *Harper's*, June 1988, 56–62. A fuller version is Richard M. Koster and Guillermo Sánchez Borbón, *In the Time of the Tyrants: Panama 1968–1990* (New York: W. W. Norton & Co., 1990). Cf. also Scranton, *Noriega Years*, 85–87; Kevin Buckley, *Panama: The Whole Story* (New York: Simon & Schulster, 1991), 21–30; and the recent fictionalized biography, Amir Valle, *Hugo Spadafora, bajo la piel del hombre* (Panama: Aguilar, Prisa Ediciones, 2013).

[43] Ardito Barletta, *Huellas*, 304–10; interviews, Apr. 10, 12, 14, 2015; Scranton, *Noriega Years*, 87–91; Frederick Kempe, *Divorcing the Dictator: America's Bungled Affair with Noriega* (New York: G.P. Putnam's Sons, 1990), 143 ff. Cf. Omar Jaén Suárez, *Diez años de administración panameña del Canal de Panamá, 2000–2010* (Panama: Autoridad del Canal de Panamá, 2011), 31–32.

nation, including prominent figures like Gabriel Lewis, Fernando Eleta, Roberto Motta, and Mario Galindo.[44]

THE NORIEGA CRISIS OF 1987–89 AND THE NATIONAL CIVIC CRUSADE

The reasons why American leaders seemed willing to accommodate strongman Noriega in the mid 1980s, with a civilian front man like Ardito Barletta, have been told many times and still echo in the memories of American news consumers from that era. Later, most of these same US leaders turned against the dictator and carried out a trenchant campaign to push him out or remove him.[45] The US press bombarded the American public with stories that demonized Noriega. *The New York Times'* Seymour Hersch had helped launch the campaign against Noriega with a blockbuster article on June 12, 1986.[46] Between then and the invasion and capture of Noriega in December 1989, thousands of stories appeared in the press around the world, prejudging him. Afterward, many "instant" trade books were published about the general and his demise, such as those by Kempe, Sánchez Borbón and Koster, Woodward, Dinges, Buckley, and Weeks and Gunson. His rise and fall in the court of public opinion could not have been more dramatic.

Some of the reasons Noriega had seemed appropriate for the role of strongman in 1983–84 evaporated in following years. For one, several other military regimes in South America, along with their national security doctrines, relinquished power. The Central American conflict moved toward resolution, no longer requiring a broker in Panama. The Cold War itself drifted toward conclusion, removing other justifications for supporting dictators. Finally, some US congressional opponents of giving the Canal to Panama played up the Noriega crisis as a strategy for annulling the 1977 treaties.[47] By 1989, Noriega had been thoroughly vilified by the US government, the press, and public opinion.

The "stability" that Noriega supposedly provided (as Torrijos had done before him) grew tenuous in the mid 1980s. Foremost among

[44] Ardito Barletta, *Huellas*, 310–12.

[45] Scranton, *Noriega Years*, 115–18.

[46] Ibid., 92–95.

[47] Ibid., ch. 6 passim. North Carolina Senator Jesse Helms played a prominent role in sabotaging the treaties. See the account by Ambassador Everett Ellis Briggs, posted in Panama during Noriega's rise, 1982–86: "Our Man in Panama," *New York Times*, Sept. 9, 2007.

troubling developments was an open break between Noriega and rival Díaz Herrera. The latter had served as chief of staff and expected to succeed to commander in 1987, as had been promised when Noriega became *comandante*. When Noriega dismissed him, he retaliated by publicly denouncing the dictator with graphic descriptions of wrongdoings.[48]

Although much of the growing opposition to Noriega originated overseas, Panamanians also mounted a serious movement against his regime that ranged from academic denunciations to street protests. Its origins went back to the 1968 coup and mobilized well-to-do professionals and their families who found their well-being threatened by the military government. During the 1970s, opposition bubbled along mostly underground, in the form of clandestine publications, student activism, antigovernment networks, and guarded newspaper columns.

La Prensa clearly served as the flagship newspaper for the opposition in the mid 1980s. It supported Arnulfo Arias in the 1984 election, denounced the death of Spadafora in 1985, calling for a full investigation, and reprinted the Seymour Hersh and other revelations from the US press in mid 1986.[49]

Student protests and repression expanded in July 1986, with street clashes, police raids on schools and the University of Panama, and mobilization of riot police nicknamed the Dobermans for their vicious tactics and black uniforms. Students denounced mistreatment and jailing of Professor Miguel Antonio Bernal and Guillermo Sánchez Borbón, a popular columnist with *La Prensa*. Police clubbed protesters and fired tear gas to disperse them, only igniting more resistance.[50]

The protest movement erupted again during the Díaz Herrera crisis of June 1987, as people opposed to the regime believed that its end was imminent. Tens of thousands demonstrated, and hundreds of civic organizations aggregated into a loose coalition, the National Civic Crusade.[51]

[48] John Dinges, *Our Man in Panama* (New York: Random House, 1990, 1991), 260–66; Scranton, *Noriega Years*, 106–08; Kempe, *Divorcing*, ch. 13; Zimbalist and Weeks, *Panama at the Crossroads*, 80–81. Roberto Díaz Herrera points to the turmoil over the Iran-Contra affair and the death of Spadafora as the key events of the era and adds other insights on militarism and Panama's relations with the US in a self-published 2009 memoir, *Estrellas Clandestinas*. Cf his *La Explosión de Panamá* (Panama: Impresos Modernos S.A., 2011); and our interview with Roberto Díaz Herrera, Nov. 23, 2014. Allan Metz reviewed this huge literature in "Manuel Noriega and the 'Panama Crisis': An Annotated Bibliography," *Reference Services Review*, Fall 1991, 7–44.

[49] "Noriega: Quién lo investiga," *La Prensa*, July 2, 1986.

[50] See front page coverage in *La Prensa, El Siglo*, and *Extra* on July 12, 1986.

[51] The Crusade and its predecessors are described by Brittmarie Janson Pérez, "The Process of Political Protest in Panama, 1968–1989," PhD diss., University of Texas, 1993, esp. ch. 5. Cf. Pizzurno and Araúz, *Panamá republicano*, 617–19.

Anti-government protesters in mid 1987 organized marches with placards and chants, pot-banging, and white scarves. Their demonstrations quickly drew attacks and dispersal by the Dobermans. Such protests, drawing students from the universities and high schools, highlighted middle-class dissatisfaction with the regime. Even some lower-class protesters made their opposition to Noriega heard.[52]

Other organizations joined in. Business associations called several general strikes in 1987, signaling their disapproval of their diminished civic freedoms and constrained economic possibilities. Civic clubs, like Rotary, Lions, Kiwanis, and the Chamber of Commerce, and others like Aurelio Barrios, also registered their opposition to the unconstitutional regime.[53] Much of this was covertly encouraged by the US State Department. Meanwhile, Noriega had *La Prensa* seized and shut down, not to reopen permanently until early 1990.

The 1989 election debacle clinched most observers' conclusion that Noriega had become a demon who should be removed from power. Noriega went on the defensive due to the US sanctions and diplomatic campaign against him, but to assuage opinion he called for a presidential election on May 7, 1989. He chose friend and business associate Carlos Duque to head the ticket. The opposition mobilized behind standard-bearer Guillermo Endara of the Panameñistas for president (Arnulfo had died the previous August). His allies Ricardo Arias Calderón of the Christian Democrats and Guillermo "Billy" Ford, of MOLIRENA and the business community, ran for first and second vice president. Few observers were sanguine about the opposition's chances to vote out Noriega, but everyone agreed that it would be a plebiscite on his regime.[54]

52 Janson Pérez, "Process," ch. 7. During these years, Alfredo Castillero Calvo and his son Alfredo Castillero Hoyos participated in Civic Crusade protests and kept author Conniff informed in private correspondence.

53 Richard L. Millett, "The Failure of Panama's Internal Opposition, 1987–1989," in *Conflict Resolution and Democratization in Panama: Implications for U.S. Policy*, ed. Eva Loser (Washington, DC: Center for Strategic and International Studies, 1992), 21–38. See the anti-government speech Carlos Bolívar Pedreschi delivered to these clubs on Nov. 28, 1987: pamphlet "Testimonio histórico," courtesy Janson Pérez. Noriega's intelligence blamed Deputy Chief of Mission John Maisto for inciting the Civic Crusade: see "Interview with Arthur H. Davis, Jr.," Library of Congress Manuscripts Division, 1991. Davis served as US ambassador to Panama from 1986 to 1990, although for most of that time he remained in Washington to signal US disapproval of Noriega.

54 Among the many accounts of the episode, see Manfredo, *La transición*, 198–201; Kempe, *Divorcing*, 350–63; Zimbalist and Weeks, *Panama at the Crossroads*, 150–53.

Because of skepticism lingering after the 1984 election, many groups offered to monitor the elections in 1989, including the Carter Center, the European Parliament, the OAS, the US State Department, the Center for Strategic and International Studies, and various former heads of state.[55] Noriega acquiesced, certain that his influence on the Electoral Tribunal and police watchers would help his candidate prevail. After a massive turnout on election day, the vote-counting arm of the Tribunal went to work, while Noriega agents alternatively stole ballot boxes and attempted to alter the results tabulated by computers. Observers witnessed gross violations of the rules and denounced them to the international press. Independent exit polls showed the opposition winning by margins so large that no amount of fraud could overcome them.

Three days after the election, Endara, Arias Calderón, and Ford led a march to the presidential palace to protest these government actions. They were attacked by irregular militiamen named dignity battalions or "digbats," who killed Ford's bodyguard. The thugs attacked and bloodied the candidates, and images of the melee went out to a shocked world.[56]

Noriega and the Tribunal cancelled the election results on the grounds that legal procedures had been violated. He installed another puppet, Francisco Rodríguez, as provisional president on September 1, 1989, the seventh to serve in eight years.[57] Less than four months later, US armed forces invaded Panama to arrest Noriega, restore constitutional government, and ensure implementation of the 1977 treaties.

ASSESSING BLAME

There was plenty of blame for the Noriega crisis to go around. Noriega himself misread US intentions until the last minute, believing that his skills at bluffing the gringos would stave off their overwhelming military superiority. He made the mistake of having his legislature declare that the United States had put Panama in a state of war, which some media quickly twisted around as "Noriega declared war on the United States." His long association with prominent figures in the US government, including now-president Bush, led him to believe he could simply outmaneuver them. His

[55] "Interview with Arthur H. Davis Jr."

[56] Scranton, *Noriega Years*, 158–64. US personnel in Panama came to call these irregulars "digbats." Cf. Pizzurno and Araúz, *Panamá republicano*, 630–32. Billy Ford provided a personal perspective in Guillermo Ford Boyd, *Valió La Pena* (Imprenta Universal Books, 2004).

[57] See the appendix of heads of state in Leonard, *Historical Dictionary*, 307 ff.

wanton execution of officers who tried to overthrow him also warranted decisive sanctions.[58]

President George H. W. Bush and his advisors also merited blame, for keeping Noriega on the payroll in the intelligence network for so long, even resurrecting him after Carter had let him go. Presidential candidate Bush killed a mid-1988 proposal that might have produced Noriega's departure, fearing that "dealing with a dictator" would harm his election chances, while ignoring the prolonged torment the Panamanian people were suffering under economic sanctions.[59] The defense establishment had encouraged Noriega's enhancement of PDF powers in 1983, arming him and giving him roles in international affairs that were inappropriate for a military chieftain. By 1985, however, the State Department and the DEA had already cranked up a campaign against Noriega.[60] Then, before Bush decided to invade, he could have taken the counsel of General Fred Woerner, head of Southcom in Panama, who did not favor an invasion. Instead the White House replaced Woerner with General Maxwell Thurman (nicknamed "Mad Max"), who colleagues described as anxious to get on with the job. Finally, the Zonians who remained in the PCC deserve some blame for making the treaty implementation as difficult as possible, in the hopes that it might be judged failed and be revoked.[61]

Most diplomats we have spoken with believe that the invasion was an unnecessary and mistaken act, a fallback to outmoded gunboat diplomacy, and a violation of international laws we were party to, including the

[58] Manfredo, *La transición*, 194, quoted Noriega as bragging: "U.S. generals will win on the battlefield, but when it's political against us, we will win because they don't have that 'Panamanian thuggery.'" Manfredo (251) reproduces the headline from *La Estrella de Panamá*, 16 Dec. 1989, regarding a state of war. Zimbalist and Weeks's "Conclusion" contains thoughtful analyses of the growing crisis shortly after the invasion. See Ambler Moss's discussion of Noriega's personality in "Interview," Library of Congress, 15–17; and former US ambassador Everett Ellis Briggs' article, "Our Man in Panama," *New York Times*, Sept. 9, 2007.

[59] Pizzurno and Araúz, *Panamá republicano*, 633–37; Michael Conniff, *Panama and the United States*, 3rd ed. (Athens, GA: University of Georgia Press, 2012), 159. Cf Ambassador Ambler Moss's scathing analysis a year before the invasion, in "Interview," Library of Congress, and Ambassador Davis's comment on the Bush campaign of May 1988: "Interview with Arthur H. Davis Jr.," Library of Congress.

[60] "Interview with Arthur H. Davis Jr." He stated that at the time of his posting in mid 1986, former ambassador to Panama Everett Briggs and Assistant Secretary of State for Inter-American Affairs Elliot Abrams pushed the anti-Noriega policy.

[61] Manfredo's *La transición* is one of the clearest accounts of Zonian intransigence and efforts to sabotage the treaty. Officers in Southcom who opposed the invasion renamed it Operation Just Because, to suggest that the White House ordered it on a whim.

charters of the UN and the OAS.[62] Assigning blame and second-guessing, however, are not historical analysis, which requires a longer view of causes and outcomes.

Like the 1984 election, the Christmas invasion of 1989 (code named Just Cause) marked a major turning point in Panama's history, unfortunately, one over which its citizens had no control. Post-invasion President Guillermo Endara told a reporter it had been like a "kick in the head ... We were not really consulted." A rich literature has accumulated about this episode, the United States' biggest military undertaking between the Vietnam War and Desert Storm.[63]

Historian Greg Grandin looked back at the invasion on its 25th anniversary, trying to gauge its longer-term causes and effects. He noted that the top members of the Bush security team found themselves uninformed about Panama and unsure what to do with Noriega.[64] They opted for a rapid, surgical invasion with overwhelming force without defining its objectives and exit strategy. When it was over, they rejoiced at its tactical success, in sharp contrast to the flawed invasion of Grenada six years earlier. They also ignored or played down the extensive civilian casualties and collateral damage to Panama City, on the heels of years of economic sanctions. Bush declared that with Just Cause, the United States had kicked the "Vietnam syndrome," that is, its reluctance to engage in military operations overseas.[65]

Grandin found longer-term implications of the invasion. The Berlin Wall had just fallen weeks before, so in hindsight Just Cause foreshadowed how the United States might deal with the world after the end of the Cold War, in its new role as sole superpower. In this context, Just

[62] Zimbalist and Weeks, *Panama at the Crossroads*, ch. 7, came to much the same conclusion after years studying the deteriorating relations between Noriega and the United States. So too did Kempe, *Divorcing*, Epilogue.

[63] Conniff, *Panama*, 167. The most authoritative account is Lawrence A. Yates's two-volume *The U.S. Military Intervention in Panama: Operation Just Cause* (Washington, DC: US Army Center for Military History, 2008, 2014). Cf. "Interview with John A. Bushnell," Library of Congress Manuscripts Division, 1997. Bushnell took over as Deputy Chief of Mission (DCM, i.e., acting ambassador) when Maisto returned to Washington. In preparation for his new role, Bushnell met often with Pentagon officials planning the invasion, and in Panama he continued to liaise with them, especially the new Southcom commander, General Maxwell Thurman.

[64] See "Interview with Arthur H. Davis Jr.," Library of Congress, on attempts to formulate an approach to the Panama crisis in late 1989.

[65] Greg Grandin, "The War to Start All Wars," *Truth-Out*, www.truth-out.org/opinion/item/28138-the-war-to-start-all-wars-the-25th-anniversary-of-the-forgotten-invasion-of-panama.

Cause was a dress rehearsal for Desert Storm a year later. And it shaped the mentality of a generation of "neo-conservative" (neocon) strategists, who militarized US foreign policy and who rose to influence under Bush's son, George W. Bush, a decade later.[66]

Panamanians who lost loved ones, property, or their liberty in Just Cause may not take much consolation from Grandin's analysis, but it shows how small nations can lose control of their destinies and be mistreated by large ones in the long sweep of history. Meanwhile, curious readers have available book-length accounts of the invasion from Panamanian viewpoints, which may be supplemented with the documentary "Invasión," by Abner Benaim, aired in 2014.[67]

CANAL TRANSITION

Implementation of the 1979 Panama Canal Act (also known as PL 9670 and the Murphy Law, after its sponsor Congressman John Murphy [D-NY]) proceeded according to a number of schedules or calendars, as established by the treaty and augmented by the law.[68] The Carter administration had drafted implementing legislation, which it passed on to President Royo in Panama for his approval. The latter, a lawyer, pointed out items where the draft diverged from the treaty and Panama's expectations.[69] The White House did not address the Panamanian complaints, and as noted in this chapter, the House of Representatives developed its own bill. The drafters were led by Representatives Murphy, archconservative Robert Bauman (R-MD), and other avowed enemies of

[66] The works of Andrew J. Bacevich, like *The New American Militarism: How Americans Are Seduced by War* (New York: Oxford University Press, 2005), have been especially influential.

[67] See Daniel Delgado, *A 25 años de la invasión de Estados Unidos a Panamá: La resistencia armada y sus consequencias* (Panama: University of Panama, 2014), esp. 82, and "25 años de la invasión a Panamá, 1989–2014," Suplemento especial de *La Prensa*, Dec. 20, 2014.

[68] This section relies on Carol Stokes, "History of the Implementation of the Panama Canal Treaties," unpublished typescript in the National Archives, RG185, A1-173, rec. 292563. After the author submitted it to the PCC in 1983, which had contracted for the study, top officials shelved it with a disclaimer to the effect that, "This material, therefore, does not in any way, reflect the official position of the Panama Canal Commission or the U.S. Government." We find it to be a serious and reliable account of the events Stokes witnessed and researched, with occasional lapses. Deputy Administrator Manfredo interacted often with Stokes and cited her study in his memoirs.

[69] FBIS, Jan. 10, 1980, N1; Carlos A. López Guevara interview, July 23, 1986. Cf. Omar Jaén Suárez, *Diez años*, 29–30.

the treaties. Rather than create an independent public corporation, as the treaty and Carter draft had called for, their version kept much closer control, especially fiscally, over Canal management. Many Panamanians and their sympathizers believed these congressmen were coached by Zonians, who hated the treaty, and were aided by Murphy's chief of staff and former Canal legal counsel, W. Merryl Whitman.[70]

The House bill made the PCC an agency of the executive branch funded by annual appropriations, subject to continuous congressional oversight, rather than a government corporation financed by its own revenues and expenses. It also made the PCC board supervisory rather than managerial, concentrating power more firmly in the hands of the administrator and his superiors in the Pentagon. Whitman then helped create a new position, that of chief engineer, who had to be a US citizen. He explained that this would make the deputy administrator, a Panamanian, redundant. Given these shifts in structure, the four Panamanian board members also became largely powerless. The Carter administration intention of binational and independent Canal management became impossible.[71]

President Carter appointed two men to lead the PCC. Dennis "Phil" McAuliffe became administrator, and his Panamanian counterpart, Fernando Manfredo, took the deputy administrator position.[72] McAuliffe had served as commander of Southcom in the Canal Zone for the previous four years and was familiar with and supportive of the treaty and transition to binational management. He held the post until 1989, under the Reagan and Bush administrations. Manfredo had served on the Panamanian treaty negotiating team in 1975–77 and was accepted by the US side to serve as deputy administrator. Nominated by Torrijos and approved by Carter, Manfredo ended up in that role throughout the 1980s and became the first Panamanian administrator in 1990, according to the terms of the treaty, albeit briefly.[73]

Michael Rhode, Jr., played a key role in drafting the Act and in Canal administration during the 1980s, a role even more critical after the 1989 invasion. Serving as secretary of the PCC's Washington, DC office, he took up duties that far exceeded his modest title: he managed liaison

[70] This section draws on Manfredo, *La transición*, 144–47. Cf. Michael Rhode Jr. interview, Feb. 2, 1994.

[71] See Stokes, "Implementation," 29–32, on the transfer of authority from the former Canal Zone Government to the new board of directors and approval of its powers in August 1981.

[72] See the organization charts in Manfredo, *La transición*, 248–49.

[73] Stokes, "Implementation," 20–26 ff; Manfredo, *La transición*, 127.

between the Canal and Congress and with numerous government agencies whose actions were critical for Canal operations. He helped to brief Ronald Reagan's 1981 nominee for president of the PCC board, William Gianelli. From Manfredo's point of view, Rhode became an eminence gris.[74]

General McAuliffe, who was not a Zonian, worked well with his Panamanian counterpart and made every effort to implement the treaty, despite the difficulties Congress threw in his way.[75] Zonians, however, never reconciled to the treaty and followed it only grudgingly, in the spirit of Spanish colonial administrators who said "obedezco pero no cumplo," i.e. I obey but do not carry out. Even if Panama eventually took over the Canal, they reasoned, they would not facilitate the process. Manfredo once remarked that the Zonians' idea of "transition" was that Zonians would run the Canal until they turned off the lights on December 31, 1999; Panamanians could come in the next day and turn the lights back on, if they could find the switch.

During the 1980s, the Canal operated under the almost exclusive authority of the US government; Panama played little part in policy decisions, despite the binational façade of the PCC. President Ardito Barletta, in office 1984–85, said Canal matters occupied little of his time. Panamanians mostly stood on the sidelines, hoping for a bountiful future of cash transfers, new jobs, and business opportunities. Most were sorely disappointed. This was especially true before many Panamanians became conversant in Canal operations and during the period the two governments sparred over the tenure of General Noriega in power. During the 1990s, as more Panamanians rose into executive roles in the Canal and better relations prevailed between the countries, board members and managers, calling themselves "canaleros" (canal men), gradually exercised more influence.

Five US and four Panamanian members comprised the board of directors of the PCC, all nominated by their respective presidents and ratified by the US Senate. The board always approved the decisions of the administrator, because its US members, a majority, were obliged to vote as their president instructed, and he in turn reported to the Secretary of the Army and the Secretary of Defense in Washington. And if that weren't enough

[74] Michael Rhode Jr. interview, June 30, 1986; Manfredo, *La transición*, 169, 171.

[75] Foreign Service Officer Sherman Henson interview, June 27, 1986. Henson had served during the treaty negotiation years and was kept fully briefed on relations through the mid 1980s.

top-down control, Congress required that the PCC capital and operating budgets be submitted annually for its approval until 1987, when they adopted a more flexible rotating fund budget.[76]

To coordinate the actions of the many US agencies with a stake in the Canal and ancillary military operations, the White House in the 1960s had established a Panama Review Committee, under the guidance of the US ambassador and the Canal Zone governor. The Southcom commander usually took an active part, also. During treaty implementation, the committee oversaw a large number of joint commissions and subcommittees to discuss and define policy across a range of matters, with special attention to environmental protection and defense. A former ambassador said that the military dominated its deliberations.[77]

Panamanian board members, despite having no real decision-making power, gained valuable experience while watching issues presented and approved, and they became familiar with the complex structures and operations of the Canal. To improve their efficacy, Manfredo suggested to Torrijos that Panama create an advisory board to coordinate Panama's participation in Canal management, autonomous like a transit authority in the United States and as a counterpart to the US review committee.

In 1978, Torrijos established the first of several such bodies. One version was the Panama Canal Authority (ACP), under the direction of Torrijos associate Gabriel Lewis Galindo, designed to centralize decision-making under the executive branch.[78] Problems arose immediately, as agencies and strong-willed politicians fought for access to returned lands and facilities. Two notable examples were the National Guard and the Port Authority, which claimed military assets, the ports, and the railroad. The Authority succumbed to such competing pressures in 1982–83 and was eventually replaced by the Executive Directorate for Canal Matters (DIPAT), charged with educating, coordinating, and advising its board members. It was lodged in the presidency at first but later moved to the ministry of foreign relations.

From the outset, Panamanian board members found themselves largely ignored and expected to play subordinate roles. But they insisted on

[76] Manfredo, *La transición*, 181.

[77] Ambassador Jack Vaughn interview, Mar. 17, 1992. See Stokes, "Implementation," ch. 4, "Binational Working Group and Post Treaty Committees."

[78] Raymundo Gurdián Guerra, "Los Tratados del Canal y su Transferencia, 1967–1999," in *Historia General de Panamá*, ed. Alfredo Castillero Calvo (Panama: Consejo Nacional del Centenario, 2003), III:II, 271–72; Jaén Suárez, *Diez años*, 30–31.

challenging the Act, especially the ways it violated the treaties. Such recriminations fell on deaf American ears, so the Panamanian board members had little influence in the early years. By its third year, however, the board settled down and became a more constructive forum for discussing Canal policies.

US ambassador Ambler Moss elucidated a major contradiction in the Board's mandate:

> Any Panamanian Government official or businessman knows what a board of directors is in a corporation. But they quite rightly question the role of a board of directors in an appropriated fund agency. It doesn't make sense; it doesn't fit legally somehow.[79]

The control Congress retained over the budget eviscerated the powers of the Board and frustrated the Panamanians' expectations of playing a part in Canal management.

The same contradiction hobbled the Coordinating Committee of division chiefs and their Panamanian counterparts. Deputy Administrator Manfredo observed that "a US representative, a bureau director in the Canal Agency, had more power than the Panamanian member who, as part of the Government of Panama's Executive Branch, was not in a position to affect the day-to-day operations of the Canal." Asymmetry undermined a sense of shared responsibility.[80]

Panamanian board members' concerns in the early years ranged from widening the Culebra/Gaillard Cut (the longer excavated portion on the Pacific side of the Canal), continued waterway maintenance, imbalance between US and Panamanian administrative authority, personnel policies, a second bridge over the Canal, limited power to raise tolls, and costly bureaucratic duplication. Again, Panamanian board members' complaints were largely ignored – one critic called them an "echo chamber" that only heard its own voices.[81]

This awkward collaboration persisted until 1985, when General Noriega asserted more control over his board members and ratcheted up conflict by appointing an iron-handed official, Major Delgado, to keep them in line. Binational cooperation only reappeared after the invasion.[82]

[79] Stokes, "Implementation," ch. 2, 38.
[80] Stokes, "Implementation," ch. 4, 84.
[81] Ibid., ch. 2, 37.
[82] Manfredo, *La transición*, 130, and interview, July 29, 1986; D. P. McAuliffe interview, July 22, 1986; Joseph Wood and James Ferrara interview, July 24, 1986.

REVERSION

The immediate turnover of lands and assets in 1979 became the big story for Panama in this period, far overshadowing the small part the nation played in Canal affairs. The assets included the Panama Railroad, the ports of Balboa and Cristobal at either end of the Canal, and 58 percent of the lands formerly contained in the Canal Zone, which ceased to exist on October 1, 1979.[83]

Administratively, the ports and railroad transferred to Panama's Port Authority, even though little business went on in these facilities.[84] The railroad and ports turned out to be white elephants, a drain on the treasury. The railroad had long been neglected and used largely for moving personnel and light cargo around the Zone. The ports handled scant trade and had not been modernized in years, especially given the containerization revolution underway. The two workforces had little to do but were protected by local unions. To spare the government of Panama from having to fire hundreds of redundant employees upon the transfer, the Canal personnel office pensioned off most of them.[85]

The reverted lands included most non-US employee housing (4,300 units), schools, recreation areas, and community buildings. The ACP began to inventory these properties and attempted to provide maintenance until they could be sold to private owners. Considerable pressure arose to show favoritism for powerful people or to sell properties at below market rates, which made the work of the ACP more difficult. This process took many years to complete, during which time critics of the treaty pointed to un-mowed grass, sweetheart deals, run-down neighborhoods, and buildings deteriorating in the tropical climate.

One property scheduled for reverting to Panama proved especially troubling. The School of the Americas (SOA), an army training facility

[83] See Charlotte Elton's chapter "Environmental Aspects of Canal Transition," in *Post-Invasion Panama: The Challenges of Democratization in the New World Order*, ed. Orlando J. Pérez (Lanham, MD: Lexington Books, 2000), 57–68, and Stokes, "Implementation," ch. 5, 1–7 ff.

[84] Manfredo, *La transición*, 128ff; Nicolás Ardito Barletta, "Áreas revertidas," *Capital Financiero*, Sept. 4–10, 2000, and "La incorporación de las Áreas revertidas (Antigua Zona del Canal)," *La Prensa*, Dec. 8, 2014.

[85] Stokes, "Implementation," chs. 16–17; Manfredo, *La transición*, 158–9, 128; Michael Rhode Jr. interview, June 30, 1986; Zimbalist and Weeks, *Panama at the Crossroads*, 54–55. Roberto Emerick's testimony provides an insider view, in Ana Elena Porras, ed., *Historias Canaleras: Doce testimonios de la transición* (Panamá: Instituto de Estudios Nacionales, Universidad de Panamá, 2007), 108–24. Cf. Richard Wainio interview, Apr. 21, 2014.

operated at Fort Gulick for Latin American military officers since the end of World War II, was not covered in the Status of Forces Agreement (SOFA) negotiated for the other US bases in Panama. Therefore, it would transfer to Panama in 1984 unless a separate SOFA was signed. Noriega, who had taken several courses at the SOA, intended for the United States to continue using the facility but did not wish to give permission publicly, for fear of protests by nationalists. Noriega wanted the SOA but without a SOFA, according to a State Department official. The Pentagon was wary of any deal without a legal basis, however, and at the last minute decided to pull the school out and relocate it at Fort Benning, GA. The incident created doubts about Noriega's ultimate loyalty to the US military.[86]

Manfredo had to deal with a particularly thorny problem with strong cultural overtones: properties built by non-profits, particularly churches, recreation centers, and clubhouses. The close-knit society of the old Zone had over 500 such organizations, which expected to purchase them at nominal prices. But the treaty only provided for a grace period of thirty months, beyond which they would have to regularize their ownership and operations under Panamanian law. In some cases, their fragile finances would not allow this, and they closed their doors. Manfredo made a concerted effort to help most make the transition, knowing that they promoted better morale in the Canal workforce and provided essential social services. He commented that half his time was devoted to handling such special cases.[87]

Most of the transferred lands, largely secondary tropical forest, lay along both sides of the Canal and to the Northeast, including the Chagres River basin, Alahuela (formerly Madden) Lake, and the southern slopes of the central Cordillera mountains. Presidents Royo, Jorge Enrique Illueca, and Ardito Barletta acted quickly to designate forest lands along the Canal as national parks, to prevent their being despoiled by developers and

[86] Conniff, *Panama*, 150; Sherman Henson interview, June 27, 1986; "U.S. military school in Panama to be closed," *Albuquerque Journal*, Aug. 18, 1984. At Fort Benning, the name was later changed to the Western Hemisphere Institute for Security Cooperation, WHINSEC. After ARI was reestablished in the 1990s, the main facilities of the School of the Americas were privatized and developed as the luxury Spanish-owned Meliá Panama Canal Hotel, a few miles from Colon.

[87] *La transición*, 135–41; Stokes, "Implementation," ch. 9; Herbert Knapp and Mary Knapp, *Red, White, and Blue Paradise: The American Canal Zone in Panama* (San Diego: Harcourt, Brace, Jovanovich, 1984), 173–81. The status of many of these organizations was finally resolved with more difficulty under President Moscoso, as described in Chapter 5.

squatters. They created several large forest reserves: Parque Soberanía in 1980, Parque Metropolitano in 1985, and Parque Camino de Cruces in 1993. For many years, the government of Panama struggled to deal with farmers and ranchers – estimated as perhaps 100,000 – who quietly penetrated the former Zone lands, because their clearings jeopardized the Canal and contributed to siltation in Gatun Lake. The establishment of a national forestry agency in 1986, INRENARE, later a part of ANAM, did not fully remedy the problem.

The joint policy committee set up for watershed protection attempted to educate the public about the potential dangers of deforestation and to create awareness among the political elite of the urgency of protecting the watershed. They established the Watershed Management Plan to accomplish this, and intellectuals and other opinion leaders embraced it.[88] They laid the groundwork for later extensive cooperation between Panamanian institutions, the Panama Canal Authority, and USAID.

The protection of the regional watershed concerned more than simply Canal maintenance. These same waters generated electricity, irrigated farmlands, and supplied consumers in the terminal cities. And ultimately, the Canal which Panama would take over in 1999, a historic patrimony of the nation, would succeed or fail largely on whether they could sustain the hydrologic system of the Chagres River basin. Eventually, the successor Autoridad del Canal de Panamá (ACP), created in the mid 1990s, assumed responsibility for protecting these lands.

Under the treaty, the remaining 42 percent of lands and waterways necessary to operate and defend the Canal was allocated to the Panama Canal Area, under the jurisdiction of the PCC, and military zones containing US bases, under the Department of Defense (DOD), for the remainder of the treaty period.

In the transferred or "reverted" areas, Panama immediately assumed responsibility for ordinary public services, including mail, police, courts, jails, fire protection, utilities, and garbage collection. In 1984, these services were extended to the whole Canal Area, excepting military bases. Within two years, the Panamanian police, their Canal counterparts, and the national courts functioned very well, a bright spot in treaty implementation. Manfredo agreed to a special pay bonus to help US employees

[88] Ardito Barletta interviews, Apr. 10, 12, 14, 2015; Manfredo interview, July 29, 1986; Joseph Wood and James Ferrara interview, July 24, 1986.

adapt to Panamanian services and stores, even though it was not authorized in the treaty.[89]

Several observers noted that the most successful phase of implementation consisted of new joint police patrols, made up of Panamanian and former Zone policemen, which began on October 1, 1979, and ended thirty months later. Their efficacy stemmed in part from the fact that for years the two forces had coordinated, cross-trained, shared intelligence, and enjoyed informal communication. This early success engendered confidence, especially among the US Canal employees, that their lives could carry on without immediate danger.[90]

Other changes in services after 1979 involved schools, hospitals, retail sales, and US housing, many of which were taken over by the Army, Air Force, or Department of Defense Dependent Schools System for the duration of the treaty. Most of these took place among US agencies and had little effect on Panama, except for Panamanians employed by the PCC or DOD.[91]

Disagreements arose, however, as to the public services available to members of the US armed forces and their dependents. Military personnel, their spouses, and DOD employees continued to run their own operations, including APO mail, police, and the coveted commissaries and PX stores. They were also exempt from paying rent on residences, which would have brought in over two million dollars a year. Finally, the embassy's surreptitious use of the diplomatic pouch for Zonian mail also rankled, because it took away hundreds of thousands of dollars in revenue from the PCC. These constituted questions of equity between Panamanian and US employees, not just budget issues.[92]

PANAMANIANIZING THE CANAL

During the early 1980s Canal managers faced multiple challenges. Foremost, they had to ramp up recruitment and training of Panamanians for positions at all levels of responsibility, with the goal of nearly 100 percent Panamanian staffing by the time the Canal was turned over in 1999. Millions of dollars were expended for this purpose, and by

89 Manfredo interview July 29, 1986. On the Panamanian assumption of responsibility for postal service, courts, fire protection, garbage, street maintenance, etc., see Stokes, "Implementation," chs. 6–15.

90 Stokes, "Implementation," ch. 12; "Interview with Ambler Moss," Library of Congress.

91 Stokes, "Implementation," chs. 19–24.

92 Manfredo, *La transición*, 179 and ch. 11 in general.

TABLE 2.1 *Panamanianization of the Canal Work Force, 1979–90*

		Panama	USA	Third Country	Total
Blue collar	1979	5,521	2,105	350	7,976
	1981	5,765	1,865	277	7,907
	1983	5,922	1,651	228	7,801
	1986	6,103	1,236	164	7,503
	1988	6,347	1,094	116	7,557
	1990	6,280	927	74	7,281
Managers	1979	8	105	0	116
	1986	42	93	2	143
	1989	47	91	5	145

Source: PCC Briefing Paper, October 1993.

1990 about 86 percent of the total workforce was Panamanian, up from 69 percent in 1979. Recruitment and training for executive, management, and senior maritime positions, especially pilots and captains, lagged, however, reaching less than a third by 1989.[93]

The PCC rolled out a wide array of special programs to prepare Panamanians for successful employment and/or advancement: apprenticeships for craftsmen, towboat mate training, pilot understudies, pilots-in-training, towboat engineer training, clerical training, career internships, upward mobility, career internships, and cooperative education tracks for college students. The first Panamanian administrator later remarked that the PCC was a veritable university of education.[94]

Canal pilots, the men who guided ships through the Canal itself, proved to be the most difficult work category to Panamanianize. Their jobs, requiring exacting skills and experience, were far and away the most demanding and paid the highest wages, comparable to senior airline pilots. It also had the strongest union. The administrator recalled that negotiations with their union in 1980, 1983, and 1985 proved very arduous. But once the other US employee unions accepted the treaty, the pilots finally acquiesced. By the late 1980s, twenty Panamanian pilots

[93] Ibid., ch. 16.
[94] PCC briefing paper, Oct. 1993.

were qualified, with another fifteen in the pipeline.[95] Still, it took many years for pilots to earn masters' papers to assume full command of ships in the Canal.

To accommodate the increase in Panamanian employees, the PCC created the Panama Canal Employment System, which reinstituted two tiers of compensation, one for US employees and a Panama Area Wage Base for new local hires. The plan, like the notorious Gold and Silver rolls that had existed through the 1940s, and the Local Rate/US Rate system through the 1970s, was intended to hold down wages so that by 1999 they would be comparable with pay scales in Panama's economy. This caused such an outcry that the PCC went back to a single pay schedule regardless of nationality. It went into effect between 1983 and 1985 and added some $3 million to the payroll. In addition, by 1986, all Canal employees except senior management were also covered by collective bargaining agreements.[96]

Panamanianizing the upper echelons of Canal management created more difficulties, as Zonians fought tenaciously to protect their high pay and benefits. Table 2.1 shows that less than a third of the managers were Panamanian after more than a decade of treaty implementation. A former Canal executive remembered that PCC board presidents William Gianelli and Robert Page supported the Zonians and attempted to block efforts by McAuliffe and Manfredo to add more Panamanians to management positions.[97]

Those Panamanians who did win appointments constituted a small but important generation critical for eventually taking over the Canal. From Manfredo on down, they faced discrimination and exclusion on the part of the Zonians. Manfredo's memoir contains myriad cases of being snubbed and ostracized, beginning with denial of housing designated for the deputy administrator.[98] He and others had to bear up under this treatment in order to persevere. In 2003–04 Ana Elena Porras collected candid testimonies by a dozen Panamanian and US officials from the transition era that recorded the anger and frustration most experienced.[99]

[95] McAuliffe interview, July 22, 1986; Porras, *Historias*, 120.

[96] Stokes, "Implementation," ch. 3; Manfredo, *La transición*, 166–67. On labor relations in general under the treaty, see interview with Ronald Seeley, July 28, 1986; and Michael L. Conniff, *Black Labor on a White Canal: Panama 1904–1981* (Pittsburgh: University of Pittsburgh Press, 1985), 147–56.

[97] Franklin Castrellón, "La panameñización del Canal," *La Prensa*, Sept. 7, 2011.

[98] *La transición*, 24–26. Cf. also ch. 16.

[99] Porras, *Historias Canaleras*.

Panamanians who earned good positions in the early transition included Luis Noli and Anel Belis, public information directors, and George Mercier, head of personnel. Assistant director positions were held by Numan Vásquez (engineering-construction), René Van Hoorde (general services), and Carlos Alvarado (marine division). They were joined by Ricardo Varela (human resource development) and Orlando Allard (pilot training). Several would become top executives after Panama took over the Canal, like Jorge Quijano, Onésimo Sánchez, Rodolfo Sabonge, and Manuel Benítez. Allard went on to represent Panama as ambassador to the International Maritime Organization and founded the Universidad Marítima Internacional de Panamá for training merchant marine officers and seamen and organized the periodic Panama Maritime conferences after the early 1990s. Executive Director Joseph Wood lauded Tilsia McTagger, Equal Opportunity Officer.[100]

To help standardize pay scales throughout the Canal area, the DOD reluctantly agreed on similar wage systems for its local employees at military installations. In the early 1980s, the Canal employment office also instituted Reductions-in-Force (RIFs in federal parlance), so that US personnel whose jobs ended due to transfer of operations to Panama could displace (bump) others below them in seniority if they qualified for the new jobs. Meanwhile, the projected exodus of US employees did not materialize: only about 100–150 Zonians left each year in the 1980s.[101] Nor did the large-scale departure of West Indian descendant employees occur as forecast: only 1,666 took advantage of 15,000 special US immigration visa slots provided by the treaty.[102]

Assuring proper maintenance of the Canal up to the time of transfer constituted another challenge facing Canal managers. Some projects chosen for funding enhanced efficiency, like widening and deepening Culebra/Gaillard Cut to allow two-way transits of Panamax ships, while others simply kept equipment in working order, like lock locomotives, tugboats, lock gates, hydroelectric plants, and dredging barges.[103] Capital expenditures, like all

[100] Ibid., includes entries by Quijano, Sabonge, and Benítez, among others. Quijano remembered being referred to as the "damn Panamanian" when he started work in the 1970s: 75. Joseph Wood interview, July 24, 1986. To this day, however, Panamanian veterans of the transition rarely criticize their former US bosses because of the valuable mentorships that many developed.

[101] Stokes, "Implementation," ch. 1, 8.

[102] Conniff, *Black Labor*, 175.

[103] D. P. McAuliffe, "An Overhaul for the Panama Canal," *Journal of Commerce*, Apr. 9, 1986; Zimbalist and Weeks, *Panama at the Crossroads*, 59–61.

outlays, came from a new Revolving Fund set up by the US Treasury Department in 1987, and they usually detracted from the meager funds available to transfer to Panama beyond treaty requirements, especially during the Noriega crisis.[104]

Panamanians had expected a windfall of income from the Canal under the treaty, and in fact treaty-designated payments to Panama rose from only three to around eighty million a year in the 1980s. In addition, the Canal injected more money into Panama's economy through a variety of means, not simply payment for use of the facility. An estimate for fiscal year 1987 appears in Table 2.2:

As employment of Panamanians rose in the 1980s, so did compensation, income tax, and social security contributions, the last two now paid

TABLE 2.2 *Gross Income to Panama 1987*

Wages and salaries paid to Panamanians	$134,000,000
Retirement and disability to Panamanians	49,000,000
Direct procurement	
Goods	21,000,000
Services, incl. contractors	24,000,000
Personal expenditures by US employees	11,000,000
Treaty payments	
Public services	10,000,000
Fixed annuity	10,000,000
Tolls/tonnage share	58,000,000
Article XIII 4(c)*	2,000,000
Total	$320,000,000

Source: PCC, Office of Executive Planning, document courtesy of Richard Wainio, prepared April 11, 1995. Some rounding and reformatting. Cf. table 3.2 in Zimbalist and Weeks, *Panama at the Crossroads*, 53.

* This article provided for giving Panama up to $10 million per year from excess of revenues over expenditures, even though the PCC was not supposed to produce "profits." In subsequent years, few funds were transferred under this treaty provision. See Chapter 3 for more discussion of this issue.

[104] Zimbalist and Weeks, *Panama at the Crossroads*, 55–56, and following chapters regarding these transfers.

to the government of Panama. The Canal also increased procurement of goods and services in Panama, anticipating the Canal turnover in 1999.

Manfredo explained that while "profit sharing" in the 1980s was minimal, the PCC did invest some $25–30 million a year in improvements, so that the Canal would be maintained and operating well in 1999. Widening the Culebra/Gaillard Cut, the biggest project slated for execution in the late 1980s, would permit two-way transits of the larger Panamax ships using the Canal during daylight hours.[105] Estimated to cost some $400 million, it was postponed due to the political conflict between Washington and Noriega and to the economic sanctions the United States imposed. It was completed in the early 2000s, along with other maintenance and improvement projects to be discussed in Chapter 3.[106]

The impact of Canal transfers and expenditures fell dramatically in 1988 and 1989, when the US government withheld all funds and business with Panama to pressure Noriega to step down from power. The GDP dropped 20 percent from previous years, and the country began to run out of cash because currency shipments (Panama has used the US dollar since 1905) were embargoed. Blocking social security payments and income tax withholding on behalf of Panamanian employees of the Canal created special hardships, from deputy administrator on down, because the Noriega regime began assessing fines on them and withholding services. They even issued an arrest warrant for Manfredo![107]

The Canal operated well during the 1980s, despite administrative friction between Panamanian and US authorities. Toll revenues increased slightly in the early 1980s due to increased traffic, especially oil tankers carrying Alaska North Slope crude to the East Coast. In 1983, 9.8 percent higher toll rates, authorized under the Act, went into effect. The following year, revenues remained about the same, as rate increases were offset by the shift of Alaskan North Slope oil to a pipeline that began operations between Panama's Chiriqui and Bocas del Toro provinces, near the western border with Costa Rica.[108]

[105] Beginning in the 1970s, shipping companies began ordering more vessels built to PCC lock dimensions, called Panamax.

[106] Manfredo interview, July 29, 1986, and *La transición*, 180. A great deal of testimony on Canal improvements in the 1980s appears in Porras, *Historias Canaleras*, and are discussed more fully in Chapters 3 and 4.

[107] Manfredo, *La transición*, 187–89.

[108] The pipeline proved profitable for six or seven years but was shut down in the late 1980s when Los Angeles refineries developed the capacity to refine the sulphur-heavy Alaska oil. D. P. McAuliffe interview, July 22, 1986; Richard Wainio interview, Apr. 21, 2014. Cf. Zimbalist and Weeks, *Panama at the Crossroads*, 61–63.

The rest of the decade the number of transits remained steady at around 12,000 a year, yet volume of cargo rose somewhat due to a growing number of larger Panamax vessels. Part of the later growth was also due to shipments of Japanese autos to the East Coast in specialized automobile carriers known as roll-on-roll-off or Ro-Ro vessels.[109]

Since the 1960s, the United States had negotiated with Panama for rights to build a sea-level Canal to replace the existing lock Canal, and the 1977 treaty had left that option open. In 1986, the PCC began considering that possibility and others, forming the Tripartite Canal Alternatives Study Group, comprising the United States, Panama, and Japan. They resurrected the sea-level studies (favored by Japan) done in the 1960s and estimated costs, ending up recommending not to pursue that course. Instead, they endorsed either enlarging the existing Canal (along the lines of the Third Locks project of 1939–42) and/or developing what they called the "Centerport," where the Canal and adjacent lands would become a marshalling center for containers, which carried an increasing share of world commerce, and other lines of commerce.[110] The added cost of port improvements, railroad reconstruction, and highway connections to achieve the Centerport would be far less than a sea-level Canal, not to mention avoiding the environmental dangers of massive excavation. One incentive to upgrade container handling was the growing competitiveness of the US "landbridge" or intermodal routes, where containers were off-loaded on the US West coast and sent by rail to Midwest and even East coast destinations.[111]

PANAMA'S ECONOMY IN THE 1980S

Zimbalist and Weeks's study of the deterioration of Panama's fortunes by 1990 devoted considerable attention to the economic story. They demonstrated that the country relied heavily on international services to earn its livelihood: the Canal, the banking center, an oil pipeline opened in 1983, ship chandlering, and the Colon Free Zone. Manufacturing and agriculture, by comparison, made up less than a quarter of the GDP.[112] Despite

[109] Ray Laverty interview, July 28, 1986.

[110] On the 1939–42 project, see Conniff, *Panama*, 93–94. For the Tripartite Commission and Centerport, see Zimbalist and Weeks, *Panama at the Crossroads*, 59–61. Japan pushed for the sea-level option but did not prevail.

[111] Stokes, "Implementation," ch. 25; Zimbalist and Weeks, *Panama at the Crossroads*, 57–58.

[112] Zimbalist and Weeks, *Panama at the Crossroads*, ch. 6.

urging by the US government, the IMF, and the World Bank, Panama found it difficult or impossible to wean itself from its role as service provider. And the economic sanctions applied by the United States from 1987 to 1989 severely hobbled the economy, which Zimbalist and Weeks described as a disaster waiting to happen.[113]

Panama had long been recognized as having one of the most unequal distributions of income in the hemisphere. This resulted from many very poor people, while wealth remained concentrated in the hands of a small elite. Urban migration only shifted poverty from the countryside to the city, rather than ameliorating it.[114]

The early 1980s had proved disastrous for Latin American economies in general, becoming what economic historians called the "lost decade," when growth stagnated and unemployment ravaged populations. The 1981–82 recession caused extreme hardship, devaluations, and debt moratoria. Panama suffered these effects as well, especially difficult after the relatively expansive years that accompanied Canal treaty negotiations. Torrijos's death and ensuing political instability exacerbated the economic distress. Fiscal deficits and heavy debt service pushed the country to the edge of bankruptcy. Thus, the 1983 presidential nomination of Ardito Barletta was partly designed to pull the economy out of its spiral. International credit would be essential.[115]

Difficulties aside, the economy rested on fairly solid foundations, because of, rather than despite, its dependence on the service sector. The banking center had grown and prospered in the previous decade, peaking at some $49 billion in assets and nearly 9,000 employees in 120 banks by 1982. It provided liquidity for other activities through loans and deposits.[116] One downside of the banking industry was its use for money laundering by a variety of clients, including General Noriega. Such activities generated profits, to be sure, but they contributed to Panama's reputation as a crime-tolerant nation and underpinned some of the indictments used to arrest Noriega. The issue has continued to occupy diplomats and bank inspectors ever since.[117]

Panama's agricultural sector remained small and stagnant during the 1980s, continuing a trend that began in the mid 1940s. It relied on a few

[113] Ibid., 27–29 and 158.
[114] Ibid., 122–27.
[115] Ardito Barletta, "La Transición Política," 82 ff.
[116] Zimbalist and Weeks, *Panama at the Crossroads*, 71–83.
[117] Ibid., 74–78.

trade goods for profits – notably bananas, sugar cane, and cattle – and subsistence farming of most staple crops for domestic consumption.[118] Concentration of land ownership became an impediment to higher productivity. During the 1970s, Torrijos carried out a land reform program, but it achieved only limited results. Basically, land cultivation grew through frontiers expanding into abundant unoccupied lands, favoring those with access to capital and technology to develop them. Low farming performance was exacerbated by steady migration of farming families to the capital and other cities.

Between 1982 and 1986 the IMF and World Bank stipulated that to receive new loans and to break out of stagnation, Panama had to adopt the austerity measures they demanded. Zimbalist and Weeks believe these agencies devised an economic straitjacket based on dogmatic adherence to neoliberal policies that later became known as the Washington Consensus. President Ardito Barletta, himself educated in such policies and a former vice president of the Bank, tried to institute them during his eleven-month administration.[119] He succeeded in winning new financing and raising the nation's credit rating, but he also stirred up labor opposition and eroded popular support for the regime. Noriega and the PDF command withdrew their support for him; the president's announced investigation of the Spadafora murder triggered his overthrow.[120]

The final chapter of the 1980s economic story includes the sanctions the United States imposed on Panama after 1987 to dislodge General Noriega.[121] They consisted of escalating measures to hobble both Panama's economy and the government's ability to conduct business as usual. Zimbalist and Weeks summarize the steps taken and their justification by US officials, and they conclude that they failed to achieve their goal. In the meantime, they plunged the economy into recession and caused widespread suffering on the part of the population: "The U.S. campaign brought the economy to its knees and an indicted drug dealer to his feet." Noriega characterized his anti-US campaign as a defense of national sovereignty. Its failure led to the Christmas invasion of 1989.[122]

118 Ibid., ch. 5.

119 Ibid., 129–35.

120 Ibid., 159–63.

121 Ardito Barletta, "The Political and Economic," 101–13; Scranton, *Noriega Years*, 132–40.

122 Zimbalist and Weeks, *Panama at the Crossroads*, 146–50, quote from 149.

THE CHRISTMAS INVASION AND AFTERMATH

Early in the morning of December 20, 1989, some 27,000 US troops invaded Panama, landing mostly in the capital and some outlying sites garrisoned by the PDF. They fought for seven days, wreaking devastation and putting an end to the standoff between Noriega and Bush.[123] The general managed to evade capture for two weeks, spending a good part of that time holed up under the diplomatic protection of the Papal Nuncio, Monseñor José Sebastián Laboa. When Noriega finally surrendered, Laboa joked that the Nunciatura might be eligible for the million-dollar reward the US army had offered for Noriega's capture.[124]

Operation Just Cause bore a resemblance to US troops landing there in November 1903, ostensibly to secure the railroad but actually to prevent Colombia from retaking its rebellious province. In both cases, the US president decided the outcome of an international stalemate and thereby the destiny of this small nation. In each case, brute force prevailed. In 1989, commanders kept the State Department out of the planning up to the very last minute. And they imposed martial law to secure the country afterward.[125] Thus military invasions neatly bracketed almost the entire century that the United States dominated the Isthmus of Panama.

Panamanians quickly stepped forward to rebuild their nation, led mostly by those who had opposed the Noriega dictatorship. Endara served as president and Arias Calderón and Ford as his vice presidents, in an uneasy triumvirate described in the next Chapter. Despite the horrors and deaths caused by the invasion, they managed to take positive steps to restore democratic government and breathe life into the ailing economy. Fernando Manfredo took over as administrator of the PCC for a short time, ensuring that the 1977 treaty would be honored. Newspapers began exercising their rights to publish information freely. The PDF disintegrated and was replaced by a police force answering to civilian authorities. Banks opened, money began to circulate, businesses opened, and people returned to work. 1990 offered a new beginning to Panamanians after a long, brutal night.

123 Scranton, *Noriega Years*, 201–07, provides a succinct account.
124 Berguido, *Vida póstuma*, 97–110.
125 "Interview with Arthur H. Davis," Library of Congress.

3

The Endara Administration: Civilians Learned to Prevail

Remember that a civilized nation cannot have just one party; if there were only one party, this would merely be a dictatorship. Politics would not advance.

Sun Yat-Sen

SECRET US PRE-INVASION SWEARING-IN OF ENDARA

The Panamanian politicians who ran for president and first and second vice president in May 1989, Guillermo Endara, Ricardo Arias Calderón, and Billy Ford, found themselves swept up in the Christmas invasion seven months later. They were summoned to a dinner at Howard Air Force base the evening before the invasion, to welcome an "important overseas visitor." The US Chargé d'affaires ad interim, Acting Ambassador John Bushnell, a veteran diplomat dispatched to handle a difficult situation, had held productive meetings with the three leaders on numerous occasions, so they accepted his invitation. When they arrived and asked who the mystery visitor was, Bushnell told them, "Like 15,000 visitors all armed to the teeth." He proceeded to tell them the invasion would start in a matter of hours.[1]

[1] Based largely on "Interview with John A. Bushnell," Library of Congress Manuscript Division, 740–48. Cf. also James A. Baker, III, with Thomas M. Defrank, *The Politics of Diplomacy: Revolution, War, and Peace, 1989–1992* (New York: G. P. Putnam's Sons, 1995), 177–94.

The Panamanians reacted with shock but resignation – it was a fait accompli. Bushnell recalled,

> Ricardo Arias Calderón, the most sensitive of the three, said, "Hundreds, even thousands of people, Panamanians and Americans, are going to die tonight. It is a terrible night for Panama." I said I hoped the resistance would not be so great that there would be a large number of deaths. After a while Billy Ford said, "The die is cast. Let's get on with what we have to do."[2]

Working closely with Southcom Commander Maxwell Thurman, Bushnell had arranged for the Panamanians to occupy a house on a nearby army base, where they would not be subject to harassment by Noriega's forces. Their families also went there for safe-keeping. Thurman had arranged for a helicopter flight, security, radio and TV cameras, and flags for a swearing-in ceremony, that would make them president and first and second vice presidents of Panama. Bushnell had to scramble to find a secure telephone so he could inform an anxious State Department what was going on.

The swearing in ceremony went as planned, media and press releases from the new president went on the air, the invasion launched a few minutes early, and the US government prevailed over Noriega in Panama.

THE ENDARA ADMINISTRATION, YEAR ONE

Guillermo Endara, a lawyer and longtime member of Arnulfo Arias's Panamañista Party, became Panama's next president almost by default. Arias had died in 1988, and the party chose Endara to run for president the following May, due largely to his willingness and personal devotion to his former boss. In the highly contentious setting of the 1989 election, he had joined in a coalition with two other opposition party candidates, Ricardo Arias Calderón and Guillermo "Billy" Ford, to run against Noriega's hand-picked candidate. They were believed to have won the election before Noriega cancelled it, alleging irregularities.[3] Later, as US authorities advanced preparations for the invasion, they decided that

[2] "Interview with John A. Bushnell," 745.

[3] On the 1989 election and demilitarization, see Orlando J. Pérez, *Political Culture in Panama: Democracy after Invasion* (New York: Palgrave Macmillan, 2011), 84–87; and ch. 5. Cf. David E. Pitt, "To Many in Panama, the New President Is an Enigma Wrapped in a Smile," *New York Times*, Jan. 28, 1990.

Endara and his two vice presidents represented the closest thing to a legitimate government available.[4]

To create the illusion of normalcy following the occupation, US authorities assembled a "shadow government" ("stood up," in military parlance), made up of US embassy and military personnel assigned to work with Panamanian counterparts to restore public services and faith in "government as usual." An early step had been to establish a secure location. At first, they operated out of the Foreign Ministry building, a cramped site with limited security features.[5] Soon Arias suggested the centrally located Legislative Assembly downtown, where executive offices could begin functioning on the border with the Canal Area and be accessible to the US military.

The embassy and army both assigned officers to work with various ministries and agencies to help them get up and running. Bushnell prevailed on the army to repair telecommunications, air conditioning, windows, and doors in the building, which had been damaged by the invasion. This operation was meant to show citizens and the world at large that the invasion was over and that Panama's leaders were now in charge: the new government was not a sham or puppet regime. The Panamanians wished to gain quick recognition from other Latin American nations.[6] Meanwhile, the army conducted a propaganda (psyops) campaign to reinforce these messages, despite the embassy's disapproval of the effort.

In early conversations, the principals settled on a rough division of responsibilities among themselves: Endara would handle politics and foreign relations, Ford economic affairs, and Arias Calderón, the only one experienced in international relations because of his Christian Democratic background, minister of justice, which included public security and police. They also, naively in hindsight, agreed to make decisions by consensus.[7]

Unquestionably the biggest challenges Panamanian and US leaders faced were what to do with the former Defense Forces (PDF) and how to bring some order to the dangerous streets of the capital. The city was plagued by lack of security, and few citizens felt safe on the streets.[8]

[4] Deane Roesch Hinton, *Economics and Diplomacy: A Life in the Foreign Service of the United States* (Washington, DC: New Academia/Vellum, 2015), 417–18.

[5] Larry Rohter, "It May Prove Difficult to Let Panama Get on With Its Life," *New York Times*, Dec. 31, 1989.

[6] "Interview with John A. Bushnell," 756–57.

[7] Ibid., 759.

[8] Richard H. Shultz, *In the Aftermath of War: U.S. Support for Reconstruction and Nation-Building in Panama Following JUST CAUSE* (Maxwell Air Force Base: Air University Press, 1993), 57–61.

Looting had begun, often led by "digbat" members joined by desperate people seeking food, shelter, or goods they could pawn.[9] By the same token, thousands of former military personnel, still armed and mobile, roamed neighborhoods.

The new leaders possessed few resources to deal with these problems, but they began to address them, working with US embassy and military representatives. They also had little experience with policing the streets – twenty-one years had elapsed since Panama had a truly civilian government. As for taking former PDF officers and troops out of circulation – the US military did that. They rounded up thousands of soldiers and officers and took them to prison compounds for processing, the largest at Empire Range. They also brought nearly a hundred Spanish-speaking reservists from the United States, who served as policemen at home when not otherwise deployed. Many of these so-called soldier/police officers ended up stationed with Panamanian police units and devoted themselves to tamping down crime and violence. Joint Panamanian–US police patrols proved most successful, as they had in the 1979–82 treaty implementation phase. Within several weeks, the shape of a new police force emerged from these operations.[10]

The question of what to do with PDF personnel and what kind of army Panama wanted in the future demanded answers.[11] The US military determined that the top echelons of the PDF officer corps had to remain in detention. John Bushnell, as a career diplomat, knew that Costa Rica had been the first, and until then the only, nation in Latin America to dismantle its army, in 1948. In early discussions, Vice President Arias Calderón and he both concurred that Panama did not need an army. They then convinced Vice President Ford to support abolishing the army. General Thurman was a harder sell, having to be convinced that Panama did not face any threats that would require an actual army. He eventually accepted the notion that most likely threats, especially to the Canal, could be best handled by police swat teams.[12] This decision to demilitarize Panama proved crucial for the nation's future.

[9] "Interview with John A. Bushnell," 760.

[10] Ibid., 778–81.

[11] Shultz covers this territory in detail: *In the Aftermath of War*, as does John T. Fishel, *The Fog of Peace: Planning and Executing the Restoration of Panama* (Carlisle Barracks, PA: Strategic Studies Institute, 1992). Fishel was assigned to help oversee the creation of the police force. Cf. Corinne Caumartin, "'Depoliticization' in the Reform of the Panamanian Security Apparatus," *Journal of Latin American Studies* 39, no.1 (2007): 107–32.

[12] "Interview with John A. Bushnell," 791.

Next up was the decision on whether to staff the police with fresh recruits or to screen former PDF officers from the lower ranks to determine who could be retrained into a new force. They decided on the latter course, even though it would be complicated and fraught with resistance. Yet the alternative – leaving thousands of former army personnel, even disarmed, on the streets without jobs – invited disaster. These discussions led to calling the new agency the Fuerza Pública Panameña (Panamanian Public Force). By mid 1990 it numbered 11,000. A Harvard-trained lawyer and fellow Christian Democrat close to Arias Calderón, Ebrahim Asvat, agreed to supervise the transition to the new force.[13] Having founded Panama's first tabloid-style newspaper, *El Siglo*, a few years earlier, Asvat also brought a populist sensitivity to the position.

These early decisions to incorporate vetted PDF officers into a police force, to include Spanish-speaking US guardsmen into police units and joint patrols, and to crack down on gangs, looters, and digbat rogues soon ended the reign of insecurity in the streets. Within a month, US forces were to begin deploying back home, to be replaced by former PDF officers and fresh recruits. These Panamanians were ready to assume responsibility for patrolling the streets, often accompanied by US personnel (reservists, advisors, MPs, instructors, etc.). Meanwhile, the private security guards who had appeared in preceding years to protect businesses and residences gradually thinned out as public policing resumed.[14]

After several interim appointees, Col. Eduardo Herrera Hassán was designated chief of the new police force. Unfortunately for peace-making, a labor protest and demonstration by officers in mid-1990 culminated in an attempted coup on December 4–6, 1990, in which Herrera Hassán was implicated. The president requested intervention by US troops, who quashed it, and Herrera Hassán was removed.[15] The embassy requested that the Military Support Group, coordinating army activities in Panama, have its deployment extended to assure stability. Southcom commander Thurman had requested that the new ambassador, Deane Hinton, regard

[13] Interview, Ebrahim Asvat, April 8, 2015; Lawrence A. Yates, *The U.S. Military Intervention in Panama: Operation Just Cause*, 2 vols. (Washington, DC: US Army Center for Military History, 2008, 2014), 2: 430.

[14] Mark Uhlig, "U.S. Yielding Its Police Role in Panama to a Rebuilt Force," *New York Times*, Oct. 30, 1990.

[15] Hinton, *Economics and Diplomacy*, 430–31; Fishel, *The Fog of Peace*, 52. See the exhaustive analysis by Margaret E. Scranton, "Possible Threats to Panama's Democratization in the Early 1990s," paper at American Historical Association meeting, Washington, DC, Jan. 4, 2014; Lee Hockstaer, "Panamanian Mutineers had Several Americans in Grasp," *Washington Post*, Dec. 6, 1990.

this support group as an integral part of the State Department team, since it exercised broad-ranging authority in the still-unsettled climate. The ambassador's legendary martinet character showed when he commented, "Quite an overlap with the embassy!"[16]

The existence of a new Panamanian government represented wishful thinking on the part of its US creators, a fiction designed to minimize the appearance of a military occupation and to show the world that Panama was whole again. It was a façade. As John Fishel, one of the best chroniclers of the aftermath, reported, the head of civil-military operations quickly realized that, given the disarray of the country, he "had no choice but lead the Government of Panama, couching its actions in the form of suggestions and recommendations to the 'government' and the Chargé."[17] General Thurman, meanwhile, told his civil-military designates, "put your uniforms away, go ahead and get your guayaberas … you're going to work for the new government of Panama."[18] Yet, as time passed, US personnel gradually pulled back, and more and more Panamanians took up vacant positions.

Inadequate funding for the new government exacerbated problems of restoring law and order. When combat operations formally ended on 11 January, Pentagon accountants shut down the spigot for war-making and shifted to force protection and training. Thurman and the Joint Chiefs were still able to shake loose money, but it was clearly going to diminish over time.

Meanwhile, President George H. W. Bush, who had promised a billion dollars in reconstruction aid, found his request languishing in Congress. Vice President Arias Calderón pressed the new ambassador, Deane Hinton, a veteran diplomat known for his influence on the Hill, for $1.5 billion. Meanwhile, when he arrived in Panama in mid-January, Hinton also attempted to assert his primacy over other US agencies in Panama, as a sort of proconsul. The military, however, did not salute him. They recognized the weakness of embassy resources and pressed ahead with nation-building as if they alone constituted the country team.[19]

[16] Yates, *Military Intervention*, vol. 2, 468; Hinton, *Economics and Diplomacy*, 421; Eric Schmitt, "U.S. Helps Quell Revolt in Panama," *New York Times*, Dec. 6, 1990. Clifford Krauss, "Rebels Are Posing Threat in Panama," *New York Times*, Jan. 21, 1991.

[17] Fishel, *Fog of Peace*, 34. The chargé referred to was DCM John Bushnell.

[18] Quoted in Yates, *Military Intervention*, vol. 2, 444.

[19] Hinton, *Economics and Diplomacy*, 428–29; Elaine Sciolino, "Bush Picks a Panama Envoy and Sends Team There, Too," *New York Times*, Jan. 3, 1990; C. Dickey,

Money never flowed as Bush pledged. Congress appropriated far less than what had been promised but at least lifted trade sanctions.[20] President Endara became so angry at the stalled recovery funding and reparations that he went on a two week hunger strike in March 1990 to protest delays.[21] Two months later, the US Congress dithered over drastically reduced aid, requiring it to be shared with Nicaragua.[22] Adding insult to injury, State and Treasury tried to use promises of aid to force changes in the country's Swiss-like bank laws to open up Panama's accounts to US scrutiny. Clearly the urgency of deposing Noriega had faded into memory. For another thing, the White House soon threw itself into the crisis caused by Iraq's invasion of Kuwait, which led to the 1991 Gulf War.

The Panamanian economy slowly recovered, little thanks to US aid.[23] The ambassador devoted most of his time to police reorganization, the tripartite Canal alternatives study, US burial remains in a reverted cemetery, and what to do with the Smithsonian Tropical Research Institute (STRI) located in Panama and not covered by the 1977 treaty.[24]

POSTMORTEM ON 1989 INVASION

Most accounts of the post-invasion actions by the US army find considerable shortcomings and outright errors committed. Fishel found major disarray, "ordered chaos," due to the missing ambassador and new Southcom commander.[25] As noted in Chapter 2, policymakers in

"Panama's high-profile proconsul," *Newsweek* 115, no. 26 (June 25, 1990): 31; Yates, *Military Intervention*, vol. 2, 461.

[20] See the table in Fishel, *Fog of Peace*, 101–02; and Hinton, *Economics and Diplomacy*, 418–20.

[21] Yates, *Military Intervention*, vol. 2, 467; Larry Rohter, "Panama's New Leader Fasts to Dramatize Need for Aid," *New York Times*, Mar. 12, 1990. Cf. interview with Endara, in Fishel, *Fog of Peace*, 60.

[22] "Interview with John A. Bushnell," 782–85; Susan F. Rasky, "Latin Aid Package Voted by Congress," *New York Times*, May 25, 1990.

[23] Richard L. Millett, "Panama's Paradoxical Progress," *North-South: The Magazine of the Americas* 4, no. 1 (1994): 21–25. Cf. Susan F. Rasky, "Bush Assails Congress for Delay of $420 Million in Aid to Panama," *New York Times*, May 1, 1990; Mark Uhlig, "After Noriega, Change Comes Slowly and Panama President Frustrated," *New York Times*, Nov. 3, 1990.

[24] Hinton, *Economics and Diplomacy*, 428–29. A 1985 agreement on bilateral cooperation in the STRI was later extended to facilitate cooperation on vital scientific installations and programs.

[25] Fishel, "Summary," in *Fog of Peace*, vii–ix, 39. See also his later analysis, "The Interagency in Panama, 1986–1990," in *The U.S. Army and the Interagency*

Washington were unprepared for such a major action. These judgments contrast with a positive assessment of the invasion itself, said to be successful, surgical, and welcomed by the people of Panama.[26] What went wrong in the aftermath? Basically, a lack of attention to what would come after military occupation. The previous Southcom commander, Fred Woerner, had dragged his feet in the two years leading up to the invasion, because he believed it was unnecessary and would cause tremendous suffering for ordinary Panamanians. Still, his staff, collaborating with planners in Washington, developed one blueprint for invasion and another for recovery/reconstruction. Woerner's heart wasn't truly in military action.

When White House staff moved toward a decision on invading, they determined that General Woerner wasn't sufficiently supportive of the plan, and they replaced him with General Maxwell Thurman (nicknamed "Mad Max"), a man described as ready for action. Thurman modified the invasion plan to speed it up, to accomplish within hours what General Woerner's plan would have taken four or five days to achieve. As it turned out, this foreshortened invasion probably averted more concerted opposition from the PDF and loss of life on both sides.[27]

On the other hand, General Thurman paid little attention to what would happen after the invasion, the so-called "stabilization operations and nation building." He dismissed these preparations, first code-named Blind Logic and later Promote Liberty, by saying, "I did not even spend five minutes on Blind Logic."[28] In addition, in several other instances cited by Yates, Thurman cast aspersions on so-called rebuilding efforts. His laser focus was getting in, capturing Noriega, defeating the PDF, and letting the rest sort itself out later. His disdain for the embassy diplomats (except Bushnell) and Washington also shone through.

Thurman clearly neglected preparations for the post-invasion. He did not foresee a shortage of vehicles and only afterward requisitioned 1,000 jeeps from depots in Germany. He did not foresee the need for Spanish-

Process: Historical Perspectives, eds. Kendall D. Gott and Michael G. Brooks (Fort Leavenworth, KS: Combat Studies Institutes Press, 2008), 65–76.

26 Yates, *Military Intervention*, vol. 2, 469–81

27 Controversy over the number of civilian Panamanian deaths continued for years and is still unsettled. Official US estimates reported losses as several hundred, whereas others ranged in the thousands. An early assessment by Larry Rohter, "Panama and U.S. Strive to Settle on Death Toll," *New York Times*, Apr. 1, 1990, suggests that President Endara took some blame for not insisting on a more strenuous accounting.

28 Yates, *Military Intervention*, vol. 2, p. 449.

speaking police and only afterward ordered up nearly a hundred such reservists serving in Southwestern police departments. He did not foresee the need to get weapons off the streets through a buy-back program, one that later netted over 60,000 guns. He did not foresee a festering crisis afflicting some 15,000 refugees when the tenement district surrounding PDF headquarters burned down. His soldiers received little training for dealing with post-invasion civilians. He assumed that after the invasion he would be chief of an occupying military government, whereas State empowered, more than a little naively, the civilian authorities who were perceived as the victors of the vitiated election. General Thurman turned out to be an over-eager commander of an invasion of a small nation under the heel of a dictator. He utterly lacked diplomatic and political skills.

Any analysis of the invasion and its aftermath needs to take account of multi-agency competition that gripped actors. One military chief noted that he had at least three headquarters to report to. Diplomats decried the fact that they had intentionally been excluded from the two-year build-up to Just Cause. The Department of Justice took over training of Panama's new police, even though they had limited resources to do so, and the army's Military Support Group did the lion's share of training. By mid 1990, many US agencies had sent personnel to Panama to cooperate in reconstruction, yet they were often ineffective.[29] And still only a fraction of the promised funds materialized.

To summarize, on December 17, 1989, President George H. W. Bush ordered military action to capture General Noriega; the US army had been planning for such an order for two years; and they executed the plan with operational success. Panamanians, suffering under a dictatorship and withering economic sanctions, hunkered down as the invasion took place, and then they celebrated the end of Noriega and shortages. Sadly, US planning for the aftermath fell far short, and women and men on the street grieved. Years passed before they believed the invasion really benefitted them.[30]

ENDARA ON HIS OWN, 1991–94

President Endara faced many obstacles as he attempted to rebuild civilian government and restore the economy. First, he had never served in an

[29] Shultz, *In the Aftermath of War*, 45–54, 63–64; Fishel, "Interagency in Panama," passim.

[30] See the 25th commemorative edition of *La Prensa* on Dec. 20, 2014, "25 años de la invasión a Panamá 1989–2014"; Fishel, *The Fog of Peace*, provides the most telling criticism of poor planning following the invasion.

executive capacity before and lacked experience as an administrator. Second, he assumed office leading a three-party coalition that broke up in mid 1991, leaving him with reduced support – even Arnulfo Arias's widow, Mireya Moscoso, abandoned him when she announced her candidacy for the 1994 presidential election. Third, he was dogged by the impression that he was a puppet of the United States, a notion that grew despite the US's fading interest in rebuilding its client state. Fourth, he found himself unable to execute programs, in part due to scant funds provided by the United States. Finally, his decisions to convert the PDF into a police force and incorporate former officers into the new agency remained unpopular, tainting his administration with the ills of Noriega's regime. His was definitely a "Mission: Impossible," and his approval rating skidded from 20 percent in 1991 to 8 percent in 1993.[31]

Endara's overweight physique and remarriage in mid 1990 to an attractive woman thirty years his junior, Ana Mae Díaz, raised eyebrows and opened him to teasing by pundits.[32] The first lady reportedly exerted influence in important presidential decisions. Meanwhile, Endara's legislative plans floundered upon the breakup of his coalition in 1991 and his inability to pass legislation or constitutional amendments.[33]

On March 1, 1990, meanwhile, the Assembly resumed activity, as dust cleared from the invasion. The Electoral Tribunal resurrected the votes from the previous year and recognized as winners the candidates for fifty-eight seats on that basis; the remaining nine seats, won by disqualified candidates, were filled in a special election the following year. The anti-Noriega spirit abroad in 1989 had handed the opposition coalition a big victory: Arias Calderón's Christian Democrats got the largest delegation (twenty-eight), followed by Billy Ford's traditional liberal MOLIRENA (eighteen), and Endara's PLA (nine). The pro-Noriega PRD got only ten seats in a special 1991 election.

These Assembly election results gave the new administration a working majority. Its leaders, taking advantage of restored democracy, immediately sought to elevate their authority, pay, and privileges, to make up for the years of military dominance. The Endara administration, on the other

[31] Margaret Scranton, "Panama's Democratic Transition," *The Midsouth Political Science Journal* 13 (Spring 1992): 114–15; interview, Ebrahim Asvat, Apr. 15, 2015; Fishel, *Fog of Peace*, 57.

[32] On commentary about the first lady, see Ana Elena Porras, *Cultura de la interoceanidad*, 2nd ed. (Panama: Universidad de Panamá, 2009), 186–88.

[33] Shirley Christian, "Panama Grows, Reaching Skyward, Yet Down Below Much Pain Remains," *New York Times*. Apr. 29, 1992.

hand, cut members' salaries (still quite high), alleging that funding was scarce. This set off a years-long tug-of-war between the legislature and the executive over budgets, perquisites, and immunity.[34]

Many observers hoped that the Endara administration, with its Assembly majority, would carry out a thorough cleanup of vice and crimes that had permeated the previous regime. When Endara's coalition broke up, however, he was unable to assert much influence. Indeed, a spirit of leniency suffused all branches of government, and the president himself issued hundreds of pardons, while courts absolved many other persons accused of pre-invasion crimes.[35]

Police reform had topped Endara's to-do list in 1990 and 1991. What he and the Americans had accomplished on an emergency basis, however, needed to be codified. His people crafted two decrees, 38 and 42, to make previous decisions official. They legally extinguished the army, created the Fuerza Pública in its stead, shifted the Investigative Police (DENI) to the ministry of justice, and amalgamated other units. Meanwhile the country's miniscule navy and air force remained under the presidency, as provided by Law 20 of 1983. All of this took place under supervision by Southcom and its various training, civil affairs, and intelligence units. As part of dismantling the army, Endara also took back the PDF bases and properties in the reverted areas, reassigning them to civilian agencies.[36]

About that time, *New York Times* reporter Shirley Christian revealed that polls showed Panamanians undecided about the treaty-driven schedule for the military to exit and the Canal to be turned over to Panama in 1999. Many believed the country to be too fragile and disorganized to take on the tasks of running and defending the Canal.[37]

In June 1992, Endara suffered another embarrassment, during a visit by President George H. W. Bush, then in his reelection campaign. Bush believed he could benefit from his image as a liberation figure in Panamanians' eyes,

[34] Carlos Guevara Mann, *Political Careers, Corruption, and Impunity: Panama's Assembly, 1984–2009* (Notre Dame, IN: University of Notre Dame Press, 2011), ch. 9 passim, 349; and "La Vida Política en el siglo XX," in *Panamá: historia contemporánea*, ed. Alfredo Castillero Calvo (Madrid: Fundación Mafre, 2014), 229–30.

[35] See Guevara Mann, *Political Careers*, chs. 10–11, passim, for many scandalous cases. On the pardons, see Pérez, *Political Culture*, 120.

[36] Pérez, *Political Culture*, 90–92; Scranton, "Democratic Transition," 119–24. For lands occupied by the PDF in the 1980s, see Raymundo Gurdián Guerra, "Los Tratados del Canal y su Transferencia, 1967–1999," in *Historia General de Panamá*, ed. Alfredo Castillero Calvo (Panama: Consejo Nacional del Centenario, 2004), III:II, 272.

[37] "Panama Questions U.S. Base Closure," *New York Times*, Apr. 19, 1992.

who seemed to give an enthusiastic endorsement of the 1989 invasion. Ignoring security warnings, Bush held his rally outdoors at the Plaza Porras, expecting an adulatory public. A couple of hundred protesters disrupted the event, however, leading to crowd dispersal by tear gas and cancellation of the speech.[38] Nearly everyone suffered embarrassment from the episode.

Meanwhile, leaders of all parties urged adoption of legal reforms to eliminate autocratic elements from Torrijos's 1972 Constitution and later amendments imposed by Noriega. Endara worked with the Assembly to compile a list of such reforms, to be submitted to a referendum in November 1992. By now, however, the Christian Democrats had exited the president's coalition, and his approval ratings slipped.[39] Accusations of corruption circulated, tarnishing his image. The referendum proved to be a disaster for Endara: turnout plummeted, and voters rejected the measures by a two-thirds majority.[40]

Endara also faced the challenge of reactivating the reversion process, which had ground to a halt during the Noriega crisis. In 1990, a legislative commission drafted constitutional reforms to create a new Canal agency, as well as the Autoridad de la Región Interoceánica (Interoceanic Regional Authority, ARI), to take over reverted properties. The latter was approved by the Assembly in 1993 and then ratified by the newly elected legislature in 1994. The Canal agency, meanwhile, would take longer to materialize.

ARI's job consisted of continuing to receive, inventory, maintain, and eventually sell or find productive uses for the former Canal Zone lands and buildings, either privatizing them or assigning them to new public purposes. Its goals were to promote the nation's economic, social, urban, and environmental development, as well as to reserve some lands for eventual Canal expansion.[41] Three factors delayed more aggressive

[38] Alma Guillermoprieto begins her excellent article, "Letter from Panama," *The New Yorker*, Aug. 17, 1992, 60–71, with the Bush speech episode. Cf. Shirley Christian, "Warnings to Bush on Panama Cited," *New York Times*, June 15, 1992; Hinton, *Economics and Diplomacy*, 434–35. This episode begs comparison with his son George W. Bush's premature declaration of "Mission accomplished" following the 2003 invasion of Iraq.

[39] Scranton, "Democratic Transition," 116–17.

[40] William L. Furlong, "The Difficult Transition towards Democracy," *Journal of Interamerican Studies and World Affairs* 35, no. 3 (1993): 24–26; Steve Ropp, "Things Fall Apart: Panama after Noriega," *Current History*, 92, no. 572 (1999): 102–05.

[41] Gurdián Guerra, "Los Tratados del Canal," 273–74; Nicolás Ardito Barletta, "La incorporación de las áreas revertidas (Antigua Zona del Canal)," *La Prensa*, Dec. 8, 2014.

exploitation of the economic potential of former Zone lands – first, delay in getting the agency up and running; second, slow planning by the Pentagon for withdrawing its bases, which largely occurred after 1995; and third, turnover in the directorship due to an unclear mandate.[42]

Authorities in charge of reverted lands, meanwhile, worried about the cost of upkeep, physical deterioration in the tropical climate, vandalism, invasions, and lack of good utilities maps in case of major breakdowns. Its board of directors visited US cities that had experienced military base closures to get ideas for Panama's coming transition.[43] ARI only became fully operational in 1995, after President Pérez Balladares nominated former president Ardito Barletta as executive director.

President Endara or his representatives also participated in meetings in the early 1990s designed to help rebuild civil society in the wake of dictatorship and invasion and to chart courses toward democracy and the Canal takeover. Between 1993 and 1994, for example, the UN Development Program (UNDP) sponsored a series of three meetings in Bambito, western Panama, to foster open debate about challenges facing the country. Leading politicians, business leaders, government authorities, and religious figures took part. Planning for Canal transfer ranked high on these agendas. These meetings were complemented by political gatherings held at the Santa María la Antigua University (USMA) in 1993 designed to soften partisan rancor in coming elections. Led by Rector Stanley Muschett, the participants sought agreements to abide by rules of decorum, mutual respect, and the public interest. Observers believed that these meetings helped to heal the wounds of previous decades and paved the way for successful public policy discussions and elections the following year.[44]

President Endara faced another humiliating episode near the end of his term. As a humanitarian gesture in spring 1994, he agreed to accept up to 10,000 Haitian refugees, who had fled after a bloody coup on their island. Many ended up in the Guantanamo naval base in Cuba, and the

[42] Ardito Barletta, *Huellas*, ch. 5. Juan Blau and José Chen Barría resigned as previous ARI directors.

[43] Richard Downes, "Panama's Historic Transition Brings High Hopes, Uncertainties," *North-South Center Focus* 6, no. 1 (1997) 3. In the early 1990s, author Conniff spent considerable time with the chairman of the ARI board, Carlos Alberto Mendoza, in Panama and the United States.

[44] Pérez, *Political Culture*, 102, 123–24; Ada Piazza and Nicolás Flaño Calderón, *Diálogo Social en América Latina* (Washington, DC: Inter-American Development Bank, 2006), 25–26.

US government put out calls for other Latin American nations to receive some of them. Endara's offer was met by a huge uproar of protests, and he rescinded his offer, one of his last embarrassments as president.[45]

Despite the Bush administration failure to deliver the promised reconstruction funding, the Panamanian economy began to grow robustly in the early 1990s, responding to the end of sanctions, increased circulation of money, foreign investment, and revived trade with the United States. In 1991–92, GDP growth rate reached double digits before falling back in 1993–95 to single digits, but still respectable. Unemployment, however, remained frustratingly high. Other positive factors were increased Canal traffic, port and highway construction, and US military expenditures (up to $300 million a year).[46]

ELECTORAL REFORMS AND OUTCOMES

The Electoral Tribunal stood as Panama's highest authority in election matters, overseeing thousands of local precincts, courts, and specialized units that carried out actual voting. (Vote *counting*, on the other hand, was conducted by the National Counting Board.) Since 1990 the Tribunal has evolved into the most trusted institution in the country, and its showy new building completed in 2013, after more than a decade of work on a property in the former Canal Zone, nicely reflects its importance.[47]

The Endara government, itself legitimized by the Tribunal based on the May 1989 election, respected the independence of the Tribunal as stipulated in the Constitution. Three new magistrates took the bench and set about reforming its operations. They adopted norms that would inspire confidence in the public, and civil society organizations also pledged their support for its actions, with counsel from the UNDP. Its first task was holding small in-fill elections for the Assembly in January 1991, which turned out to be a test run for burnishing its tarnished system. They went well.

[45] Howard W. French, "When Neighbors Aren't Friends," *New York Times*, July 10, 1994.

[46] Juan Moreno Lobón, "El proceso económico en el siglo XX," in *Panamá: historia contemporánea*, ed. Alfredo Castillero Calvo (Madrid: Fundación Mafre, 2014), 4. Shirley Christian provided a good snapshot in "Panama Reaches High but Stays Mired in Pain," *New York Times*, Apr. 29, 1992.

[47] The best source on the 1990s is Margaret Scranton, "Electoral Reform and the Institutionalization of the Electoral Tribunal in Post-Invasion Panama," in *Post-Invasion Panama: The Challenges of Democratization in the New World Order*, ed. Orlando J. Pérez (Lanham, MD: Lexington Books, 200), 101–24.

The magistrates then turned to a general overhaul of their procedures, led by a special appointed commission. This effort elicited participation by an array of organizations, from civic groups to university leaders. By the end of 1992 they had developed broad agreement on principles, yet they had to delay reforms to hold a national referendum.[48]

The Endara administration, encouraged by civic groups, the US embassy, and its own need to stabilize the nation, worked up a list of constitutional amendments to address pressing needs. Among the most important was dissolving the army and replacing it with the Public Force, as discussed. Other changes altered some of the autocratic elements of the military-era 1972 Constitution. The commission did not, however, heed calls for an entirely new constitutional convention.

The 1992 referendum proved a success for the Tribunal but a disaster for Endara. It flowed smoothly without major difficulties, showing that the reforms discussed until then worked fine. It also rolled out a unique feature – shifting command of the Public Force to the Tribunal during the week ahead of the election, so the executive branch could not use it to manipulate its outcome. The successful execution of the referendum showed up in favorable newspaper editorials.[49]

The referendum hit a sour note for the new government, with exceptionally low turnout and a two-thirds rejection rate. The turnout reflected faulty data in the electoral registry but also the public's disapproval of the country's leadership. Endara himself was widely seen as responsible for negative attitudes toward the government's direction. US foot-dragging on funding reconstruction and high unemployment compounded his disapproval ratings.[50]

With the successful execution of the referendum under its belt, the Tribunal pushed ahead with its reform package. The Assembly passed it as Ley 17 in 1993, including the Public Force shift in command, a single ballot for each type of race, popular elections for mayors, and obligatory resignation of candidates from public office six months ahead of elections.[51]

48 Ibid., 107–09.

49 On the referendum, see Miguel Antonio Bernal, "Evolución constitucional desde la separación de Panamá," in *Historia General de Panamá*, ed. Alfredo Castillero Calvo (Panama: Consejo Nacional del Centenario, 2004) III:I, 44.

50 Scranton, "Electoral Reform," 109–11; Shirley Christian, "Referendum Defeat: Panama Leader Loses Expectations Game," *New York Times*, Nov. 22, 1992.

51 Scranton, "Electoral Reform," 111–12.

Former Tribunal magistrate Guillermo Márquez Amado later credited Ambassador Hinton and the USAID-financed advisors for preventing Endara's comptroller Rubén Carles from undermining its work. Under the guidance of technical director John Palm, the Tribunal protected its political neutrality and achieved managerial sophistication.[52]

The Tribunal's next major hurdle was conducting the presidential election of 1994, the first transparent one in over a quarter century. Public anticipation surged, and so did participation by civil society. To assure a clean campaign, the groups that had been engaged in the Bambito and USMA talks coalesced into a more formal organization to hammer out a code of conduct for candidates and parties. It came to be called the Ethical Code of Santa María la Antigua, named after the university whose rector led the effort. The code won support from the UNDP, church leaders, civic groups of all sorts, and eventually the candidates and their parties. Adherence to the code became a badge of honor, and the meetings provided forums for early airing of accusations and complaints.

By late 1993, several politicians stepped forward to run for president. Mireya Moscoso (widow of Arnulfo, running under her re-married name Gruber) seized the reins of the Arnulfista Party from Endara and took over the top of its ticket. Rubén Carles, former comptroller of the nation, ran on the MOLIRENA ticket, a pro-business liberal party favored by established politicians. Businessman Samuel Lewis Galindo ran on the ticket of the Solidarity Party. Ernesto Pérez Balladares took control of the PRD and won its backing. A newcomer, singer/actor Rubén Blades, tossed his hat in the ring, debuting in his new party, Papa Egoró, which meant mother earth in the Guna Yala language. Three more candidates from smaller parties joined the race in early 1994, hoping to make deals with the front-runners.[53] Oddly, neither of the two vice presidents tried to run for president.

[52] Interview, Guillermo Márquez Amado, Nov. 26, 2014.

[53] This election received deep coverage due to its historic nature, and author Conniff served as an observer with the Carter Center delegation. See Margaret E. Scranton, "Panama's First Post-Transition Election," *Journal of Interamerican Studies & World Affairs* 37 (Spring 1995): 69–99; Scranton, "Electoral Reform," 112–14; Centro de Estudios Latinoamericanos (CELA), "Encuesta elecciones 94, Boletín #5," (1994); Hinton, *Economics and Diplomacy*, 436–37. Two of the minor contestants, Balbina Herrera of the PRD and Ricardo Martinelli of Cambio Democrático, became perennial candidates and faced off in 2009, when Martinelli won. A positive story about Moscoso appeared in a front-page article of *La Prensa* on May 7, 1994.

FIGURE 3.1 Sample ballot for May 1994 presidential election. Note that three candidates (Edy, Samy, and Toro) used their nicknames. Authors' collection.

Pérez Balladares, a tall, handsome figure who had been an executive with CitiBank in the region, had helped found Torrijos's PRD and remained in its leadership cadres throughout the 1980s. After the invasion, he shrewdly disassociated himself from Noriega and his PDF element of the party, claiming to represent the legacy of Torrijos and the PRD nationalist wing. He held MS degrees from Notre Dame and the Wharton School so presumably was pro-United States. He promised to be a good steward for the economy and to guarantee a stable business environment. His constituents included civil servants, union members, and businessmen who had aligned with the government in the 1980s. He mounted an efficient, competent campaign and led the polls heading into the contest.[54]

Mireya ran as heir to her former husband and appealed more to rural voters, traditional constituents of the Arnulfista Party, as well as to women. Observers wondered why she didn't run with the Arias name, traditional in Panama, choosing instead the non-Hispanic name Gruber.

[54] See the coverage by Howard W. French of the *New York Times*: "Panama Journal: Democracy at Work, Under Shadow of Dictators," Feb. 21, 1994; "Panama Likes Ruben Blades but Not, It Seems, as Leader," Mar. 17, 1994; "Panama Race Gets Tighter: Ruben Blades Salsa Star Maverick," Apr. 5, 1994; "Businessman Appears to Oust 'Old Guard' in Panama Election," May 9, 1994.

She had little experience in electoral politics but could count on legacy votes and substantial financing. She came in second in most polls leading up to the election and finished second in votes.[55]

As a newcomer, Blades ran an unorthodox campaign that appealed to younger voters and persons who had lost faith in politics. Observers called Blades quixotic and a maverick, but he did well in polls. He touted his success as an entertainer, emphasizing the entrepreneurial skills he had developed, and promised to pursue economic growth if elected. His party's name, "Mother Earth," highlighted his commitment to environmental protection. His face seemed fresh, in part because he had been away for twenty years, first pursuing a law degree at Harvard and then building his music and film business in the United States. He finished third in the final count.[56]

The 1994 election decided many issues and marked a new beginning for Panama's democracy. It followed to the letter the voting reforms instituted the year before and resulted in one of the cleanest elections in the entire region. Turnout came in much higher (nearly three-quarters). The voting rolls had been updated, a spirited campaign ensued amid world-wide scrutiny, and the results confirmed the election of Pérez Balladares without question. He took office on September 1st.

PANAMA'S ROLE IN CANAL MANAGEMENT

The 1977 Treaty stipulated that in 1990 a Panamanian appointee would take over as administrator of the Panama Canal, an issue that stirred up conflict in 1989 when Noriega announced his intention to appoint someone other than Deputy Administrator Fernando Manfredo, who had been groomed for the job. The treaty gave the US Senate the power to approve such appointments, and the prospect of a long, contentious succession had exacerbated tensions between the two countries.[57]

[55] Manuel Álvarez Cedeño, "Mireya de Gruber: Todavía hay tiempo para la unión," *La Prensa*, May 7, 1994. Moscoso later blamed Endara, who remained neutral in the campaign, for her defeat and in 2004 did little to back him as unsuccessful nominee for the Supreme Court. *Panamá América,* Dec. 19, 2017.

[56] Barbara C. Cruz, *Rubén Blades: Salsa Singer and Social Activist* (Springfield, NJ: Enslow Publishers, 1997), ch. 7.

[57] Noriega's choice was Tomás Altamirano Duque, a business associate, owner of *La Estrella* newspaper, and allegedly a bagman for the general's payoffs. He later served as first vice president under Pérez Balladares.

The Christmas invasion obviated the problem, and Manfredo won approval as administrator in January 1990. Still, Manfredo's association with Torrijos tainted him in the eyes of the triumvirate that took power during the invasion, so the latter sought someone both capable and politically acceptable. They chose an apolitical businessman trained in engineering, Gilberto Guardia Fábrega.[58]

Guardia wound up in the second-most important job in Panama until 1996, running the Panama Canal (although obviously not alone). He had earned engineering degrees in the United States and ran his family business for years. His association with Vice President Billy Ford and *La Prensa* owner Bobby Eisenmann caused his name to surface during the controversy over choosing the first Panamanian administrator in 1989. Guardia had also supported the Cruzada Cívica, as had many businessmen, so had anti-Noriega credentials. At the time of the invasion Guardia was in Miami with his ill mother, but on December 31 he received a call from Billy Ford offering him the job. Little did he realize the gauntlet he would have to run to secure his approval.[59]

The Endara administration nominated Guardia to US President Bush in March 1990. This entailed some awkwardness, because Fernando Manfredo had just assumed the job two months before. Yet Manfredo's PRD past undermined his candidacy, and the Ford and Eisenmann endorsements prevailed. Manfredo bowed out gracefully. In May, Guardia had to make his appearance in Washington, to meet President Bush and other top officials. He had already obtained the endorsement of Panamanian members of the PCC board and took the customary orientation tours of the Canal. His final vetting occurred before the US Senate, where he was escorted by Michael Rhode Jr., Secretary of the PCC. Other PCC honchos took part in his "anointment." Unpleasantness only arose when Senator Jesse Helms (R-NC) and other diehard foes of the Canal treaties used their time to denounce them. Still, at the end of the day, Guardia was ratified and had to swear a loyalty oath to the United States, which proved awkward but not insurmountable. He was fully confirmed in September, six months after his nomination.[60]

When Guardia took over the administrator job, his predecessor, Ray Laverty, stepped down to the deputy administrator job. Laverty welcomed

[58] Hinton, *Economics and Diplomacy*, 427.

[59] Nadhji Arjona, *Una misión histórica: Gilberto Guardia Fábrega* (Pànama: Ed. Libertad Ciudadana, 2003), 87–94.

[60] Ibid., 95–147.

Guardia and took him under his wing. Cordial and informative, he set about showing Guardia the ropes. He and his colleagues, James Ferrara, Joe Wood, and Richard Wainio, showered him with information, data, rules, and traditions that would essentially lock him into business as usual in Canal management.[61] In addition, they saddled him with petty problems regarding reverted properties and employee benefits that distracted him from larger issues. Guardia also signed on to a very active schedule of meetings and public speeches, presenting the Canal and its future plans, especially to his fellow countrymen. No wonder he had little chance to ask larger questions about how the Canal operated. In addition, his "bosses," Michael Rhode Jr. and PCC Chairman Robert Page in Washington, likely didn't want him asking delicate questions about Panama's benefits under the treaty.[62]

Guardia's confirmation came in time for him to issue the administrator's message for the FY 1990 *PCC Annual Report*. In it, he noted that Canal had survived the 1989 invasion unscathed and that democracy had been restored in Panama. Tonnage through the Canal was slightly down, caused by global economic declines, but revenues were up, due to an increase in toll rates. Capital improvements included widening the Pacific entrance channel, overhauling the Gatun lock gates, and purchasing two new tugboats. The PCC had acquired fiber-optic cable to lay a line across the Isthmus, promising to greatly improve internal communications. Panamanians made up over 86 percent of the workforce, while US employees constituted 13 percent. Elsewhere, the report noted that President Endara had nominated, and the US Senate approved, four new Panamanian board members: Cecilia Alegre, J. J. Vallarino, Alfredo Ramírez, and Luis Anderson. Chairman Robert Page would be replaced by M. P. W. Stone, Secretary of the Army.[63]

In Guardia's first months as administrator, he dealt mostly with personnel and housing issues, intensified by more US employee retirements after 1990. He also authorized continuing to pay a 15 percent hardship

[61] Sabonge and Guillermo Van Horde interviews, in Ana Elena Porras, ed., *Historias Canaleras: Doce testimonios de la transición* (Panama: Instituto de Estudios Nacionales, Universidad de Panamá, 2007), 47–56, 141–47.

[62] Gilberto Guardia Fábrega, *El Canal de Panamá: transición y perspectiva, 1990–1996: presentaciones y conferencias* (Panama: Editorial Libertad Ciudadana, 2003), compiled and edited by Nadhji Arjona. The difficult questions to be avoided from the Zonian perspective had to do with the overall purpose of the Canal and its business operations, fully discussed in Chapter 7.

[63] *Annual Report 1990*, i–ii, 5–25 passim.

bonus to US citizen employees, even though it created inequities between them and Panamanians. Training and apprenticeships for Panamanians needed more attention, especially for positions in the higher grades. The Canal spent so many millions on these programs that he wrote, "The Canal is a great university." He relied on María Luisa "Maruja" Langman, who had served as secretary to previous administrators, to capture some institutional memory and gauge personalities and relationships.[64] Perhaps he didn't perceive the extent to which Laverty, Ferrara, Wood, and Wainio hedged him in regarding policy initiatives, or he lacked the political clout to counteract them.[65] After all, it continued to be a US government agency.

Land use issues also confronted Guardia soon after taking over as administrator. First, many of the military bases claimed lands contiguous to the Canal, creating operational and security vulnerabilities. The fact that Endara took reverted bases from the PDF eased the problem but left US-base encroachments unsolved. Guardia proposed transferring such areas to PCC jurisdiction. The issue went to negotiation between the Pentagon and State and dragged on for years – DOD rarely liked to give up any rights or assets. As former ambassador Moss stated, "it's a well-known Pentagon habit that you don't give up an inch, even if you don't need it."[66] Eventually the issue would go away in 1999.

Second, Panama had not taken effective control of many reverted areas, allowing intruders and squatters to move in, even on former firing ranges with unexploded ordinance (UXO). The Endara administration, struggling to get traction in politics, did not wish to rile up opponents over problems it had little power to solve. Guardia also had limited success. It, too, would drag on for many years.[67]

Change on the Canal progressed slowly. The year 1992 saw a slight drop in both traffic and revenue, and in following years business seemed to level out. That year, Congress authorized a toll increase, which many hoped would allow the Canal to carry out long-postponed projects like widening Culebra/Gaillard Cut and upgrading aged equipment. Guardia proposed undertaking these expenditures, which could mount into billions of dollars, in stages to avoid "sticker shock." A bid went out to plan for the widening,

64 Arjona, *Una misión*, 156–63. Re training, Joseph Reeder communication, May 22, 2016.
65 Len Kujawa, interviews, Feb. 24, 27, 2016.
66 Ambler H. Moss Jr., "Interview with Ambler H. Moss Jr.," Library of Congress Manuscripts Division, 1988, 11.
67 Guardia, *Canal de Panamá*, 165–68.

a multi-year project. More powerful locomotives built by Mitsubishi went on order. Older lock gates began to undergo overhauls. Tugs and dredges also came up for maintenance or replacement. Finally, Panamanians now made up 88 percent of the workforce, and a special training program had produced 100 new Panamanian ship pilots, who now constituted 43 percent of all pilots.[68]

Since Panama wished to expand its national product and employ more citizens, not just live off the proceeds of Canal transits, it needed to grow beyond being a simple "path between the seas." In 1991, Guardia helped host the first of what would become periodic industry gatherings, called Panama Maritime, that have brought together shippers, port authorities, waterway operators, builders, academics, and government officials ever since. In this spirit, he paid visits to the St. Lawrence Seaway, often cited as a model for binational canal management, in 1991 and 1994.[69] Guardia also lectured and cajoled in public and private circles, to beef up the national Ship Registry business, train more seamen (at a new Maritime Academy), and install factories and plants at former military bases, mostly abandoned. In the mid 1990s, this role of pushing business development fell to ARI.[70]

The biggest challenge facing both Guardia and Endara was setting up an institutional home for the Canal after 1999, under what came to be known as the Organic Law of the Panama Canal (1997). To foster dialogue on the issue in 1991, Endara had created the Comisión Ad Hoc (renamed Comisión Presidencial in 1993) for Canal organization, chaired by prominent businessman and PCC board member J. J. Vallarino.[71] The Southcom commander offered to give tours of the bases to commission board members, to familiarize them with what existed for eventual turnover. Meanwhile, Endara and Vallarino convened two high-level retreats, Contadora I and II, to build on the Bambito I resolutions regarding the Canal and to develop strategies for taking it over and operating it successfully.[72] These new meetings, held on a resort island in the Pearl Archipelago that the government wished to develop, were meant to foster knowledge about, and eventually consensus on, how Panama would manage the Canal.

68 Ibid., 172–77; Agustín Alberto Arias interview, *Historias canaleras*, 81–2; *Annual Report 1992*, i–ii, 2.
69 Arjona, *Una misión*, 205–06.
70 Ibid., 178–83. See Chapter 4 on ineffectiveness of ARI in its first years.
71 Quijano, calling himself a "canalero," interview, *Historias canaleras*, 68–69.
72 Guardia, *Canal de Panamá*, 153.

Guardia's many speeches and guided tours served to educate the public, government officials, and Assembly on what would be needed for the nation to take over the Canal. Meanwhile, in the 1990s, Canal managers had ordered up several studies by international consultants to advise on the waterway's future and reverted lands (e.g. Louis Berger, Arthur Anderson, GAO, Nathan Associates), and the Tripartite Canal Alternatives study was finally delivered in 1993. The Canal Area became one of the most studied patches of land on earth.

For their part, the Zonians harped at their Panamanian counterparts about avoiding politicians' getting their hands on the Canal, which could ruin it. A consensus on the need for an independent agency free from political pressure and manipulation began to emerge during Guardia's term as administrator. Although the law (Ley Orgánica de 1997) would not be finalized until after he stepped down, he set in motion discussions that led to its adoption. In this role, he served as a bridge between the outgoing PCC leadership and the Panamanian cadres that would take over in a few years.[73]

Guardia adopted a theme first uttered by Manfredo: "We have to change Panama so it operates like the Canal," i.e. with checks and balances, accountability, and decentralization. He believed that Panama would "come of age" when it finally took control of the Canal. He also expressed a mantra meant to reassure the public and ship operators: the transition to Panamanian operation of the Canal would be "imperceptible," usually translated into English as "seamless."[74] Thanks to his and his successor's efforts, and those of his US allies, it was widely regarded as a success.

Guardia also participated in the critical 1994–95 transition in Canal management, during personnel changes under US President Bill Clinton. Until that time, the top Zonians – Laverty, Ferrara, and Wainio – kept tight control over major policies on the Canal, using their influence to prevent major financial transfers to Panama. They believed that Congress only intended to give Panama the Canal free and clear and did not authorize large capital improvements on the eve of the turnover, which Panamanians had not earned nor deserved. They believed many Panamanians wanted "something for nothing," which they opposed.[75]

[73] Guardia, *Canal de Panamá*, 186–88; Quijano interview, *Historias canaleras*, 79.
[74] Guardia, *Canal de Panamá*, 189–97, 202–6.
[75] Len Kujawa, interviews, 24, 27 Feb. 2016. Wood retired in 1993.

A Panamanian executive of the PCC, calling himself a "canalero," referred to the US executives as a Zonian clique pitted against Panama's interests, and another referred to a war between Zonians and Panamanians.[76] The Zonians did so openly during Manfredo's term as deputy administrator, then more subtly under Guardia.[77] Recruitment, training, and promotion of Panamanian managers and pilots lagged, so that the 1999 turnover stood in some jeopardy. The *canaleros* also feared that Zonian foot-dragging could leave the Canal in poor physical shape by then.

Zonian executives also exploited a contradiction between the treaty and Panama Canal Act to block major financial transfers to Panama. The Act stipulated that the Canal was to operate on a cost-recovery or non-profit basis, yet article XIII 4c of the treaty determined that in the event the Canal produced a surplus of revenues over expenses, Panama should receive a share, up to $10 million per fiscal year. Zonian managers created an "accounting gimmick" to move any surplus into an account labeled "capital replacement," that would be held in reserve for major expenditures, like equipment purchases or waterway improvements. Between 1988 and 1994, when Panama might have received up to $70 million under article XIII4c, it got only one payment, $875,000 in 1992.[78] During the Noriega crisis this action fit into the larger sanctions imposed by the United States, but after 1990 it hindered reconstruction following the invasion. And monies for capital improvements did not begin to flow until 1995.

PANAMA REBOUNDED

Panama began the 1990s conquered and occupied by the US army, following the Christmas invasion. President Guillermo Endara and his two vice presidents had little authority over the remnants of the government, and disorder in the streets made life hazardous for ordinary citizens. Communications virtually halted except for military traffic and some rogue radio stations. The planning and execution of the invasion,

[76] Agustín Alberto Arias interview, *Historias canaleras*, 83–84; Rodolfo Sabonge interview, *Historias canaleras*, 51.

[77] See Guardia's comments in *Una mission histórica*, 219, that "everything we got from the Canal was like administered by an eyedropper. Nothing was easy."

[78] Interview Richard Wainio, Apr. 21, 2014 and PCC spreadsheets; interviews, Len Kujawa, Feb. 24, 27, 2016. See the various annual PCC transfers to Panama, including under Article xiii, 4c, 1980–99, in Gurdián Guerra, "Los Tratados del Canal," 267.

recounted in vivid detail by Lawrence A. Yates and others, had left little to chance. Planning for subsequent occupation and restoring peace, however, proved deplorable. Code-named Operation Promote Liberty, the plans for "stability operations and nation building" turned out to be largely an afterthought. In addition, the invaders had conquerors' mindsets, unprepared to deal with messy civilian affairs in their wake or even understand the language of those they liberated from dictatorship. (See section "Postmortem.")

President Endara made the best he could of a terrible situation and worked with US authorities to reestablish orderly government. He faced withering challenges, like attempted coups and the breakdown of his coalition. Still, he abolished the army, got a semi-new police force in place, oversaw the recovery of the economy, put Canal treaty implementation back on track, took up the issue of reverted lands, and lent support to an overhaul of election procedures that, ironically, led to his losing a major vote on constitutional reforms in 1992. He also suffered from two image problems: that he was a puppet of the United States and that he was a lame duck executive, both of which had considerable truth. He was more than a caretaker but far less than a forceful administrator.

Regarding the administrator position of the PCC, Endara recommended to the US president an apolitical engineer, Gilberto Guardia. As we have noted, the latter faced major obstacles at the helm of this gargantuan public utility. To be sure, the Canal operated just fine under existing management, but the Zonian executives found ways to obstruct progress toward a successful Canal turnover in 1999. They also managed to withhold funding from Panama and slowed efforts to upgrade the Canal before the eventual turnover. Finally, they did little to facilitate recruitment and training of Panamanians who would soon fill executive and management positions on the Canal. As former administrator Manfredo noted, some Zonians thought their duty was simply to turn off the lights as they left on December 31, 1999, and let the Panamanians figure out how to manage the Canal the next day. They showed little commitment to prepare for a successful transfer of ownership.

In the early 1990s, Embassy economic counselor John Dawson "examined how the Canal would do were it run as a private business. His study concluded it would do exceedingly well." Zonian Wainio also predicted that the Canal could be enormously profitable if run as a business. Time would prove them exceptionally prescient.[79]

[79] Hinton, *Economics and Diplomacy*, 436.

By 1994, Panama had turned the corner on military dictatorship and US occupation. Its economy grew robustly, despite high unemployment, and the business community had regained its footing. The country still lacked a decisive leader and direction for the future. The election of Ernesto "Toro" Pérez Balladares that year led the country around the next corner.

4

The Pérez Balladares Administration: Return of the PRD

[T]he Pérez Balladares government will be clean, serious, democratic, and dedicated to bettering the quality of life of Panamanian citizens.[1]

Gabriel Lewis Galindo

THE PÉREZ BALLADARES INAUGURATION

Ernesto "Toro" Pérez Balladares stood in the reception line shaking hands with well-wishers and exchanging quiet words with many. Tall and handsome in a dark suit, he exuded strength and confidence during his inauguration as Panama's new president. His 1994–99 administration would stretch almost to the date the United States transferred the Canal to full Panamanian ownership. The actions he would take to ensure democratic stability and a successful Canal transfer required all his skills and authority.[2]

* * * *

Five years earlier, few would have predicted that Pérez Balladares would emerge victorious in the 1994 election. He was a founder and leader of the Partido Revolucionario Democrático (PRD) since its inception in 1978. He had even presided over it during the disastrous 1989 election, which

1 This was the key message that the foreign minister-designate and former Canal negotiator carried to a panoply of high-ranking US officials during a whirlwind five-day trip to Washington, DC, just after the 1994 election: María Mercedes de la Guardia de Corró, *Gabriel Lewis Galindo: Hasta La Última Gota* (Cali, Colombia: Cargraphics, S.A., 2009), 290.

2 Author Conniff attended Pérez Balladares's inauguration on Sept. 1, 1994.

Manuel Noriega had nullified months before the United States invaded to capture and prosecute the general. After the invasion, thousands of PRD leaders and followers went to jail or suffered other punishments, and it appeared that the party would remain moribund or on the fringes of politics for a long time.

Surprisingly, however, the PRD arose from the ashes of the invasion to rebuild its organization and membership. It did so largely by claiming the legacy of General Omar Torrijos and eschewing that of Noriega. Pérez Balladares also benefited from missteps by the previous administration and from the US failure to deliver economic assistance promised after the invasion. Voters seemed attracted to the option of alternating the party of the executive, in this case from the Arnulfistas to the PRD. Finally, voters preferred a strong leader at the helm of state during the years leading up to turnover of the Canal. Pérez Balladares seemed to be that forceful figure.

THE PÉREZ BALLADARES ADMINISTRATION

In his campaign speeches, Panama's future president promised to move definitively beyond the Noriega era. He intended to steer the economy toward more openness and participation by foreign investors, hoping that a revived business sector would draw in more money than could be expected from the United States, as it wound down Canal operations. He emphasized balancing the national budget, privatizing major public-owned corporations, lowering tariffs by joining GATT/WTO and seeking other free trade partnerships, and encouraging exports and foreign investments but discouraging imports. On social development, he pledged to create a national commission to overhaul education, address deficient public health services, build more low-cost housing, and lift the poor out of poverty through more and better jobs. He said the new Public Force (Fuerza Pública) needed continuous attention, as did high rates of crime and deplorable conditions in prisons. He promised pardons for persons in jail for political crimes, which would benefit mostly his PRD associates. He stated that he would approach the World Bank and the Inter-American Development Bank to finance these and other programs.[3] His ambitious platform had won public approval in the recent election and editorial endorsements by most newspapers.

[3] See the summary in *La Prensa*, Sept. 3, 1994, and the PRD campaign brochure, "Ideas para la acción." Richard Downes provided a competent overview at the administration's midpoint, in "Panama's Historic Transition Brings High Hopes, Uncertainties," *North-South Center Focus*, 6, no. 1 (1997).

FIGURE 4.1 President Ernesto Pérez Balladares meeting with Jacques Santer, foreign relations chief of the European Union. © European Union, 2018.

Almost immediately, Pérez Balladares confronted a delicate situation in responding to a US request to allow some 10,000 Cuban refugees to be housed for six months at military bases near the Canal Area. President Bill Clinton needed a way to secure and screen Cuban *balseros* (rafters) who had been picked up in the Florida Strait and taken to the US naval base at Guantanamo in eastern Cuba.[4] Just two months, earlier Pérez Balladares had criticized his predecessor for agreeing to house 10,000 Haitian refugees temporarily and then backtracking on the offer. Yet after Pérez Balladares was sworn in, working with his foreign minister Gabriel Lewis Galindo, who was well liked in the United States, he agreed to allow the Cubans in, as a good will gesture toward the United States.

By December, conditions in the camps festered, and only a fraction of the refugees had been resettled to the United States. The majority, young males, despairing of ever reaching US land, rioted, fled the camps, and some even attempted suicide. Pérez Balladares endured considerable criticism in the press for acceding to US requests. The last Cubans traveled

[4] Clinton was criticized in 1980 when, as governor of Arkansas, he had accepted thousands of Marielito refugees, who later rioted over poor treatment. He blamed his failed reelection partly on this episode. His policy in 1994 discouraged resettlement while he was trying to normalize relations with Cuba, unsuccessfully it turned out.

back to Guantanamo in February 1995.[5] As another accommodation to the United States, in October 1994, Pérez Balladares agreed to allow Lt. Gen. Raoul Cedras and nine members of the recently deposed junta in Haiti to take up exile in Panama.

Pérez Balladares also confronted the problem of jailed officials of the deposed Noriega regime. His predecessor had already pardoned over a thousand persons convicted of political crimes to heal old wounds, and the new president immediately issued pardons for another 222.[6] Still, thousands of digbat members, PDF officers, and local officials remained incarcerated. A proposal to pardon nearly a thousand more in 1996 drew rebuke from prominent religious and human rights leaders in Panama and even from Amnesty International, and the president backed off.[7]

Pérez Balladares also had to deal with a thorn in the side of the United States, the case of Pedro Miguel González, the son of Gerardo González, who became president of the PRD in 1997. Pedro Miguel had been charged with killing an American soldier in June 1992, but his father and other powerful figures managed to keep him out of the hands of the law for three years. Eventually, Gerardo turned his son over to newly elected President Pérez Balladares. Pedro Miguel went into custody in a posh prison and avoided prosecution for two years. He and two accomplices finally won acquittals in late 1997, to the dismay of US and human rights officials.[8]

As a former banker and businessman, Pérez Balladares enthusiastically took up the challenge of stimulating economic growth and putting more people to work. He announced a five-year modernization effort to restore economic vitality. The plan included privatizing (he called it corporatizing) major public utilities that either lost money or provided inadequate

[5] Larry Rohter, "Panama's People Don't Want Haitians, or 'Gringos'," *New York Times*, July 9, 1994; "Llegarán 10,000 cubanos a Panama," *La Prensa*, Sept. 3, 1994; Eric Schmitt, "Suicide Attempts on the Rise Among Cuban Refugees," *New York Times*, Jan. 23, 1995. The episodes resembled the controversy that arose when General Torrijos accepted the deposed Shah of Iran in 1979 as a favor to Jimmy Carter.

[6] Orlando J. Pérez, *Political Culture in Panama: Democracy after Invasion* (New York: Palgrave Macmillan, 2011), 120; Larry Rohter, "Some Familiar Faces Return to Power in Panama," *New York Times*, Feb. 9, 1995; Larry Rohter, "Panama Amnesty Plan for Abuses Draws Fire," *New York Times*, May 14, 1996.

[7] Meanwhile the State Department began putting PRD officials formerly in the Noriega regime on a no-visa list.

[8] Carlos Guevara Mann, *Political Careers, Corruption, and Impunity: Panama's Assembly, 1984–2009* (Notre Dame, IN: University of Notre Dame Press, 2011), 247–51; Larry Rohter, "G.I.'s Slaying in '92 Entangled in Panama's Politics," *New York Times*, Aug. 24, 1997.

service. These included the phone system, power plants, the electric power grid, the water company, the ports at either end of the Canal, and the Panama railroad. He also pledged to supplement the national highways by allowing private contractors to build and operate toll roads. Finally, he promised to loosen some labor laws, corporate taxation, and banking regulations that discouraged new business investments. This package of reforms, he promised, would deliver a major stimulus to the economy.[9] Pérez Balladares was able get the necessary legislation through the Assembly, where his party had put together a majority coalition.

The president's choice of highly respected and US-educated economist, Guillermo Chapman, founder of the Panama Stock Exchange in 1990, as minister of finance, sent a positive signal to investors and international bankers. His nomination of former Panama president and World Bank vice president Nicolás Ardito Barletta as director of ARI, to manage development of former Zone assets through the reversion process, also reassured financial observers.[10] He nominated the former dictator's nephew Hugo Torrijos to head the Port Authority. The president kept these and other top officials working smoothly through the complex agenda he set out for himself. He also began restructuring the foreign debt to assure that new capital would be available to support his ambitious plans. Finally, by adopting an orthodox, pro-business economic program, he unfroze loans that had been held up by the World Bank and the Inter-American Development Bank – at which point some $800 million began to flow.[11] His plans to join the international trade pact GATT (and later World Trade Organization) signaled his intention to attract foreign investment and to open Panama's economy to outside competition.

Panama's GDP began to grow again in 1996, at nearly 6 percent a year, in large part stimulated by Pérez Balladares's expenditures, expansion of the Colon Free Zone, rising trade with the United States, PCC expenditures on Canal improvements, and a sharp rise in Foreign Direct

[9] Downes, "Panama's Historic Transition," 3–5; Calvin Sims, "Panama Chief Seeks to Prod the Economy," *New York Times*, Nov. 3, 1994.

[10] Chapman earned BA and MA degrees at Louisiana State University. He also cofounded and remained the managing partner of the respected economics consulting firm, INDESA. Foreign Minister Lewis Galindo and his vice minister Omar Jaén Suárez recommended Ardito Barletta to the president, who forwarded his name to the ARI board, which exercised its authority to appoint him.

[11] Juan Moreno Lobón, "El proceso económico en el siglo xx," in *Panamá: historia contemporánea*, ed. Alfredo Castillero Calvo (Madrid: Fundación Mapfre, 2014), 449–55.

Investment. On the negative side, income inequality remained the worst in the hemisphere, and unemployment stood at 13 percent.

The privatization campaign shook the economy to its foundations. Long inefficient and unprofitable utilities, like the electric power company and grid, phone company, water works, ports, and railroad, all drained the treasury because of subsidized prices and bloated payrolls. Pérez Balladares auctioned off these and a handful of smaller public businesses, promising to invest the earnings in social development and more growth. It turned out to be a messy business, but it spurred immediate growth and created a more flexible and entrepreneurial economy.

The railroad ended up purchased and totally rebuilt by the US firm Kansas City Southern Railway, in partnership with MiJack International, a manufacturer of container flatbeds. The line, long in disrepair, got all new rolling stock, rails, double-track and double-stack capacity, and new signaling and security equipment. The railroad focused on container transport between terminal ports but soon also added passenger service, at the insistence of the ARI director.

The ports proved more complicated. First, a bidding war took place for the Canal ports. In the end, a major Hong Kong consortium, Hutchison Whampoa, won the largest and only two-ocean concessions, for Balboa (at the Pacific Canal entrance) and Cristóbal (on the Caribbean). Earlier, Seattle Stevedoring of America (SSA) had won a 1991 concession to transform a former Colon seaplane base into a major container port, Manzanillo International Terminal (MIT). It was soon to be joined by Taiwan's Evergreen, which converted a former military base on the Atlantic side into another container marshalling yard (now the Colon Container Terminal, CCT). Within a few years, they handled millions of containers. Huchison Wampoa-owned Panama Ports, which operated Balboa and Cristóbal, also began installing container cranes and later a new cruise ship terminal in Colon. Panama was on the way to converting the "path between the seas" into an international commercial hub.[12] The banana port at Puerto Armuelles, in the southwest province of Chiriqui, also passed into private ownership in 1998.[13]

Some controversy surrounded the sale of the railroad and ports in the mid 1990s. US construction giant Bechtel Corporation submitted a

[12] Alberto McKay, "El Canal, los puertos, movimientos e industrias marítimas," in *Historia general de Panamá*, ed. Alfredo Castillero Calvo (Panama: Consejo Nacional del Centenario, 2004), III:II, 93–114; Downes, "Panama's Historic Transition," 4.

[13] It had been nationalized by Torrijos in the 1970s.

preliminary bid, proposing to operate both the ports and the railroad. The cabinet rejected the bid for failing to meet the terms of the tender. The government held a second round of bidding, and Bechtel again insisted on the railroad-port package, upon which it was disqualified. The fact that the company's CEO was former US Secretary of State George Schultz raised the political stakes considerably and prompted claims of insider treatment until the government rejected Bechtel's bid. In addition, some US members of Congress criticized the ports award to Hutchison Whampoa, on the mistaken grounds that it was a Chinese company and would threaten US interests in Panama. In fact, it was a Hong Kong firm, with strong British roots, which was taken over by Chinese entrepreneur Li Ka-shing with some capital from the mainland and which successfully operated ports in many parts of the world.[14]

Telephone service took more work to sort out, due to the recent innovation of cell phones, but, in the end, British-owned Cable and Wireless took it over and introduced new and better services, at substantially higher prices. Meanwhile, in 1998, the government began work on a fiber-optic cable alongside the Canal to improve telecommunications and later facilitate connections to global networks that were being laid across the world's oceans, to keep costs down.

The electric power system ended up split into six generating companies, plus their corresponding distribution grids. Even so, the Panama Canal continued to supply an important part of the nation's power needs from its hydro- and thermo-electric plants, as well as most of the water for residents in the transit zone, who constituted nearly half the national population. Today, the Canal's continuing role as utility provider sits awkwardly with its main mission of running the maritime facility.[15]

Pérez Balladares's infrastructure ministry issued contracts for the construction and operation of two major toll highways in and around Panama City, one of the most congested in Central America. The return of economic growth in the mid 1990s, along with the availability of

[14] Some observers believed that Pérez Balladares and his team wished to avoid putting too much economic control in one company, especially one so closely connected with US interests. US ambassador Ambler Moss recalled his first meeting with the Panama Ports CEO. The latter, a Briton, said, "If you want to know who I am, I'm that red scare you're been talking about." Talks by Governor Bob Graham and Ambassadors Ambler Moss and Simon Ferro, *Panama Considered Conference*, University of Florida, Mar. 20, 2014.

[15] Interview, Manuel Benítez and Oscar Vallarino, Apr. 8, 2015. Political pressure forced the president to suspend the sale of the water company, Instituto de Acueductos y Alcantarillados Nacionales (IDAAN). Aquilino Ortega Luna, "Gobierno abandona idea de privatizar el IDAAN," en *Panamá América*, Sept. 11, 999.

inexpensive autos from Asia and Russia, multiplied the number of vehicles on city streets. Corredor Norte highway pushed through the north of the city, crossed the Transisthmian Highway, and curved east to Tocumen International Airport, serving the lower-middle-class suburbs of San Miguelito, Nuevo Veranillo, and Nueva Gorgona. Corredor Sur skirted the shoreline from Punta Paitilla to the airport, opening up new land for development. The Mexican firm PICSA won both bids, built the roads, and continued to operate them for years. In partial payment and to open land for construction, it received seventy-four acres of splendid shoreline property in Punta Paitilla, vacated when the government moved a small general aviation airport to the site of former Albrook Air Base in the Canal area. The highway construction firm eventually oversaw a new development of high rise condos, called Punta Pacífica, next to the existing neighborhood, and opened the door for the virtual satellite city of Costa del Este.[16]

Albrook, ceded by ARI to investor Alfredo Alemán, underwent a major expansion in the late 1990s. The airport runways were outfitted for general aviation traffic transferred from Paitilla, making it an important hub. The Corredor Norte (and later Metro line 1) served it, a huge new bus terminal handled inter-urban passengers, and a major shopping mall attracted a variety of retail shops and a hotel. Albrook became a veritable "poster child" for ARI's development plans.[17] Colon got a similar but smaller commercial center called Cuatro Altos.

Pérez Balladares also needed to finalize the conversion of the PDF into the Public Force, carried out by his predecessor through executive decrees but not sanctioned in law. For better or worse, the PDF-staffed police force had taken root, amid public skepticism. Levels of common crime and corruption had diminished, especially after 1994. The PRD's strong bench in the Assembly allowed it to approve Law 18 of June 3, 1997, institutionalizing the changes made since the invasion. Despite some tinkering around the edges, the Public Force has remained largely unchanged since then and firmly under civilian control.

Pérez Balladares suffered another embarrassment in these years, a revelation that his 1994 presidential campaign had accepted funds from

[16] Viodelda Barrías, "Proyecto de Punta Pacífica costará B/. 500 millones," *Panamá América*, Sept. 11, 1997; and Carlos David Castro-Gómez, "Mega Crecimiento de la Ciudad de Panamá y Su Impacto sobre el Habitat y la Vivienda Popular," *CLACSO* (Quito), 2012.

[17] Nicolás Ardito Barletta, *Huellas: Contribuciones públicas nacionales e internacionales, memorias* (Bogota: Panamericana, 2016), 199–200.

the Cali drug cartel. Although the route the money took was circuitous, it led directly to the candidate's election account, a fact he later affirmed, without admitting knowledge of its origin nor responsibility for the decision to accept it.[18]

Looking ahead to the 1999 elections, Pérez Balladares, on a roll with multiple construction and reform projects underway, and enjoying a major economic boom, decided to have his party propose a constitutional amendment to allow him to run for a second term. The amendment went through two favorable votes in the Assembly and then to the public in an August 1998 referendum. In the meantime, the Electoral Tribunal had made important procedural changes and spent millions on training voting officials and educating the public. The government skirted the rules and supported campaigns in favor of the referendum, yet the public rejected presidential reelection by almost two-thirds.[19] The president's loss made him a lame duck and threw the election coming in less than nine months into an uproar.

REVERSION CONTINUED

Although many complications arose in the 1990s regarding the handoff of former Zone assets, Panama worked hard to capitalize on the transfer of over 500 square miles of prime real estate, especially its buildings and infrastructure, estimated to be worth between $3 and $30 billion, depending on the source. These lands, which lay beside the two principal cities of Panama and Colon, promised to help Panama convert its economy from a mere accessory to the Canal to a global commercial and financial hub by building on myriad business opportunities. The stakes could not be higher.[20]

[18] Larry Rohter, "Drug Scandal Taints Panama's Reform Chief," *New York Times*, June 12, 1996. For the array of allegations against Panama in the 1990s, see the memoir of Pérez Balladares's ambassador in Washington: Eduardo Morgan Jr., *Memoria de una embajada* (Panama: Editora Sibauste, 1998).

[19] Margaret Scranton, "Electoral Reform and the Institutionalization of the Electoral Tribunal in Post-Invasion Panama," in *Post-Invasion Panama: The Challenges of Democratization in the New World Order*, ed. Orlando J. Pérez (Lanham, MD: Lexington Books, 2000), 101–24; Carlos Guevara Mann, "La Vida Política en el siglo XX," in *Panamá: historia contemporánea*, ed. Alfredo Castillero Calvo (Madrid: Fundación Mafre, 2014), 163–248; Larry Rohter, "Leader's Loss in Panama Clouds Future of the Canal," *New York Times*, Sept. 1, 1998. Cf. Miguel Antonio Bernal, "Evolución constitucional desde la separación de Panamá," in *Historia General de Panamá*, ed. Alfredo Castillero Calvo (Consejo Nacional del Centenario, 2004), III:I, 42–46.

[20] Larry Rohter, "Bonanza: Panama Canal Zone Up for Sale," *New York Times*, Nov. 18, 1995.

The Endara administration had begun reversion work after the creation of the Ad Hoc Commission and the Autoridad de la Región Interoceánica (ARI) in 1993, but the agency had barely initiated work by 1995. Pérez Balladares nominated as ARI general administrator Nicolás Ardito Barletta, who was soon appointed by the board, presided over by business titan Stanley Motta. The nominee brought major political, administrative, and intellectual experience to the job.[21] A former president, treaty negotiator, finance minister, World Bank vice president, and consultant, Ardito Barletta enjoyed close relationships with the president, new finance minister Guillermo Chapman, other PRD ministers, and top economic authorities around the world. He embraced the job of ARI director with gusto, enjoying the chance to dig his hands deep into the soil of Panama's economic future. Chapman, meanwhile, promised to carry out the program of privatizing public utilities and liberalizing trade the president announced, in coordination with ARI's initiatives.[22]

ARI's inventory included forested lands, lakes and rivers, buildings, townships, former military bases, industrial plants, public facilities, and much more, most already turned over but some scheduled to be "reverted" in the next several years. Ardito Barletta estimated a total of 7,000 entities would be handled by ARI before the 1999 Canal turnover. Luckily for him, the interagency feuds that had sprung up over these assets in the early 1980s had either been settled or now were his responsibility to solve. For guidance, he contracted with international consulting firms for two studies: a general plan for utilization of the reverted lands, passed into law in 1997, and another to develop the areas in and around Fort Amador, adjacent to the Pacific entrance to the Canal, for tourism.[23]

Ardito Barletta laid out his plans in a mid-1995 speech on the future of reverted lands. He was guided by the study he oversaw in 1970, *Estrategia para el Desarrollo Nacional*, to take advantage of returned lands and buildings. He began by stressing the need to protect the hydrographic basin so that the Canal would have continuous supplies of water. He also emphasized developing the region around Colon, at the north end of the

[21] This section draws on Ardito Barletta, *Huellas*, ch. 5; interviews on Apr. 10, 12, 14, 2015; "Informe del Administrador General," *ARI Memoria 1997–98;* his op-ed articles in *La Prensa* on Sept. 4–10, 2000, and Dec. 8, 2014; and his *Estrategia para el Desarrollo Nacional: Visión, realización, actualización* (Panama: Editorial Exedra, 2012), chs. 10–11.

[22] Downes, "Panama's Historic Transition," 4–5; Ardito Barletta communication, Mar. 11, 2016.

[23] Ardito Barletta, *Estrategia*, ch. 10.

Canal, to support a larger and more prosperous city. In this regard, he noted that since 1991 a multinational group had created Panama's first container port, MIT, near the Colon Free Zone. Telfers Island adjacent to the existing port of Cristóbal, was now being converted into a container facility and would also host a marine fuel bunkering station.[24] Former Fort Davis was being rebuilt as an industrial park by Taiwanese manufacturers, to focus on exports. Former Fort Sherman stood to become an area of urban expansion for Colon.

At the southern end of the Canal, other military sites would revert soon, opening new possibilities for nearby Panama City and the port of Balboa. Ardito Barletta foresaw that business growth on the Pacific side would cause the capital city to expand to the west and incorporate the towns of Arraiján and La Chorrera. This development needed careful planning to avoid environmental degradation. Proceeding with reversion, he stressed, required zoning regulations and cost-benefit analyses. He recommended a robust information campaign to let domestic and international investors know what assets and opportunities existed. That campaign could help replace the bad image Panama had gained during the Noriega dictatorship with one emphasizing democracy, civil liberties, and stability, the way Costa Rica had. This image-making should also stress that the Pérez Balladares administration welcomed foreign investment by promoting greater productivity, competitiveness, and exports.

At the Pacific end of the Canal, ARI also explored development of new ports at Corozal and Farfán and licensed a pipeline to move bunker fuel from the Arraiján storage tanks to former Rodman naval base, to serve commercial vessels. Other facilities were proposed, such as shipyards, liquid natural gas (LNG) export facilities, and dry docks.

To ensure that reversion led to economic growth, Ardito Barletta urged that the government create a pro-business environment by reducing regulations and making transparent those that remained. Included would be labor-management relations that boosted productivity, with wage growth tied to output. Business development also required public safety and efficient delivery of basic utilities.

Finally, Ardito Barletta listed priorities that would guide ARI decisions. First, Panamanian businesses should provide the many services ships required while in Panama's waters. The country's two public ports were woefully obsolete but when privatized would participate in the global

[24] See Ardito Barletta, *Huellas*, 133–36, on container ports.

explosion of container traffic.[25] To support this transition, the railroad had to be privatized and rebuilt to carry containers, and the Transisthmian Highway needed to be rehabilitated or replaced to allow trucks to carry containers between ports.

Second, ARI would encourage the development of several more industrial parks to operate as bonded warehouses (called maquiladoras in Mexico), like in the Colon Free Zone. These would purchase foreign inputs and export finished products. They would capitalize on access to Panama's banking and transportation facilities.

Third, ARI would push for more tourism to take advantage of appealing historic, recreational, and natural sites. Indeed, the Canal itself already attracted over a quarter of a million visitors a year transiting on cruise ships, but few disembarked due to US legal restrictions. After 2000, those restrictions would be relaxed so Panama could build and refurbish numerous sites to entice cruise ship and international travelers. These included the colonial ruins at Panama Viejo, Portobelo, and Fort San Lorenzo, plus the colonial-era neighborhood of Casco Antiguo. The nation's splendid beaches and rainforests also could be developed for tourists. Ecotourism, a boom industry in Costa Rica, could be pursued, particularly in places like the Gamboa rainforest. (See the hypothetical tourist map that opens Chapter 10.)

Ardito Barletta also announced that he would shortly sign with a planning company, Nathan Associates, to develop a tourism program for Fort Amador, along the southern entrance to the Canal, with Inter-American Development Bank financing. The Amador plan called for tourist attractions on the causeway/breakwater bordering the south approach to the Canal. A yacht marina and cruise ship basin would be proposed for the three linked islands at the end of the causeway, supplemented by restaurants, hotels, and shops for tourists. One of the boldest undertakings at Amador was a biodiversity museum, featuring Panama's tropical flora and fauna, as well as its unusual geologic history. Ardito Barletta, Vice President Dominador "Kaiser" Bazán, business magnate Stanley Motta, *La Prensa* owner Bobby Eisenmann and his brother Rodrigo, and businesswoman Pilar Arosemena de Alemán campaigned to raise $100 million for it and to attract world-famous museum architect Frank Gehry to design it. (Gehry's wife was Panamanian.) It would take

[25] This was done by ARI's sister agency, the Autoridad Portuaria Nacional (APN), which had jurisdiction over ports. In 1998, the APN was transformed into the Autoridad Marítma de Panamá (AMP).

many years to bring the project to fruition, but with so many attractions, Amador would become a major destination for tourists.[26]

Fourth, ARI would turn the US Army base at Fort Clayton into the City of Knowledge (Ciudad del Saber), to attract and house organizations, students, and researchers from around the world. This idea had been floated in 1992 by media owner Fernando Eleta and later was proposed to the president by ministers and Jaén Suárez Lewis in 1995. It would promote cultural, scientific, and technological development the way the Smithsonian Tropical Research Institute had done for decades. Ardito Barletta estimated that within ten years of opening, the City of Knowledge would draw in 10,000 students, professors, and researchers, replacing the 10,000 soldiers who would soon be leaving the bases being closed. Lawyer and writer Juan David Morgan presided over the board set up in 1995 and created a foundation to raise money for its operations. The Assembly passed Law 6 in 1998 to formalize its creation, once the base was turned over in November 1999. Sociologist Jorge Arosemena became its longtime executive director and Guillermo Castro its academic chief.[27]

Ardito Barletta outlined the criteria that would guide ARI in selecting clients and projects for the reverted facilities. ARI would choose activities that generated jobs, exports, domestic demand, and profits for investors. He emphasized jobs to address the nation's stubbornly high, then 13 percent, unemployment rate, and he stipulated that businesses had to be profitable for the nation as well as for stockholders. Choices also would take into consideration the impact new developments would have on the nearby cities and hopefully enhance their livability. Thus, planning and smart zoning had to be done beforehand to provide roads, utilities, access to transportation, and residential areas for new employees and their families.

Environmental impact also would be analyzed before approving any new concessions, due to the fragile character of tropical lands and the importance of maintaining the Canal watershed. Residential zones to be reverted could continue to include green areas, like European "garden cities." Some neighborhoods should have limited density for better quality of life.

The final criterion would be accommodating future expansion of the Canal itself. Culebra/Gaillard Cut was being widened, and plans were

[26] Ardito Barletta, *Huellas*, 201–04.
[27] Ibid., 205–07.

under development for a third set of locks much larger than existing ones. Panama could not possibly jeopardize its maritime future.

Over the next two years, ARI pushed ahead on many fronts, especially matchmaking potential investors with promising business opportunities. Some other entities gave support. For example, upon learning of the City of Knowledge, the European Union committed funding to create a research park in the reverted lands, and the Inter-American Development Bank put up $4 million. Taiwanese conglomerate Evergreen made its port in Coco Solo, on the Atlantic side, a principal hub for its container business in the western hemisphere. Many complex deals had overlapping jurisdictions that required the president to mediate and bring other ministers and the APN to the bargaining table, not to mention US authorities overseeing their exit from the former Zone, primarily the PCC, DOD, and State. The railroad was a good example. The APN, which had inherited the decrepit line, had to work with ARI, the Comptroller's office, and other agencies to put together a tender and host international bidding.[28]

To make good on environmental and tourism promises, ARI set aside land for recreation areas, preserved existing golf courses, and allocated over eighty square kilometers for reforestation/timber harvesting. It applied rigorous reviews of environmental impact to protect the watershed. In one area, however, it was stymied – unexploded ordinance (UXO) remained on former military bombing and artillery ranges, constituting about 7 percent of the former useable Zone. The Pentagon had fenced off and lightly patrolled these areas but refused to initiate a cleanup that would make the lands useable. Even years later, the issue continued on diplomatic agendas, as will be discussed in later chapters.[29]

Meanwhile, ARI made accommodations for non-governmental organizations to acquire buildings and lands for non-profit work in public health, education, and sports, and for low-cost public housing and sustainable agriculture. Many properties were assigned to government agencies to relieve crowded conditions in existing offices. ARI calculated that new public offices represented an investment of $500 million.[30] Many reverted residential neighborhoods, meanwhile, were sold through open bidding, although some existing occupants assumed ownership. Parks and plazas

[28] On the railroad, see Ardito Barletta, *Huellas*, 136–37. The APN, in these years, was directed by Hugo Torrijos, Omar Torrijos's nephew.

[29] John Lindsay-Poland, *Emperors in the Jungle: The Hidden History of the U.S. in Panama* (Durham: Duke University Press, 2003), ch. 5.

[30] Ardito Barletta, *Huellas*, 218–20.

were assigned to urban jurisdictions in Panama and Colon. Finally, some lands were sold to residential developers to add to the nation's housing stock. It was a busy time for ARI.[31]

Two years later the Assembly unanimously passed Law 21 to adopt the Regional Plan for the Development of the Interoceanic Region and Plan for the Use, Conservation, and Development of the Canal Area, which gave Ardito Barletta legislative authority to push ahead with his agency's work. He listed a dizzying array of projects: ports, transportation, commerce, tourism, manufacturing, education, health, housing, sports and recreation, and agricultural settlements. All, he asserted, followed the selection criteria and approval processes outlined before.[32]

At this juncture, and given the vertiginous pace of events in government, ARI, and the Canal in the mid 1990s, the UNDP decided in 1996 to follow up on the successful Bambito and Santa María la Antigua meetings. It sponsored three wide-ranging discussions about all these developments and welcomed community opinion and input on how they should be embraced. Leading civil society figures again participated, at the beach resort setting of Coronado, two hours west of the capital. The first meetings, called Visión Panamá 2000, in May and July 1996, focused on the Canal Organic Law being debated, land use, and ARI's progress. The following year, it sponsored a Visión 2020 to look ahead to long range challenges, including global trends, Canal turnover and expansion, democracy, and political reconciliation. Although observers believed that airing these big issues stimulated healthy debate, it did not produce concrete outcomes.[33]

FINAL YEAR OF ARI UNDER ARDITO BARLETTA

The frenetic final year of ARI in the Pérez Balladares administration found General Administrator Nicolás Ardito Barletta scrambling to close deals and attract investors to develop business opportunities in the former Canal lands. By 1998, he had accomplished a lot: several intermodal ports were operating or under development, largely on the Atlantic side; the railroad was being rebuilt; thousands of homes had been sold and hundreds designated for government or NGO offices; the Colon Free Zone had expanded physically and would soon be joined by other bonded

[31] Ibid., ch. 5, passim. See Guevara Mann's discussion of favored property transfers to Assembly members, in *Political Careers*, 224–25.

[32] Ardito Barletta, *Estratégia*, ch. 11.

[33] Pérez, *Political Culture*, 127–30.

assembly plants; and hotels, schools, and hospitals were being set up in former PCC facilities. Ardito Barletta estimated that 6,000 new jobs had been created through these activities, more than replacing the Panamanian jobs lost when the last military bases closed. Most of these accomplishments, of course, required close collaboration with other agencies.[34]

To accomplish these actions, ARI lobbied hard for streamlined processing of paperwork so that properties never before registered in Panama could be legalized quickly. Still, this required 4,600 appraisals, 2,800 lot surveys, 3,700 inspections, 3,000 property descriptions, and 1,350 registries. All these records were duly computerized by 2000.

In addition to the City of Knowledge, several other post-secondary schools were set up in the former Zone. Florida State University, which had operated a school for military dependents at Albrook, converted to a Panamanian institution and took over the former Canal Zone College.[35] The University of Panama and the Technological University both gained sites for branches at either end of the Canal. Eventually many European and US schools set up operations in the City of Knowledge. Finally, one of Panama's premier science promotion authorities, SENACYT, established in 1997, located its headquarters in the City of Knowledge after the turnover.

Disposition of military bases lagged despite advance planning by ARI. Howard, Clayton, and Rodman did not revert until 1999. Howard proved especially contentious because the US Department of Defense pushed hard to base an anti-narcotics air surveillance center there. ARI, meanwhile, explored the development of an industrial park in the sprawling site, either by European or US investors. By the time the military negotiations failed in 1998, planning was clouded by the PRD referendum on a second term for Pérez Balladares and by presidential elections in May 1999. Howard remained in abeyance. After Mireya Moscoso won the presidential contest, she requested that ARI postpone any agreement concerning Howard. In the end, a London firm won the concession in 2004, to create the Panamá Pacífico business park.

Clayton reverted in November 1999, and soon received City of Knowledge tenants. Rodman, at first used for bunker fuel docks, and as

[34] This section is based largely on Ardito Barletta, *Huellas*, ch. 5; "Informe del Administrador General," *ARI Memoria 1997–98*, Panama 1998; "Áreas revertidas," *La Prensa*, Sept. 4–10, 2000; and "La incorporación de las Áreas revertidas (Antigua Zona del Canal)," *La Prensa*, Dec. 8, 2014.

[35] "Panama Canal College Seeks Role for Era After the U.S. Withdraws," *Chronicle of Higher Education*, May 16, 1997.

a Panama coast guard operations center, eventually was taken over by container port operator PSA. A small portion of Corozal, which had reverted in 1982, remained under US jurisdiction because it had a military cemetery containing remains of US servicemen. Other areas were used as a leprosarium, for the ministry of education, and for private development adjacent to the shops and service facilities of the ACP.

In 1998, ARI also took over operation of the fiber-optic cable installed in 1991 and commercialized it for global communications. By 1999, six new fiber-optic cables were established next to the Canal across the Isthmus, converting Panama into the main such trunk in the Western Hemisphere.

By mid 1999, tourist attractions advanced on both coasts. Wealthy Swiss developer Herman Bern took on the task of building an eco-hotel beside the Canal in Gamboa, providing visitor trails through the rainforest and converting a former radar tower into a lookout and birdwatching station. The Spanish hotel chain Meliá, meanwhile, had taken over former Fort Gulick and rebuilt it to accommodate tourists interested in tropical settings. Tourism numbers boomed, as visitors came from around the world.[36]

After President Mireya Moscoso took office, she sent an advisor, the outspoken University of Panama law professor Miguel Antonio Bernal, to request Ardito Barletta's resignation. Although this was illegal (he was appointed by the ARI board of directors), he submitted his resignation in January 2000, to avoid her threat to change the autonomy, nature, and mission of ARI.

CANAL MANAGEMENT

In mid 1993, the new US President Bill Clinton nominated a Texas lawyer, Joe R. Reeder, to serve as the Army's new Undersecretary. Once confirmed, Reeder took Army Chief of Staff General Gordon Sullivan's place on the PCC board and was elected to serve as its chairman. Administrator Guardia noted that the appointment of a civilian to chair the board showed sensitivity to the leaders of a nation recently rid of a military dictator. Reeder immediately collaborated with Guardia, his Panamanian staff, and their PCC board members, as had his predecessor. He also made it clear that he would drive events toward treaty-mandated Canal

[36] David Adams, "In Panama, Change of Heart," *New York Times*, June 6, 1999, Travel Section.

turnover in 1999. Reeder showed no patience for the foot-dragging of certain Zonian executives who were perceived by many as uncommitted to the effective change in control that the treaty mandated. He forced the retirement of deputy administrator Ray Laverty and put Richard Wainio on notice to get on board with turnover planning. His arrival brought a sea-change in policy on the PCC board and throughout Canal administration.[37]

Reeder recommended appointment of Joe Cornelison to replace Laverty and began cooperating with *canaleros*, as the Panamanian Canal executives referred to themselves. Cornelison in turn named Rodolfo Sabonge head of the Treaty Division, and the pace of implementation picked up markedly. With State Department support, Reeder, even if at times skeptical, was called upon to make hard decisions to ensure a smooth and seamless final transition, treaty-mandated to take place on December 31, 1999. Zonians were now on their way out the door, and some, like Wood, took retirement in 1993. Still, some Zonians continued to sabotage the path to 1999. Jorge Quijano believed they wanted to subvert treaty implementation or at the very least turn over an obsolete Canal. Moreover, Zonians warned *canaleros* not to get together with Panamanian officials in ways that could appear conspiratorial.[38]

In 1995, President Pérez Balladares appointed a Transition Commission for the Transfer of the Canal, to take up planning where Endara's Presidential Commission had left off. Its duty was to design laws, policies, and institutional structures for eventual Canal takeover. Its foremost product was the 1997 Organic Law of the Panama Canal Authority (ACP). One of the commission members, Adolfo Ahumada, symbolized the continuity in Panamanian leadership related to the Canal, since he had participated in the 1964 student demonstrations.[39] Several other commission members were later also appointed to the ACP board.

Under PCC chairman Joe Reeder, Panamanian (four) and US (five) board members, effective immediately, ceased to caucus separately before

[37] Raymundo Gurdián Guerra, "Los Tratados del Canal y su Transferencia, 1967–1999," in *Historia General de Panamá*, ed. Alfredo Castillero Calvo (Panama: Consejo Nacional del Centenario, 2004); III:II, 271–72; Richard Wainio interview, Apr. 21, 2014; Ken Kujawa interview, Feb. 27, 2016.

[38] Interview, Rodolfo Sabonge, July 9, 2014; Quijano, "Intrigas en el Canal durante la transición," in *Historias Canaleras: Doce testimonios de la transición*, ed. Ana Elena Porras (Panamá: Instituto de Estudios Nacionales, Universidad de Panamá, 2007), 64–79; Roberto Roy interview, Oct. 7, 2016.

[39] Gurdián Guerra, "Los Tratados del Canal," 275.

PCC board meetings and worked as "One Team, One Mission." By a unanimous vote, they strongly advocated for and brought about significantly greater investments in Canal maintenance and upgrades and ordered an inventory of all such projects to be completed well before 1999. Reeder responded by creating a Panamanian Blue Ribbon Commission of prominent engineers to work side-by-side with the US Army Corps of Engineers, which had been chosen to contract with the PCC to conduct a comprehensive audit of the Canal's entire infrastructure.[40]

Outside engineering expert Alberto Alemán Zubieta headed up the Blue Ribbon Commission. *Canaleros* used this Commission to lobby for upgrades, such as completing the widening of Culebra/Gaillard Cut, replacing the navigation signals system, finishing the locks overhauls, dredging the entrances to accommodate larger ships, and purchasing new tugboats and other floating equipment. The overall cost to the PCC of implementing all recommended upgrades exceeded a billion dollars, paid by US taxpayers, and was largely completed prior to the 1999 turnover.[41]

In order to monitor progress on projects identified by the Blue Ribbon Commission, Reeder directed his staff to create a Milestone Plan, which included literally thousands of action items, large and small. Each action item included by name the person responsible and the deadline for completion. This list was made available to the government of Panama, the legislature, and the press, so that progress was completely transparent to officials and private citizens alike. In its final *Annual Report*, the PCC announced the successful accomplishment of the 200 largest Milestone items, including US enabling legislation, a new corporate structure, a financial plan, public relations and marketing efforts, and draft regulations for the ACP.[42]

In October 1995, meanwhile, recognizing the changing climate in the PCC and the return of the PRD to power, Canal administrator Guardia discussed succession in his job with President Pérez Balladares. Among other considerations, if he remained for his full term, the country could face a huge adjustment in 1999, when the Canal changed ownership and

[40] Roberto Roy interview, Oct. 7, 2016.

[41] Joe Reeder communication, May 22, 2016; interviews by Sabonge, Quijano, and Cardoze in *Historias canaleras*, passim.

[42] Sabonge interview in *Historias canaleras*, 56; Joe Reeder communication, May 22, 2016; Panama Canal Commission, "Milestone Plan for the Transition of the Panama Canal," Oct. 1, 1997, summarized in *Annual Report Supplement*, Oct.–Dec. 1999, 41.

the country got a new president and administrator. Better, he reasoned, to appoint a new administrator now so he or she would continue through the turnover. Guardia was confident that his successor, who turned out to be Alberto Alemán, would be a competent replacement. He submitted his resignation letter to President Clinton.[43]

The following July, PCC board chairman Reeder hosted a gala dinner in honor of Guardia and conferred on him the Distinguished Service Award, noting his willingness to overlap with and provide invaluable mentoring to Alberto Alemán, pending Alemán's confirmation as Canal administrator. Alemán's nomination was formally approved by the US Senate in August. His engineering degree from Texas A&M, leadership of the Blue Ribbon Commission, and experience in the family construction business stood out among his qualifications.

At chairman Reeder's urging, in 1996, the PCC board recommended and the Army and US Congress approved shifting the Canal to a corporate management basis, to foreshadow Panama's concept for organizing its operating agency. This shift obviated the need for many of the remaining Congressional oversights and approvals built into the Panama Canal Act and allowed more flexibility in the final years of what now functioned as a joint operation. Among other things, the PCC could raise tolls without presidential approval. That same year Fort Amador, a jewel of Army property on the southern end of the Canal, was turned over, whetting Panamanian appetites for recreational and tourism development there.[44]

Two other developments occurred under Reeder's watch. The PCC instituted a reservation system whereby ships could pay a premium to move up on what previously was a "first come, first served" schedule, an essential move for cruise ships and vessels carrying time-sensitive cargoes. It made the Canal more responsive to clients' needs, a move long advocated by the market-sensitive *canaleros*. The ship pilots' union, meanwhile, seeing that under Reeder's leadership the Canal would almost certainly be turned over in 1999, decided to pressure the administration to raise wages and benefits to lock them in before the turnover. The pilots, who already earned substantial salaries and enjoyed special perks, had usually been able to force management to meet their demands, since

[43] Nadhji Arjona, *Una misión histórica: Gilberto Guardia Fábrega* (Pànama: Ed. Libertad Ciudadana, 2003), 228–37.

[44] Joe Reeder communication, May 22, 2016; Gurdián Guerra, "Los Tratados del Canal," 277–78; PCC Secretary Michael Rhode, interview, Feb. 2, 1994; Larry Rohter, "Panama Still Wants Yankees to Go Home, But Not Right Away," *New York Times*, Oct. 1, 1996.

slowdowns (strikes were not permitted) could cause delays in ship transits, angering shippers and disrupting the flow of global trade. The PCC stood up to the pilots this time, so that their earning packages would not be too far out of alignment with those of all other Canal employees, already higher than corresponding salaries in the rest of Panama.[45]

The Assembly, meanwhile, completed legislation for administering the Canal, entitled the Organic Law of the Panama Canal, in 1997.[46] The resulting agency, called Autoridad del Canal de Panamá (ACP), would assume Canal control from the US on December 31, 1999. By many accounts, the partnership between the PCC's able administrator, Alberto Alemán, and chairman Reeder and his successor was productive from beginning to end. Alberto Alemán would lead the ACP into the future. The ACP composition had been debated for years and developed by several commissions. In the end, the Assembly sought to keep a high wall between Canal operations and the day-to-day business of the government. For years, advisors had warned of the potential risks of allowing politics to seep into Canal operations, and the Assembly took them to heart.[47] Political representation would be restricted to two directors, one, appointed by the president, would serve in the cabinet as Minister of Canal Affairs and president of the board, and another who served at the pleasure of the Assembly. Nine board members, approved by the cabinet and ratified by the Assembly, were to serve staggered nine-year terms, with three members being replaced every three years.

The administrator would serve a seven-year term and be eligible for a second term. The administrator could be removed by a majority of board members and would be back-stopped by a deputy administrator, making the position extremely secure and fairly immune from political pressures. At the end of each year, the ACP would transfer its operating profits to the treasury, minus the usual funds kept in reserves. It had total control of its budget, subject to both ordinary and external audits and oversight. Given the fact that the Canal served an international clientele, it would be advised periodically by an outside board. The law also set up a labor regime separate from the government's, based on merit and with wages and benefits roughly at levels existing before the turnover. It prohibited

[45] Joe Reeder communication, May 22, 2016.

[46] https://panCanal.com/eng/legal/law/chap2-1.html. Cf. Larry Rohter, "Panama Charting a Course to Run Its Canal," *New York Times*, Dec. 15, 1996; interview with Eloy Alfaro, Apr. 12, 2015.

[47] Interview, Michael Rhode, Feb. 2, 1994.

strikes and slowdowns to guarantee continuous service. The final sections of the law concerned maintenance and the environment. It assigned overall protection of the Canal watershed to the ACP.

When President Pérez Balladares released the names of his ACP board nominees in late 1997, a chorus of objections erupted, because several nominees were either his relatives or close associates. *La Prensa* and the leader of the Christian Democratic Party, Ricardo Arias Calderón, criticized the choices, which nonetheless sailed through the Assembly. In their defense, Joe Reeder, who overlapped for over two years with these nominees, was effusive in his praise for each one of the four, who brought distinct skills and backgrounds to the table.[48]

Meanwhile, President Pérez Balladares boosted the stature of his principal appointee on Canal matters, Foreign Minister Jorge Ritter, to Minister for Canal Affairs and vice president of the PCC board. With Reeder's departure from the Pentagon, Secretary of Defense (former US Senator) Bill Cohen decided to replace him on the PCC board with Army Secretary Togo West. This change in leadership gave the impression that the locus of authority over the Canal was already shifting from Washington toward Panama.[49]

The government also laid institutional foundations for Panama's new role as operator of the Canal by creating the Panama Maritime Authority (AMP) in 1998. This agency accumulated existing and new functions related to the nation's maritime vocation: port operations, ship registry (an old and lucrative business), enforcement of international laws regarding the sea, training and certification of merchant seamen, and development and pursuit of a national maritime strategy. It, like its predecessor APN, continued to work closely with ARI on reversion of lands and buildings. In 1997, based on earlier favorable legislation, ship-flagging services covered nearly 14,000 vessels, the largest such fleet in the world and source of considerable income to the government.[50]

[48] Larry Rohter, "Panama Leader Accused of Cronyism Over Appointees to Run the Canal," *New York Times*, Sept. 28, 1997. The original appointees, today considered godfathers of the transition, included Adolfo Ahumada, Eloy Alfaro, Roberto Roy, Emanuel González-Revilla, Moises Mizrachi, Fernando Cardoze, Samuel Lewis Navarro, Jorge Ritter, Alfredo Ramírez, J. J. Vallarino, and Luis Anderson.

[49] Larry Rohter, "As Panama Canal Transfer Nears, More Jockeying to Fill a Power Vacuum," *New York Times*, Oct. 5, 1997.

[50] Ricardo González J., "Registros de naves supera los B/. 30.7 millones," *Panamá América*, Finanzas, Sept. 11, 1997.

To publicize these developments and Panama's future position as Canal operator, the government sponsored a four-day meeting in September 1997, the Universal Congress of the Interoceanic Canal. They invited a wide array of shippers, commercial agents, waterway experts, government representatives, and academics – some 1,300 attended. Its purpose was to reinforce public awareness of the impending transfer of Canal ownership and to reassure the world that Panama would do a good job running it. President Pérez Balladares appointed Fernando Manfredo to chair the organizing committee, and the former administrator mobilized his prodigious contacts to put on the conference, whose papers were later published. PCC planning staff, meanwhile, went into overdrive to formulate designs for future Canal expansion, at the administrator's request, for presentation at the Congress. In addition, the PCC staff held hearings and made outreach efforts to inform shippers of coming changes and to elicit their views on Canal services.[51]

During the Congress, President Pérez Balladares inaugurated the Panama Canal Museum in the Casco Antiguo district, in the revitalized building that had once served as the headquarters of the French canal project. This event recognized Panama's imminent ownership of, and growing pride in, the waterway, showing that the country embraced the legacy of the Canal.[52]

Canal tolls had been increased several times since the 1977 treaty, helping to generate capital for improvements and payments to Panama for services in the former Zone. One egregious toll situation remained, however: the treatment of container cargoes, an ever-growing component of Canal transits. Under US management, the toll structure, called the Panama Canal Universal Measurement System, charged one-price-for-all, based on cargo space enclosed below decks.[53] After the so-called container revolution of the 1980s, however, more and more cargo ended up loaded above decks. Under the existing PCC toll structure these cargoes were exempt from tolls, so shippers and ship-builders took advantage by

[51] *Proceedings of the Universal Congress of the Interoceanic Canal,* ed. Melva A. Raven and Gloria Manfredo (European Commission, 1998) and preceding academic conference, *El Canal de Panamá en el siglo XXI* (Panama: n.p., 1998); Richard Wainio interview, Apr. 14, 2014, and Oct. 8, 1977, memo to Administrator Alemán; Joe Reeder communication, May 22, 2016; Wilfredo Jordán Serrano, "Crean ente supervisor del tercer juego de esclusas," *La Prensa*, Sept. 10, 1997. Vice Minister Jaén Suárez suggested holding the Universal Congress.

[52] Author Conniff presented at the academic meeting and attended the museum inauguration. Manuel Àlvarez Cedeño, "Presidente inaugura Museo del Canal," *La Prensa*, Sept. 10, 1997.

[53] www.panCanal.com/eng/op/tolls.html.

designing container vessels with most of their cargo above deck and hence free of tolls. This created an unequal toll burden, where some (cruise ships and Ro-Ros, for example, with most space enclosed) paid high tolls and others (container ships) paid low ones.

Pressure from the *canaleros* led to a 1997 revision in rate calculations whereby containers on deck began to pay tolls as if in enclosed cargo space. Zonian managers had defended the older system saying that the Canal should not make a profit and that low tolls provided a welcome subsidy to shippers, many of which were US owned. This breakthrough in charging for all cargo, not just in enclosed space, led to a total overhaul of tolls after 2000, based on Canal utility and profitability to shippers. Chairman Reeder remarked that the PCC knew it would be a pitched battle but well worth the fight to get the new approach accepted by Congress and the container shippers.[54] (See Chapter 7 for rate structures after 2000.)

Canal business, despite personnel and administrative changes, continued on an even keel in the mid and late 1990s, as modernization and widening projects proceeded. The gradual increase in Panamax vessels boosted cargo handled to record levels in 1999, and given the toll increases, so did gross revenues, which surpassed a half-billion dollars.[55] The Chiriqui oil pipeline closure in the mid 90s boosted cargo totals as well. By the late 1990s, the capital improvements ordered up by Reeder neared completion and contributed to general growth in Panama's economy.[56] A big question mark hovered, however, over the impact of base closings and the withdrawal of the last US military and civilian personnel and the money they spent.

FINAL YEARS OF THE PANAMA CANAL COMMISSION

During 1998 and 1999, the PCC worked feverishly to address items remaining on the Milestone list before the Canal turnover. Secretaries of the Army Togo West and later Louis Caldera oversaw operations from Washington, while day-to-day management ran out of the Canal Administration Building in Balboa. Administrator Alberto Alemán increasingly looked ahead to taking full control of the Canal, and his deputy, Joe Cornelison, carried on the

[54] Richard Wainio interview, Apr. 21, 2014; Ken Kujawa interview, Feb. 27, 2016; Joe Reeder communication, May 22, 2016.

[55] PCC, *Annual Report Supplement*, Oct.–Dec. 1999, ch. VII and passim.

[56] Moreno Lobón, "El proceso económico," 450–55.

preparations and reforms set in motion by Joe Reeder. Since Pérez Balladares lost his bid to run for reelection in mid 1998, nobody knew who would be elected in May 1999 or what surprises would be in store for the Canal in the last months before its turnover. The hope was that all the preparations had been sufficient to protect the Canal for at least a while.

By the end of 1999, the Canal workforce, which had been shifting to local hires for twenty years, reached 96.7 percent Panamanian. Only 250 US employees remained on the payroll. (See Chapters 2 and 3 for previous years' data.) It took special efforts to recruit, train, and retain Panamanians for executive positions and high-skill jobs like pilots and tug captains.[57]

By virtually all measures, the Canal had prospered in the late 1990s, a reflection of both internal efficiencies and global demand. By then, the ACP, led by Panamanians, formed a shadow administration waiting in the wings. Its future leaders, of course, participated fully in the Canal's day-to-day business. The big job still facing them, concluding the widening of Culebra/Gaillard Cut, underway since 1992, to allow two-way, 24-hour Panamax transits, was scheduled for December 2002. Meanwhile, maintenance and upgrading had transformed floating equipment, locks, power plants, and myriad other working parts of the complex enterprise. The total cost of these capital investments stood at about a billion dollars.[58]

Some special enhancements had been added to the Milestone to-do list. Oracle and other IT contractors upgraded the core management computing system, and precautions were taken for potential disruptions by turn-of-the-millennium Y2K threats. Outreach and public education efforts had generated a huge surge in Canal interest on the part of Panamanians anxious to see what their country was about to inherit. The beefed-up visitor and orientation center at Miraflores Locks handled 127,000 visitors in the three months before the turnover. The ACP's International Advisory Board (which came to include PCC board alumni Joe Reeder and Al Nahmad), established pursuant to the unanimously enacted Organic Law, met for the first time on December 13, 1999, the day before the formal turnover. And the ISO 1400 Environmental Management System set up earlier prepared to transition into the ACP, providing ongoing training and certification for managers. The two decades of preparation for the turnover, while not always smooth (especially during the Noriega crisis), produced a remarkably seamless hand-off of Canal

[57] PCC, *Annual Report Supplement*, 33.
[58] Ibid., 19–22.

operations from Americans to Panamanians. The final *Annual Report* gave everyone involved a well-deserved pat on the back.[59]

The last few months of US operations saw mild slowdowns in Canal business, due perhaps to shipper concerns and to the early onset of what became a generalized recession in 2000–01. (For the Canal under Panamanian management, see Chapter 7.)

MULTINATIONAL COUNTER-NARCOTICS CENTER

Another question mark in the late 1990s concerned whether Panama would negotiate an agreement that would permit the United States to leave behind some military forces, especially assets devoted to fighting the drug war in the region. From the early 1990s, the US Department of Defense (DOD) contemplated the possibility that some troops would remain in Panama. As justification in the post–Cold-War era, they argued that hemispheric counter-narcotics operations could be run most efficiently out of Panama, specifically overflights of the crucial transit zones along both of Colombia's coasts from the huge Howard Air Force base in the southwest corner of the former Zone. That was already a major duty of the military stationed there, and from the Pentagon point of view, it made sense to continue operations there. Less prominent but extremely important were radio, satellite, and radar surveillance facilities installed in Panama. The DOD expected Panama to cede the air base and buildings at no cost and to agree to a Status of Forces Agreement (SOFA) to authorize their presence and protect US personnel from prosecution under local laws. For much of the mid 1990s, President Pérez Balladares expressed willingness to negotiate an agreement for such a program, called CMA, the acronym for its Spanish name, Centro Multinacional Antinarcóticos.[60]

The CMA negotiations dragged on, much to the irritation of DOD negotiators, who believed they had a right to remain there. The White House was caught in a bind, vulnerable to criticism if it agreed to lease back a base it was giving Panama free of charge. Panamanians, for their part, nationalistically counted the days until the last US soldier left their soil, and any president who permitted their continued presence did so at his or her peril. Not only was public opinion against troops remaining,

59 Ibid., 28–29, 37–43.

60 The episode is discussed in many works cited in Margaret Scranton's excellent, "Knowing When to Fold a Bad Hand: Saying No to Bases in Panama," LASA Conference Mar. 2000. Cf. Conniff, *Panama*, 180–83.

powerful figures in the PRD, who had slogged through the years of negotiations and implementation, got their hackles up at the prospect of a continuing military presence. Pérez Balladares undoubtedly inclined to mollify the United States on troop continuation, as in many other areas, but he had a difficult path to walk.

In the months leading up to April 1998, the deal – earlier thought to be nearly concluded – fell apart and generated considerable tension on both sides. A leaked draft of the agreement stirred up local and hemispheric opposition, since it contained vague wording that authorized 2000 US military personnel to carry out operations beyond simply drug interdiction. The proposed SOFA would hold soldiers exempt from Panamanian courts, bringing back images of servicemen swaggering down the streets during Just Cause. Another stumbling block was Panama's expectation of big lease payments, which the White House ruled out. The fact that Japan paid billions each year for US bases stationed on its territory would have made lease payments to Panama a major policy contradiction. Pérez Balladares displayed his anger with his US counterparts by refusing to accept the credentials of the new US ambassador, Simon Ferro, for sixty days, a serious affront.[61]

President Pérez Balladares also expressed his ire with the United States through slights to Ambassador Ferro and even to the local US troop commander. When the ambassador learned of a major scandal in the president's cabinet, in which ministerial-level officials were profiting from bribes paid by Chinese nationals to obtain visas to Panama, to continue on to the United States, he threatened the president with exposure if the frosty climate didn't thaw. The threat worked to a degree, but after Pérez Balladares's term ended, the State Department permanently cancelled his and some associates' ability to travel to the United States because of the visa scandal.[62]

After another failed attempt to negotiate the CMA with Panama's new President Moscoso in 2000, the Pentagon gave up and established other air surveillance basing arrangements in Ecuador, Aruba, and El Salvador, which cost hundreds of millions of dollars more than what would have been required in accepting Panama's terms. (See Chapter 5.)

[61] Larry Rohter, "In Panama Accord, G.I.'s Would Stay," *New York Times*, Dec. 25, 1997; and "U.S. Accord with Panama on Troops Hits a Snag," *New York Times*, Apr. 26, 1998.

[62] Joe R. Gregory, comp., "Panama: U.S. Revokes ex-Leader's Visa," *New York Times*, Nov. 27, 1999; Eloy Alfaro, interview, Apr. 12, 2015; Berta Thayer, interview, Aug. 16, 2014; talks by Governor Bob Graham and Ambassadors Ambler Moss and Simon Ferro, Mar. 20, 2014, *Panama Considered Conference*, University of Florida.

1999 ELECTION

Less than nine months after the failed 1998 reelection referendum, Panama went to the polls again on May 2 to choose its next president. One of Omar Torrijos's sons, Martín, who had served as deputy minister under Pérez Balladares, took over leadership of the PRD and captured the nomination. He also instituted the first-ever primary ballot for candidates running for the Assembly. Bright and well educated in the United States, Martín Torrijos had never run for office before, but he enjoyed residual support from citizens who credited his father with securing the 1977 treaty. He promised to continue the policies of the incumbent and to see justice done by receiving the Canal from the United States in 1999. Rubén Blades's Papa Egoró supported Martín Torrijos this time.

Mireya Moscoso also threw her hat into the ring, under the banner of the Arnulfista (formerly and again after 2005 Panameñista) Party, but only after a divisive fight in which wealthy banker Alberto Vallarino sought the nomination and then ran as the candidate of a coalition of small parties led by the Christian Democrats. She campaigned with the slogan "Mireya is Change," promising to roll back privatization and free trade and to help elevate the standard of living of the rural poor. The Liberal MOLIRENA and two splinter parties aligned themselves with her as well.[63] One commentator said it was a contest between the ghosts of two dead men, represented by the son of one and the widow of the other.

Voters seemed to repudiate the PRD, as they had nine months earlier, by giving Moscoso a resounding 45 percent of the national tally, followed by a respectable 38 percent for Torrijos and 17 percent for Vallarino.[64] PRD candidates for the Assembly, however, fared much better and captured a majority of the seats. The election proved to be one of the most honest in history, reflecting years of assiduous work by the Electoral Tribunal.

* * * *

63 Ebrahim Asvat, *Bitácora del presidente* (Panama: El Nuevo Siglo, 2010), 49–50, discussed the difficulties she faced in choosing a vice presidential candidate in 1999, as part of her coalition-building strategy.

64 Orlando J. Pérez, "The Past as Prologue? Political Parties in Post-Invasion Panama," in *Post-Invasion Panama*, ed. Pérez, 137–41; Mireya Navarro, "Woman in the News: Mireya Elisa Moscoso; Earnest Icon for Panama," *New York Times*, May 4, 1999; David Gonzalez, "In Panama's New Dawn, Woman Takes Over," *New York Times*, Sept. 2, 1999; Eloy O. Aguilar, "Panama Welcomes New Leader," *Miami Herald*, Sept. 2, 1999.

As the momentous events of 1999 unfolded, Panama faced major challenges on the horizon – seating a new president, the Canal turnover, unsettled relations with the United States, and the ACP's as-yet-untested ability to manage the huge maritime facility without US participation. Still, in the previous decade, the nation had moved far beyond the dictatorship of Manuel Noriega. The constitution had been amended for Zone and Canal transfer, solid foundations existed for honest elections, the army had been replaced by police under civilian control, several political parties helped to aggregate the interests and demands of the electorate, and the 1977 treaty implementation had almost run its course.

Even more remarkably, Panama had adopted innovative methods to restructure government itself, modeled on US and European forms. Foremost was the "authority," or autonomous agency. The ARI, ACP, AMP, TSE, and others took control of major sectors of public management and largely removed them from the political machinations that dogged the executive branches of government. The once-dreaded threat of socialism that many associated with the PRD had also been removed and was instead replaced by a modernized and more competitive form of market capitalism open to the world. No system, of course, could entirely divorce administration from politics, but, in the late 1990s, the *autoridad* approach and respect for competitive markets gave hope of more efficient and productive government and society. The model came directly from thousands of special districts in the United States that governed ports, transportation systems, utilities, and other services that overlapped local and state political jurisdictions. The New York Port Authority was a good example, going back to the early twentieth century, when all manner of local transportation services, cutting across municipal and state lines, were organized by Robert Moses.[65]

Panama modeled another innovative structure on a uniquely US institution, the office of the Inspector General, which goes back to when German General von Steuben served in this capacity during George Washington's command of the continental army. This official, called the Public Defender (Defensor del Pueblo), operates independently of the chain of command and is available to whistle-blowers. He or she reports to both the President of Panama and the Assembly about fraud, waste, and

[65] Robert A. Caro, *The Power Broker: Robert Moses and the Fall of New York* (New York: Knopf, 1974). Panama's experience recalled the reforms ushered in by José Figueres's 1948 revolution in Costa Rica, which rolled out numerous autonomous agencies (*entes autónomos*) as a way to limber up bureaucratic sclerosis and decentralize government

abuse. Paid by the state, the Public Defender serves like an ombudsman but is empowered with unfettered discretion to report any irregularities. The Canal first appointed an ombudsman in the late 1970s, and the position remained in place under the PCC and the ACP.[66]

Panama's Contraloria also served as an independent agency to assure that public monies were spent properly. Many observers believed that such autonomous bodies have prevented the tendency of the executive branch to wield autocratic power. An indirect and overlooked outcome of having such a long period of forced coexistence with US agencies was the ability to observe, modify, and adapt some foreign institutions to national purposes.

In comparison with most other "colonial withdrawals" in the twentieth century – e.g., Britain from India and China, Portugal from Africa and India, Holland from Southeast Asia – the US exit from Panama proved efficient, constructive, and (with the exception of Just Cause in 1989) peaceful. That put responsibility for effective post-1999 Canal operations fairly and squarely on the shoulders of the Panamanians who had been integrated into the PCC as full-fledged partners throughout the 1979–99 period of treaty implementation.

[66] PCC, *Annual Report Supplement*, 33.

PART II

INTRODUCTION TO PART II

The second half of this book, covering the period since 2000, opens with Chapter 5 recounting the tough start that the Moscoso administration had, even though Panama's takeover of the Canal turned out seamless, as planned. The troubles came mostly from opposition by the outgoing PRD and the majority they retained in the Assembly. These were compounded by a global economic downturn exacerbated by loss of expenditures by US base closings. Gradually, the new corporate management of the Panama Canal Authority (ACP) boosted government revenue and attracted foreign investment.

While Moscoso inaugurated a restored Panama Railroad and sought to exploit assets from the former Canal Zone, the two countries increased security cooperation, especially after the 9/11 terrorist attacks. A new security agreement extended counter-narcotics cooperation, collaboration on international shipping and port protection, and border security. Yet the slow economic recovery and corruption scandals undermined support for Moscoso's Arnulfista Party. The youthful opposition leader, Martín Torrijos, son of the former dictator, won a decisive victory in May 2004 and returned the PRD to power.

Chapter 6 describes how the advent of a PRD Assembly majority led it to initiate constitutional reforms even before Torrijos's inauguration. With continued economic growth, the new president enjoyed a prolonged honeymoon. Sweeping tax and government spending reforms, a successful referendum on Canal expansion, and other actions launched the highest rate of economic growth in Latin America. Yet he faced corruption scandals, severe weather events, and damaging health crises. A popular opposition movement blocked social security and other reform efforts. Torrijos positioned the nation as a hemispheric leader at the UN and in the clean energy and climate change movements. Yet despite his popularity and the booming economy, Torrijos could not get the PRD candidate elected in 2009, and instead billionaire businessman Ricardo Martinelli won by a landslide.

Chapter 7 reviews Panama's management of the Canal and its expansion, authorized by the Torrijos referendum in 2006. Led by Alberto Alemán Zubieta, the ACP team formed during the treaty implementation took over the Canal on January 1, 2000. It maintained good relations with former managers, the US Army Corps of Engineers, and the US Coast Guard. Panamanian managers overhauled the toll structure, marketing relations with the shipping industry, and personnel systems to link the waterway more closely to the national economy. They adopted cost savings and made efficiency gains, enabling the ACP to begin a growing revenue stream to the treasury. Over the next decade, fiscal contributions swelled by more than 600 percent, even before the $5.25 billion expansion was completed. Meanwhile, traffic volume rose while efficiency and safely also improved. The transfer of leadership to Jorge Quijano in 2012 did not alter the reliable operation or expansion work, completed in 2016. The ACP adjusted appropriately to shipping changes and continued building links with the national economy. Panamanians' expectations about the Canal as a powerful motor for national development came true.

Chapter 8 covers the five years of economic expansion led by the populist Ricardo Martinelli and his Cambio Democrático (CD) party. While promising a businessman's approach to government, he combined giveaway programs for the masses, such as universal scholarships, a Metro for Panama City, and other public works, with a controversial bid to attract foreign investors and contractors. Early criticized for nepotism and appointing former private employees to public positions, he rode a wave of economic expansion to maintain early approval ratings. Sweetheart deals with foreign investors and environmental carelessness, however, soon aroused popular push back. Harsh treatment of demonstrators only escalated the opposition and forced Martinelli to abandon three major initiatives. The administration also suffered from internal rivalries and ambitions. Martinelli sacked vice president Juan Carlos Varela from his role as foreign minister, and super-minister Jimmy Papadimitriu resigned under presidential pressure. As rumors of other corruption cases multiplied, Martinelli handpicked a CD loyalist to run as his successor in the 2014 election and inserted his wife as candidate for vice president. Despite lavish campaign spending, a still-buoyant economy, and an apparent lead in the polls, the CD lost. For the sixth time, Panamanian voters turned against the incumbents to favor an opposition figure, in this case Martinelli's former vice president/foreign minister, Juan Carlos Varela.

As of this writing, Varela has months left as president, and his accomplishments since 2014 are described in Chapter 9. Although elected by a slim margin and only backed by the third largest party in the Assembly, Varela has achieved surprising successes, including four majority legislative coalitions. Similarly, many independents and coalition partners in the cabinet have fortified the administration, enabling Varela to weather challenges. He pushed prosecution of Martinelli-regime corruption cases, managed the Panama Papers episode, inaugurated his predecessor's botched and unfinished public works, and oversaw the completion of Canal expansion.

Varela worked closely with his vice president and foreign minister, Isabel de Saint Malo, whose background as a UN development expert helped to revive a national planning effort committed to humane sustainability goals. She also positioned Panama as a leader of the tropical forestry alliance vital for achieving the Paris climate change accords. Although the full story of the Varela years is still unfolding, the president hoped to complete social security reforms, host Pope Francis's global youth celebration in January 2019, and preside over mid-2019 elections that at one point featured over twenty presidential candidates, including a half-dozen prominent women.

Chapter 10 presents conclusions about the dramatic transformation of Panama since 1980. Bio-diversity and tropical exuberance flourish throughout its territory, while Panama City has become a bustling, skyscraper-topped metropolis comparable to Miami or Singapore. The military dictatorship gave way to a vibrant democracy in which the deck may still be stacked against incumbents. The economy boomed, as shipping and logistics connections multiplied, and Panamanians became among the richest citizens in Latin America. Steady progress brought more humane living conditions to Panama's poor, although inequality persisted. Dependence on, and a forced alliance with, the United States was replaced with global maritime leadership and better security cooperation. Corruption scandals, uneven development, and international criminal networks remained challenges. Yet the professionalism shown in the management of the Panama Canal offered an alternative path toward the centuries-old dream of becoming the crossroads of the Americas.

5

The Moscoso Administration: Millennial Transitions

Now it is yours.

Jimmy Carter to Mireya Moscoso on Canal turn-over

TURNOVER OF PANAMA CANAL

On December 14, 1999, at the first of three official events, former US President Jimmy Carter quietly acknowledged to new Panamanian President Mireya Moscoso that the Canal had finally become the country's property. The simple ceremony at the Miraflores Locks was attended by the King of Spain, presidents of six Latin American countries, several former presidents and other dignitaries, and a granddaughter of Ferdinand De Lesseps. Over 600 foreign journalists beamed the historic act to the world.[1]

On the afternoon of December 30, 1999, US ambassador Simon Ferro officially lowered the American flag over the Panama Canal for the last time, in a modest, unpublicized proceeding before an audience of about 200 people.

Then, at noon on December 31, 1999, on the steps of the imposing Panama Canal Administration Building, the formal transfer called for in the treaties that General Omar Torrijos and Carter had signed in 1977 finally took place. Secretary of the Army and out-going chairman of the Panama Canal Commission, Louis Caldera, represented the United States at the

[1] David Gonzalez, "Carter, Proclaiming 'It's Yours,' Celebrates New Era for Panama," *New York Times*, Dec. 15, 1999.

ceremony hosted by President Moscoso. Hundreds of thousands of spectators and well-wishers had been expected, but just tens of thousands showed up.[2]

* * * *

These three events culminated a series of more than fifty public occasions and milestones that took place in Panama to mark the transfer of the Canal, starting in April. They included an international cultural festival, diplomatic ceremonies with the foreign ministers of the Caribbean Community, and others with the Organization of American States and the United Nations. Special art displays, book presentations, and performances by 100 of Panama's leading entertainers, headed by singer/actor/politician Rubén Blades, regaled the country for months. At the final celebration, the large crowd roared approval outside Canal headquarters, and several Panamanians described it to foreign guests as being like independence day. Moscoso had traveled to the United States five weeks after taking office to prepare for Clinton's trip to Panama. Yet for many, the celebration evoked frustration as well. President Bill Clinton and his secretary of state Madeline Albright declined to go to Panama. The December 14 ceremony had been scheduled to accommodate Clinton, whose staff averred the need to deal with Y2K disruption on the December 31 date. Many world leaders RSVPed they would still come, as shown in the accompanying photo. Then just a few days before the event, word came that Clinton and later Albright had to attend to business in Washington.[3]

Although the Clinton administration never admitted it publicly, it worried about negative backlash from treaty opponents. Moreover, fear arose that demonstrations against the United States due to the 1989 invasion and other historic grievances could occur. When noisy protests broke out after the December 14 ceremony, Ambassador Ferro advanced the date for the special flag lowering twenty-four hours rather than risk a commotion.[4] Panama reacted nationalistically by adding a special flag display with over 2,000 students at the December 31st event in honor of the 1964 Day of the

[2] The Panama Canal Authority (ACP) provided an official chronology of fifty-seven actions and events that took place in the transfer of the Panama Canal to Panama.

[3] Frederick A. Becker, "Interview with Frederick A. Becker," Library of Congress Manuscripts Division, 2006, 187–204, detailed his experience as deputy and acting chief of mission for the United States in Panama from 1999 to 2002. About the participation of major administration officials, he said, "no U.S. political leader had the backbone ... to hand over the symbolic trappings of Canal ownership to the Panamanians."

[4] The concern for anti-American protests was prudent, as shown by events at the University of Panama in January 2001. An off-duty American officer, Major Anthony Dana Williams,

FIGURE 5.1 Mireya Moscoso and Jimmy Carter, center, joined by international dignitaries, celebrate the transfer of the Panama Canal to the Republic of Panama. Panama Canal Museum, University of Florida Library, courtesy of Angus Grover Metheney.

Martyrs. Behind the otherwise cheerful celebrations, both sides worried that past misunderstandings might foreshadow future problems.

Bobby Eisenmann, a senior advisor to President Moscoso and founder of the *La Prensa,* voiced the disillusionment of Panamanians, saying that the absence of Clinton and Albright in the transition ceremony had spoiled a beautiful occasion.[5] Former vice president Ricardo Arias Calderón also worried that the action might symbolize the end of Panama's special relationship with the United States.

accompanied a close friend to the campus. When some students noticed his Army t-shirt, they surrounded him and began to badger him with questions. As more students arrived, they grabbed his camera, accused him of gathering intelligence, and then severely beat him. Press accounts called it a "lynching." Williams, who knew the country well, understood the roots of the hostility and believed that a few extremists were to blame. During a subsequent meeting with journalists after he left the hospital, Williams pardoned even the extremists and helped create an improved atmosphere for US cooperation with the University of Panama.

[5] The disappointment was not just on the Panamanian side. Author David McCullough was one of many who urged high-level US participation. See his editorial in *The New York Times,* "A Canal Worth a Trip," Nov. 10, 1999, urging Clinton to go.

FIGURE 5.2 Mireya Moscoso with other regional presidents attending the 2001 3rd Summit of the Americas in Canada. Roberto Schmidt/AFP/Getty Images.

For many thoughtful Panamanians, gaining control of the Canal fulfilled their nation's aspirations for true independence and the end of the forced alliance.[6] Yet the economic impact of the closing of US bases had already had a negative impact on the economy, as feared by many Panamanians.

* * * *

The transition of the Panama Canal was just one of the many trials which confronted the Moscoso administration. The economy was stagnant, security problems were increasing both within the country and in the Colombian border region, and merely getting the new government in place turned out to be major hurdles.

TOUGH START FOR THE FIRST WOMAN IN CHARGE

The out-going Pérez Balladares administration left a nasty legacy for Moscoso's in-bound team. The Arnulfista victory had robbed the PRD of

[6] The first and second editions of Michael L. Conniff's study, *Panama and the United States*, were sub-titled "The Forced Alliance" (Athens and London: University of Georgia Press, 1992, 2001.) The third edition, published in 2012, is sub-titled, "The End of the Alliance."

presiding over the ceremony turning over the Canal to Panama that the party of Omar Torrijos had struggled to obtain. Serious political fighting escalated soon after the votes were counted, reminding observers of the chronic incivility that had plagued the country for much of the twentieth century.

When Moscoso's inauguration day came on September 2, 1999, Pérez Balladares declined to participate. Many members of his government went out of their way to sabotage the new administration, by emptying the treasury and filling hundreds of vacancies with PRD stalwarts at the last minute.[7] The more than forty years of enmity between the supporters of his PRD and her Arnulfista Party led departing civil servants to wipe out the hard drives of their computers, hide the records of their offices, and otherwise undermine the new government.[8]

Yet the greatest discomfort for the new government occurred even before the inauguration, when Pérez Balladares proposed legislation to add a fifth chamber to the Supreme Court, to allow him to pack it with his partisans. The 1972 Constitution established a Supreme Court with four chambers, made up of nine justices nominated by the president and approved by the Assembly to serve staggered ten-year terms. Three judges each oversaw the civil, penal, and administrative chambers, and all nine served together in the fourth general chamber, in charge of corruption and government oversight. A judge from one of the three chambers was elected as the president of the entire court for renewable two-year terms.

In proposing the addition of a fifth chamber to the Court, with three more justices who he hoped to nominate, Pérez Balladares tried to create a solid majority to perpetuate his influence on the court and protect his allies from judicial scrutiny. This last-ditch court packing attempt, as much as the election campaign itself, set the stage for further transition mischief.[9]

The final details of Canal turnover under the 1977 treaties also remained to be resolved, despite the more than twenty-two years already dedicated to the process.[10] Many complications arose because four of the most important military properties, Howard Air Force Base, Forts Kobbe

[7] David Gonzalez, "In Panama's New Dawn, Woman Takes Over," *New York Times*, Sept. 2, 1999.

[8] Eloy O. Aguilar, "Panama Welcomes New Leader," *Miami Herald*, Sept. 2, 1999. Robert C. Harding, *The History of Panama* (Westport, CN: Greenwood Press, 2006), 33–37 and passim, describes rising partisan rivalry in the post-WWII era and under military governments.

[9] Grisel Bethancourt, "Sala Quinta: ¿fracaso o impasse?" *Panamá América*, May 29, 1999.

[10] Ambassador Ferro later recalled (in a talk on Mar. 20, 2014, at the University of Florida) that he visited former president Carter in Plains, GA, to clarify some ambiguities in the treaty. Carter said he didn't know and to consult Ambler Moss, a treaty negotiator and

and Clayton, and the Farfan housing complex didn't revert to Panama until November 1999, and Rodman Naval Base preceded them by just a few months. Under the leadership of Ardito Barletta, ARI had devoted a great deal of planning for Panamanian uses of these facilities, but when Moscoso replaced Barletta with Alfredo Arias, a protégé of her former husband, many of the experienced incumbents found themselves replaced by inexperienced persons.

The final reversions suffered further complications from US pressures and lobbying for agency interests. For instance, the Pentagon lobbied for Panama's naval police unit, the National Maritime Service (SMN), to retain use of Rodman so it could collocate its Pacific coast operations there. Florida State University (FSU) leaders, with support from the US embassy, pushed to preserve its La Boca campus. Local interests, combined with US meddling, slowed down decision-making and delayed other programs. Thus, years lapsed before the Port of Singapore Authority (Singapore PSA) developed its container terminal at Rodman, the Panama International Maritime University (UMIP) took over the former community college site in La Boca, and FSU relocated to the City of Knowledge.[11]

Similarly, the Pentagon and military officials in the US embassy at first insisted on locating quasi-security functions at Howard Air Force Base, ranging from police training to national emergency services (SINAPROC), evidently with the intention of resurrecting the facility as a regional air base.[12] Some hoped that US firms might also obtain concessions for property development there. Despite helpful efforts by the Moscoso government, nothing concrete emerged. In the end, the original ARI vision of the Panamá Pacífico International Logistics Center, managed by an energetic British firm, won approval in 2004, launching a major buildup there under the next administration.

US efforts to influence decisions about bases proved only minor irritants when compared to the American refusal to address the unexploded ordinance (UXO) problem. As noted earlier, Panama feared that the explosives and live ammunition left behind on the firing ranges and coastal islands may have contaminated as much as 7 percent of the

later ambassador to Panama in 1978–82. At that point, Ferro simply pushed ahead on his own.

[11] Author Bigler was responsible for oversight of reverted properties for the US embassy and consulted extensively with ARI director Alfredo Arias and other officials on these issues between 2000 and 2003.

[12] See Chapter 4 for the failed efforts to create a multinational anti-narcotics center at Howard.

reverted lands. A few isolated tragedies had already befallen Panamanians who had stumbled onto bombs, artillery shells, and grenades. The presence of UXO in areas of high value for future projects, including tourist development on San José Island and near the future centennial bridge over the Canal, put those projects at risk. It also jeopardized routes for the Canal's expansion.

The Moscoso administration hoped to revive close relations with the United States by putting forward friendly figures, especially after Pérez Balladares and others fell into disrepute over the sale of visas. For example, the government highlighted common interests by celebrating Panamanian jockey Laffit Pincay Jr.'s achievements in thoroughbred horse racing.[13] Moscoso also assigned second vice president Dominador Kaiser Bazán to oversee bilateral relations, since he was a West Point graduate and had served as ambassador to Washington. Accordingly, and in view of no progress under the previous administration, Moscoso redoubled efforts to negotiate UXO removal.

If the first few months of the Moscoso term had not been trying enough, their first year brought even more problems. Authorities discovered almost four hundred Colombian refugees in the remote Darien province, victims of drug conflicts. The withdrawal of the US military and the loss of assistance with border security led groups like the Commission on Justice and Peace, mentioned in Chapter 3, to call for the immediate creation of a special Darien border force like that of Costa Rica.[14]

A few days later, the government confronted demonstrations by Greenpeace anti-nuclear activists that threatened to paralyze the Canal over the transit of radioactive cargo on the British vessel *Pacific Swan*.[15] The Canal had been used for decades to move reactor fuel between France, England, and Japan, and then to return radioactive waste to Europe. Suddenly, the same activity aroused the old debate over the neutrality of the Canal as well as questions about potential dangers. The ACP managed the *Pacific Swan* transit without a hitch, but its very professionalism contrasted with the government's poor handling of Darien border problems.

[13] Beth Harris, "Pincay Breaks Shoemaker Record, *Washington Post*, Dec. 10, 1999.

[14] "Gobierno de Mireya no despega," *Crítica,* Dec. 9, 1999; and "Moscoso enfrenta protestas en sus primeros 100 dias," *Panamá América,* Dec. 9, 1999.

[15] Elizabeth Becker, "Panama Steps Up Security for Ship With Atomic Waste," *New York Times*, Jan. 15, 2000.

The new millennium also surprised the Moscoso team with news that the former administration had not resolved international concerns about Panama as a tax haven and center for money laundering. The timing of the announcement by the Organization for Economic Cooperation and Development (OECD) that Panama had been placed on a "grey list" of fifteen uncooperative countries compounded fears about the new government's inability to revive the economy.[16]

In early 2000, Panama's faltering economy raised increasing concern: unemployment hit 16 percent, and growth became anemic. GDP rose slightly but fell on a per capita basis. This contrasted with the usual upsurge of production and improved outlook during the onset of dry season and school vacations. In fact, a wave of pessimism set in and forced the postponement of many new projects for a year or more.

Bad news continued, this time from a leaked classified report by the US Customs Service that concluded that Panama failed to control drug trafficking and money laundering within its borders.[17] Although the report focused on the decline in drug seizures and lack of important arrests at the end of the Pérez Balladares years, the specific allegations about problems in the Colon Free Zone, Tocumen International Airport, and the ambivalence of the Moscoso government in working with the United States magnified doubts about her administration.

BACKROOM POLITICS AND OVERCOMING A TROUBLED START

Even though President Moscoso had never held public office before, she turned to traditional methods to manage the myriad demands that beset her. The two decades she spent as Arnulfo Arias's wife, as well as the work she did rebuilding the party after his death, made her a capable politician – she even proved more successful in retaining power than the old caudillo had.[18]

The electoral alliance the Arnulfistas had forged for the campaign, the Union for Panama, produced an electoral victory on this, Moscoso's second

[16] Joseph Kahn, "15 Countries Named as Potential Money-Laundering Havens," *New York Times*, June 23, 2000; and Joseph Kahn, "Rich Nations Issue Black List of Tax Havens," *New York Times*, June 27, 2000.

[17] David González, "Panama Still Failing to Stem Narcotics Trafficking, U.S. Report Asserts," *New York Times*, June 9, 2000.

[18] Enlightening comparisons emerge in William Francis Robinson, "Panama for Panamanians: The Populism of Arnulfo Arias Madrid," in *Populism in Latin America*, ed. Michael L. Conniff, 2nd ed. (University of Alabama Press, 2012), 184–200.

try. The alliance also proved crucial for forming a cabinet and coping with the opposition majority in the Assembly. Jobs in the new administration and other forms of patronage figured clearly in the composition of her new cabinet. The three minor coalition partners – Movimiento Liberal Republicano Nacionalista (MOLIRENA), Cambio Democrático (CD), and Movimiento de Renovación Nacional (MORENA) – together contributed just over a third of her votes but got six of the thirteen ministries and an even larger share of the vice minister appointments.

Moscoso expanded patronage jobs through a series of political actions, including:

- Creation of a mega-cabinet by including vice ministers in the cabinet, so the cadre of prominent leaders rose from thirteen to thirty-three. With eleven women, including three as ministers, the composition became more female, as expected, while many thirty-something vice ministers added a youthful flair.
- Formation of a brains trust by recruiting prestigious citizens as presidential advisors. These included Bobby Eisenmann, jurist Mario Galindo, industrialist J. J. Vallarino, and even maverick academic Miguel Antonio Bernal. They played visible roles in government, if only briefly for Eisenmann and Bernal.
- Expansion of her political tent by including important independents in the cabinet, such as her first minister of public works, Moisés Castillo de León.
- Addition of positions for longtime Arnulfistas (renamed Panameñistas in 2004) and personal confidants, such as Alfredo Arias in ARI, Arnulfo Escalona in Fondo de Inversión Social (FIS), Bolívar Pariente in the National Bank of Panama (BNP), and Jerry Salazar in the Panama Maritime Authority (AMP).[19]

Although she deployed little coalition-building rhetoric, Moscoso made efforts to befriend non-PRD members of the Assembly. While

[19] Besides loyalists, the president drew on family and hometown connections to fill important jobs to such an extent that many considered nepotism and personalism to be the real glue of her government. Her older sister, Ruby Moscoso, was formally the First Lady. Ivonne Young, her sister-in-law, was the minister of the presidency. Several cousins served as secretaries and in other staff functions. Carlos Barés, the head of the National Police, was from her hometown of Pedasi and had been a longtime collaborator of her husband. Many of Arnulfo's family members, including Harmodio Arias, first deputy foreign minister and then minister, Alfredo Arias, and others also played prominent roles in her administration.

PRD candidate Martín Torrijos's New Nation Alliance won a clear forty-one-seat majority in the seventy-one-seat chamber, Arnulfistas gained just eighteen seats and added six more belonging to partners in their Union for Panama. The seven legislators belonging to the Solidarity and National Liberal Party, however, who had supported Torrijos during the election, were immediately targeted by Moscoso's people to explore collaboration on specific issues. Similarly, Arnulfistas approached six other Assembly members, mostly Christian Democrats, who had supported banker Alberto Vallarino in the 1999 presidential election.

First-time legislators in all the parties showed eagerness to get resources for their constituents. The only sure way to get something for individual districts, even for PRD legislators, was to snare government funds, called district shares, which required cooperating at least some of the time with the government. Such district shares, originally intended to support constituent services, were often converted into petty patronage and gifts to constituents, like food baskets and construction materials. As a candidate, however, Moscoso had promised to eliminate them. Once in office, she realized that constituency support programs were crucial, so, in the end, she compromised by pursuing logrolling. This political tradition promised support for others' projects if they reciprocated by helping with hers.[20]

At least during her early months, Moscoso's logrolling proved to be just the approach needed to get things done and loosen PRD control of the Assembly. It worked well in revoking the creation of a fifth chamber and promised success for other Arnulfista plans. The government's prowess in coalition building could be witnessed in the expensive Cartier watches that many legislators sported after Christmas visits to the Las Garzas presidential palace. Thus, what started as clever politics appears to have veered toward outright corruption.[21]

The Moscoso administration failed to achieve some crucial goals despite its well-oiled maneuvers. For example, a package of economic reforms and compromises, designed by presidential advisor Mario Galindo to jump-start the economy and reverse some of the Pérez Balladares privatization projects, went down to defeat. They did derail

[20] This practice may be compared conceptually with earmarking funds in the US Congress. This and other forms of clientelism in Panama are described in detail in Carlos Guevara Mann, *Political Careers, Corruption and Impunity: Panama's Assembly, 1984–2009* (University of Notre Dame Press, 2011), 104–13.

[21] Guevara Mann, *Political Careers*, 218–20.

the scheme to pack the Supreme Court, but they failed to win confirmation of former president Endara as justice.

On balance, the government seemed to lose more than it won. Without increased access to credit that the reform package would have provided, the economic doldrums stretched far beyond Moscoso's first year in office. In addition, getting all the coalition partners to agree on key appointments proved difficult, so that a year into the new administration, many positions were still not filled. Some agencies and ministries struggled to get up and running.[22]

The mega-cabinet also proved awkward to coordinate, and some ministries, especially those controlled by powerful political allies, such as education, housing, and Canal affairs, seemed to go their own way or relate minimally to the rest of the cabinet. Politically, the new administration also had trouble defining its economic future and how closely it wanted to be aligned with the United States. Although Moscoso had pledged to continue efforts to join the World Trade Organization (WTO) and to liberalize economic policies, begun in the 1990s, she also sought to uphold the traditional Arnulfista emphasis on national self-sufficiency. Her rural roots led her to maintain or increase protection for agricultural products and other segments of the economy facing increased international competition.

Thus, it came as no surprise when Moscoso announced her unwillingness to participate in the WTO procurement regime that required transparency and competitive bidding on government contracts. This became a particularly important issue for the United States and other countries, whose companies bid on ACP contracts. It led to disagreements over economic and financial reform measures and to a separate effort to convince the ACP to adopt the WTO standard on its own. Indeed, ambivalence about trade policy lasted for years, especially in the use of regulatory and other non-traditional measures for agricultural protection.

Still, the lagging economy needed a jolt. The defeat of her early reform package and her economics minister Víctor Juliao's commitment to traditional Arnulfista protections seemed the heart of the problem. In August 2000, Moscoso surprised observers by moving Juliao to the

[22] Author Bigler observed this when he took up diplomatic duties in June 2000. Some ministries still sought to get rid of unwanted appointees while simultaneously recruiting key staff for political and professional positions. In August, the entire cabinet resigned in a show of support for Moscoso: "Renuncia el gabinete de Mireya Moscoso," *El Universal*, Aug. 17, 2000.

ministry of public works, where he could still direct patronage to loyal members of the party. To take his place, she promoted the progressive young economics vice minister, Norberto Delgado Durán. Then she confirmed her shift toward pro-business and trade promotion by moving another thirty-something, Meliton Arrocha, from vice minister of the presidency to vice minister for foreign trade in the ministry of industry and commerce (MICI). These shifts won applause from the business community.

The government finally seemed ready for more decisive action on the economy and lined up important private-sector support in the Colon Free Zone and the tourism sector. Getting a handle on how to deal with the United States took longer to work out.

NOT QUITE THE END OF THE "SPECIAL RELATIONSHIP"

As her second year in office started, President Moscoso looked forward to Panama hosting the 10th Ibero-American Summit as a means of bolstering the country's image and getting beyond the US shadow.[23] Then suddenly, global connections blew up in her face. On September 24, 2000, the former head of Peruvian security services, Vladimiro Montesinos, fleeing revelations of his use of bribery, extortion, and worse, to help president Alberto Fujimori control his opposition, unexpectedly showed up in Panama seeking political asylum.

Montesinos belonged to a long line of strongman rulers and US allies who previously sought refuge in Panama. This practice by Panama, part of a broader pattern of US impositions that, in turn, earned the country special attention from Washington, started in 1956. The first asylum case occurred when the wounded dictator of Nicaragua, General Anastasio Somoza García, arrived at a US military hospital in the Canal Zone. This type of quid pro quo was supposed to have ended, however, with the departure of US forces. Then suddenly Montesinos, who had been Fujimori's bagman and worked with US forces to crush the Shining Path guerrillas, invoked the Latin American tradition of asylum that the

[23] In July 2000, the Atlantic Council, represented by former ambassadors Charles A. Gillespie, Jr., Thomas E. McNamara, and other Latin American specialists, issued a special report entitled, "The United States and Panama: End of the 'Special Relationship,'" see www.css.ethz.ch/en/services/digital-library/publications/publication.html/44648. US embassy officials understood this as a very strong signal that any request for attention or support for Panama would be viewed skeptically.

US helped impose on Panama.[24] The Peruvian's offshore banking experience and Panama's reputation for lax financial controls, rather than any direct connivance with US officials, appeared to have prompted his choice of Panama.[25]

For the next few weeks, a relentless stream of backchannel and sometimes high-level communications took place between US and Panamanian leaders about how to handle this delicate case. Since the recently re-elected Fujimori had shown more openness to reform, the United States wished to avert a coup there. Meanwhile, vivid media reports added more details about Montesinos's abuses and Fujimori's corruption. Ridiculed by a *Los Angeles Times* story about serving as a dustbin for dictators, Panama also came under greater scrutiny. Moscoso gradually turned against letting the colonel stay.[26] This time, the United States also seemed to endorse Panama's cold shoulder to Montesinos because of his record of misdeeds. Rather than granting safe haven right away, Panama let the controversial Peruvian stay without any formal action. The government even used as an intermediary OAS Secretary-General César Gaviria, who had been working to organize a national dialogue in Peru over the controversial re-election of Fujimori, to announce that Panama would issue a declaration within a few days.[27]

Rumors flew that Montesinos had been an agent of the CIA in Peru but had gone rogue and supplied arms to the FARC guerrillas in Colombia. Public opinion mounted against granting asylum to Montesinos. Details of his career raised discomforting comparisons to the Noriega story. With such a cloudy outlook for him in Panama, Montesinos suddenly disappeared. Months later, a surprising collaboration of US and Venezuelan authorities led to his arrest there and extradition to Peru, where he and Fujimori served many years in prison.[28]

[24] Other cases in Panama included President Bucarám of Ecuador in 1998, General Cedras of Haiti in 1994, Jorge Serrano of Guatemala in 1993, the Shah of Iran in 1979, and President Arosemena of Ecuador in 1963. When General Anastasio "Tachito" Somoza Debayle fled from the Sandinistas in Nicaragua in 1979, he decided to go to Paraguay rather than Panama, believing, incorrectly, as it turned out, that he would be better protected there. Cedras, Bucarám, and Serrano were all still living in Panama when Montesinos arrived, but all left within a year or two. Perhaps significantly, in 2005, when Lucio Gutiérrez was overthrown in Ecuador, he chose to go to Brazil rather than Panama.

[25] Larry Rohter, "Peru Spy Chief Flies to Panama Looking for Asylum," *New York Times*, Sept. 2, 2000.

[26] Mary Beth Sheridan, "Panama Tiring of Status as Dustbin for Dictators," *Los Angeles Times*, Oct. 4, 2000.

[27] "El asilo de Montesinos en lo jurídico," *Panamá América*, Sept. 25, 2000.

[28] The strange story of Chávez's support for US assistance to Peru in locating and arresting Montesinos is told in Stratfor, "Montesinos Arrest Could Lead to Trouble for Chavez,"

Less than a month after the Montesinos flap, the world learned that a gang of anti-Castro Cuban-Americans had come to Panama to assassinate Fidel Castro during the Ibero-American Summit. In almost keystone cops fashion, police chased the conspirators while Castro vociferously denounced their villainy. Authorities identified the notorious Luís Posada Carriles as the ringleader and quickly linked him to the US-based Cuban American National Foundation. At the height of the Summit, he and his three accomplices were taken into custody.[29] Venezuelan president Hugo Chávez demanded extradition of the plotters, and the events completely overshadowed the diplomatic proceedings and the good will Panama had hoped to garner. Moscoso decided to bring the Cubans to trial in Panama, where they were convicted and imprisoned, which prevented their being extradited to Cuba or Venezuela. She eventually pardoned them at the end of her term, causing both Cuba and Venezuela to break diplomatic relations. Since her decisions pleased the US State Department, they seemed reminiscent of the era of the special relationship.[30]

More unpleasant surprises greeted Moscoso as her second year in office began. Investigators discovered what appeared to be the remains of Father Héctor Gallego, a once politically active priest and critic of the Torrijos government. The evidence, uncovered on the grounds of a former military facility where he was long believed to have been assassinated, raised an immediate clamor for investigating hundreds of other persons who had disappeared during the military era. Given an opportunity to prove her commitment to human rights, President Moscoso appointed a respected National Truth Commission to investigate. She gave it considerable resources and a charge to look into all pending cases. The final results of the investigation took more than two more years to complete.

Meanwhile, the government's handling of these politically sensitive matters stirred some sympathy in Washington on the UXO issue. Rather abruptly, the Department of State announced that it would work with Panama to train its citizens to remove UXO. The new attention focused on

Worldview, July 11, 2001, www.stratfor.com/analysis/montesinos-arrest-could-lead-trouble-chavez-0.

[29] ABC News, "Castro Assassination Attempt Quashed," Nov. 17, 2000. Posada had earlier been convicted of bombing a Venezuelan airliner on its way to Cuba but managed to escape from prison and holed up in Central America. Fidel Castro called the CIA-trained exile "the most notorious terrorist in the area."

[30] David González discusses similar Moscoso administration ambivalence in dealing with the United States in terms of counter-narcotics cooperation in "Panama Still Failing to Stem Narcotics Traffic, US Says," *New York Times*, June 9, 2000.

offshore islands where Panama hoped to develop tourist facilities. After yet more rounds of discussions, however, the Pentagon withdrew support for fear that a concession in Panama could boost UXO removal requests in the United States. Refusing to deal with the UXO issue and deeming it an exclusively Panamanian problem signaled a desire on the US side to end the special relationship.

Part of the limited US responsiveness to Moscoso derived from the absence of an ambassador. Although Ambassador Simon Ferro had gotten relations between the two countries off to a good start, as a political appointee of the Clinton administration he was obliged to resign in May 2001. Deputy Chief of Mission Frederick Becker, a respected career officer, became the Chargé D'Affaires or Acting Chief of Mission and ran the show so well for the next twenty months that Panama in many respects just seemed to drop off Washington's radar.[31]

THE SPECIAL RELATIONSHIP BECAME A SECURITY PARTNERSHIP

Despite the embassy's reduced clout, other Washington attention focused on Panama due to its involvement in drug trafficking, money laundering, and spillover from Colombia's civil war into the Darien.[32] The Pentagon increased support for the development of Panama's naval police, donating several patrol boats and more than doubling their capacity. Panama's special police unit for the border region also expanded and got US jungle-warfare training. Finally, in the summer of 2001, negotiations produced a bilateral law enforcement treaty, called the Salas-Becker Agreement after Minister of Government and Justice Aníbal Salas and Chargé Becker.[33]

[31] Becker, "Interview," 203. In his oral history, Becker refers to a series of continuing issues and negative attitudes toward Panama and the mission there by the Washington bureaucracy that had arisen under politically appointed ambassadors to Panama.

[32] Christopher Marquis, "New Drug Plan Shifts Focus on Latin America," *New York Times,* May 16, 2001.

[33] The negotiations for the agreement were completed under minister Spadafora, with Ambassador Marcel Salamín leading the Panama delegation. The formal signing could not be arranged before Spadafora was nominated to the Supreme Court, however, so he was replaced by Salas, who had been Moscoso's private attorney. Author Bigler represented the embassy on the US team. It was formally called the US-Panama Supplementary Arrangement on US Coast Guard Assistance, rather than a treaty per se, to avoid the possibly controversial ratification processes that would be required. See Victor D. Torres, "Panamá y EU firman hoy acuerdo contra el narcotráfico," *La Prensa*, Feb. 2, 2002.

The new accord restored "ship-rider" cooperation – the deputizing of vessels from partner navies – and other collaborative law enforcement practices from the Canal Zone era. The new arrangement stirred up controversy in Panama, however, sparking claims the United States wished to "remilitarize" the country and that the agreement should have been ratified by the Assembly. Still, agreed-upon procedures for expeditious rendition of prisoners to the United States and for sharing air as well as maritime intelligence, including over the Darien, proved mutually beneficial, and the cooperation has been repeatedly upgraded since.[34]

The new Panama–United States security cooperation had not kicked in fully when the September 11, 2001, terrorist attacks occurred in New York City and Washington, DC. Even while the attacks were under way, President Moscoso summoned Chargé Becker and Counselor Gene Bigler to meet with her team to discuss the vulnerability of the Canal to terrorism and what next steps should be taken to protect it. They agreed that a delegation from the National Security Council and the ACP would consult with counterparts in Washington to upgrade protection of the Canal, thus launching a new arena of binational security cooperation.

The outpouring of sympathy for the United States in the wake of the 9/11 attacks (in which several Panamanians perished at the World Trade Center) lasted for weeks and served as an antidote to accusations of remilitarization. Two months later, during Independence Day celebrations, Panama invited three New York firefighters to participate in the National Firemen's Day parade.[35] One of them, Captain Erick Weekes, Commander of Fire Station 126 in Queens, was a Panamanian who had emigrated with his family to New York. When this became public, the guest firefighters were feted as national heroes.[36]

[34] For example, the rendition provisions allowed for prisoners taken at sea to be transferred to Panamanian judicial authorities and then to US officials for air transport to US courts in Miami and San Diego. This saved US vessels from having to leave their patrol stations for months at a time to transport the prisoners to US ports and relieved the SMN of having to extend its resources far beyond their optimal operational range. The critical reaction was elaborated in José H. Santos Aguilera, "Las relaciones entre Panamá y los EEUU en la era de la globalización," *CELA – Centro de Estudios Latinoamericanos Justo Arosemena,* 2008, http://biblioteca.clacso.edu.ar/Panama/cela/20120717112658/causas.pdf.

[35] Since Panama had no military forces at the time it declared its independence from Colombia in 1903, the Caracas fire brigade was converted into the new country's national defense force and still forms an integral part of independence celebrations. Firemen are symbols of Panamanian patriotism, like Minutemen in the US.

[36] The 2001 celebration also gave rise to annual commemorations of 9/11 by Panamanian firefighters: Grisel Bethancourt, "Bomberos recuerdan 11 septiembre," *Panamá América,*

The positive symbiotic relationship between Panama and the United States became even more palpable during the January 9, 2002, commemoration of the Day of the Martyrs of 1964. Whereas previous demonstrations had anti-American tones, this time only a handful of protesters with stones and paint cans approached the US embassy. They were blocked by thousands of cheering countrymen, many dressed as firefighters or in other pro-Yankee apparel. Surprisingly, Panamanians celebrated closer ties to the United States, which reciprocated by focusing most of the increased good will on security cooperation.[37]

Throughout the remainder of the Moscoso term and beyond, the two countries supplemented Salas-Becker with other agreements and assistance. This included expansion of law enforcement and maritime and border security collaboration that would have been unlikely before 2001. A status of forces agreement restored the ability of US soldiers to conduct in-country training, and a new pact for combatting drug trafficking stiffened that effort. Panama also welcomed a large two-week joint training mission called New Horizons, reminiscent of 1960s civic action tours, in which US National Guard members carried out a series of school-building, public health, and veterinary projects with the indigenous population of Chiriqui province.

Panama also assumed a major role in the development of a new International Shipping and Port Security Code by the International Maritime Organization (IMO). The code completely restructured its approach to maritime security in the face of global terrorism. In July 2002, the United States and Panama issued a Joint Declaration on Maritime Safety, Security, and Protection of the Marine Environment, and, in 2003, the two countries sponsored the Panamax multinational naval exercises for protecting the Panama Canal. Remarkably and without fanfare, growing trust of the United States and other countries as active partners supplanted the notion that neutrality was the Canal's best protection.[38]

Sept. 10, 2006. See also, "Panamá brinda bienvenida de héroes a bomberos de Nueva York," US Embassy Panama Press Release, December 14, 2001.

[37] Panamanians still remember January 9 for heroic youth and national pride, but anti-Americanism has all but disappeared on its anniversary. Public support was matched by various forms of official and private-sector cooperation, including collaboration by offshore banks to search out flows of funds to terrorists. David González, "Changed Panama Banks Root Out Terror Funds," *New York Times*, Oct. 26, 2001.

[38] New patterns of cooperation arose with each of these developments. Panama's ambassador to the IMO, Captain Orlando Allard, built on years of service as a Panama Canal pilot to spearhead work with US officials at the IMO in London. US Coast Guard officials

Just before leaving office, the Moscoso administration took two more important actions. First, it upgraded border protection that had started with a US-trained special force of 500 police in November 2000, after Colombian bandits savaged the border town of Nazaret. That action and increased humanitarian cooperation with the United Nations High Commissioner for Refugees, an important element of Moscoso policy from the start, had reestablished a sense of Panamanian control of the Darien region. Border control suffered again in late 2002, when a series of attacks killed several Panamanians and the flow of refugees spurted. In response, Moscoso led a team of six ministers and her chief of police, Carlos Barés, to stand up another US-trained and equipped force, the Reconnoiter and Combat Unit, comprised of 150 police in the town of Paya. She issued a virtual declaration of war against irregular Colombian forces in the region.[39]

Second, Panama supported US efforts to approve a controversial agreement, the Proliferation Security Initiative, launched by Ambassador to the UN John R. Bolton. This included interdiction of trafficking in materials that could be used to produce weapons of mass destruction. Progress on this front never overcame sovereignty reservations by many nations, but this did not prevent Panama from intervening later, as described in Chapter 8, to seize a North Korean shipment of illicit arms.[40]

The Moscoso administration also worked closely with the United States in other areas, most notably a program to control screwworm infestations. These pests had devastated cattle and other livestock populations in the United States and Mexico during the 1920s and 1930s, at a cost of hundreds of millions of dollars. In the 1950s, these countries developed a production facility in Mexico to breed infertile screwworms, to spread sterilized bugs in North and Central America that prevented healthy ones from reproducing.

assigned to the ACP instigated the maritime agreement and then helped the US Navy enter the Panamax security system. Five nations joined in the first Panamax event, and, by 2015, cooperation had grown to sixteen: Mahlet Tesfaye, "Panamax 15 Exercise Brings Nations Together," Aug. 5, 2015, www.army.mil/article/153379/panamax_15_exercise_brings_nations_together.

39 The humanitarian response was reflected in the EFE article, "Panamá da refugio a desplazados colombianos," Jan. 7, 2000, and the later security emphasis in "Moscoso declara la guerra a irregulares colombianos," *La Prensa*, Feb. 7, 2003.

40 Judith Miller, "'Panama Joins Accord to Stem Ships' Transport of Illicit Arms," *New York Times*, May 11, 2004. Just over sixty nations had acceded to the treaty when Panama and Liberia joined, covering almost half of the world's merchant marine.

In the early 2000s, Caribbean and US authorities determined that a new production center based in Panama would work more efficiently. Accordingly, the United States and Panama built a joint facility in 2002–04, worth about $100 million, near Tocumen airport. Employing over 400 workers, the new plant increased preventive coverage across the entire Caribbean Basin. This investment also complemented Panama's efforts to stimulate the economy.[41]

The Moscoso administration's new relationship with the United States proceeded in fits and starts. The 9/11 attacks had spurred cooperation in the security arena and opened the door for advances in other areas, if not yet to the degree that Panama sought in trade and economic policy.

GETTING THE ECONOMY ROLLING AND THE FREE TRADE ROUTE TO GLOBALIZATION

President Moscoso's restructured cabinet in 2000 presaged a more vigorous approach to economic growth.[42] Without a central bank, Panama could not resort to monetary expansion, but the National Bank of Panama, the Banco de Desarrollo Agropecuario, and other public entities expanded credit as rapidly as budget constraints allowed. Additionally, the government promoted private borrowing and worked to speed up foreign investment already under way in the ports, infrastructure, and tourism.[43]

Moscoso authorized two mega projects to attract foreign investment and tourism, the $400 million dollar CEMIS undertaking and the Figali Convention Center. The first aimed to buttress the Atlantic side of the Canal by connecting a multi-modal industrial service center to the Colon Free Zone (CFZ) and the new ports that Pérez Balladares had launched. The second, a more modest enterprise on the Amador Causeway, was

[41] US Department of Agriculture, Animal and Plant Health Inspection Service (APHIS), "USDA Seeks Comment on Proposal to Recognize Panama as Free of Screwworm," May 15, 2008. The importance of the program in Panama and central America appeared when the pest returned to the US in 2016, possibly from Cuba. Sarah Zhang, "Flesh-Eating Worms Have Returned to Florida," *The Atlantic*, Oct. 7, 2016.

[42] All thirteen ministers submitted resignations to signify their willingness to support more drastic action. Taking emergency measures to combat drug trafficking and solidify government finances were also considered crucial after the government's credit rating was reduced and tax haven practices were criticized. "Renuncia el gabinete de Mireya Moscoso," *El Universal*, Aug. 17, 2000.

[43] Mireya Navarro, "Panama Converting Canal Zone for Tourism," *New York Times*, Aug. 29, 1999.

a major events center to attract more hotels, marinas, upscale housing, and other venues, while complementing the future Biodiversity Museum (Biomuseo) under development there. Both projects, launched with surprising speed, quickly aroused controversy and charges of corruption that abruptly stopped CEMIS and slowed progress on the Figali Center. Political scheming and corruption, not philosophical issues, prevented these Moscoso initiatives from achieving their intended impact during her term.[44]

Free trade promotion also made its way onto the Moscoso agenda. At first reluctant to follow the path started by the Pérez Balladares economic team, she nonetheless raised the issue of trade advantages on her first trip to Washington. Panama stood at the forefront of Central American nations seeking US support in a new "banana war" against the European Union over preferences given to growers in former colonies. Despite earlier hesitation, in December 1999, the United States suddenly sided with the Central Americans and buttressed Panamanian commitment to trade promotion.[45]

Following changes in her economic team in 2000, Moscoso began to press for the inclusion of Panama in economic integration schemes, starting with Central America and the Dominican Republic. Then she sought bilateral free trade agreements with special targets of opportunity, including Taiwan, Singapore, and the United States. In each case, Panamanian motives for the bilateral trade arrangements seemed aimed more at promoting investments by prospective partners than free trade expansion per se. Meanwhile, Panama imposed protectionist measures, such as health and phytosanitary regulations, to control and occasionally exclude imports of US food products, a blatantly contradictory stance.

The Moscoso administration's approach to financial policy, banking, and other economic matters remained ambivalent for a time. Its measures not only faced resistance in the Assembly but often virulent labor union and even civil society reactions too. For instance, bus owners and operators opposed any reform of the free-wheeling system of Diablos Rojos (Red Devils), the independently operated buses named for the vivid designs painted on them and aggressive driving by their operators. Reformers overlooked the fact that these buses were vital for the working

44 Guevara Mann, *Political Careers,* 222–23. Ebrahim Asvat commented on the Afú and CEMIS scandals in several columns dated August 2003, in his collected newspaper columns, *Bitácora del presidente* (Panama: El Nuevo Siglo, 2010), 56–59.

45 See Chapter 2 for the first banana war, against US importers.

and low-income population. In September, when the administration announced a fare increase to support reforms, thousands participated in protests and over 100 demonstrators suffered injury.[46]

Similarly, administration attempts at banking, finance, and other reforms met strong opposition, especially from the PRD majority in the Assembly. They also had to deal with new scrutiny from the OECD's Financial Action Task Force, whose denunciations of drug trafficking and money laundering in Panama, called a "shame campaign," overshadowed their promotion of tourism and investment opportunities. With few options, the Moscoso administration boosted international cooperation and financial information sharing. They also undertook less controversial banking and tax measures. These responses led the OECD to remove Panama from the "gray list" of tax havens and money launderers in 2002.[47]

About midway through the Moscoso administration, some good news came when the new Colon cruise ship terminal suddenly blossomed. Initial concerns about crime, the dilapidated look of the city, and even scarcity of English-speaking taxi drivers faded as news about the restoration of the Panama Railroad and successful management of the Canal spread. Indeed, the railroad became a magnet for tourists from all over the Caribbean and was voted the most popular mainland attraction in the Caribbean. Additionally, a lobbying campaign to make the Amador Causeway the home of the Miss Universe Pageant helped raise awareness of Panama's attractions. These and other positive signs grew partly out of new foreign investment and plans for large scale construction projects. One of these, a second bridge over the Canal (named Centennial for its opening on the 100th anniversary of independence), amazed observers because it was scheduled for completion in a mere twenty-nine months, by the end of Moscoso's term.

Favorable external conditions also began to support economic expansion. For example, investment and global markets drove growth in the fishing and mining industries in 2000. Then civil construction expanded steadily. Slowly, improvements spread to tourism and other sectors. By far

[46] Observatorio Social de América Latina (COSAL), "Panamá: Cronología del conflicto social, septiembre a diciembre de 2002." The impetus for urban transportation reform continued with the Torrijos administration but did not end the Red Devils until the Martínelli administration about a decade later, as discussed in Chapters 6 and 8.

[47] Panama has been off and back on both gray lists and black lists of the OECD and FATCA several times over the years. A recent report reflects the continuing challenge, "Panamá supera lista gris del GAFI (FATCA), aún falta Ocde (OECD)," *Panamá América*, Feb. 19, 2016, that will be revisited in later chapters.

the most important development, detailed in Chapter 7, was the steady increase in ACP payments that swelled government coffers each year. Thus, little by little, Panama's economy perked up slightly during 2001, though not enough to keep up with population growth at first.

Other successes came along. The City of Knowledge grew and the railroad and tourism boomed. The latter's management had first offered passenger service on the railroad at ARI insistence and because container handling in the ports grew more slowly than anticipated. But tourists soon flocked to cross the Isthmus and to new facilities on the Amador Causeway, helping to generate profits and complement growth in the cruise ship industry. Similarly, despite the problems with the CEMIS mega project in Colon, work on the Convention Center and its surroundings progressed enough to add momentum.

By late 2002, the new projects underway engendered real growth in the economy and produced the first substantial per capita GDP increase in three years. By 2004, the expansion reached a robust level, above 6 percent. Proof of the strength of the turnaround came in 2003, despite major setbacks like Chiquita Banana's abandonment of operations in Chiriqui. The company had sold out to the government in 1976, but leased back 15,000 hectares to continue production. Most of the other lands went into private hands, while a small portion became a government-owned banana company in Bocas de Toro, which did survive the Chiquita shut down.[48]

Despite good growth figures, unemployment persisted at about 12 percent, so ordinary people felt a sense of economic insecurity. On the eve of the 2004 election, 73 percent of the people polled reported that unemployment, poverty, and other economic troubles were the country's most important problem.[49] Evidently, a structural dualism – i.e. the rich prospered and the poor fell behind – kept most of the population from enjoying the benefits of economic expansion.

[48] On the first banana takeover, see Chapter 1, note 31, and Sandra W. Meditz and Dennis Michael Hanratty, eds. *Panama: A Country Study* (Washington, DC: Federal Research Division, Library of Congress, 1989), 156–58. These later transitions in the industry during the Moscoso administration are reported in an AFP article, "Chiquita venderá plantación bananera a cooperativa de trabajadores," June 21, 2003, www.emol.com/noticias/economia/2003/06/29/116077/chiquita-vendera-plantacion-bananera-a-cooperativa-de-trabajadores.html.

[49] Orlando J. Pérez, Marco A. Gandásegui, Jr., and Mitch Seligson, "The Political Culture of Democracy in Panama: Public Perceptions about the Political System," Latin American Public Opinion Project, March 2004, p. 59, www.vanderbilt.edu/lapop/panama/2004-politicalculture.pdf.

Toward the end of Moscoso's administration, Panama got off the OECD watch list of "gray economies." Free trade negotiations produced agreements with Central America, Taiwan, and Singapore, reinforcing the view that the world had become increasingly open to Panama. The United States, which at first put off proposals for bilateral talks, agreed to negotiations in the context of the Free Trade of the Americas proposal. Observers saw this as the United States acknowledging Panama's success in operating the Canal and improving international maritime security.

The nation's rising international stature got a boost from other events in the capital. In 2001, Mayor Juan Carlos Navarro presided over a ceremony proclaiming Panama City a UNESCO World Heritage site. Ambitious plans to clean up Panama Bay and other environmental undertakings won positive attention abroad. In 2002, the Smithsonian Institution's board of directors held a meeting in Panama to acknowledge the binational cooperation and progress on construction of the Biodiversity Museum. At the same time, the World Wildlife Federation partnered with Panama to create the Coiba National Park and Marine Protection Zone, covering the former prison and 38 other offshore islands. The UN Development Program's study of Human Development in Panama pointed to successful approaches to civic participation. Finally, Supreme Court chief judge Adán Arjona's plan for judicial reform, in conjunction with Transparency International, won broad approval. In 2003, the second Miss Universe Pageant held in Central America brought global attention to the completed Figali Convention Center on Amador Causeway. Luxurious new marinas and seaside restaurants welcomed international participants and television audiences. The Center also hosted a string of major concerts and events, despite construction delays and rumors of corruption. Good news seemed to crop up across the Isthmus.

Such international success also pushed the Moscoso administration toward a more open economy. Whereas in 2000 commitment to trade languished, by 2003 Panama proposed to replace Miami as the headquarters for the Free Trade Area of the Americas negotiations. Moreover, its growing maritime ambitions and initiatives forged a consensus about how to move the country forward.[50]

[50] Christopher Marquis, "Panama Challenges Miami as Free Trade Headquarters," *New York Times*, Nov. 11, 2003.

A MARITIME STRATEGY FINALLY EMERGED

The idea of Panama as a regional hub or emporium for the Americas dates back at least to Simón Bolívar's famous 1815 Letter from Jamaica. Many episodes in the intervening centuries seemed to advance that dream. The Panama Railroad, built during the California Gold Rush, refreshed these hopes, but foreign control of the line made it an enclave with limited impact on national development. French Canal construction in the 1880s again raised hopes, later to be dashed by the company's bankruptcy. As discussed in Chapter 1, the Panama Canal, built and operated by the United States, had more impact on the country, but the enclave system imposed by the United States prevented it from achieving the emporium dream promised by Panama's unique geography.

Panama's acquisition of the Canal in 1999 renewed discussions about a broader national maritime strategy or vocation to take advantage of its role in world commerce. Certainly, the idea played an important role in shaping the national imagination and influenced every episode of renegotiation of its treaties with the United States. As discussed in Chapter 1, Ana Elena Porras recounted the many ways Panamanians found to describe what she calls *interoceanidad,* or the fact of living between two oceans. Gradually, the intelligentsia that emerged during the negotiations of the 1960s and 1970s created a framework that economist Nicolás Ardito Barletta and others articulated as a vision for the linkages between the waterway and the rest of the economy.[51]

Historians, meanwhile, had been developing the concept of *transitismo* and its adjectival form *transitista*, referring to the structuring of the entire nation around the canal and its transit zone, to the neglect of other regions and activities. Even before the canal turnover, a small elite could influence government, the economy, the media, and international relations through their control over the flow of business through the Panama-Colon corridor. Once the canal became the prime national asset after 2000, this concentration of power could only grow. As the elite pursued the broader goals of making Panama a hub, the canal and its related enterprises came to represent an overwhelming share of the national product. Those

[51] *Cultura de la interoceanidad: Narrativas de identidad nacional de Panama, 1990–2002* (Panama: Universidad de Panama, 2009). Cf. also the discussion in Chapter 1. Ardito Barletta's ideas are elaborated most fully in *Estrategia para el desarrollo nacional* (Panama: Editorial Exedra, 2012). References to the approach are also discussed with respect to meetings in Bambito and Coronado in Chapters 3 and 4.

outside the elite enjoyed little chance to spread the benefits or break up the monopoly.[52]

The Moscoso administration eventually enhanced the path toward maritime development, partly spurred by the ACP's success managing the Canal. In 2001, it charged the Panama Maritime Authority (AMP), under Administrator Jerry Salazar, with bringing the country's entire sector together to develop a national strategy. At last, Panama committed to transform the dream of a maritime vocation into practical action. As important as the Canal and commercial activities were, they still only amounted to 10 percent of GDP. If these and new activities being planned could be synchronized around the Canal, their share of the economy would be much higher. And the whole could be greater than the sum of the parts.

Salazar convened about thirty public and private entities in a strategic planning process. They embraced the obvious maritime sectors, such as the ACP, admiralty lawyers, longshoremen, seamen, and naval authorities, but they also invited representatives of transportation, tourism, education, commerce, environment, business, and government organizations. The Japanese International Development Agency gave the group a grant of $2.5 million dollars for research. The staff formulated a plan to advance Panama's global economic connections. Its draft, completed at the end of 2003, won the approved of the Moscoso cabinet the following February.[53]

Elaboration of the plan itself proved more important than its actual implementation, because it forced disparate players to focus on broader development goals instead of their own institutional interests. It also compiled measurements and data about the role of the maritime sector in the economy. Continuing studies, based on the pioneering work of Nicolás Ardito Barletta's Intracorp, showed that the percentage of Panama's GDP generated by these activities grew from just over 6 percent to more than 10 percent during the half century between 1950 and 1999. They also demonstrate that, after 2000, national authorities succeeded in

[52] Alfredo Castillero Calvo, "Transitismo y dependencia: el caso del istmo de Panamá," *Lotería* 210 (July 1973): 35–50; and the essays in "Transitismo y la cuestión social," in *Antología del pensamiento crítico panameño contemporáneo*, eds. Gandásegui et al. (Buenos Aires: Consejo Latinoamericano de Ciencias Sociales, 2018), 147–290.

[53] Author Bigler participated in many of these discussions and assisted in arranging contributions sought from US government sources. Ebrahim Asvat discussed the national maritime strategy in "La ACP: Estrategia marítima nacional," Aug. 20, 2003, in his collected newspaper columns, *Bitácora del president*, 51–52.

linking as much of society as possible to the maritime engine of growth. The results were striking: the share of GDP generated by the maritime sector just fifteen years later, and even before the expansion of the Canal, had grown to more than a third of the national economy.[54]

Decisions about maritime development made by the Pérez Balladares administration became realities after 1999.[55] On the Colon side, the Moscoso administration pushed Panama Ports to elaborate on its designs for a new passenger facility to attract the Caribbean cruise ship industry. In addition, Seattle's Stevedoring Services of America (SSA) was urged to quicken the pace and expand the Manzanillo International Terminal (MIT). By 2003, previously unskilled Panamanian workers had been transformed into international-award-winning dock workers and enabled MIT to be recognized as the fastest growing and most efficient port in the Americas. On the Pacific side, Panama Port's Balboa terminal was given more space and connected seamlessly across the Isthmus after the Panama Railroad began carrying containers between the two sides. In 2002–03, with the Panamanian Coast Guard and US interests finally out of the way, Singapore PSA took over the naval facility at Rodman and started converting it into the nation's fourth major container port. During the mid 1990s, all the ports in Panama moved about 200,000 containers a year; they handled over two million annually by the end of the Moscoso years.

Development of the Amador Causeway, the six-kilometer breakwater connecting three tiny islands to the mainland next to the Pacific entrance of the Canal, also got moving in 2001. Previously, its attractions were limited to the STRI Marine Research Station, the ruins of a WWII naval battery, one of Noriega's homes left in ruins after the invasion, and three rustic seafood shacks adjacent to the beaches. One could ride a bike down the center line undisturbed by traffic at almost any time of day or night. As if overnight, however, a variety of tourist facilities, hotels, restaurants, and shops sprang up along the Causeway. Next came yacht harbors and boatyards. Work advanced on the Figali Convention Center and the Biodiversity Museum. The government erected a statue to celebrate the six major groups of immigrants who arrived and mixed with native peoples. Panamanians and tourists alike soon flooded the Causeway with 24/7 traffic, forcing the widening of the roadway. Nearly five

[54] Wilfredo Jordan reported on the growth of the maritime sector in *La Prensa*. See for example "Maritime Sector of Panama's Economy," Sept. 20, 2015, https://ioepanama.wordpress.com/2015/09/20/martime-sector-of-panamas-economy/

[55] Achievements by the ACP are described in Chapter 7.

centuries after the founding of Panama City, the Causeway became a global playground by the sea.

Other developments, responding to growth of the maritime sector, came more slowly. Prior to 2000, the largest global connections were provided by the Colon Free Zone, the petroleum pipeline in Chiriquí (shut down in 1993 after a decade in service), and the international banking center. The most impressive new enterprise under the Moscoso administration was the Panamá-Pacífico International Logistics Center, which got off the ground in 2004. It hosted new factories, tourist facilities, beachfront resorts, and residential condominiums. The groundwork was also laid for the transformation of the Nautical School into the Panama International Maritime University (UMIP). Meanwhile, the boom in high-rise construction in the capital moved beyond Punta Paitilla and Punta Pacífica to other areas of the city, like Costa del Este on the Corredor Sur.

In 2000, the government authorized Global Crossing to lay new fiber-optic cables to link the Atlantic and South American networks, as had been planned for years and described in Chapter 4. This resulted in enormous new bandwidth availability in Panama and almost immediately attracted high tech companies and international call centers. Dell Computers led the way for high tech businesses moving to Panamá-Pacífico. After 2002, these communications links and high tech services drew a wave of regional organizations, multinational firms, and shipping companies to Panama that continued beyond the Moscoso years. Meanwhile, the explosion in high-rise construction made office space available at competitive prices.

ADJUSTING THE SOCIAL DEVELOPMENT AGENDA

The 1999 presidential campaign called attention to poverty and the dual economy, as we have seen. The rich had obviously gotten richer under Pérez Balladares, so inequality and social neglect dominated the electoral agenda. Mireya Moscoso's humble roots in small-town Pedasi had made her the more popular candidate for addressing these challenges. A few days after her inauguration, in an address at the UN General Assembly, she confirmed her pledge to keep the struggle against poverty as her top priority.[56] Key advisors, led by Bobby Eisenmann, echoed the president's anti-poverty commitment. They had written a plan for combating poverty and creating jobs, called "The Social Agenda of Mireya Moscoso and the National

[56] Leandro Avila, "Mireya en la ONU," *Panamá América*, Sept. 24, 1999.

TABLE 5.1 *Access to Sewage and Refuse Services in Panama by Poverty Level (numbers in cells are percent of population enjoying access)*

Poverty level	Sewage or septic tank	Latrines or other basic installations	No installations	Garbage collection
Non-poor	70%	28%	2%	73%
Urban poor	44	48	8	77
Rural poor	6	80	14	6
Indigenous/poor	8	32	60	0

Source: Encuesta de Niveles de Vida de Panamá, Contaloría General de la República, 1997.

Society." It called for reducing poverty by 3 percent and illiteracy by 2 percent a year, goals they hoped would be adopted by the Assembly. A key element of the plan embraced the US Brady Bond Program for debt relief in developing countries, which aimed to channel resources for fighting poverty, as well as a substantial increase in funding from the Inter-American Development Bank and other international financial institutions.[57]

The need was glaring. Lack of access to sewage and hygiene by a large part of the population constituted the most serious problems, especially in rural areas. Table 5.1, based on a government survey, shows that the requirements for barely 20 percent of the poor for basic sewage and garbage services were met in 1997. Since about four in ten Panamanians were classified as poor, about half of the population lacked such basic services.

Although some improvements in standards of living had occurred during the 1990s, socioeconomic disparities combined with election rhetoric spurred more vigorous action. For instance, literacy in the adult population rose from 88 to 92 percent but was still under 85 percent in rural areas. Access to potable water in cities rose from 80 to 90 percent, but in rural areas it stood at 75 percent. Panama City developed a plan to clean up Panama Bay and increase potable water for its residents, but little was done to deal with the drought brought by El Niño weather in 1997–98. With respect to the proportion of families with incomes below the poverty level, change came slowly, dropping

[57] Carlos A. Rodríguez y Víctor Santos, "Lucha contra la pobreza: una cruzada que compromete a todos," *Panamá América*, Sept. 19, 1999; and David Carrasco, "Panamá: Gobierno inicia cruzada para reducir la pobreza," *Inter Press Service*, Nov. 11, 1999.

from 31 to 25 percent nationally and barely falling in rural areas. Government studies indicated that over half of families could not afford to purchase basic necessities in 2000.[58]

President Moscoso failed to win approval for her social agenda in the Assembly, preventing her administration from allocating more money to fight poverty. Fraud accusations against the director of the Social Investment Fund early in 2000 dealt another blow to her program. As a result, social development actions advanced in fits and starts. Each ministry and agency went ahead with little regard for Eisenmann's agenda or any other unifying rationale. Meanwhile, the sluggish economy and the US withdrawal drove up unemployment. The poor continued to suffer.

By the end of 2000, with her approval ratings at only 25 percent, Moscoso needed a new approach to social issues.[59] Perhaps as a distraction, she threw herself wholeheartedly into the campaign to determine the murderers of popular priest Héctor Gallego. Her National Truth Commission won broad support because many of its members were lifelong adversaries of the PRD and military governments. Its charge to identify wrongdoers, substantial powers, and considerable resources gave it deep credibility. It also signaled a quiet abandonment of efforts to address poverty.

During the eighteen months of the commission's deliberations, rumors and leaks about its findings circulated widely. Its final report confirmed long-held suspicions about the 148 disappearances investigated. It documented seventy murders, with many noteworthy confessions, largely by Guardia officers. Forty other disappearances, however, remained inconclusive. The commission continued to work for the rest of the Moscoso term, with only modest results, and some observers believed that more could have been accomplished. Some still advocated for more action by an extended commission, while others believed the exercise to be too partisan.[60]

In early 2001, Moscoso decided to shift attention from poverty to human development, in partnership with the UNDP. They tried to revive broad participation by the citizenry, as had occurred in the 1980s and 1990s.

[58] All data are from the statistical appendices of Programa de las Naciones Unidas para el Desarrollo, *Informe Nacional de Desarrollo Humano: Panama 2002*.

[59] Results of polls between January 2000 and February 2001 appear in Jean Marcel Chéry, "Aceptación de Moscoso cae al nivel 'más crítico,'" *Panamá América*, Feb. 20, 2001.

[60] Orlando Pérez, *Political Culture in Panama: Democracy after Invasion* (New York: Palgrave Macmillan, 2011), 121–22; Harding, *History of Panama*, 134–35; and Defensoría del Pueblo, *Informe Final de la Comisión de la Verdad*, www.defensoriadelpueblo.gob.pa/index.php?option=com_flippingbook&view=book&id=6:informe-final-de-la-comision-de-la-verdad&catid=6:informes&Itemid=151.

She appointed the energetic minister of economics and finance, Norberto Delgado, to work with Elizabeth Fong of the UNDP. They hoped their campaign would result in consensus building. Respected social scientist Paulina Franceschi, serving as coordinator, brought together many social activists to hold public forums around the country. They undertook national assessment studies to serve as benchmarks. The work also turned attention from a narrow family-income approach to a broad-spectrum one involving education, opportunities for women, nutrition, quality of social services, housing, health care, and other measures. The project included rural and indigenous communities. Its data-driven methodology incorporated the UN-formulated Human Development Index to measure achievements.

Despite the fanfare that accompanied its first report in 2002, the Human Development project did not distract attention from Moscoso's meager record in reducing poverty, nor did it create a sustainable social movement.[61] The report did, however, cast light on some attributes of Panama's approach to social progress.[62] For instance, it found that:

- Educational spending was regressive. Greater benefits went to higher income families rather than to less well-off ones. In addition, spending became increasingly regressive as students rose through the grades. Therefore, government spending on education perpetuated the county's high level of inequality.
- Panama's social spending in nearly every field proved less efficacious than in many less well-off countries. For example, Costa Rica spent less on social development than Panama yet had higher levels of human development.

A SCANDAL-STREWN PATH TO THE 2004 ELECTIONS

The Moscoso administration found itself enveloped in a cloud of scandal and corruption, despite some efforts to curb it. She had halted the perilous

[61] Telephone interviews with ambassador Linda Watt, Aug. 1, 17, and 23, 2016. Ambassador Watt, who accompanied President Moscoso on many trips, was impressed by her personal empathy for and outreach to impoverished Panamanians, especially in the countryside, but also noted a sense of stoicism that more could not be done for them.

[62] PNUD, *Informe Nacional de Desarrollo Humano, Panama 2002, El Compromiso con el Desarrollo Humano: Un desafío nacional,* June, 2002. Also see the report, José Emilio Champasur y Manuel Ferrer, "Grandes gastos, pocos resultados," Fundación para el Desarrollo de la Libertad Ciudadana, 2004, on the Social Watch website, www.socialwatch.org/es/node/10340.

FIGURE 5.3 Centennial Bridge, several miles north of the Bridge of the Americas. Danny Lehman/Getty Images.

fifth chamber scheme to pack the Supreme Court, yet to do it she bribed legislators with fancy watches. The Ibero-American Summit showcased Panama's management of the Canal to many attending heads of state, but the subsequent donation of seventeen luxury Cadillacs, purchased for the visitors, to vice presidents and ministers set a new standard for the transportation of senior officials. Moscoso's completion of the majestic Centennial Bridge over the Canal in record time was marred by its delayed inauguration because improperly mixed asphalt melted away on access roads.

In these and other cases, the taint of scandal revealed a pattern of privilege or entitlement that those governing enjoyed. Moscoso's international travel also raised concerns. In 2000, she led a large delegation on a week-long trip to Rome. Meetings at the Vatican, with the Italian government, and at the headquarters of the UN Food and Agriculture Organization certainly justified more than an overnight visit, but the six-day stay and the size of the entourage suggested junketeering more than public business. A later excursion to Taiwan elicited even more criticism.[63] The president also protected persons who fell under suspicion of wrongdoing, by moving them into even higher positions and foregoing investigations. For instance, when a scandal arose over the contracting

[63] "Moscoso defiende a compañeros de viaje," *Panamá América*, Sept. 7, 2000; and Meredith Serracín, "Viaje de Moscoso repercute en prensa internacional," *Panamá América*, July 11, 2000.

procedures of the FIS early in his tenure, its youthful director, Arnulfo Escalona, promptly rose to be vice minister of the presidency and the charges against him were ignored.

In another case, a leased helicopter carrying two cousins who worked on the president's staff had to land at sea due to mechanical difficulties about halfway between the president's Pedasi vacation home and the capital. The presidential helicopter and SMN (maritime police) units rescued the passengers, but then the story got complicated. As the police removed several black satchels, they saw a wad of hundred-dollar bills in one. Before further action could be taken, however, the police were ordered to sink the leased helicopter, because it could be a marine hazard. The cousins remained on the staff, the presidency reimbursed the leasing company, and no investigation occurred.[64]

Amid rising concern over corruption, an unexpected turn for the better occurred in 2001. Judge Adán Arnulfo Arjona won election as president of the Supreme Court. Arjona, then just 38 and the youngest justice ever to be elected by his peers for a two-year term, had been appointed to the high court two years earlier because of his leadership of judicial reform and modernization of lower courts. Observers welcomed his choice as a sign of hope for the judiciary, and he went to work gathering international financing for a broader strategic reform of the courts.[65] Court reform, supported by the US Agency for International Development (USAID), focused on reducing pre-trial detentions that accounted for over two-thirds of the inmates in Panama's prisons. The Inter-American Development Bank and several European donors also financed reform efforts led by Arjona and others, especially to modernize procedures and create computer-based archives and record keeping. Although USAID involvement in this area would soon end, the embassy applauded achievements like the creation of a Panama affiliate of Transparency International.

[64] Monica Palm, "El misterioso caso del HP1430," *La Prensa*, Apr. 19, 2001; and Juan Ignacio Blanco, "Gobierno hundió el helicóptero HP1430," *Panamá América*, Aug. 28, 2001.

[65] Author Bigler represented the US embassy or supervised embassy involvement with the Panamanian judiciary and developed a close relationship with Arjona. Arjona's dedication to the development and independence of the judiciary is reflected in the two-volume collection he organized for the celebration of Panama's centennial, *Justicia Panameña: (1) Historia y Biografía; (2) Perspectivas Históricas* (Panama: Órgano Judicial de la República, 2003).

At the time of Arjona's election as president, the Court faced a stalemate due to evenly divided Arnulfista and PRD justices and a difficult case of corruption in the Panama Maritime Tribunal. The Maritime Law Association, similar interest groups, and law firms had already worked behind the scenes to sideline a judge considered a liability for the profession. Given the judge's partisan backers, however, the parties sought a compromise. Rather than fighting to remove him, they created a Second Maritime Tribunal to protect the quality of admiralty law and its role in the expansion of the industry.[66]

Incidents like this may have convinced the Moscoso administration of the importance of loyalty in the Supreme Court and helped to explain the otherwise surprising nominations of minister of government and justice Winston Spadafora and Arnulfista deputy Alberto Cigarruista, shortly after Arjona's election. While both were members of Moscoso's inner circle, they also carried heavy baggage and aroused rivalries related to the court that would carry over to the next government, as we shall see in Chapter 6. Critics believed Cigarruista paid deputies for pro-administration votes in the Assembly. Spadadora, popular for strong law enforcement as minister and the earlier family crusade against Noriega, lost credibility due to accusations that he used his influence to have the government build a costly access road to a family property. Still, Moscoso approved both nominations on the eve of the biggest scandal yet.

When the leader of the PRD delegation in the Assembly, Balbina Herrera, arranged to expel Carlos Afú for having voted in favor of the Spadafora nomination, Afú responded with an even greater bombshell. He accused PRD secretary general, and already presumptive presidential nominee, Martín Torrijos, of taking money (possibly passed on by Cigarruista), from the government and distributing it to the PRD deputies to approve CEMIS, their landmark project for the development of Colon. Press investigations soon revealed a series of problematic aspects of the CEMIS project and questions about the more advanced Figali Convention Center. The resultant public outcry over seemingly minor or quirky cases of corruption tarred both government and opposition figures.[67]

Controversy continued for months and eventually killed the CEMIS project, but the Supreme Court abruptly halted further investigation of the Afú accusations. Chief Judge Arjona and several other justices voted not

[66] Law 23 in 2001 created the second maritime tribunal, see www.monografias.com/trabajos81/tribunales-maritimos-panama/tribunales-maritimos-panama.shtml.

[67] The Afú episode kicks off Guevara Mann's *Political Careers*, 1–2. Cf. also 222–23.

to intervene, but two thirds argued that the investigations violated the parliamentary immunity of the accused deputies. Arjona and his allies continued planning to reform the justice system and presented the project in 2003 to coincide with the centennial of Panama's independence. After Arjona lost re-election as president, however, it was abandoned. A bipartisan group of justices vetoed Arjona's efforts to clean up the judiciary, at a time when polls showed that four-fifths of the people believed that their government was corrupt.[68] He would revive the effort later, however, in response to actions by the Torrijos administration.

More corruption scandals surfaced as the Moscoso administration wound down, one implicating minister of the presidency Ivonne Young.[69] Still, most damage to the public trust resulted from the lingering sense of economic vulnerability, unemployment, crime, spillover from the Colombian drug wars, and the migration of Colombians to Panama. Indeed, as the skyline of Panama City became crowded with high-rise buildings, conventional wisdom held that most were financed by Colombian drug money. The government reacted by cracking down on crime and illegal immigration, an operation aptly named *mano dura* or heavy hand. Results proved meager at best.

2004 ELECTION

The unusually early start of 2004 election campaigning highlighted myriad issues, including public concern with crime.[70] The PRD candidate for president in 1999, Martín Torrijos, laid claim to his party's nomination fourteen months before the general election.[71] While crime and border

[68] Arjona's proposal for judicial reform can be found in *Justicia Panameña: Perspectivas Históricas* (Órgano Judicial de la República de Panamá, 2003), "La Justicia Panameña ante el Nuevo Siglo," 281–310. See also Pérez et al., "The Political Culture of Democracy in Panama." 97–105, www.vanderbilt.edu/lapop/panama/2004-politicalculture.pdf.

[69] On the third anniversary of the administration, the editorial staff of a leading newspaper summarized the litany of scandals, "Lo que no se olvida," *Panamá América,* Sept. 1, 2002. The Minister was accused of having approved a campaign of telephone intercepts against more than a hundred persons: "Ministra Ivonne Young acude a la Procuraduría," *La Prensa,* Nov. 22, 2002.

[70] Author Bigler held meetings with Martín Torrijos from 2000 to 2003, the last a spontaneous one during a fishing tournament on Lake Gatun during the summer of 2003, a few months after he won his party's primary election. Torrijos believed that his 1999 candidacy suffered from the short seven months it had to gather momentum.

[71] Martín Torrijos used his position as Secretary General of the party to reform its internal procedures in preparation for the primary election of March 2003. Many believed that the outcome of the PRD convention in 2002, which Bigler attended as an observer,

security remained salient in the campaign, observers also remarked on the image of corruption that the Moscoso government showed to the world. In response, the president's energetic foreign minister, José Miguel Alemán, passed his chancery duties to his longtime deputy, Harmodio Arias, to get his own campaign started.

Just as formal campaigning got underway in Fall 2003, two events framed thinking and commentary about the nation. First, the United States uncharacteristically waded into local politics. At the October convention of the National Chamber of Commerce, Industry and Agriculture, attended by President Moscoso and members of her cabinet, US ambassador Linda Watt delivered a scathing indictment of political corruption. The envoy argued that the United States was not slowing negotiations for a free trade agreement, but rather that Panama's corruption undermined its global competitiveness.[72] Neither the president nor her foreign minister responded to Watt – rather, the minister of the presidency, Ivonne Young, declared that they would demand an explanation from the State Department. At the same time, vice president Dominador Kaiser Bazán showed some sympathy with Watt's statement, noting, ironically, that "one cannot block out the sun with one's hand."

The second event occurred in early November, during a visit by US secretary of state Colin Powell, ostensibly to honor the centennial of Panama's independence. The media gave his presence heavy coverage, even though he was outranked by many visiting heads of state. His remarks made two points: that Panama was doing a good job running the Canal and that he agreed with Ambassador Watt's earlier remarks regarding corruption.[73]

Despite media attention to corruption and crime/security issues, polling showed that more people were upset that they did not benefit much from economic growth. A Latin American Public Opinion Poll conducted in March 2004 showed that about half the people named unemployment

enabled Torrijos to increase his control of leadership positions and decided the victory he obtained over his four rivals. His percentage of the vote in the PRD primary, however, rose from 56 percent of 368,000 votes in 1998 to 98 percent of 480,000 ballots in 2003, reflecting his overwhelming popularity.

[72] Telephone interviews with Ambassador Linda Watt, August 1, 17, and 23, 2016. She explained that the speech was to inaugurate a new embassy program of support for civic society anti-corruption efforts. She did not remember either the president or minister Young raising objections to her about it.

[73] Ambassador Watt explained during her interview that the mention of corruption by Powell was at his own initiative because the hurried nature of his trip and arrival did not allow her to brief him before the ceremony.

and about one in five other economic difficulties as the most important issues in the election. Only 12 percent cited corruption and 11 percent crime. Yet candidate Alemán could not have been pleased when new reminders of the Moscoso scandals arose as the campaign drew to a close. Word leaked out that the United States had revoked visas, allegedly for corrupt practices, for Supreme Court magistrates Spadafora and Cigarruista, as well as Bertilda Garcia, the director of the Panama Maritime Authority.

The long election campaign ended up delivering a sound rejection of the Moscoso administration. Alemán, the president's favorite among her retinue of young ministers, ended up splitting the party and alienating former president Endara, prompting him to run on the rival Solidarity ticket. The final vote tabulation showed that Endara far outstripped Alemán, 31 vs. 16 percent of the vote.[74] Seventy-seven percent of eligible voters flocked to the polls, an unusually high turnout even for Panama, to declare their desire to partake more in the country's increasingly visible progress. PRD presidential candidate Martín Torrijos won over 47 percent of the vote, the greatest plurality yet under the restored democracy, and enabled his party to re-establish a majority in the National Assembly.

The Arnulfistas, now calling themselves Panameñistas, did almost as poorly in Assembly races as they did at the head of the ticket. After having pieced together coalition after coalition to hold their own for five years, the party barely elected seventeen deputies, less than a quarter of the seats available. Clearly, if the electorate wished to deliver a message to the Moscoso administration, it conveyed its deep disappointment with her five years in office.

* * * *

At the start of the new millennium, the transition to Panamanian control of the Canal, as detailed in Chapter 7, worked out more smoothly and to the benefit of Panama than even the well-managed election process. Although the government party was rebuffed in the election, president Moscoso had overcome recalcitrant opposition and a troubled start to move the country ahead.

Despite the difficult economic conditions, empty treasury, and sabotage by many outgoing officials, Moscoso turned out to be a capable dealmaker who advanced much of the Arnulfista agenda for Panama. Right at

[74] Ebrahim Asvat discussed the situation in "Ejercicio presidential, simpatía por Endara," Aug. 4, 2003, in his collected newspaper columns, *Bitácora del president*, 50.

the start, she avoided the PRD attempt to pack the Supreme Court, and throughout her term she patched together a variety of coalitions in the Assembly to pass budgets and other key bills despite her party's legislative weakness.

Panama's special relationship with the United States came to a confusing conclusion, with Panama frustrated over its inability to get the US to remove unexploded munitions (UXO) from the Canal area. Yet some of the Moscoso's most noteworthy achievements came unexpectedly in security cooperation with the United States. Not only did she secure access to financial and material support, but her administration facilitated defense of the Canal, advanced the Salas-Becker accord on law enforcement cooperation, and enabled Panama to join with the United States on reforming the global regime on maritime security. Support provided by the United States also helped to upgrade Panama's security forces and underwrote their border security and air and naval assets.

The sometimes painful, always controversial, and hopefully healing work of the Truth Commission helped to elucidate crimes and abuses by the military governments from 1968 to 1989. Its revelations assisted the families of some of the victims, documented the excesses and human rights abuses, advocated for transparency and accountability in government, and buttressed the traditionally weak public support for the independence of the media and judiciary.

Moscoso all but abandoned her early goal of alleviating poverty due to early economic difficulties, so, as in the past Panama continued its lopsided economic progress, favoring business and professional elites and foreign investors. Growth for the country rose largely due to the revenue stream from the Canal, and foreign investment increased and opened the economy further to global commerce and tourism. Perhaps most significantly, the Moscoso administration did advance the country's long-term aspiration to develop a maritime economy based on the country's interoceanic position. Yet the lack of more widespread participation in the country's increasingly visible prosperity and a sense of regime corruption and insecurity all but guaranteed the overwhelming defeat of Moscoso's party in the 2004 election.

6

The Torrijos Administration: Uneven Progress Spread Discontent

[T]he Panamanian people can be proud of what they have accomplished over the last ten to fifteen years to put this democracy on such a stable basis.
US Secretary of State Colin Powell[1]

MARTÍN TORRIJOS'S INAUGURAL ADDRESS

President Martín Torrijos's inaugural address on September 1, 2004, took just over a half hour. In it, he made up in programmatic ambition for its short length. He declared war on corruption and impunity, pledged to reduce government debt and to put public finances on a sound footing, and to increase citizen security by fighting crime. He also promised to harness globalization for Panama's benefit by promoting free trade and more jobs and by taking advantage of Panama's strategic location. The less fortunate in society would enjoy pensions and access to health services through Social Security reform. He would hold a referendum on the expansion of the Panama Canal. Finally, he promised to amend the constitution so that even the humblest citizens could participate in programs to improve their lives. Torrijos's speech clearly reiterated campaign themes yet surprisingly distanced him from past errors and excesses of the PRD. He did, however, evoke his father Omar Torrijos's legacy, which he construed as deep socioeconomic changes, not simply the Canal treaties. The inauguration drew many world leaders, including US Secretary of State Colin Powell, ten presidents of neighboring countries, and global partners of the Panama Canal, such as Taiwan. Torrijos expressed

[1] Statement during an interview with Luz Maria Nolli of Panama's TVN Channel 2 the late afternoon following the inauguration ceremony on Sept. 1, 2004.

disappointment, however, at the last-minute withdrawal of Fidel Castro and Hugo Chávez, who severed diplomatic relations because outgoing President Moscoso had issued last minute pardons for four Cuban terrorists convicted of plotting to assassinate Castro at the 2000 Ibero-American Summit there (see Chapter 5).

Many international business and maritime leaders also attended the inauguration, attracted by Panama's booming economy and high expectations for a dynamic young president, whose governing coalition was strong enough to amend the Constitution even before he could undertake his ambitious inaugural agenda. The amendments had been made possible by the strong PRD victory and the unusually long period (May–September) between the election and inauguration. Besides, the degree of discontent with the outgoing Moscoso administration contributed to a wave of public support for reform. Thus, in the interim, Torrijos's Patria Nueva electoral coalition took full advantage to begin the new government with a set of constitutional amendments ready for formalization.

PRD legislators launched their constitutional reforms on June 24, more than two months before the inauguration. They proposed a long list, fought for them during the next five weeks, and got final approval for major changes, including at least minor revisions in fifty-seven articles of the Constitution, at the end of July. Their most significant achievements included:

- Reducing the number of seats in the Legislative Assembly from seventy-eight to seventy-one;
- Authorizing constituent assemblies to amend the constitution;
- Eliminating immunity of members of the Legislative Assembly from criminal prosecution;
- Removing the position of second vice president and second alternates for deputies after 2009;
- Advancing presidential inauguration from September 1 to July 1;
- Prohibiting cabinet and assembly member nominations to the Supreme Court;
- Requiring a referendum to approve the expansion of the Panama Canal.

Despite controversies surrounding some of these reforms, they won widespread endorsement and support across party lines.

Beyond these popular reforms lay citizen indignation at the judiciary's failure to take action against Carlos Afú and other legislators who either admitted to wrongdoing or where there was prima facie evidence of crimes.[2] Foremost among them were legislators involved in the most corrosive scandals of the Moscoso administration – the appointment of Alberto Cigarruista and of two former ministers of government, Winston Spadafora and Aníbal Salas, to the Supreme Court.

Canal expansion also weighed heavily in the public consciousness during the election, especially the possibility that it was not feasible or would detract from public funding for the poor. To neutralize these fears, presidential candidates Torrijos, Alemán, and Endara had promised a referendum before proceeding with any project. Thus, one of Panama's youngest presidents began his administration with an ambitious agenda for fundamental change.

A TORRIJOS RODE AGAIN

When Martín Torrijos finally assumed the presidency, accompanied by a majority coalition in the Assembly, the package of constitutional reforms

FIGURE 6.1 President Martín Torrijos and counterpart George W. Bush in White House meeting. Jim Watson/AFP/Getty Images.

[2] Carlos Guevara Mann, *Political Careers, Corruption, and Impunity: Panama's Assembly, 1984–2009* (Notre Dame, IN: University of Notre Dame Press, 2011).

passed earlier was sure to be confirmed in the new session. With a 75 percent approval rating, Torrijos's chances of rapid accomplishment seemed assured.[3] Still, people were pining most for action on the economy. Two months before the election, some three quarters of the population identified economic problems as the country's most important challenge, and 56 percent said unemployment concerned them most. In contrast, just 12 percent said that corruption was the most important issue, and 11 percent said crime and delinquency. Despite high rates of economic growth preceding the election, over half the electorate still believed that the economic situation was bad or very bad – clearly the benefits of growth were not widely felt.[4]

Torrijos enjoyed several months of lead time to put together his governing team. His electoral coalition, called Patria Nueva (New Homeland), had already produced results in the constitutional reform package. He also counted on loyal support from his first vice president, Samuel Lewis Navarro, a respected business leader and son of Gabriel Lewis Galindo, the shepherd of the Carter-Torrijos Treaties. His second vice president, Rubén Arosemena, had brought on board the Partido Popular, with its historic links to the Christian Democrats. It was a formidable team.

Ten days before the inauguration, President Torrijos presented his future cabinet in an unconventional fashion, apparently to demonstrate his ambitions and bona fides. He staged it in Jimmy's, one of Panama City's most popular open-air restaurants.[5] The event suggested that his team exuded technocratic quality, macroeconomic expertise, and business friendliness, often based on US educations as well as professional records. World-class entertainer Rubén Blades became minister of tourism; ACP financial whiz Ricuarte (Catín) Vázquez stepped up as minister of economics and finance and also of Canal affairs; Alejandro Ferrer, the brilliant young lawyer who had ushered Panama into the GATT a decade earlier, took over the ministry of commerce and industry; Carlos Vallarino, Panama's first superintendant of banks, promised to clean up

[3] Steven R. Weissman and Ginger Thompson, "Panama's New Chief Sworn In, Inherits a Diplomatic Tempest," *New York Times*, Sept. 2, 2004.

[4] Orlando A. Pérez, Marco A. Gandásegui, and Mitchell Seligson, "La cultura política de la democracia en Panamá, 2004," Vanderbilt University, Proyecto de Opinión Pública en América Latina, Sept. 2004.

[5] Cynthia Sánchez, "Martín Torrijos Define Gabinete," *La Prensa,* Aug. 21, 2004. Examples of the educational connections include Vázquez with a PhD in managerial economics from Rennselear Polytechnic Institute and Ferrer with a Master's in International Law from the University of Michigan.

corruption in the ministry of public works; international business guru and first vice president Samuel Lewis Navarro, who came of age during the Panama Canal negotiations, also served as minister of foreign relations; the ministry of health was led by the respected clinician and professor of medicine, Camilo Alleyne; and the minister of the presidency, Ubaldino Real, was a highly successful businessman as well as a personal confidant of the new president.[6]

The technocratic nature of the new team distracted attention from its strong connections to the PRD that many Panamanians disliked. Thus, while the light shone on past achievements and credentials, the PRD "old guard" tint of the cabinet was obscured. Minister of government and justice Héctor Alemán, minister of housing Balbina Herrera, and minister of labor Reynaldo Rivera spent nearly their entire careers as PRD militants, as did technocrats Vázquez, Vallarino, Alleyne, and education minister Juan Bosco Bernal.

Torrijos heightened the impact of his cabinet announcements by including thirteen new vice ministers, most notable for their business and technocratic connections.[7] He also appointed international lawyer, publisher, and Harvard graduate Ebrahim Asvat as secretary for planning and ministerial coordination. Finally, he revealed his intention to have new and yet unfilled positions for national secretaries of innovation in the technology of state and for the social integration of the disabled. It was a tour de force that he had spent months planning.

President Torrijos's first few months, in contrast, seemed quite undramatic, except for a national emergency caused by torrential rains, to which housing minister Balbina Herrera responded quickly and effectively.[8] Most new officials concentrated instead on organizing their new staffs. Vice president and foreign minister Lewis Navarro emphasized rebuilding the country's international relations, starting with Cuba and Venezuela, which were soon restored at the consular level. The Legislative Assembly, meanwhile, dominated by the PRD's delegation, approved the

[6] Samuel Lewis Navarro interview, Nov. 14, 2017, stressed the importance of showing that macroeconomic expertise was being marshaled to overcome the sense of economic stagnation that remained in people's perceptions despite the growth that had been achieved.

[7] The cabinet included only two women as ministers, but four more were added as vice ministers.

[8] Carlos Estrada Aguilar, "MIVI atiende pugna por titulación de tierrras," *Crítica*, Sept. 13, 2004; and Katherine Palacio P., "No quieren vivir entre aguas negras," *Panamá América*, Jan. 25, 2005.

constitutional reform package passed earlier, which needed ratification in a new session.

In November, US Secretary of Defense Donald Rumsfeld visited and stirred up controversy over the potential for remilitarizing Panama, but with the ministry of government and justice firmly in the hands of civilian leaders, the revival of the PRD military wing seemed less imminent. Critics' major concern focused on the number of police receiving US military training, a practice that harkened back to the 1980s military dictatorship. During the late 1990s and first years of the Moscoso government, from twenty to as many as seventy-five Panamanian police each year undertook some training, ranging from pilots and naval officers, to mechanics and communications technicians, to cadets in military academies and advanced schools for officers. Then suddenly in 2002 and 2003, the United States trained over 900 Panamanian police yearly, making the program the largest for Latin America.[9]

Rumsfeld's visit helped shift attention to increasing threats to Panama's border regions and a broader conceptualization of national security that the government was advancing. The threats included penetrations by paramilitary groups, drug traffickers, and international criminals and terrorists, which required more maritime and technological sophistication available from the United States, as well as seeking broader European cooperation. Joint security planning called for regimental-size police units and upgrading technology, especially in communications and surveillance. Torrijos reassured the nation that increased security cooperation with the United States was working well.[10]

Finally, Torrijos took a stab at addressing long-festering corruption in the judiciary, a major source of public repudiation of the previous administration. He began by removing César Pereira Burgos from the presidency of the Supreme Court, on the technicality that he had exceeded the mandatory retirement age of seventy-five. This gave the impression of action yet also installed a person of his personal confidence, Esmeralda Arosemena de Troitiño, as president of the Court.

[9] Betty Brannan Jaén, "Un Programa Masivo para Militarizar a Policías," *La Prensa*, Nov. 14, 2004.

[10] Lewis Navarro interview, Nov. 14, 2017; and "Torrijos niega que se pretende re-militarizar a Panamá," *La Nación* (Costa Rica), Nov. 18, 2004.

CONSTRUCTION DROVE THE BOOM

Panama's rate of GDP growth during 2004, rising from just over 4 percent to 7.5 percent by the end of the year, did not seem to benefit the working class much nor create a sense of shared prosperity because unemployment remained high, at 13 percent. Yet the high-rise buildings springing up all over the city, new shopping centers, hospitals, hotels, universities, and casinos being advertised or under construction, attracted international attention. The building boom exacerbated traffic snarls, even causing bottlenecks along the Amador Causeway. Inflation also returned, after a lull during the Moscoso years. The slow economic recovery of the new millennium finally showed clear signs of improvement, at least for investors in the construction sector.

In 2003, the various economic sectors had participated unevenly in GDP: for example, construction contributed 3.4 percent, while the transportation, warehousing, and communications sector was much larger, accounting for 17 percent. By 2009, these two sectors had jumped from 20 to just over 28 percent of the total economy. The share of construction almost doubled, growing at a phenomenal 18 percent a year, while transportation increased steadily to over 21 percent. Thus, construction and transportation together roughly replaced about half the combined contribution of the agriculture, manufacturing, and fishing sectors in just six years. Sector share changes of this magnitude rarely occur so quickly.[11]

Since the Canal contributed most of the change in transportation, warehousing, and communications growth, much was also beyond the public's immediate view. Most people believed that high-rise construction alone was driving the increasing signs of a boom. Construction cranes gradually outnumbered even the phalanx of existing high-rise buildings and spread across the city, from centrally located Balboa Avenue (now blossoming into the Cinta Costera expressway) and Punta Paitilla into new areas, especially Costa del Este, just off the highway to Tocumen International Airport.

Political developments in Panama City accompanied the real estate boom. Mayor Juan Carlos Navarro managed to win reelection in 2004 and forged stronger links between the city and Torrijos, with which

[11] Sector data from the Contraloría General de la República de Panamá. Financial services also grew steadily until 2009 and then fell back. Most of the fifteen sectors were steady or had small erratic changes. The overall pattern of increasing dominance of service activities has continued, rising from 74 percent of GDP in 2004 to 79 percent in 2010, while the primary and manufacturing sectors declined.

Navarro enjoyed close party, personal, and generational ties. The two cooperated on waste disposal, cleaning up Panama Bay, and restoration of historic Casco Viejo. Launching the first project to clean up Panama Bay in October 2005, after years of delay, generated special pride in local and national leaders.

Budget restrictions, required to address deficits inherited from the previous administration, limited Torrijos's ability to keep the boom going through infrastructure spending. On top of that, the public works ministry inherited a major scandal after the inauguration of the Centennial Bridge at the end of the Moscoso years. Finally, rumors surfaced that the flood of new foreign investment, especially from Colombia, originated in drug profit laundering. Thus, despite the strong increase in economic growth in 2004, Torrijos resisted promising more spending at a time when the public was going to be asked to approve major investments in Canal expansion.

REFORM AFTERSHOCKS ENDED THE HONEYMOON

The slow pace of modernizing actions by the new government aroused critical commentary, so in early January 2005, Torrijos got the new year off to a good start by announcing an ambitious plan for tax and fiscal reform. Upon taking office, he had discovered an alarming deficit of about $720 million or almost 5 percent of GDP. This had already hampered his ability to respond quickly to the extreme weather and flooding in September. After the presidential announcement, economics minister Vázquez began wielding the budget ax. Both also emphasized the need for greater equity in taxation along with austerity in spending, but their announcement of increased fees for offshore corporations succeeded mainly in mobilizing powerful opposition from the business and legal communities before any fiscal benefits could be achieved.

Vázquez went on to explain that the greatest equity advance would be to reduce the tax burden on salaried workers and to remove it entirely for those earning less than $800 a month, the legal minimum wage. At the same time, tax increases on offshore corporations, non-salaried business (professionals), and individual incomes, including a new tax on representational benefits of higher income individuals, would offset reductions for lower income persons. He added that eliminating the 5 percent sales tax on purchases in restaurants would help low income families. Finally, he proposed major public sector layoffs, by returning to 1999 staffing levels.

In all, these reforms sought to equalize the tax burden and reduce the fiscal burden from 5 to 1 percent of GDP within three years.

When Torrijos announced these reforms, he also stated his intention to hold public debates on social security reform and the expansion of the Panama Canal. The fiscal reform alone, however, aroused plenty of controversy, especially from the business community, which dubbed it the *saca plata* (grab the money) law. When Vázquez succeeded in ramming it through the required debates in the Assembly and getting Law 6 signed on February 5, opposition and adverse opinion proved daunting. Still, the measures stood and, ironically, the sudden velocity of government action worked to undermine Torrijos's approval ratings.[12]

The next storm erupted a few weeks later over charges and counter charges between Supreme Court judges over corruption. A civic watchdog group, Panama Anti-Corruption Front, accused former court president Adán Arnulfo Arjona of influencing the appointment of four officials in the office of the Solicitor General, Ana Matilde Gómez. Justice Arjona reacted swiftly, declaring that the real corruption was committed by three magistrates, Winston Spadafora, Arturo Hoyos, and Aníbal Sánchez. He then detailed how they had ordered the release of two notorious international drug traffickers without justification, as well as impeded investigations of weapons trafficking and of the misuse of $25 million donated by the Taiwan Foundation for hospitals.

Given the gravity of these accusations, Gómez called on the Legislative Assembly to investigate the charges. Meanwhile public opinion turned sour. Gómez muddied the waters by reminding the Assembly it needed to resolve the CEMIS scandal pending from the Moscoso administration. Tensions escalated when former president Endara described the court as a mafia, and the president of the bar association, respected jurist Carlos Vázquez, said "the Supreme Court has become an insane asylum which makes the whole country hope the magistrates will submit their resignations." Summarizing the sense of public disgust, the National Association of Business Executives (APEDE) described the whole situation as shameful and called on all supreme court judges to resign.[13] To calm the waters,

[12] ACAN-EFE, "Torrijos propone histórica reforma fiscal," *La Nación* (Costa Rica), Jan. 11, 2005; and Kathy Martínez, "Torrijos aumentará impuestos a empresarios en Panamá," www.mrt.com/news/article/Torrijos-aumentarU-impuestos-a-empresarios-en-7593466.php.

[13] AFP, "Denuncian corrupción en Corte Suprema de Panamá," *ABC Color*, Mar. 5, 2005, provides the fullest account. See also AFP, Escándalo amenaza Corte Suprema de Panamá,"

Torrijos created a special commission to propose reforms to assure the independence, transparency, and efficiency of the judiciary.[14]

Given the already rising distrust of government, Torrijos's proposed social security reforms unleashed a storm of protest. His approval ratings dropped precipitously from three quarters to less than a quarter of the population. The Assembly debated the proposal and introduced 142 changes. Yet the predictable approval by the government's large majority gave the impression that yet another measure had been ramrodded through the Assembly against public opposition.

During the broad debates over the reforms, opponents skillfully recast their intent. Rather than rescuing the social security system from imminent bankruptcy, they ridiculed the demographic adjustment the government sought as a "death law," postponing benefits until people were dying. Men would have to reach age sixty-five rather than sixty-two to retire, and women sixty. These changes, plus higher co-payments, would go into force by 2007. The fact that it might lead to staff reductions of some 45,000 positions was branded as harsh neoliberalism, rather than as the purging of feather-bedding, as the government tried to explain.

Torrijos faced a tsunami of unexpected opposition. The construction workers' union, SUNTRACS, joined with teachers, university students, and civil servants to form the National Front for Defense of Social Security (FRENADESSO), which also means "stop this" in Spanish. Protest marches and wildcat strikes erupted and spread around the country, resembling the 1987 campaign against Noriega. By May 26, as the second debate on the bill took place in the Assembly, about fifty organizations joined the front, and national coordinator Andrés Rodríguez declared a national strike. Undeterred, the PRD majority in the Assembly passed the law on the night of May 31, or between midnight

Hoy, Mar. 4, 2005; and ACAN/EFE, "Magistrados de la Corte Suprema cruzan acusaciones de corrupción," *La Nación* (Costa Rica), Mar. 3, 2005.

[14] The Torrijos administration's democratic accountability reforms stand as noteworthy in recent years. He reinstituted the Transparency Law that Moscoso had suspended, eliminated the prosecution of disrespect (desacato) and the National Censorship Board, and created new information and participation mechanisms, including Consensus-Building (Concertación) in National Development: see Fernando Martínez García, "El Poder de los Medios," in *Por qué nos odian tanto? Estado y medios de comunicación en América Latina*, ed. Omar Rincón (Bogota: Centro de Competencia en Comunicación para América Latina, 2010), 137–38. On the other hand, Professor David Acosta ("La Corte Suprema y el caso Arjona," *La Prensa*, Oct. 17, 2005) stated that "the comments by Arjona would have caused a social explosion in other countries, but here in Panama, everything just goes along as normal, a commission was named and will issue a report, but the Assembly won't take action."

and the rooster's call, as opponents put it. President Torrijos signed it the next day.

Strikes, protests, and school closures spread from Panama City to three provincial capitals by June 2 and gradually to most of the rest of the country. Violence also escalated, and organizers claimed that more than 1,500 supporters were arrested. The weeks of escalating opposition and urban chaos wore the government down, and on June 25, after the Episcopal Conference helped bring the two sides together, the president announced that he would suspend the reforms and hold dialogues on future changes.[15] This major step back by the government chastened Torrijos and likely delayed the referendum on Canal expansion by another year.

The successful campaign for approval to expand the Canal is told in Chapter 7, as part of the history of Panama's management of this valuable national asset. The Torrijos administration tried to re-establish public trust in its use of the resources provided by the Canal, beginning in January 2006. The president issued a decree creating PRODEC, a ten-year program to invest up to $50 million a year from Canal transfers for local infrastructure improvements at the municipal (corregimiento) level.[16] Final choices of the projects would take place in public assemblies (cabildos comunitarios). In this way, every community in the nation benefitted directly from the success of the Canal.

PANAMA STROVE FOR GLOBAL STATURE

The last-minute pardons of would-be assassins by Moscoso and the rupture of diplomatic relations with Cuba and Venezuela frustrated the new government, which saw Cuba and especially Venezuela as traditional allies of the PRD. More importantly, the 2004 formation of the Alliance of Bolivarian Nations (ALBA), under the leadership of Venezuela and Cuba,

[15] Juan Rivas, "Panamá: el seguro social es la primera derrota popular de Martín Torrijos," *Rebelión*, June 26, 2005; EFE, "Torrijos sanciona polémica ley pese al rechazo de los sindicatos," *Noticias del Mundo*, June 2, 2005; ACAN-EFE, "Torrijos acepta suspender mediante ley de reforma a seguro social," *La Nación* (Costa Rica), June 25, 2005. This dialogue produced Law 51 of Dec. 25, with most of the original provisions, plus a guarantee of no privatization and changes to stave off another financial crisis. These changes were not made, however, and the Varela administration recognized in 2016 that more reforms would be needed to prevent insolvency by 2021. See Chapter 9 and Salvatore Bacille Ladaris, "A diez años de la reforma a la Ley Orgánica de la CSS," *Estrella de Panamá*, Mar. 16, 2016.

[16] Samuel Lewis Navarro, communication, Apr. 2018.

FIGURE 6.2 Attending the inauguration of the expanded canal locks project in December 2006, front row L to R, Samuel Lewis Navarro, Martín Torrijos, Rosalynn and Jimmy Carter, and Alberto Alemán Zubieta. Teresita Chavarria/ AFP/Getty Images.

posed a dilemma for Torrijos. Should Panama seek a bigger international role in ALBA or continue promoting a US-oriented hemisphere? To keep their options open, Torrijos and Lewis had contacted Cuba and Venezuela before the inauguration and reestablished consular relations promptly, as we have seen.

Foreign minister Lewis, as one of the key developers of the Trans-Panama Pipeline, saw the potential benefits to Panama of closer relations with petroleum powerhouse Venezuela. He hosted a meeting of the fifteen members of the Caribbean Common Market (CARICOM) to discuss oil supplies. Soon afterward, Panama, Cuba, and Venezuela restored full diplomatic relations.

In the spring of 2005, the election of a new Secretary General for the Organization of American States (OAS) offered Panama an opportunity to advance its position in the region. After Lewis was elected president of the General Assembly, the ALBA countries supported a revolt in favor of Chilean José Miguel Insulza against a US-backed candidate from El Salvador. When neither candidate could prevail, the United States shifted its support to Mexican foreign minister Luis Ernesto Derbez. The OAS had never elected a Secretary General not favored by the Americans. Through round after round of votes, stalemating at seventeen to seventeen, Lewis kept the OAS together in search of a solution. A few weeks later, during a meeting of over 100 foreign ministers in Chile, Panama helped work out a deal acceptable to most, and Derbez withdrew his candidacy. In the end, only traditional Chilean rivals Peru and Bolivia, with one abstention, failed to endorse the hemispheric consensus.[17]

In mid 2005, Torrijos prepared for Operation Miracle, a Cuban goodwill program to provide free eye care for low-income persons in Latin America. In November, he escorted a planeload of poor Panamanians to Havana, where they received cataract operations and ophthalmological assistance. Additionally, he arranged for Cuba to send an eye care team to Panama in March 2007, despite opposition from local doctors. In coming years, over 5,000 Panamanians traveled to the island for eye care and another 44,486 benefitted from the work of the resident Cuban team in Panama. This was accompanied by broader cooperation in education and other medical fields, and the administration was impressed by Castro's appreciation of the importance of Canal expansion and its willingness to bet heavily on the modernization and expansion of the port of Mariel.[18] The Martinelli administration abruptly cancelled the medical cooperation program in January 2010.

The Torrijos administration boosted its international stature in two important ways. First, it helped overcome another hemispheric cleavage to provide an acceptable candidate for a seat on the UN Security Council (UNSC). Second, the country became a significant actor in climate change and energy cooperation.

As one of the fifty original signatories to the 1945 United Nations Charter in San Francisco, Panama took pride in the historic role their foreign minister Roberto Jiménez and others played in the organization. Over the years, Panama had served on the UNSC four times, including three during the presidency of Omar Torrijos. Its fourth turn was unexpectedly gained under Martín Torrijos.

[17] "Derbez e Insulza disputan la secretaría de la OEA,"*ABC Color* (Asunción), Apr. 10, 2005; "Insulza, Secretario General de la OEA, *El Universo* (Mexico), May 2, 2005; Samuel Lewis Navarro communication, Apr. 2018.

[18] Samuel Lewis Navarro, interview Nov. 14, 2017, conveyed this impression of Castro; Ohiggins Arcia, "Las dos caras de la 'Operación Milagro,'" *Panamá América*, Jan. 7, 2006; and "Cuba y Panamá se enfrentan por operativo médico," *América Económica*, Feb. 2, 2010.

As during the controversy over the OAS election a year and a half earlier, the ALBA countries and many CARICOM allies united in support of Venezuela's candidacy for the UNSC seat. The United States and the rest of the hemisphere, meanwhile, supported Guatemala, which had never held the seat. When Hugo Chávez alluded to President George W. Bush as "the devil" in his General Assembly speech, the competition suddenly became polarized.

Voting for the open UNSC seats began in early October. All other regional vacancies filled quickly, but round after round of votes cast for the Latin American representative dragged out. No country could get the required two-thirds of the potential 192 votes. Finally, on the sixth day and forty-eighth round, the stalemate ended. Ecuador, then under the government of Lucio Gutiérrez, chaired the Latin American block and was embarrassed by the deadlock. Historic close ties between Panama and Ecuador, long dependent on the Panama Canal, as well as coinciding interests in free trade negotiations with the United States and in coping with Colombia's guerrilla and drug wars, prompted Ecuador to back Panama as a consensus candidate for Latin America. Panama's good relations with both Guatemala and Venezuela helped seal the deal. It finally won the seat with 164 votes, representing most of the world except a few of Venezuela's oil-dependent Caribbean allies, who felt one of them should have it. Panama proceeded to use its victory to play a vigorous role in the UNSC for the next two years.[19]

Parallel with its campaign for the UNSC seat, Panama wooed UN agencies to locate in the City of Knowledge. As a result, in December 2006, the United Nations Development Program formally named Panama as a regional center and opened several new offices there. The following year, the new UN secretary general, Ban Ki-moon, confirmed Panama's growing status by traveling there to inaugurate the new UN Regional Hub at what was once the US Army's Fort Clayton. Panama's heightened international posture also paid dividends when Torrijos participated in the Regional Summit on Drugs and Security Cooperation in Colombia and took advantage of the trip to sign an agreement for interconnecting the two nations' electrical grids. Torrijos's growing stature also attracted significant international visitors, including

[19] Bill Brubaker, "Panama Wins UN Security Council Seat," *Washington Post*, Nov. 7, 2006; and William M. Reilly, "Analysis: Panama Gets UN Council Seat," *UPI*, Nov. 8, 2006. The timing of Panama's candidacy may have been just right, because Rafael Correa rose to power in Ecuador in 2007, joined ALBA immediately, and became a strong supporter of Venezuela. He probably would not have supported Panama.

President Felipe Calderón of Mexico as well as the presidents of Uruguay, Bolivia, and Taiwan.

Panama's role in international climate change cooperation expanded during the Torrijos administration and remained on the agendas of subsequent administrations. Its actions had been buttressed by the transition from US to Panamanian control of the Canal and the assumption of responsibility for watershed management in the 1990s. The PRD committed to the sustainability movement in the Socialist International and incorporated environmental activism into its platforms.

In the 1990s, Panama's foreign ministry had participated in the development of the United Nations Framework on Climate Change and in the Kyoto Protocol, though without taking a leadership role. When the latter entered into force in 2005, however, the Torrijos administration became more active, spurred by extreme weather events in the mid 2000s that left tens of thousands homeless and scores dead. Climate change activism gained urgency and became a political obligation.

At an OAS forum on Energy for Sustainable Development in 2007, hosted by Panama, and in the UN Climate Change Conference later that year, Torrijos emerged as a leading advocate for private–public cooperation in renewable energy, as well as for mechanisms by which wealthy countries would support the efforts of developing ones to reduce carbon emissions. The next year, he chaired the International Socialist conference on sustainability in Chile, again promoting private–public cooperation to reduce emissions. In 2009 Panama created one of the first national committees on climate change in the hemisphere, bringing together seventeen private and public institutions to form a network for action. These efforts also laid the foundation for Panama's later path-breaking role in the coalition of tropical forest countries.[20]

BUSH'S REFUGE IN LATIN AMERICA

The positive relationship with the United States developed during the Moscoso administration grew even closer under Torrijos, who had graduated from Texas A&M University. During his five years in office, Torrijos had five working meetings in the White House, received President Bush for a substantial visit in Panama (the most exchanges of

[20] "Torrijos e Insulza resaltan importancia de promover alianzas con el sector privado para fortalecer el desarrollo energético," OAS, Press Release AG-06–7, June 1, 2007, and Chapter 9.

presidential visits during one term of office in Panamanian history), and fostered many other high-level consultations.

US ambassador Linda Watt helped her superiors to recognize Panama's success in managing the Canal and to pursue mutual economic and security interests, and this rapport was reflected in the presidents' relationship. As often happens when foreign leaders studied in the United States, university connections opened doors to closer associations. The ambassador had such school ties in Panama, first with ACP administrator Alberto Alemán and later with Torrijos and minister of the presidency Real, all Aggies. The Bush family ties to Texas A&M led to a special reception for Torrijos's first official visit to Washington in 2005, including an intimate private working dinner in the White House.[21]

President Bush's first visit to Panama later that year witnessed more advances in the bilateral relationship, and the new ambassador, Bill Eaton, built on his predecessor's rapport. In addition, Torrijos hosted US officials Colin Powell and Donald Rumsfeld, oversaw the month-long Nuevos Horizontes humanitarian military mission in Los Santos and Herrera provinces, and advanced negotiations for a bilateral trade agreement.

Bush's 2005 trip to Argentina, Brazil, and Panama sought to repair relations that had become frayed by the war in Iraq. He hoped that the 4th Summit of the Americas in Mar del Plata would advance the US proposal for the Free Trade Area of the Americas (FTAA) agreement, a hemispheric customs union. He would then reach out to Brazil's left-leaning Luiz Inácio "Lula" da Silva in a side meeting and finish up in Panama to support the proposed expansion of the Canal. Before Bush was even airborne, however, Hugo Chávez and his allies removed FTAA talks from the agenda and promoted anti-American demonstrations there and in other countries. Bush's conciliatory stance fell flat at the Summit, and the FTAA died a quiet death. Then, in Brazil, despite Bush's praise for Lula's leadership and numerous cabinet talks with his entourage, billed as the most important since FDR and Getúlio Vargas formed an alliance in WWII, Lula declined the offer of closer ties.[22]

[21] Interviews with Ambassador Linda Watt, Aug. 1, 17, and 23, 2016. The George H. W. Bush Presidential Library is located at Texas A&M University.

[22] Tim Padgett, "Why Latin America Bashes Bush," *Time*, Nov. 4, 2005; and Howard LaFrenchi, "At Summit of the Americas, no trade pact for Bush," *Christian Science Monitor*, Nov. 7, 2005.

In contrast, Bush's two-day presidential stopover in Panama could not have been more cordial. As the *New York Times* put it, "the friendly reception here was in sharp contrast to some of the hostility that Mr. Bush had encountered on a four-day trip to Latin America." Although some isolated anti-American protests occurred, the overall reception was both warm and interactive. Several Panamanian big-league ball players engaged the former owner of the Texas Rangers in a baseball clinic for children. Besides touring the Panama Canal and meeting with its executives, Bush also held discussions with Canal staff and strongly endorsed the expansion plan being developed. The President praised the country's management of the Canal and assured his counterparts that their quest for a tree trade agreement, by this time called a trade promotion agreement, would not be prejudiced by the deal with Central America that US congressmen believed Panama should have joined.[23]

Although President Bush did not return to Panama, his wife Laura Bush visited to promote inter-American cooperation in fighting breast cancer and a bilateral "English for Life" education program. Bush's Secretary of State Condoleezza Rice also chose Panama to host the ministerial conference on Pathways to Prosperity in the Americas in December 2008. Altogether, the bilateral cooperation and the many encounters between Bush and Torrijos created an unusual degree of trust between the two leaders that enabled Torrijos to serve as a trusted backchannel to Cuba and the ALBA countries on many issues.[24]

POISONED DRUGS AND MORE STORM CLOUDS

Just as the Torrijos government celebrated the favorable popular vote in the referendum on the Canal and in election to the UNSC in October and November of 2006, several calamities struck the country. The political crises of 2005 had prompted the government to schedule ample time and a level playing field for the referendum, mainly by leaving responsibility for an extensive public information campaign about expansion completely up to the Panama Canal Authority (see Chapter 7). It also reduced collateral opposition by diminishing the role of minister of canal

[23] Elisabth Bumiller, "Bush, Meeting Panama's Leader, Endorses Widening the Canal," *New York Times*, Nov. 8, 2005; and "George W. Bush in Panama," *Boletín Informativo de la Embajada de los EEUU*, Panama, Nov. 2005: photos/state.gov/libraries/panama/11567/2005/abushvisit.pdf.

[24] Interview with Samuel Lewis Navarro, Nov. 14, 2017.

affairs Catín Vázquez, still unpopular for a controversial tax reform in April.[25] Both the maneuvers and campaign worked well, and the vote was overwhelmingly favorable.

Just before the vote on Canal expansion took place on October 22, however, a series of news reports captured headlines, as Panamanians began dying due to a mysterious illness. After fifteen deaths from diarrhea, high fevers, and paralysis, the government issued an epidemic alert. Then, just days before the referendum, as the death toll reached twenty-six, with many more getting emergency treatment, the government revealed that poisoned cough medicine was the suspected cause of the epidemic. As special treatment centers were ramped up, dedicated Panamanian epidemiologists, with the help of the Center for Disease Control in Atlanta, discovered that diethylene glycol had been unwittingly substituted for glycerin in cough syrup dispensed by the public health system. Panamanian public officials, intent on helping people get through what was turning out to be another severe rainy season, had distributed some of the tainted medicine.

Later, the *New York Times* and others traced the cause of at least 365 deaths in Panama, and thousands of illnesses, to the illicit substitution of cheap and hard to detect antifreeze-like liquids for expensive glycerin in Chinese chemical plants. Spanish and Panamanian intermediaries paid Chinese firms top dollar for the barrels of what they believed was the glycerin Panama needed. Yet, before the Chinese government was willing to accept responsibility for the dangerous public health practices and lack of proper control over the exporting firms, Panama was rocked by new concerns over tainted toothpaste. Fortunately, an alert Panamanian consumer noticed some toothpaste from China that even listed the deadly diethylene glycol as an ingredient. Prompt action by Panama's director of customs, Daniel Delgado Diamante, resulted in the seizure of thousands of tubes of the questionable toothpaste, first in Panama and then through rapid international cooperation, much larger shipments to the United States, Dominican Republic, and other countries.[26]

[25] The government also replaced minister of government and justice Héctor Alemán with Olga Golcher, so the former, an experienced PRD legislative leader, could return to the Assembly, and made another PRD stalwart, Benjamín Colamarco, minister of public works. Victor D. Torres, "Las tareas del nuevo ministro de economía, Carlos Vallarino," *La Prensa,* May 6, 2006; and Kathia Martínez, "Panamá: Cambios de gabinete por tema del canal," *My Plainview,* Apr. 27, 2006.

[26] Articles in the *New York Times*: Walt Bogdanovich and Jake Hooker, "From China to Panama: A Trail of Poisoned Medicine," May 6, 2007; Jake Hooker and Walt

In this troubled environment, citizens learned that former dictator Manuel Noriega might be returned to Panama. With his sentence in US prison about to end, the government of France sought extradition for his involvement in money laundering. The government of Panama argued that the United States should first turn him over to them for prosecution of the far worse crimes he committed there. Vice president/foreign minister Samuel Lewis stated that Noriega had faded into history and that the pending judicial action in Panama would keep him from making mischief. Yet many Panamanians and foreign observers expressed concern that he might still have hidden resources and connections that he could use to disrupt the process. For example, sitting minister Colamarco had been the head of Noriega's feared Dignity Battalions, and Herrera had been a close collaborator and defender of Noriega after the invasion. The latter, a leading contender for the PRD presidential nomination, if elected, could commute Noriega's sentence.[27]

In the end, the United States extradited Noriega to France, allaying concerns about him, but the machinations within the PRD revived worries about political conflict. A top concern was the PRD Assembly delegation's insistence on electing Pedro Miguel González to preside over the Assembly. The United States had clearly signaled its continuing opposition due to González's alleged role in the assassination of US soldier Zak Hernandez in 1992 (see Chapter 3). Less than two weeks after the election of González, US Secretary of Commerce Carlos Gutiérrez stopped in Panama on a trip considered a prelude to the US Senate vote on trade agreements with Colombia and Panama. He explained clearly, as did several congressmen in press briefings, that approval of the treaty with Panama would be very unlikely if González occupied such a prominent position, and, in fact, the treaty took another four years for approval.[28] Clearly, an assertive new wing was on the rise in the PRD, and the lines of partisan conflict were also hardening as electoral maneuvering for 2009 increased.

Bogdanovich, "China Says Two of Its Companies Played a Role in Poisonings," June 1, 2007; Walt Bogdanovich and Jake Hooker, "Poisoned Toothpaste in Panama Is Believed to Be From China," May 19, 2007; and Walt Bogdanovich, "The Everyman Who Exposed Tainted Toothpaste," Oct. 1, 2007.

[27] Marc Lacey, "Panama Weighs Debt and Threat of Noriega," *New York Times*, July 29, 2007.

[28] Gustavo A. Aparicio, "Secretario de Comercio de EE.UU. aborda el tema de González," *Panamá América*, Sept. 12, 2007.

MORE UNEVEN PROGRESS ON HUMAN DEVELOPMENT

Torrijos showed his desire to improve the quality of life of the poor and disadvantaged by creating a new cabinet position, that of secretary for the social integration of the disabled (SENADIS). Martín and Vivian Torrijos, themselves parents of a disabled child, knew firsthand the struggles families faced to obtain services. With progress on social policy moving ahead slowly despite over two years in office, Torrijos decided to pursue a reset of his administration in 2007. His entire cabinet resigned in August to allow him to reorient his programs. He replaced five ministers and substituted nine other officials to give more emphasis to social progress. He appointed his second vice president, Rubén Arosemena, as minister of the presidency to implement these changes.

Observers familiar with the first couple recognized that Vivian Torrijos had been a driving force in the campaign for social improvements from the beginning. She pushed for the creation of SENADIS and urged it, in cooperation of the ministry of health, to conduct a census of the disabled. This was followed by a program of assistance through both families and institutions. Soon she carried her crusade to the rest of the Americas as well.[29]

Vivian Torrijos, the daughter of one of Panama's most renowned publicists, Tony Fergo, had worked alongside her father and was naturally gifted in public affairs.[30] Her personal appearances and genuine empathy for Panama's underprivileged became a campaign that embraced AIDS sufferers, Special Olympics, and Habitat for Humanity. She carried her message to the Pan American Health Organization during her husband's first presidential trip to Washington. The following year she keynoted the annual meeting of the health ministers of the Americas and succeeded in adding assistance for the disabled to their agenda.[31]

[29] The census found that 11 percent of households included at least one person with some disability, that only 2 percent of these persons had access to any special education to overcome the disability, and that 80 percent were not productively employed. SENADIS, "Estudio sobre la prevalencia y caracterización de la descapacidad en la República de Panamá," Ministerio de la Presidencia, Octubre 2006. By 2008, 2,100 families were receiving $50 monthly support payments, and the Fondo Nacional de Descapacidad provided institutional supports.

[30] Yovanska Spadafora, "Vivian Torrijos, una panameña más," *Panamá América,* Jan. 25, 2004.

[31] EFE, "Primera Dama de Panamá busca crear conciencia sobre descapacidad," *La Nación* (Costa Rica), Sept. 25, 2006.

Martín Torrijos complemented his wife's labors on behalf of the poor and disabled, even if with a little less savoir faire in this arena. He also delegated some of this work to other officials, as when he asked Balbina Herrera to take the lead in helping the homeless. As time went on, he increased his involvement in humanitarian actions to the point that it took clear priority over other administration goals. In late 2008, for example, he cut short a trip to Spain to direct field support operations for thousands of persons left homeless by another round of severe flooding.

In hindsight, Torrijos's progress on human development turned out more modest than he had hoped, despite levels of economic growth averaging 9.1 percent between 2004 and 2008. For one thing, much of the growth simply did not reach a large segment of the population. According to government figures, the percentage of the population living in extreme poverty in 2003 declined about one third by 2010, from 18 to 12 percent, while those in poverty fell from 40 to 30 percent. Poverty reduction could have been more pronounced had the increases in public investment been spread more evenly. As it turned out, by the end of Torrijos's term, almost a third of the population still lived poor, and an eighth were very poor.

Statistical indicators of human development showed some improvements over the period since 1990, while at the same time they reflected the challenges still facing the country. Life expectancy at birth averaged seventy-two years in 1990, rose to seventy-four in 2000, then jumped to nearly seventy-seven years in the 2010 census. The percentage of all households with functioning services in the home (water, sewer, electricity) rose from 45 percent in 1990 to 52 percent in 2000 and continued rising to 60 percent in 2010. Literacy rose from 88 percent in 1990 to 92 percent in 2000 and then to 94 percent in 2010. Finally, the average years of schooling also showed almost the same incremental rate of improvement, from eight years in 1990, to nine in 2000 and then nearly ten in 2010. The president could feel good about these results.[32]

THE BOOM BECAME MORE MARITIME

The Torrijos administration expanded Panama's participation in the global shipping industry. It already had the world's largest ship registry, accounting for as much as a quarter of all the tonnage navigating the

[32] Census data reported in the UNDP Human Development reports for Panama, 2002, and 2014.

high seas, and oversaw the regulation, training, and safety of more than one and a half million workers employed as seamen. Still, the registry had little direct impact in the country because not many Panamanians went to sea, few ships stopped in the country's ports before 2000, and the country had generally played minor roles in maritime organizations.[33] The Moscoso administration increased its engagement in the International Maritime Organization (IMO) maritime security regime and increased merchant marine training and port activities, as discussed in Chapter 5. Torrijos continued these policies and, moreover, engaged the International Labor Organization (ILO). The Panama Maritime Authority (AMP), especially due to the leadership of Fernando Solórzano, contributed more vigorously to global efforts to regulate the merchant marine. This resulted in the development of the International Convention on Maritime Labor, signed in 2006 and fully implemented in 2013, an important global achievement.

The nation continued to host Panama Maritime conferences, which had started in the 1990s, giving it an opportunity to show off its commercial vocation. These biannual trade shows featured lots of lawyers and service providers eager for closer relations with the officials of the ACP and AMP and in hope of contacts with an expanding clientele of international visitors. The 2009 conference, Panama Maritime IX, attracted an array of such attendees and signaled that Panama had come of age as a shipping powerhouse. High-level authorities included the secretary general of the IMO, Efthimios Mitropoulos; the international affairs director of the ILO, Cleopatra Dumbia-Henry; the vice commandant of the US Coast Guard, Rear Admiral Brian Salerno; the naval commander of Southcom, Rear Admiral Joe Kernan; and a vice president of the World Bank, Pamela Cox. Several shipping magnates, such as Philip Empiricos, and the CEOs and presidents of such conglomerates as INTERTANKO and INTERCARGO, container shipping giant, CMA-CGM, and a long list of representatives from international insurance firms, shipping service representatives, and maritime financial service providers also attended. Panama, no longer just a crossroads for global shipping, had become a true global hub for the maritime industry, which, in turn, helped drive the domestic economic boom.[34]

33 The registry included 6,654 ships at the end of 2005: "Interview with the Director General of the AMP," *World Investment News*, Dec. 2007, www.winne.com/pa/interviews/fernando-a-solorzano.

34 Joachim Bamrud, "Panama: Outlook Good," *Latin Business Chronicle*, Oct. 20, 2008, emphasizes that, because of Panama's booming maritime sector, the country's economy is

New evidence that Panama's location had developed a broadened logistical appeal emerged in 2007 and 2008 as the country attracted a whole new category of international business connections. The Torrijos government, like its predecessors, had worked hard to make the country more attractive for an array of international business activities, but it was not until the shift of Proctor & Gamble's Central American headquarters that the campaign succeeded beyond the traditional realm of maritime and banking enterprises.[35] With the relocation of over a thousand expatriate employees to the Isthmus, all the activities they directed across the region shifted to a base in Panama and to deepening partnerships there. The door was now open and the pathway created for a corporate migration to add to Panama's business boom.

MORE SPILLOVER FROM THE DANGEROUS NEIGHBORHOOD

When President Torrijos replaced his cabinet in 2007, he promoted former PDF official Daniel Delgado Diamante from the head of customs to minister of government and justice. Delgado had gained renown for dealing with the toothpaste scandal and enjoyed a reputation as a security expert with military and legal experience. This choice for justice minister partly reflected security threats facing the country. Many attributed these to criminal activity in Colombia and to political deterioration and outmigration from Venezuela, Cuba, and Haiti. The symptoms included drug trafficking, money laundering, tax havens, human trafficking, and a steady stream of refugees crossing the Darien into Panama.

Yet before addressing security problems, Delgado faced a partially dysfunctional criminal justice system. Since an incomplete court reform in 1997, jails and prisons had been overcrowded with detainees who, in more than half the cases, were unable to get to trial before their time served exceeded the term of incarceration for the crimes they were charged with. The legal community had come to accept that the best replacement for the existing inquisitorial system would be an accusatorial penal code, more like that of the United States, Chile, and other Latin American countries. With a working majority in the Assembly in 2008, the new minister got approval for Law 63 that substituted a new penal code for the existing one.[36]

not yet facing the effects of the global recession that started earlier in the year in the United States.

[35] Interview with Samuel Lewis Navarro, Nov. 14, 2017.

[36] "Panama Unveils New Penal Code," *Latin America Weekly Report*, May 29, 2008.

Delgado also dealt with emergency response mechanisms, shown to be lacking during recent severe weather events. He reorganized the Civil Defense System (SINAPROC) through a presidential decree. Finally, to grapple with rising levels of criminal activity and violence, he appointed Jaime Ruíz, also a former PDF officer, as chief of police and increased the penalties for attacks on the police and other violent crimes.[37]

To address worsening external security, Torrijos continued his predecessor's policy of cooperation with the United States in the new Central American thrust of Plan Colombia. This involved upgrading some of Panama's military equipment, beefed-up training for security forces, and more extensive cooperation with US military and law enforcement organizations. This initiative led to several historic drug seizures and increased cooperation with Colombia.[38]

Finally, led by Delgado and other former PDF officers, the administration undertook a major reorganization of the security apparatus that required a year of intensive planning and used executive authority during the Assembly recess of mid 2008. The five decree laws Torrijos enacted were described by Orlando Pérez as the first major reorganization of Panama's national security forces since the early 1990s. They responded directly to efforts by the Revolutionary Armed Forces of Colombia (FARC) to extend their operations to Panama.[39] The package of reforms started with the creation of a National Intelligence Service (SENIS) and instituted the National Police Law, which allowed former military officers to head the national police. This added fire to the controversy over the interim appointment of Jaime Ruíz to that position a few months earlier. The previously separate police coast guard, naval, and air services were combined into a single National Air-Naval Service. Lastly, the rapidly expanding police border forces were formed into a distinct National Border Patrol, and the Council on Security and National Defense spun off as a separate entity. Critics labeled the reforms a "velvet coup" and organized yet more demonstrations against the government, alleging that the reorganization constituted another step toward remilitarization.[40]

37 *Revista Pensamiento Penal*, Apr. 16, 2007, www.pensamientopenal.com.ar/legislacion/32344-pampa-codigo-procesal-penal.

38 The Salas-Becker Treaty is described in Chapter 5.

39 Orlando J. Pérez, *Political Culture in Panama: Democracy after Invasion* (New York: Palgrave Macmillian, 2011), 97.

40 "President Martín Torrijos' Velvet Panamanian Coup," *Council on Hemispheric Affairs*, Aug. 29, 2008.

Before he could implement these changes, however, Delgado faced allegations that he had been involved in a 1970 murder, forcing him to take a leave of absence and, in November 2008, precipitated the seventh round of changes in the cabinet. Minister of the presidency Dilio Arcia became the fourth minister of justice, and Rafael Mezquita, the fourth minister of the presidency. Vice president/foreign minister Samuel Lewis and tourism czar Rubén Blades remained the only pillars of stability, serving throughout Torrijos's entire term in the same positions.

POLITICS IN THE MUD: THE 2009 ELECTION

The presidential election started much earlier and eventually became the most vituperative two-way race in recent Panamanian history.[41] The soon-to-be billionaire supermarket magnate Ricardo Martinelli started his campaign immediately after winning 5 percent in the May 2004 contest. The businessman had first surfaced politically in the 1990s, serving as director of the social security agency in the Pérez Balladares administration. He had to resign when his attempt to privatize it and cut deficits prompted huge protests and marches, reminiscent of those against Noriega in the 1980s and the FRENADESSO demonstrations of 2005 and 2008. Still close to Pérez Balladares, Martinelli resurfaced by organizing the Cambio Democrático (CD) party in 1999 to support his patron's ill-fated attempt to pass a constitutional amendment so he could run for reelection.[42]

When his first political ally faltered, Martinelli repositioned his party to support Mireya Moscoso for president in 1999, earning himself an appointment as minister of the Canal and chair of the ACP board. In those roles, he oversaw the transfer of ownership and publicly advocated for the expansion project even before the ACP and the government were ready to move ahead. In 2003, he resigned from the cabinet to revive his political party and organize his 2004 election campaign against his Arnulfista colleagues. Such shifts in allegiance and outbursts of political energy gave rise to charges that he was an opportunist or a "rightist

[41] Martínez García, in "El poder de los medios," 139–41, held that "If something defines the electoral tournament that ended on May 3, 2009, it is the total absence of ethics and the absolute prevalence of money as a motor for voting." He went on to describe examples of "the systematic use of lies, calumny, insults, fabrication of events, personal attacks, and rumors," and the refusal of the Martinelli campaign to sign a pact of ethical conduct promoted by the Catholic Church.

[42] In 1998, Martinelli purchased a lucrative sugar mill privatized by the government, causing public outrage over insider influence.

populist" without ideology or scruples. Some even questioned his mental stability.

The 2009 campaign started with Martinelli taking off for the US Republican Convention in New York City in the summer of 2004. Working closely with his personal adviser, Demetrio "Jimmy" Papadimitriu, Martinelli opened doors to ideas, resources, and relationships with GOP stalwarts even before Presidents Bush and Torrijos began their remarkably close association.[43] During the next three years, and before any other candidate emerged, Martinelli used his private foundation and personal fortune to raise his public visibility by showering scholarships, school supplies, and other benefits on poor students across the country. He also took vigorous public stands critical of government policies and actions and financed other leaders he recruited to his hitherto tiny CD party.

Encouraged by his showing in 2004 and general dislike of the PRD government, former president Guillermo Endara announced his candidacy for 2009. His relatively early move, however, cost him the support of the Solidarity Party, which had sponsored him in 2004. This party was now being led by former vice president Billy Ford and former minister José Raúl Mulino but had no clear presidential candidate yet.

The contest for the candidacy also developed early in the Panameñista Party, perhaps because of their 2004 fiasco. With seven candidates seeking the nomination, the aspirants for the mantle were forced into the party's first primary election in July 2008. Despite the longer records of former candidate Alberto Vallarino, Marco Ameglio, and others, party president Juan Carlos Varela emerged with a decisive victory, winning fifty-five votes to Vallarino's thirty-five. Suddenly Varela became a serious rival for Martinelli.

In September the PRD nominated party stalwart Balbina Herrera for president. She had served several terms and presided over the Assembly, was a popular housing minister, and managed party politics in the poorer neighborhoods of the capital city after emerging as the mayor of San Miguelito during the Noriega era. Her early resignation from the cabinet enabled her to secure the leadership of the party ahead of her rivals for the

[43] Born in Panama to Greek immigrant parents, Papadimitriu, like Martinelli, finished high school and attended college in the United States. His fascination with politics led him to stay on in Washington, DC, to work for years in Republican offices in Congress. When he returned to Panama early in the 2000s, he joined the family import business while pursuing a role in politics. After being spurned by the major parties, he eventually went to work for Martinelli almost a year before the 2004 election.

PRD nomination, Panama City mayor Juan Carlos Navarro and vice president Samuel Lewis. When Lewis decided to leave the field to his cousin, the mayor, and close friend since childhood, Herrera's stronger position in the party enabled her to defeat Navarro, despite the latter's support from former President Pérez Balladares.[44] Although Torrijos stayed above the fray to reduce internal divisions, the contest became so heated that months passed before Herrera could calm passions and convince Navarro to be her candidate for vice president. Now, the veteran grassroots dynamo woman and handsome young environmental champion created a formidable team.

Herrera and Navarro seemed to face an uphill battle at the start of the campaign to counteract the wavering popularity of Torrijos's government.[45] The PRD platform promised to continue the outgoing administration's policies and a scattershot of new programs to attract voters: subsidized energy rates, low mortgage interest rates for low-cost housing, and more jobs to address unemployment. They also had to deal with the late-emerging negative effects of the US Great Recession, including the first bout of inflation in years. In response, Herrera echoed the familiar language of the development agencies, stressing inclusionary and human development programs.

Martinelli's 2009 campaign spent well over $35 million (an estimated five times more than the PRD), a huge amount for such a small country. Polls in 2008 showed a clear early lead for the PRD candidate because of its much larger membership base and her personal popularity, with Martinelli in third place. After Martinelli's vigorous and vicious campaigning won the support of the Patriotic Union and then MOLIRENA, he suddenly forged ahead of both Herrera and Varela, whose candidacy seemed to be stuck with about the same percentage of support (15 to 19 percent) that had won a weak third place in 2004.[46]

After months of pressure from Alberto Vallarino, Moscoso, and others to forge an alliance with Martinelli, Varela met his rival at an apparently coincidental meeting at the US ambassador's residence, opening the door

[44] Herrera won 48 percent of the September 2008 primary vote, Navarro 43 percent, and Laurentino Cortizo 9 percent.

[45] Ironically, popular approval of the Torrijos government recovered and hovered between 50 and 60 percent in the waning days of the administration, far ahead of the PRD ticket in the election.

[46] Martínez García provided monthly tracking polls during 2008. By the end of the year, with the competitors and their programs clearly defined, Martinelli was about six points ahead of Herrera.

for a merger. The two stepped into a side room and worked out the details for the expansion of the Martinelli Alliance for Change coalition, adding Varela as the candidate for vice president. Martinelli eventually won a landslide 60 percent of the vote, to Herrera's 37 precent (and Endara's 2 percent). His platform stressed major infrastructure projects worth $6 billion, like a subway system called the Metro, a children's scholarship program like the one his private foundation supported, and promises to battle against poverty, crime, and corruption. He also pledged a more conservative, pro-business approach to running the country, as detailed in Chapter 8.[47]

While Martinelli's electoral advantage rose soon after the merger of his campaign with Varela's, the dimension of his landslide seems to have been influenced by events later in the campaign that reinforced the country's predisposition against succession (*continuismo* in Spanish) by the governing party.[48] These included continuous attacks and disruptive political mobilizations by the left, government corruption scandals, a dramatic drug money accusation, and the sudden global economic downturn accompanied by an enormous spurt in oil and gasoline prices.[49] Thus, in addition to the impressive growth of the Martinelli coalition, the PRD candidates ran into a "perfect storm" of negative forces that reminded the people of Panama that they always throw out the incumbents, the one way this election was most like its predecessors.

* * * *

[47] Marco Gandásegui, blogs "Candidatos a la Presidencia sin plan de gobierno," Mar. 5, 2009; "Campaña con la misma propuesta económica y social," Mar. 29, 2009; "Martinelli y el giro a la derecha en Panamá," May 7, 2009; "La izquierda panameña y las elecciones," June 18, 2009.

[48] Panamanian scholar Raúl Leis R. called the Martinelli strategy a project to prevent leftist continuismo but explained that it was a contest of *caudillos* (political bosses) and not ideology, quoting the Organization of American States official observer report: "The negative campaigning obscured the political debate about government programs." See his article "Caja negra electoral," *Nueva Sociedad*, July–Aug. 2009.

[49] FRENADESSO organized mass protests against the government in February 2009, gasoline prices went through the roof, inflation hit 8 percent and much higher for basic necessities. In March, a Colombian criminal who had been arrested in Panama and extradited to the notorious high-security La Picota Prison in Bogotá, David Murcia, was inexplicably able to grant an exclusive interview to a Panamanian journalist to reveal that he had given $6 million in bribes to support the campaigns of Balbina Herrera and the PRD candidate for mayor of Panama City, Roberto Velásquez. Until that time, Velásquez had been far ahead in the polls but also lost: see Santiago Fascetto, "Murcia calienta elecciones presidenciales en Panamá," *Semana* (Bogotá), Mar. 11, 2009.

Contrary to the fears of many of their countrymen, Panama's civilian democracy survived and thrived under a second Torrijos-led government. The size of his opponent's victory suggests a dismal failure, yet the administration led by the son of the former strongman took office facing great expectations and performed remarkably well, despite some serious rough spots and frustrations. In fact, the list of regime accomplishments compares well with any of its predecessors. The PRD-led government

- achieved a broad set of important constitutional reforms and new Penal Code;
- reduced public budget deficits and created a fairer tax system;
- kept the Social Security system solvent and more inclusive;
- increased government transparency and citizen participation in policy-making;
- recognized the disabled and started the delivery of vital assistance;
- convinced citizens to endorse Panama Canal expansion, which it then launched;
- established Panama as a hemispheric, maritime, and environmental leader;
- maintained steady progress on human development and poverty reduction;
- continued development of vital infrastructure in the capital; and
- strengthened national security institutions and law enforcement cooperation.

In the face of such an objective set of achievements, the political frustration with which the PRD and its allies faced the election defeat may be traced to a long list of ironies that provide a counterpoint to Torrijos's legacy.

Strong PRD party loyalty may have caused some of its greatest setbacks. The election of Pedro Miguel González to the presidency of the Assembly delayed implementation of the FTA with the United States for four years. The nomination of PRD jurist and supreme court president Graciela Dixon for a vacancy on the International Criminal Court brought on widespread and international opprobrium for Panama's judicial corruption. The selection of rival presidential contender Juan Carlos Navarro as a vice presidential candidate helped restore party unity but may have prevented opening the door to a competitive electoral coalition like the one that triumphed in 2004.[50]

[50] Rafael Pérez, "Secuela de una candidatura: el malogrado paso en el terreno internacional," *La Prensa*, June 1, 2008.

The election of Martín Torrijos aroused old Panamanian fears of excesses of the left in government. Yet the leftist opponents of the regime time and again mobilized massive public opposition, demonstrations, work stoppages, and conspiracies to impede social security reform, to prevent coalition building for transportation modernization, to undermine development planning, and to sap the energy of the government and the patience of the people to cope with so much turbulence. Torrijos deserved some blame for not curbing these elements. He assembled an initial cabinet of remarkable prowess. Yet circumstances beyond his control often produced unfortunate conditions. Repeated torrential rains multiplied homelessness, the poisoned medicine catastrophe overwhelmed the health care system, and frequent cabinet replacements and scandals undermined the potential for meritocracy and created the sense of a revolving-door government.[51]

Despite the strides Panama made to overcome troublesome international relationships, those same connections still contributed to the 2009 electoral debacle. The unprecedented level of cooperation with the Bush administration was abruptly supplanted by the right-leaning Martinelli campaign. In contrast to the administration's rebuilding bridges to Cuba and Venezuela, domestic advocates for these moves proved the most disruptive force in Panamanian society, paralyzing Colon and much of the country just two months before the election.[52] Again, some of these wounds appeared self-inflicted.

Those who observed the perennially calm, thoughtful, and approachable duo of Martín Torrijos and Samuel Lewis, with their democratic approach to government, were perplexed by the turmoil and controversy that marred their term in office. This perplexity would be heightened by the flamboyant administration of Ricardo Martinelli.

[51] The revival of thirty-eight-year-old charges, later dismissed, against Daniel Delgado Diamante certainly appeared suspicious: Denise Lara, "Delgado Diamante responde a acusaciones de asesinato," www.Telemetro.com, Oct. 20, 2008.

[52] *"Panamá: Hoy es el sepelio del obrero asesinado, SUNTRACS hace nuevas denuncias,"* *lahaine.org*, Feb. 20, 2008, www.lahaine.org/mm_ss_mundo.php/panama_hoy_es_el_sepelio_del_obrero_ases.

7

Panama's Canal: Better than Ever

Great things are not done by impulse, but by a series of small things brought together.

Vincent van Gogh

KICK-OFF OF NEW LOCKS PROJECT

On September 3, 2007, president Martín Torrijos and former president Jimmy Carter set off an enormous controlled explosion to mark the beginning of the construction of the third set of locks, to more than double the capacity of the historic waterway Panama took control of on December 31, 1999.

On June 26, 2016, the vessel *COSCO Shipping Panama* completed the first transit of the expanded Canal's third set of locks, fourteen days after it left Greece on the way to China, and sixteen years after Panama took over the Canal. The pathbreaking voyage from the new Agua Clara Locks on the Atlantic to the new Cocoli gateway to the Pacific was witnessed by the entire country as well as sixty-two international delegations led by the King of Spain. Almost a thousand journalists also helped turn the world's attention to the enormous vessel. Meanwhile, the century-long daily parade of thirty some smaller ships through the two original channels between Gatun (Atlantic) and Miraflores (Pacific) portals was suspended for just one day.

Originally christened as the *Andriokonos* and renamed to honor the expansion, the enormous vessel carried 9,472 containers, more than twice the number on the typical Panamax-size vessels still lining up in the other channel. Yet by adding the new lane, five to ten of these neo-Panamax – the new name for the larger – vessels would add significantly to the total volume of cargo that the Canal could handle.

* * * * *

Explosions and operational milestones have been an integral part of the history of the Panama Canal. The original construction carried out by the United States in the early 1900s utilized sixty-one million pounds of dynamite and involved thousands of explosions. The recent expansion of the Canal also started with a huge detonation, but the rest of the work proceeded quite differently. In order to avoid unintended blasts and future hazards, the Panamanians first had to conduct a costly and painstaking removal of unexploded ordinance (UXO) left behind on former artillery and bombing ranges used by the US military. Like the original construction, the expansion cost more and took longer to complete than forecast, yet only six lives were lost.[1]

Just as remarkably, and despite the complications of thousands of workers laboring right next door on the expansion, the waterway continued to reach operational milestones. The one millionth transit occurred on October 14, 2010. New records for tonnage also continued right up to FY 2015, when just over 340 million tons (PC/UMS) were carried between the oceans. The Canal had not reached its first hundred-million-ton year until the late 1960s, nor the second until the early 1990s. Yet by that time, a remarkable period of expansion in global shipping made it possible to reach the third hundred-million-ton milestone in 2003. The expensive and risky bet on continued growth in demand appeared to be paying off as the work was being completed.

Data for the first two years after the expansion suggest that Panama won its bet on growth in demand. Other new records piled up. The *Mol Benefactor*, an enormous container ship out of Hong Kong, passed the

[1] Originally expected to be completed on the Canal's centennial in August 2014, but two more years were required. Final cost data are not yet available, but the worst-case projections placed the final bill at about a third over the original estimate of $5.25 billion or something over $7 billion. This compares with a cost completion index of 2.0 for the original Panama Canal construction, not including the cost of clearing enormous landslide debris before it became fully operational in 1920, six years after the formal opening in 1914. The expansion also compares favorably with the Erie Canal (1.5), Bay Area Rapid Transit System in San Francisco (1.6), the Washington, DC, Metro (1.8), the Miami Metrorail (2.1), and the Boston Big Dig (2.9). See Noel Maurer and Carlos Yu, *The Big Ditch: How America Took, Built, Ran, and Ultimately Gave Away the Panama Canal* (Princeton: Princeton University Press, 2011), 98–99.

long-standing threshold for the highest toll ever for a single vessel: on July 1, 2017, it paid $829,468. This was just the tenth trip by a neo-Panamax ship through the new third lane. Then, in mid-July, the huge new *Maran Gas Apollonia* carried liquefied natural gas (LNG) for the first time from the rapidly developing US facilities in the Gulf Coast on its way to East Asia.

On August 22, 2017, the *Theodore Roosevelt,* with a record 14,863 containers, made its way to the newly raised Bayonne Bridge in New York harbor facilities after paying a Panama Canal toll record of almost $1.2 million. By April 2018, three LNG ships were able to use the new locks in a single day, and a policy of reserving at least one slot a day for the new category of vessels had to be established. Even better than forecast, the Canal handled 403.8 million tons (PC/UMS) during the 2017 fiscal year ending September 30th (see Figure 7.1, the chart of volume of Canal tonnage and number of ship transits). These bigger ships now get through the passage as quickly and safely as smaller ones, while the contributions to Panama's treasury and the development of the country under Panama's management of the Canal achieved unprecedented levels.

PANAMANIANIZING THE ASSET

Once Panama's managers took exclusive control over the waterway at the end of 1999, they made clear to all their constituencies that they intended to make major changes in how they ran the Canal.[2] Panama and the US had already publicly embraced the idea of a "seamless transition," and it was on display at the transfer ceremony. They also emphasized that business would proceed as usual, so the absence of high-level US political leaders made it more a corporate than political event. Everything continued to work smoothly, in part because 97 percent of the employees were, by that time, Panamanian up and down the personnel roster.

Panamanian managers were determined to show not only continuity in operations but also improvements they intended to make. The three specific indicators chosen by the ACP to demonstrate this were efficiency, safety, and the amount of income from tolls paid to the government. All three measures were available and easy to update and understand: the ACP got ships through the Canal quicker by reducing the transit time by 9 percent the first year; reduced accidents from twenty-six to seventeen by

[2] This chapter relies heavily on Omar Jaén Suárez, *Díez años de administración panameña del Canal* (Panama: ACP, 2011).

2002; and increased the revenue generated by the tolls.[3] How better to contrast the ACP's new corporate efficiency with the more bureaucratic ways of the Panama Canal Commission's (PCC) old order. Yet instead of unflattering comparisons or criticizing the PCC, ACP officials expressed pride in their organizational heritage and commitment to carry on its predecessor's tradition of excellence in civil engineering.

The ACP's business approach to running the Canal had emerged in the mid 1990s, especially after changes in leadership instituted by Pérez Balladares (1994–99). The third Panamanian administrator, Alberto Alemán Zubieta, and the majority of directors who joined the PCC/ACP after 1995, had extensive private-sector experience.

Alemán, clearly the organizational pace setter, exuded a corporate mind-set that spread across the organization, while his charisma helped infuse the drive for excellence through the ranks. The scion of one of Panama's leading construction families, he went off as a teenager to study civil and industrial engineering at Texas A&M, where he embraced the Aggie esprit de corps. Upon his return, he ran the family business so successfully that Pérez Balladares selected him to lead the study by Panama's Blue Ribbon Engineers (see Chapter 4). The respect he won in working with the US Army Corps of Engineers, the shipping community, and US officials paved the way for him to be appointed administrator in 1995.

Alemán drew the ACP into close collaboration with the private sector in Panama, and at the same time he welcomed into the ACP professionals from the many trades critical to maritime transportation business. His personal drive for excellence fit well with the Canal's merit-based traditions and gradually became the basis for a new ethos of corporate social responsibility and operational excellence.

Other new directors who joined the ACP in the late 1990s managed engineering firms, construction companies, banks, and other businesses, in contrast to the bureaucrats, military men, and engineers who ran the PCC as a public utility for the United States.[4] Alemán and his new board

[3] Toll revenue increased 1 percent that first year, from $569 to $574 million. Since the amount collected from tolls varied, however, the amount of profit transferred to Panama better reflected its value to the overall economy. Such fiscal transfers could also be compared to the amount the PCC had paid to Panama. The ACP could boost the size of payments by cutting costs or instituting new efficiencies. In its first six years, the ACP contributed more to Panama's treasury than had the United States in eighty-five years.

[4] ACP Board members Roberto Roy and Guillermo "Billy" Quijano had construction industry experience like Alemán's. Samuel Lewis Navarro, Emanuel González Revilla,

members faced high expectations. Their own priorities were profitability, efficiency, and customer service, yet the party that appointed them, the PRD, also set progressive social goals first enunciated by Omar Torrijos. Thus, the ACP also began to pursue corporate social responsibility in its approach to business.

The Organic Law which created the ACP also established an international advisory board comprised of representatives of shipping companies and others in the global maritime community to reflect even more the concern shown for Canal customers, first demonstrated during the 1990s. The advisory board held its first meeting in Panama, just before the transfer in 1999. The next year, the board started a pattern of holding alternating biannual sessions in centers of the global shipping industry, starting in London, where its new chairman, and still leader at this writing, Canadian William A. O'Neill, also served as the secretary general of the International Maritime Organization following his distinguished leadership of the St. Lawrence Seaway. The United States was represented by Joe R. Reeder, who, in the 1990s had chaired the PCC board (see Chapter 4). Other American board members included a former admiral, scholars, and transportation experts, as well as leaders from finance and business, while shipping magnates, industrialists, entrepreneurs, and bankers made up the remaining international members.

SAFER TRANSITS AND GETTING NOTICED

For business as well as financial reasons, Panamanian managers had begun preparing to raise transit safety long before the turn of the century, in light of the burgeoning size and deepening draft of ships transiting the Canal. Knowing that the world would be watching when they took over, they raised the priority of safety even higher than under US administration. With help from the US Coast Guard, which provided a senior safety specialist as a consultant, they achieved a reduction in accidents, incidents, and delays. They mounted campaigns that recorded the months and then calendar quarters without accidents in dangerous sites. The ACP, aware that accidents caused disruption of business and

Moisés Mizrachi, and Raúl Montenegro Vallarino also had extensive business backgrounds, like earlier figures Fernando Manfredo and Gabriel Lewis Galindo. They contrasted with the more lawyerly, intellectual, and public-sector backgrounds of most of the other early Panamanian directors and treaty negotiators.

increases in insurance costs for shippers, made safety a signature program to demonstrate added value to clients.

The leading safety metric, number of accidents serious enough to merit formal investigation, achieved the steady decline that the operations division and others aspired to. Despite numerous record cargo volumes and the continued high number of transits from 1996 to 2006, the annual number of accidents fell from thirty-six in 1996 to twenty-seven in 2000, and then plunged sharply to just sixteen in 2001 and record lows of less than ten each in both 2004 and 2006. Under ACP management, the Canal suffered as few serious accidents during the first few years of Panamanian control as the Canal had in the early 1920s, when less than a third as many crossings were made by much smaller ships. Meanwhile, the decline in insurance costs and increase in crossing efficiency created a downward trend in shipping costs which helped restore the rising volume of Canal cargo, after a downward blip for the global recession in 2008–09 (see the Figure 7.1).[5]

ACP managers worked to make immediate gains in other areas, because polls showed that a majority of Panamanians doubted the ability

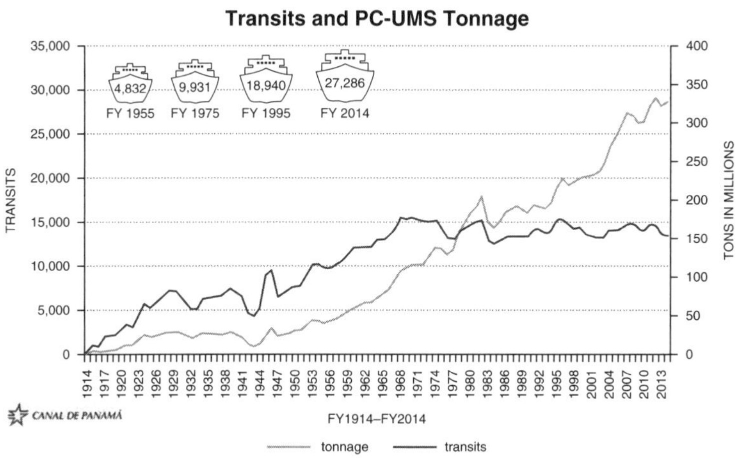

FIGURE 7.1 Chart showing numbers of ship transits and tonnage carried on Panama Canal. Autoridad del Canal de Panamá.

[5] Accident numbers are from ACP annual reports. Shipping agents and other maritime industry specialists reported the reduction in insurance costs to author Bigler in discussions about ACP performance.

of the ACP to do a good job with the sophisticated task of running the waterway. So they set out to reduce transit times and retain standards of excellence the Canal had always enjoyed, to boost their countrymen's confidence. They also diligently publicized their achievements in increased efficiency, cost savings, and other measures.[6]

In addition, the ACP promoted occasions for testimonials by prominent individuals, like the US ambassador and international visitors, and worked with the maritime media such as *Lloyd's List,* to point out Panama's growing capacity for handling nuclear cargoes and for bringing more women into the maritime industry.

Attainment of international performance standards spread across the organization, via approval under the ISO quality management system, a test first applied to the Safety and Environment Division under the PCC. After the ACP takeover, the next unit to qualify for the ISO 9001 standard was the maritime operations division, directed by Jorge Quijano, which covered the core work of ship transits and waterway maintenance. Second was the human resources and training division, under Ana María de Chiquilani, the first female senior executive. Later, nearly every division of the ACP achieved similar high standards of management performance.

At about the same time, the Canal's website began to attract attention as one of the best in Central America. Originally created and maintained by Francisco Loaiza, www.pancanal.com and its webcams that showed the progress of ships through the locks provided invaluable information to shippers, contractors, and citizen observers, while continuing to win international recognition. Gradually, such praise became so commonplace that some Panamanians ironically said it proved that the ACP may not really be Panamanian.

Long-range planning and market monitoring, established in the PCC in the 1990s, expanded under the ACP, directed by veteran *canalero* Rodolfo Sabonge. The organization complemented planning with a "corporate university" to integrate formal academic achievement into personnel development. These innovations, part of a new human resource plan targeting executive staff, middle management, and the general labor force, later rolled into the organizational master plan launched in 2004.

[6] When the ACP reduced the large supply inventories it inherited from the PCC, some predicted bottlenecks and service interruptions. In fact, the move cut costs – disposal of surpluses contributed to boosting transfers to Panama. While serving in the embassy from 2000 to 2003, author Bigler observed and reported on the ACP to the US government.

Finally, ACP leaders encouraged the adoption of business terminology to help reshape workplace values and conduct.

MARKET RESPONSIVENESS AND CANAL REVENUE

ACP managers repeatedly revised the reservation system for transits and created a segmented tolls market, showing further sensitivity to the needs of the shipping industry. Modifications in the reservation system, first introduced during the 1980s, allowed ships to reduce costly delays by paying more to move up on the transit schedule. Then, in the first decade of Panama's management, the ACP introduced over a dozen changes that increased the number of appointments for transits, allowed for changes, moved up scheduling, accommodated delays, permitted day-time-only transits, and ultimately offered auctions.[7] If getting through on a schedule was sufficiently urgent, why not provide a mechanism to jump to the front of the line? As the average fees for typical transits rose to well over $100,000 prior to expansion, the winning bids for jumping to the front of the line on occasion rose to nearly $500,000, mostly for passenger liners and some container and chemical products carriers.

Segmentation of the market proved just as important as reservations to the evolution of the Canal's operations. Under the pre-1979 Panama Canal Company, the same tolls had applied for all users and employed a special measurement to roughly equate vessel volume to tonnage for calculating tolls.[8] It only reduced fees for small ships or those sailing "in ballast," that is, empty. The original "one price for all" policy kept tolls down and indirectly subsidized the Panama route to favor US inter-coastal commerce. Tolls were meant only to cover the Canal's operations and maintenance costs.[9]

Panama's goal of operating the Canal to generate a greater surplus for the benefit of the nation led the ACP to base tolls on the value of the Panama route as perceived by its clients, what Panamanian managers

7 The PCC first instituted a reservation system with a single flat fee of $1,800 in 1983, but relatively few of the available reservations were used. After the number of large ships rose in the late 1990s, the ACP expanded the number of reservations for them. In April 2006, the ACP started an auction system to allow vessels to move to the front of the line for a fee of $25,000. This new service attracted more shippers, as shown by winning bids jumping from $186,000 to $220,000.

8 The Panama Canal Universal Measurement System (PC/UMS).

9 The policy of price neutrality, dating back to Woodrow Wilson, responded to British diplomatic pressure: Maurer and Yu, *The Big Ditch*, 146–47.

referred to simply as "the value of the route." ACP studies of ship traffic revealed the increasing variety of the vessels that used it: those with refrigerated cargo ("reefers"), different types of liquids and gases, grains and bulk cargos (break bulk), container ships, automobile carriers ("Ro-Ro"), and liquefied natural gas (LNG). Each type of ship generated a different rate of return for their owners. In addition, each type of vessel and market/product had different operational priorities when using the Panama waterway.

ACP managers decided that they should vary tolls not only by whether ships were full or not and by the total volume/displacement of the vessel, but also by the type of cargo carried.[10] The market that originally consisted mainly of general cargo vessels, tankers, and passenger liners became incredibly specialized and differentiated.[11] From the late 1970s through the1990s, the prominence of dry bulk carriers, especially grain ships so important to the US Midwest, shifted first to petroleum tankers, back to grain ships, and then steadily to container ships as the years progressed.

Besides market segmentation, the ACP also began to charge for additional services required by complicated transits, such as the number of locomotives and tow lines needed, arrangements for dangerous cargos, inspections, tug assistance, and so on. When the Canal opened in 1914, the original Westinghouse locomotives that kept ships steady as they passed through the locks cost $13,000, and rarely were more than four required for a vessel. Since the turn of the century, fourth generation locomotives made by Mitsubishi cost $2.2 million each, and Panamax vessels need as many as ten to make their way through the locks.[12] Given the huge size of the post-Panamax vessels now called neo-Panamax, the expanded third set of locks have done away with locomotives and depend exclusively on enormous tractor tugs, mooring lines, and the ships' own

[10] As described earlier, the first major change involved measuring the volume of cargo carried in containers stacked on deck, considering whether they were full or empty. Ultimately, the ACP simply charged for the total number of containers. This new measurement system began in 1997 and was fully implemented by 2005. The ACP held extensive public hearings well in advance of rate increases. The PCC began such hearings in the l990s to smooth the transition to Panama's jurisdiction. See Chapter 4.

[11] The latest variation of the toll structure, announced in 2014 for implementation on April 1, 2016, grew even more complicated. The number of different categories of vessels rose from seven to ten to recognize additional cargo considerations, including the number of passengers on cruise ships rather than the number of berths.

[12] The ACP assembled 14 of the 100 new locomotives in Panama and built barges, dredges, other vessels, and major pieces of equipment in situ to increase the skills of its workforce.

engines. Slowly, the ACP also began to develop explicit consciousness of its role in serving cargos, and not just ships.[13]

The ACP introduced its new system of tolls and service fees with modest rate increases in 2002 and 2003. Even so, these market-oriented changes immediately boosted revenues, a portion of which passed through to the national treasury. In 1999, the PCC paid Panama just over $138 million as a result of Canal operations, excluding other transfers, by far the highest payment ever made. At the end of the first year under Panama's mandate, this payment jumped to $167 million. Bigger rises in the following years reflected early ACP cost savings and drove government income above $300 million by 2004. At that point, the toll adjustments, added service fees and tonnage growth accelerated the rate of revenue increase still more, surpassing $800 million by 2007. Toll segmentation also continued to be refined as further specialization took place among shippers.

A modest decline in collections resulted from sensitivity to the US economy and a global shipping slump after the start of the Great Recession in 2008, but they fully recovered by 2010. Global market recovery and other factors boosted revenue above the billion dollar level for the first time in 2011, and then stabilized just below that level as the work on expansion was being completed.

By 2014, even after the increased costs of investment in expansion during recent years, payments to the country's treasury again slightly exceeded a billion dollars and continued at that level as the expansion was being completed. With the third lane fully operational for FY 2017, the fiscal contribution to the government of Panama again jumped to a whole new level: $1.65 billion (almost as much as the US had paid in eighty-five years) and the total revenue of the ACP reached almost $3 billion.

CONTINUOUS MODERNIZATION

Converting the Canal into an engine of national development could not be achieved with mere management adjustments. As studies undertaken

[13] Roberto Roy interview, Oct. 7, 2016. The August 8, 2017, announcement of toll changes showed the same sensitivity. Rather than increases, most of the toll changes were adjustments and discounts for load conditions, completing round trips within a given period, and changes in ship categories based on comments made by shippers at the July 12 public hearings: see ACP press release, "Panama's Cabinet Council Approves Panama Canal Tolls Structural Modifications."

during the mid 1990s had shown, the century-old waterway needed to undergo continuous modernization to meet the changing needs of global shipping. As Chapter 4 explained, in the mid 1990s the PCC undertook an extensive program of maintenance and improvements. Yet planners believed that the real challenge would be to accommodate larger and more numerous ships in coming years.

The waterway operated at near capacity in the 1990s, and much of its technology had become dated. The increasing use of Panamax ships did not permit continuous two-way traffic through the Culebra Cut. Locomotives and even railroad tracks that kept ships in position in the locks were strained to the limits by the size of vessels and rhythm of transits. The legendary hydraulic system for opening and closing the locks sorely needed upgrading. Computers and communications needed updating, as did lighting, navigation systems, and safety equipment.

Ship tonnage growth and watershed limits also required an increase in the capacity of Lake Gatun, along with deeper dredging of the shipping channel through the lake and entrances at both ends. Most of the tugboats, dredges, floating cranes, and other maintenance equipment predated World War II.

Finally, the ACP undertook a major expansion of training, educational, and human resource development facilities to replace those no longer available through US agencies and to provide ones needed for the ambitious new human resource development plan being implemented.

Despite revenue increases, the ACP had to budget carefully to cover both national and internal needs. Just the expenditure on modernization projects grew from slightly over a hundred million to several hundred million dollars a year, even before the referendum on Canal expansion. At that point, the ACP still continued comprehensive programs begun in the 1990s to further modernize and improve operations, increase the revenue paid over to Panama, and keep pace with increases in vessel capacity. Although not comprehensive, Table 7.1 enumerates major modernization projects that were largely carried out on time and within budgets.[14]

Modernizations allowed the ACP to continue expanding output, as the Canal had done historically, as seen in Figure 7.1.[15] Although the number of vessels using the Canal did not increase significantly after 1969, cargo tonnage rose steadily. In 1999, the last year of US management, the cargo volume reached a then-record of 227.5 million tons.

[14] This list is based mainly on the study by Jaén Suárez, *Diez años*, esp. 167–80.

[15] The ACP provided this graph of Panama Canal/Universal Measuring System tonnage that passed through the canal. During the 1930s, the Canal neared its then-estimated capacity

TABLE 7.1 *Major Modernization Projects, 1997 to 2010*

- Upgrading of locomotives and replacement of all track
- Installation of modern hydraulic systems for locks gates
- Replacement of electrical mechanical control systems with fiber-optic electronic communications and control boards for the operations of the three sets of locks
- Installation of a new locks illumination system to permit night transits of Panamax vessels
- Renovation of the motor pool and incorporation of hybrid vehicles
- Removal of 30 million cubic meters of material to widen and deepen major channels to 14.2 meters
- Deepening of the channels in the Culebra Cut and Lake Gatún from 10.4 to 11.3 meters
- Completing the widening of the Culebra Cut to permit 500-meter line of sight required by Safety of Life on the Seas (SOLAS) Treaty standard
- Acquisition of the Mindi suction dredge to deepen Lake Gatún
- Expansion of tugboat fleet from 20 to 32 higher power vessels and acquisition of 29 other new marine service vessels
- Installation of a comprehensive perimeter security system and state of the art command and control system

Following completion of the Culebra Cut widening in 2003, cargo volume rose to an all-time high of 333.7 million tons in 2012, and the proportion of the difficult-to-service Panamax vessels rose from 29 percent in the mid 1990s to 62 percent of the vessels crossing the Isthmus in 2014. The average size of the vessels, measured in terms of their tonnage in 2014 (27,286 tons), was almost 50 percent larger than the average in 1995 (18,840 tons) and almost three times the 1975 average (9,931 tons). Thus, the ACP accomplished its goals of making the Canal an asset of increasing national value and of maximizing the economic benefits of the country's

of 80 million tons (PC/UMS) of cargo a year. An expansion project began in 1939 but ended in 1942, anticipating victory in World War II. Many gradual improvements to the Canal, such as deepening and widening the channels, permitted increases in tonnage, even after the number of vessels did not. That is, 14,000 transits occurred first in 1969, and has remained at that level ever since. As the size of vessels has grown, however, the total volume carried by the Canal first surpassed 100 million tons in 1969, 200 million tons during the late 1990s, 300 million tons in 2001, and is expected to reach 500 million tons by 2020.

strategic location. The recently completed third set of locks is, in many respects, a larger-scale version of the modernization program.

MAKING THE CANAL MORE THAN A PASSAGEWAY

Panamanians had long felt frustrated with US operation of the Canal because of their exclusion from it for most of the century. From the sidelines, they watched the great waterway carry all these ships across their country. Few Panamanians had been hired to help build it (357 out of more than 45,000). Once it opened, only a token cohort of Panamanians were involved: in 1979 only 48 out of more than 500 in highly paid positions. Panamanian business was kept at arm's length, and the supplies needed to support its operations were channeled through the Zonian community that made the Canal such a large and irritating presence in their country.

To Panamanians, the US approach to running the waterway was called "pro mundi beneficio" (for the benefit of the world), when they thought it should be "pro Panama beneficio."[16] Worse, the Panamanian public knew the Canal Zone and all the wonderful facilities that it provided to a very limited population. Clearly, the transition period, as described in Chapters 2–4, provided an unprecedented opportunity to get Panamanians into the Canal work force. To make sure that the Canal would then provide more than a passageway, the ACP designed a vast array of citizen, corporate, and national engagement activities. These fit into five broad realms of interaction: commercial, national enterprise, environment and natural resources, corporate social responsibility, and national culture, arts, and recreation.

The Canal had always done much more business with the world than with Panama, so to remedy this, the ACP made concerted efforts to expand its commercial links to the country. It sought to influence business practices and spur development of the country's maritime vocation, activities related to the sea, shipping, and foreign trade. A complete overhaul of purchasing procedures increased competitiveness in the local market, decentralized acquisitions, encouraged transparency, and gave preference to local sourcing. The ACP began conducting its purchasing on its website and tried to end cronyism, insider trading, and patronage systems. It even went so far as to experiment with building its own heavy equipment, starting with barges and other maritime gear, to create precedents for industrialized production in the

[16] The impact of this experience on the development of Panama's identity is described in detail in Chapter 1.

country. It also tried to maximize automation of its purchasing system, which would advance information technology in Panama. The ACP became one of the first practitioners of online buying in Panama.

The ACP began to take an active part in many of Panama's professional and business organizations with global interests, such as the Maritime Chamber of Commerce, Panama Maritime Exhibitions, and the Panama Association of Business Executives (APEDE). Through its sponsorship and participation of its senior staff, the Canal promoted private–public cooperation and encouraged the creation or reform of new entities, like the Panama Maritime Authority (AMP) and the Panama International Maritime University (UMIP).

The ACP inherited many public services, including the two largest municipal water systems in the country and a hydro-electric generation grid based on its two large damns, a public enterprise responsibility it could not disregard. Some ACP directors and senior executives questioned the wisdom of keeping these operations because of the potential for political demands related to them and the lack of fit with the Canal's new corporate model. Nevertheless, they ended up retaining them with the intention of acting only as wholesale supplier, to minimize their political exposure and continue providing valuable services to the public. Another advantage to retaining water and electric power was it dodged the pitfalls of controversial privatization efforts in other sectors, which had sparked scandals and claims of mismanagement. Finally, this way the ACP avoided allowing outside operators of water and electric utilities into the heart of its watershed and environmental efforts.

Environmental and natural resource management became a core ACP responsibility, larger than for its predecessor pre-1979 Panama Canal Company. Instead, it emerged as a shared transition activity of the two countries largely due to the environmental awakening of the late 1970s, which moved both countries to work together to reverse some of the previous deterioration of the watershed. Ultimately, such cooperation became a poster child for binational cooperation during the transition era and led to the emergence of Panama as a global climate change activist.[17]

[17] The most important study of the Canal watershed was completed in 1999, by Panama's national environmental authority, ANAM, the Smithsonian Tropical Research Institute (STRI), and USAID. The executive summary, *La Cuenca del Canal: Deforestación, Urbanización y Contaminación*, was edited by Stanley Heckadon-Moreno, Roberto Ibáñez D., and Richard Condit (Panama: STRI, 1999). The PCC did not participate directly in this study, but, after the Canal turnover, ACP became the prime actor in all environmental projects related to the watershed.

Juan Héctor Díaz, the pioneering head of the ACP's environment and safety division, formed a felicitous alliance with AID, whose conservation funding expanded in the 1990s. On the face of it, environmental protection seemed marginal to the ACP's job of moving ships from one ocean to another. It was also fraught with political sensitivities because it disturbed illegal land occupancy, rights to natural resources, rights of indigenous communities, and even centennial controversies related to the creation of Lake Gatun and the losses of homes and lands by a significant portion of the country's population. Still, the ACP partnered with AID and its contractors, and they exchanged a great deal of technical and developmental expertise plus financing. This produced major assessments, action research, and implementation programs.

ACP managers, grappling with environmental issues, learned to operate in the "parry and thrust" of national politics. They had mastered important skills, like surveying, land titling, reforestation, and resettlement, meant to benefit the watershed's population, yet they had to earn political capital to succeed. Just the announcement of new studies for potential new dam sites provoked protests and demonstrations.

As the environmental steward of the most populated and productive region of the country, the ACP became a key player in a whole new realm of national policy and action. It played the key role in the formation of the Interinstitutional Council for the Canal Watershed in 2000 and helped implement its programs. These included reforestation, conservation, and public education. Partly through this work, the ACP fostered Panama's ecotourism business, which now rivals that of Costa Rica, long the leader in the region. It also has become a major force behind the country's progressive role in global climate change politics, starting with Martín Torrijos's administration.

Although the 1997 Organic Law intended to shield the ACP from political influences, and its corporate approach implied apolitical management, in truth Canal directors, by the very nature of their calling, had to wade into political affairs. Most early ACP Board members and much of the senior leadership believed in the progressive ideology of Omar Torrijos, yet those beliefs ran counter to the apolitical charge of the law and the corporate ethic, generating quiet yet noticeable tension. Surprisingly, UN Secretary General Kofi Annan provided a solution in 2002, when he began a worldwide campaign to increase corporate social responsibility (CSR) in the business world. This provided the perfect antidote for the ACP's dilemma, and the ACP management enthusiastically embraced his crusade. UN officials in turn lauded the ACP approach as a perfect example of the effort Annan wished to inspire.

Corporate social responsibility nicely linked the ACP's need to persuade poor rural *campesinos* to protect the watershed forest with its larger mission to ensure adequate runoff for waterway operations. It also justified major investments in education to convince the public that they now owned a stake in the Canal. The ACP *canal de todos* (everybody's canal) campaign was partly public relations but also educational, addressing a crying national need. This campaign set up public information kiosks with internet access in provincial and even remote areas to allow citizens to learn more about the Canal. It also donated computers to schools to educate rural and low-income children about the Canal and in so doing also opened the world of the Internet to them.

Meanwhile, the National Secretariat for Science and Technology (SENACYT, mentioned in Chapter 4) financed extensive internship programs in higher education and signed a cooperative agreement to work with the ministry of education. This included dispatching Canal staff to classrooms, publicizing careers needed by the Canal, and creating the new national maritime university. Because about 95 percent of its staff was concentrated in and around the passageway, ACP educational and outreach activities touched the majority of the urban population.

Finally, the ACP embraced Panamanian culture in new ways. For example, it named its first human resources training center for one of the students killed in the flag riots of January 1964.[18] In addition to symbolic acts, the ACP disseminated information about the Canal in the national media and facilitated student and public visits to the Miraflores Locks Visitors' Center. These efforts featured a website and a biweekly newsletter, *El Faro,* which has also been a key source of information for this chapter.[19] In 2003, the ACP piggybacked on Panama's independence centennial commemoration to get out news about their newly acquired waterway. That same year they opened a remodeled visitors' center, with exhibits loaned by the renowned Panama Interoceanic Museum.

To further educate the public about their Canal, the ACP launched an outdoor cultural program, with a festival-in-the-park that featured many

[18] The PCC tradition of human resource development continued in the ACP's priorities, especially in its Ascanio Arosemena Training Center. An example was a new navigation simulator for instructing Panama Canal pilots. Once operational, it was adopted by the US Navy for training US nuclear submarine personnel in underwater maneuvers.

[19] *El Faro* helps keep a record of events at the ACP. Like its predecessor, the PCC's *The Spillway*, it serves as an official house publication.

of the country's leading music and pop stars.[20] Held on the ceremonial grounds of the Canal headquarters, it helped to overcome the perception of the ACP as an aloof enclave of technocracy and global business. Salsa and pop music suggested that the Canal also rocked. The popularity of this event led to road show editions to other cities. Celebrities like baseball star Mariano Rivera of the New York Yankees and boxer Roberto Durán often took part. When film and recording star Rubén Blades took over as minister of tourism in 2004 under President Torrijos, these festivals became true showcases for national popular culture.

PUTTING PLANNING ON STEROIDS

During its first few years operating the Canal, and despite efforts to continually modernize, the ACP still faced a series of potentially game-changing events:

- Climate change raised the potential for extreme weather events, such as a strong El Niño, which could dramatically reduce rainfall and force the ACP to impose draft limits on cargo ships if the water level of Lake Gatun dropped. The proliferation of deep-draft Panamax vessels also meant that restrictions would affect a larger portion of clients. Another drought like that of 1997–98 might force shippers to seek alternate routes or to pressure the ACP to divert water supplies from other clients.[21]
- In 2001, container ship tonnage for the first time equaled that of dry bulk cargo vessels, for decades the Canal's main customers. How far would the trend continue, altering the total volume and the types of ships using the Canal? Would the change increase the size of vessels? Would growth of container traffic affect the other services needed, especially for transshipment or intermodal transportation?
- The sudden rise of China in the late 1990s, and especially the flood of container cargo exports to the US, portended major shifts in traffic and markets after the turn of the century, as well as complications for Panama's traditionally close relations with Taiwan. Yet how far and fast would China continue to grow? To what extent

[20] Panama's summer or dry season starts in late December and extends into late April or May.

[21] The 2015–16 El Niño also produced a drop in the water level of Lake Gatun. Fortunately, further dredging and returning rains avoided the need for restrictions on cargos in 2015, but they were required briefly in 2016.

might Japan recover its traditional second place position for the Canal? And what other changes by the Asian Tigers or elsewhere in the region would be important enough to alter market trends?

- Dockworkers' strikes at US West Coast ports in 2002 and 2005 drove more container ships to Panama and shook up planners' understanding of the business. The Canal's capacity limits meant that sudden upsurges in demand could undermine existing efficiency and operational parameters. Thousands of manufacturers and importers on the East and Gulf Coasts of the US suddenly turned to the Canal to restock inventories depleted by the strikes. Their prior reliance on the so-called land bridge, containers forwarded from West Coast ports by rail, now stood in jeopardy.[22] Canal planners saw that without capacity to handle the increased traffic, business might move elsewhere.

ACP managers reacted to these events by broadening their ability to cope with changing circumstances. The most important measure, a master plan to guide decision-making through the year 2025, gradually took shape under the guidance of Rodolfo Sabonge and later Stanley Muschett and Francisco Miguez. The ACP then created the Canal Capacity Project, under the direction of Agustín Arias, later with Roberto Roy, the chief designer of Panama's new Metro, to address the perennial question of expanding the Canal. Separate teams worked in a parallel and closely coordinated fashion to advance both efforts.

These initiatives produced hundreds of studies and reports in the early 2000s. The issue of traffic capacity (and possible expansion) zeroed in on water resources and ways to increase them. It incorporated extensive conservation studies, looked at raising the level of existing lakes, and considered incorporating more distant rivers and new dams into the water supply system. With at least six new rivers to consider, this rapidly became one of the most intensively studied issues, as well the most controversial. Despite the good will won by the ACP rural outreach

[22] The Panama Railroad, built during the California Gold Rush, 1851–55, was the major link between the US West Coast and the Atlantic world until the first US transcontinental railroad was completed in 1869. Despite the success of the Panama route, the opening of the land bridge across the United States almost put the railroad out of business. The best history is Aims McGuinness, *Path of Empire: Panama and the California Gold Rush* (Ithaca: Cornell University Press, 2008). See also the fictionalized account by Juan David Morgan, *The Golden Horse* (Minneapolis: Two Harbors Press, 2014).

initiatives, like land survey and title programs, many watershed residents and some indigenous groups vehemently rejected the idea of any new dams.

With an eye to new technologies that might be needed to operate enlarged locks, the ACP contracted with the US Army Corps of Engineers (USACE) for consultation and applied research. When critics complained of a single source contract awarded to a US government agency, the ACP asserted that the USACE's special expertise and record of collaboration with it on alternative technologies for new locks and gates justified the action. The valiant message was that technical expertise trumped nationalistic preferences.[23]

The ACP also made sure that it understood the trends, assessed the controversies, evaluated the resources, and framed the costs and benefits associated with choices made. Looking back, its most astute forecasts held that container traffic and the Chinese connection would become major motors of change and revenue for Panama. By the time expansion began, container ship traffic had grown as predicted to produce just over half of the waterway's greatly expanded toll revenues. The remainder was generated by nine other types of vessels/market segments with dry bulk at about a fifth, vehicle ships (Ro-Ro) a tenth, chemicals just over a twentieth and petroleum behind them, and five categories at one or two percent.

The soundness of increased and adjustable market segmentation for planning and decision-making was also demonstrated by the ACP's experience with the commodities underlying the market segments. For years, the impact of petroleum-based products on the Canal was difficult to recognize because it was divided by the types of vessels and the form in which it was carried, i.e., as chemicals, LNG, and so on. Since the Canal did not handle large super tankers, its significance in the field was neglected. Gas discoveries in the Gulf Coast, however, and the opening of the third lane of the Canal to accommodate LNG shipments changed everything. Thus, in 2017, the tonnage of petroleum products transiting the Canal suddenly surpassed even that of the cargos on container ships. In the early 2000s, when the details of the revised toll structure were being developed, some believed that dry or liquid bulk cargos would retake the lead or that vehicle carriers or some new traffic combination would surge. LNG had not been expected, and container ships accounted for less than a fifth of tolls. ACP projections proved sound, however, and they

[23] The USACE had created a record of trust and collaboration in its work on the Blue Ribbon Commission, described in Chapter 4.

determined that the Canal could base its expansion plan at least on rising container traffic, driven especially by the China-to-East-Coast connection. As their predictions were proving sound, the arguments favoring an expansion plan became more immediate.

Yet Canal expansion also hinged on access to more water to support the larger third locks, an issue that could undermine ACP plans, as environmental and indigenous community activists suggested. If each transit required 55 million gallons of water, where would the water come from to accommodate even larger ships and greatly expanded locks? The 2004 presidential election barely raised the expansion issue, yet a great deal of controversy during the campaign centered on the potential for incorporating more rivers and dams into the watershed to supply additional water. Thus a new challenge arose that was already shrouded in controversy.

A RIGHT-SIZE EXPANSION PLAN

ACP managers became convinced that the time for expanding the Canal had come as the new century advanced. Evidence of this included increases in the size and specialization of ships and port facilities and the steady rise of their cargo volume. In particular, transit surges during the 2002 and 2005 West Coast dock strikes and intermittent closures of one of the Canal's two lanes for modernization and maintenance work argued for building a larger set of locks. Already, long queues of ships waiting to transit the Canal, especially in 2005, made some question whether the decision had been too painstaking, jeopardizing their preference for orderly growth and efficiency. Managers shifted from capacity studies to a plan for expanding the Canal itself.

Newly elected president Martín Torrijos soon also took up the banner of expansion. Many senior officials in his government also provided a bridge to the ACP. Ricaurte "Catín" Vásquez had worked under president Pérez Balladares for years before becoming the chief financial officer and also deputy administrator of the ACP during the Moscoso administration. In 2004, he became minister of finance as well as canal affairs and the chairman of the board of the ACP. Additionally, vice president and foreign minister Samuel Lewis Navarro, son of lead treaty negotiator Gabriel Lewis Galindo, had served on the ACP board. His senior advisor, Adolfo Ahumada, was virtually a lifelong advocate for expanding Panama's role in the Canal. He belonged to the generation of 1964 martyrs, had served as labor minister for the PRD, supported the treaty negotiations, and participated in writing the Organic Law that created the ACP. He spent more years on the ACP board than any other member.

Given the administration's close alignment with and support for the ACP, the path toward expansion became more definite; in August 2005, the ACP board unanimously confirmed Alberto Alemán for a second seven-year term as administrator. His success in leading the implementation of new corporate and national leadership roles for the ACP earned him the board's, and increasingly the nation's, trust as the chief architect for the emerging expansion plan.

In addition to this liaison team, Torrijos's vision of Panama and its road to economic development, detailed in Chapter 6, rested on continued Canal progress and making his country a business hub for the Americas. In contrast to his predecessor, president Moscoso, who had kept her distance from the ACP, Torrijos used a ceremonial visit to the ACP at the beginning of his term to broadcast his view of the importance of the waterway for Panama's development. Even US president George W. Bush contributed to the cheerleading for Canal expansion and actively engaged Canal personnel during his visit in November 2005 to promote a free trade agreement between the two nations.[24] Finally, his PRODEC program helped link the Canal's financial success to local development efforts.

Once Canal expansion became a public issue, which would be decided in a national plebiscite, backers had to establish a formula to achieve their goals and convince the public. How large would the new locks be? How would the water supply be provided? What system of gates would they use? Would still larger and costlier locomotives be needed? How would the ACP cover construction costs and still raise the flow of revenue to the government? These and many other questions had to be resolved, and a gigantic public education campaign would be required to answer the doubts they aroused.

The ACP and other agencies studied such questions, examined laws and precedents, consulted experts, and tried to resolve them. They reviewed earlier expansion efforts and undertook hundreds of new studies. From early on, they pledged to seek transparency and public approval for the enterprise. The contest for popular support was engaged.

[24] This expression exaggerates the cooperation engendered by the Bush stopover in Panama in November 2005. He did have lengthy discussions with Canal employees about their work on and the future of the waterway.

The Canal expansion debate, which ended in approval, stimulated heated controversy and emotional outbursts. Part of the heat came from government and ACP-financed publicity in favor of the project. In the end, the plan underwent serious modifications. Most of the changes resulted from continued examination of the issues by the ACP, and, not surprisingly, most of them had been anticipated beforehand by staff. Examples of some major adjustments in the original designs and educated guesses about what prompted the adjustments include:

- Opposition to new dams and careful study of technological alternatives prompted the ACP to discover and adopt an ingenious system for water recycling basins that could operate the larger locks with about the same amount of water.
- Claims that the expansion would only benefit the wealthy led to a scaled-back design, far less than the original estimate of $8 billion or more, so that transfers to the treasury would begin earlier, presumably for the benefit of the poor.[25]
- Concerns that private capital markets would profit unduly from the expansion led planners to rely on public international and domestic funding for the project.[26]
- Criticisms about the lack of educational and social spending induced the government to agree that some of the Canal revenues be earmarked for these purposes.

After a remarkable public debate on general ideas about expansion, Torrijos unveiled the final plan for the third locks in an April 2006 event at the Atlapa convention center. Over the next few weeks the government rolled out a public information campaign that would lead to a referendum in October. Over 200,000 persons, about one out of every ten adults, participated in forums organized all over the country. Media covered the debate, mostly sympathetic to the government. Still, not everyone went along.

[25] Locks large enough to handle emerging mega ships (greater than 14,200 TEU capacity) would have cost over three times more and taken much longer to build. The ACP adopted a prudent compromise, calculating that mega ships would represent only a tiny share of global shipping during the first fifteen years after the expansion.

[26] The ACP's high investment grade rating allowed it to borrow $2.3 billion at favorable terms, well under half the cost of the project, avoiding costlier bond emissions and private financing. A consortium of international financial institutions provided the funds for twenty years, with a ten-year grace period: the Japan Bank for International Cooperation ($800 million), the European Investment Bank ($500 million), the Inter-American Development Bank ($400 million), the Corporación Andina de Fomento ($300 million), and the International Finance Corporation ($300 million).

Opponents included Fernando Manfredo, respected for his role as deputy administrator of the PCC during the first decade of reversion, and a number of independent professionals; opposition political leaders, such as later President Juan Carlos Varela, and most of his Panameñistas; and several small parties representing leftists and organized labor.

The referendum on Canal expansion occurred at a propitious moment. World trade was growing strongly, and US shippers increased their reliance on the Panama route. During the 1990s, the US share of Canal business had dropped to about 60 percent but then rebounded to 69 percent, about where it has remained since 2006. Global enthusiasm for the expansion also generated favorable attitudes in Panama. For instance, a June 2006 report by US shipping expert Asaf Ashar, for the National Ports and Waterways Institute, argued that the value of the Panama route already justified the higher costs expansion would entail.

Just a month before the vote, ACP marketing guru Rodolfo Sabonge laid out the details of Panama's competitiveness. Despite recent toll increases, the value of cargoes and tolls rose because of economic advantages the Canal provided. He did the math for his countrymen: shippers from Japan and China were saving $30,000 to $50,000 a day on the fourteen to eighteen fewer days they spent at sea by using the Panama route, rather than the Strait of Magellan passage to the US east coast.[27] The shipping industry would pay the higher tolls needed to finance most of the Canal expansion. Thus, expansion would be a boon for the country, not a burden, and shippers would be quick to accept even higher tolls.

The national referendum on the expansion of the Canal, held on October 22, 2006, took place at 4,414 polling places. Turnout was much lower than general elections, just over 43 percent of the 2,132,842 eligible voters, but comparable to other referenda. The government's arguments prevailed with a 78 percent victory. Apparently, a large majority of the people accepted that the country's fate was strongly tied to keeping their Canal competitive by enlarging it.

A REALLY BIG DITCH

Actual work on expansion commenced in September 2007, when huge explosions paved the way for the widening and deepening of the

[27] Sabonge's "Competitividad de la Ruta por Panamá" appeared in *El Faro* no. 18 (Sept. 15, 2006): 6–7 and was reprinted in many other media. Ashar's study, "Ampliar, el único camino," was printed in *El Faro*, no. 11 (June 9, 2006): 7.

waterway's main channel. In some respects, this huge engineering feat impressed observers much like the original, albeit perhaps less pathbreaking in today's world of the Three Gorges Dam, International Space Station, and Khalifa Tower. Yet the passageway still depends on gravity-fed water from Lake Gatun and on the Culebra Cut for most of the trip. Now, however, it has deeper approaches and 2.8 times larger locks on both ends, as can be seen in this schematic comparison created by the ACP.

The new locks are 180 feet wide (instead of 110 feet), 1400 feet long (versus 1000 feet), and 60 feet deep (rather than 42 feet). The greater beam is especially important for container vessels because it allows for more rows to be stacked on deck. Meanwhile, the greater depth is important for container ships but even more so for the new carriers of liquefied natural gas (LNG), as well as new "Mini-Capesize" dry cargo grain carriers, which will become prominent in the coming decade.[28] The expansion opens the door for a new age of mega-ships that will gradually add new dimensions to global shipping.

The design of the expansion project elicited plaudits from engineers around the world, both for its size and sophistication. The new gates, for example, had to be built in a factory in Italy and transported on special ships to Panama before being installed. The gates have a totally different design from the 1914 originals: European-style sliding partitions instead of swinging ones. They are 190 feet long, 26 to 33 feet thick, up to 110 feet high, and weigh 4,200 tons. As far as gates go, they can appropriately be called Brobdingnagian, as Jonathan Swift would have described them in *Gulliver's Travels*. Opening and closing these enormous structures has been compared to sliding an 11-story building back and forth across a distance the equivalent of a twelve-lane expressway.

In contrast to the original waterway, a project of the USACE with contractors mainly from the US, Panamanians built the third set of locks, with considerable help from abroad. Once the overall project was approved, the ACP put one of its most senior and respected engineers, Jorge Quijano, in charge. When he assumed leadership of the expansion, he brought over thirty years of increasingly responsible duties and achievements at the Canal, including his work as director of the maritime division starting in 1999.

[28] Mini-Capesize refers to one of the many categories of neo-Panamax and still larger mega ships that are being built today.

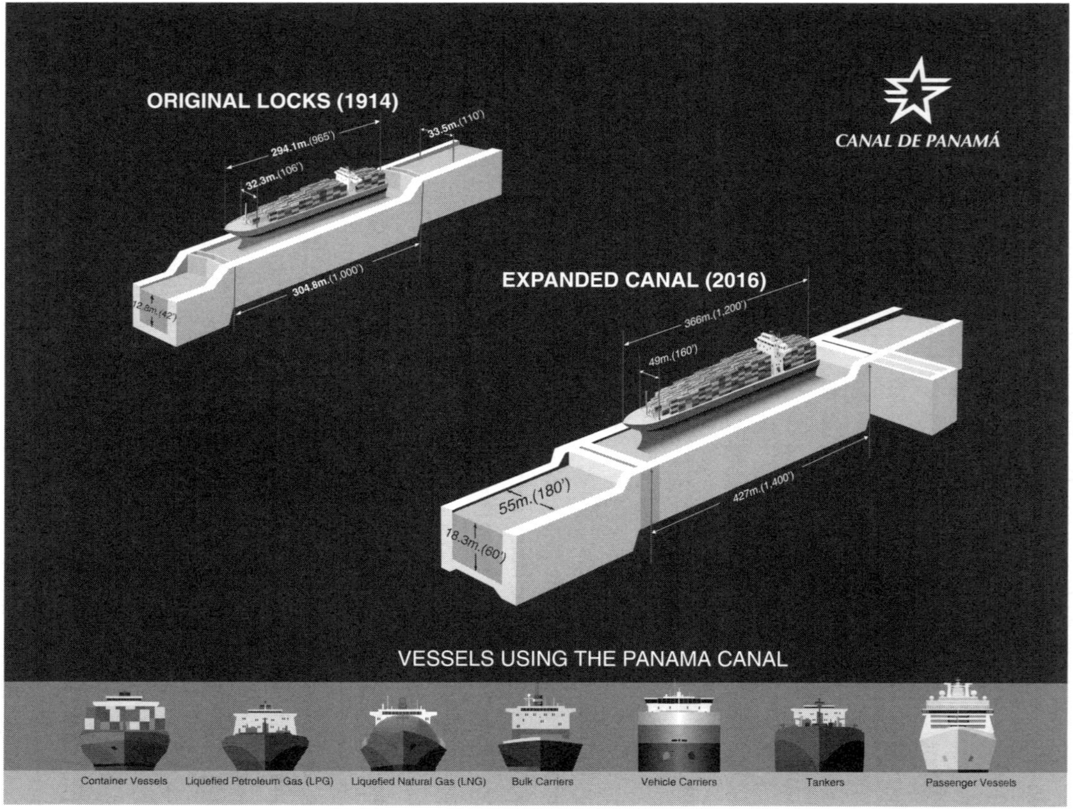

FIGURE 7.2 Chart comparing dimensions of old and new canal locks, plus maximum ship sizes. TEU = twenty-foot equivalent, a standard measure for container sizes. Autoridad del Canal de Panamá.

Like many Canal senior managers, Quijano grew up in an upper middle class family heavily involved in the construction industry. In contrast to many of his contemporaries with links to either the PRD or the Panameñista Party, his family had been tied to the more historic Liberal Party. He attended some of Panama's better schools, and, with family support and his own high academic standards, he went abroad to college. He studied industrial engineering at Lamar University in Beaumont, near the heart of Texas's oil industry. After graduating, he returned to Panama to begin his professional career at the Texaco refinery in Panama. In 1975, Quijano started work at the Canal, well before the new treaties pried the doors more open for Panamanians. He rose steadily through the ranks in the apprentice-like training system, taking advantage of opportunities for graduate and advanced management study at important international institutions, including Northwestern University and the Federal Executive Institute operated by the US Office of Personnel Management. After overseeing the first five years of the expansion project, Quijano rose to succeed Alberto Alemán as the third Panamanian Administrator (2012 to 2019) of the ACP.

Ilya R. Espino de Marotta then moved up to vice president for engineering and programs management, taking charge of the expansion project. She graduated from Texas A&M University at Galveston in marine engineering and went right to work for the ACP. While on the job, she completed a master's degree in economic engineering in Panama and later did graduate management training at INCAE in Central America and at the Kellogg School in Illinois. Over her thirty plus years at the Canal, she has occupied a number of different roles, including work related to engineering design, valuation, and investment. When the ACP was formed, her work concentrated on the administrator's master planning project and then development of the expansion plan itself.

Panamanians made up over 90 percent of the rest of the expansion workforce of about 35,000, in contrast to the more than 56,000 mainly West Indians a century ago. Workers' high pay helped boost the rate of growth of the Panamanian economy to the highest rate in Latin America over the last decade, averaging over 6 percent a year.

Comparisons of the third locks and original Canal construction yield surprising similarities. The early 1900s work required the excavation of 7 billion cubic feet of material and pouring 113 million cubic feet of concrete. The recent expansion excavated 5.5 billion cubic feet and required 155 million cubic feet of concrete.[29] In contrast, work on the original waterway stretched across the fifty-mile width of the Isthmus, while this time most of it took place around the two miles of navigational access channel and locks on the Caribbean side and the five miles of access channel and locks on the Pacific side.

International contributions to the expansion focused on design, financing, and management and organization of specific segments of the project. Besides the US Army Corps of Engineers, New York-based Parsons Brinckerhoff took a major role in the design work. The contract for overall project management went to the Colorado-based engineering firm, CH2MHill, while that for construction of the locks and navigation channels went to a consortium called the United Group for the Panama Canal (GUPC), led by the Spanish firm Sacyr Vallehermosa, joined with Impreglio of Italy, Jan de Nul of Belgium, and Panama's Constructora Urbana, S.A. (CUSA).

Disputes with the ACP's management and cost overruns by the GUPC delayed project completion two years beyond the original target date of 2014 and raised the cost from the original $5.25 billion to about $7 billion. Skepticism about the ability of the GUPC to complete the work on budget arose shortly after they won the bid, partly because it came in a billion dollars below that of Bechtel International and about half the cost of the highest bidder. Yet the ACP had a history of probity and transparency in its contracting and also of bringing projects in on time and at cost, so the work went forward.[30] Problems over contract execution worsened in 2013, and GUPC instituted a work slowdown, blaming delays and overruns on demanding standards for concrete quality and lack of nearby supply for some materials. Most of the disputes with the GUPC were arbitrated in favor of the ACP. The ACP took advantage of

[29] This comparison is based on the description by Rick Jervis, "U.S. Ports Prepare for Panama Canal Expansion," *USA Today*, Apr. 19, 2015.

[30] Joe R. Reeder, "Panama Exceeds Expectations on Contracting," *Journal of Commerce*, 2009. Some Panamanians and foreign observers raised questions about ACP favoritism toward GUPC because it included CUSA, one of Panama's leading construction firms, run previously by Alberto Alemán and still controlled by his family. The ACP contracting process was thoroughly scrutinized, however, including previous contracts won by CUSA, without finding improprieties, poor performance, deficient value to cost, or undue influence. On the contrary, CUSA's record, especially in large-scale excavation projects, demonstrated strong performance by a well-qualified national firm. Panama's rules for competitive bidding allowed the participation of such family firms, and most observers believed that the selection process was conducted without undue personal influence. In this respect, the informal vigilance and trust in the ACP's board of directors helped maintain confidence in the ACP.

a large insurance bond to get work going again in 2014 and made additional financial concessions later to keep up progress. A *New York Times* article on the eve of the inauguration on June 26, 2016, chronicled many of the problems, emphasizing criticism of the ACP.[31]

In 1906, Theodore Roosevelt aroused global interest in the original Panama Canal by visiting the site, the first overseas trip by a sitting US president. His trip helped propel a flood of journalists and tourists to visit Panama. As many as 15,000 tourists a year, mostly from the US and Europe, streamed into the tiny tropical country and produced a vast amount of coverage by magazines and newspapers around the world. Excitement about the Canal spurred plans for the Panama-Pacific International Exposition, held in San Francisco in 1915, the first world's fair in the Pacific Basin, an earlier one in San Diego, and Panama's in 1916.[32]

Public and international interest in the expansion also ran high, so the ACP built a new visitor center overlooking the Caribbean locks. The Pacific-side Miraflores Visitor Center, meanwhile, provided somewhat less viewing of the new navigation channel and Cocolí locks that open on the Pacific. Together, the two centers have hosted over a million visitors during the construction, but this time most have been Panamanians.

International attention to Canal expansion has mostly been from the specialized international maritime and commerce sector. In the United States, the principal reaction has been the investment of tens of billions of dollars in port and infrastructure improvements to accommodate the larger ships that use the new locks. Expansion may again spur tourism to Panama, as it did during the first years of last century, but so far the growth of new hotels and facilities for tourists has exceeded the number of visitors. Around the region, similar responses brought construction or planning for new mega-ports in Cuba, Costa Rica, Mexico, Puerto Rico, Chile, and Brazil. Meanwhile Nicaragua, Guatemala, Colombia, and Mexico have considered both wet and dry (railroad) canals, ports, and other projects.[33]

[31] Walt Bogdanich et al., "The New Panama Canal: A Risky Bet," *New York Times*, June 22, 2016. Some observers speculated that rival interests of some US West Coast ports and of Panamanian tugboat captains seeking higher pay may have influenced the negative perspective of the article.

[32] Michael L. Conniff, "Promoting Global Trade: The Panama-Pacific Expositions," in *Panamá cosmopolita: La exposición de 1916 y su legado*, ed. Adrienne Samos (Panama: Panama City and UNDP, 2017), 18–77.

[33] Although work on the Nicaragua canal was supposed to start in 2015, the Chinese company holding a generous concession from the Ortega government, billionaire Wang Jing's HKND, had not completed environmental impact studies for the 170-mile project. Designed for the largest mega-ships afloat, it would cost more than $50 billion. See

Panama's delay in opening the third locks from 2014 to 2016 proved controversial. Polemics over the urgency of completing the expansion actually started in 2012, when Maersk, the world's largest container shipper, announced it would divert many of its ships from the Panama to the Suez Canal. Their rationale stressed the savings that would result from using neo-Panamax vessels right away, even if the route was longer.[34] At that point, the extent of delays caused by the difficulty of the contractors meeting the required high-quality concrete work were uncertain, but the Maersk action was also widely understood as a means of pressuring the ACP to speed up the expansion and to head off future toll increases. The ACP expressed surprise that the move by Maersk had not come earlier, since the vessels had been available for several years. It suggested that most shippers were willing to accept marginally higher costs to preserve the integrity of established routes, made possible by keeping the Canal open throughout the expansion process.

The contracting controversy with the GUPC caused the greatest delay in the expansion work. Then more troubles arose in 2014–2015, due both to labor and climate demands, and finally to leakage as the locks were first filled with water. A severe El Niño drought briefly required reduced load limits on ships in 2016. With the locks completion on the horizon and contractor disputes still pending, Panama's largest labor union, SUNTRACS, added new wage and benefits claims, potentially further escalating final costs.

This convergence of challenging events in 2014–16 must at times have seemed as discouraging to the ACP's managers as the experience of Colonel George Goethals and his colleagues a hundred years earlier. World War I broke out just after the first complete transit of the Canal in 1914, raising security issues, and huge landslides in the Culebra Cut delayed commercial use of the Canal for another six years.

The fact that the Panamanians had prepared for most of these contingencies eased many difficulties. They avoided major reductions in cargo required in the 1997–98 El Niño by having already dredged Lake Gatún to

Michael D. McDonald, "China's Building a Huge Canal in Nicaragua, but We Couldn't Find It," *Bloomberg News*, Aug. 19, 2015.

[34] Maersk can save money by rerouting its neo-Panamax ships from the East Coast to Asia via the Panama Canal instead of through the Suez Canal. For example, the New York to Shanghai route is 1,788 miles shorter via Panama and New York to Yokohoma is 3,727 miles shorter. Besides the obvious fuel and administrative cost savings, the considerable reduction in GHG emissions of the shorter routes are increasingly emphasized by the global shipping community.

more than thirty-nine feet, and the rains returned before draft limits affected business. So while the labor and contracting disputes dragged out and the schedule for completion seemed hectic, the planned transition from two locks handling 300,000 tons of cargo a day to three locks able to carry over 400,000 tons a day went ahead as expected. Because of this steady progress, Maersk announced plans to reroute its neo-Panamax container ships back to Panama even before having the precise date for the opening.

Notwithstanding operational challenges and concerns about the expansion project, those who observed the celebrations accompanying the inauguration of the new locks reported widespread public relief and joy over the accomplishment. The corporate model for management of the Canal adopted by the ACP stressed the importance of long-range planning and actions, such as expansion, that must be taken and needed to be understood in that context. The completion of the expansion and the immediate demonstration of its utility to enable neo-Panamax ships to use the passageway vindicated the new approach and the faith the public expressed when they approved the referendum a decade earlier.

FROM ENGINEERING WONDER TO BUSINESS JUGGERNAUT

Since the days when Teddy Roosevelt had his famous photo taken on a giant steam shovel, the Panama Canal has been known for the engineering prowess that its construction required. Some of the unprecedented accomplishments included creating the world's largest man-made lake, excavation of ship channels through mountain barriers, raising and lowering huge vessels eighty-five feet from the ocean to Lake Gatun and back to the ocean, and development of some of the dynamo industrial companies of the twentieth century, such as General Electric. Together, such achievements helped establish the reputation it achieved as "the eighth wonder of the world."

Panama's new managers respected the engineering tradition of the Canal and diligently incorporated this value into the new enterprise as they gradually took control. With the expansion working as designed, the issue of Corozal Port still not resolved (see Chapter 9), and Jorge Quijano's appointment as administrator ending in 2019, the ACP took time to evaluate and again adjust its administrative structure in 2017–18. The new design streamlines the executive structure but focuses the organization even more clearly on the two business drivers of the organization, the core transit business and the complementary enterprises, such as port development, that have driven the expansion of the country's maritime sector. As the ACP press release explained, the new design more clearly emphasized the strategy for future growth scheduled to begin in October 2018.[35]

Notwithstanding these recent adjustments in management structure, Panamanian managers always envisioned the Canal to play a more powerful role in the nation than under their American predecessors. Their ambition hinged on transforming the waterway into the centerpiece and motor of their country's economic development. They did not just want to create a business that would provide more jobs, business opportunities, and revenue to the government. They wanted to make the Canal into an engine for national progress. Like the first great warships of the modern maritime era, when the Canal was being dug, they designed a business juggernaut to drive their society forward.[36]

ACP's efforts to raise civic engagement and economic interconnectivity brought the Canal deeper into the lives of Panamanians. Increasing revenues poured by the Canal into the national income stream created new resources for government programs and infrastructure modernization. Burgeoning growth and diversification in Panama's other maritime activities increased the pace and spread the impact that the ACP has had on Panama's destiny. At the turn of this century, the ACP's contribution to GDP measured about 6 percent, and the entire maritime sector contributed about 10 percent to national income. Under US Canal management, the enterprise contributed only marginally to GDP.

As discussed in Chapters 5 and 6, after 2000, national economic growth first moved from anemic to a modest recovery fostered by construction spending in 2002–03. Then, after 2004, Panama took off on one of the greatest booms in Latin American history, as we will describe in the later chapters. Driven by the business juggernaut created by the ACP, economic growth averaged well over 6 percent per year, by far the highest in the Americas for more than fourteen years. Throughout the administrations of Torrijos, Martinelli, and Varela, Canal expansion and the

[35] ACP, "Canal de Panamá alinea su estructura a su estrategia de crecimiento," Jan. 22, 2018; and "Canal reestructura su administración," *La Prensa,* Feb. 5, 2018.

[36] Concepts of national identity and development are discussed in Chapter 1. Roberto Roy, minister of canal affairs and director of the Metro under both Martínelli and Varela, recalled that a Zonian PCC executive in the 1990s said that the Canal could become a gold mine for Panama if managed well. Likewise, in the 1850s and 1860s Panama Railroad's stock eclipsed all others on the New York Stock Exchange, leading investors to call the line the Golden Horse.

associated maritime business engendered by the Canal drove the economy at a feverish pace. Even after the expansion was completed, growth only moderated a little, gradually falling back toward a rhythm well above that of regional and global economies. Not even the Great Recession of 2008–10 interrupted Panama's historic boom, which only slowed down for slightly over a year.

During Panama's years of hyper growth, ACP's financial contribution rose by about two thirds, to account for over 10 percent of the national economy. The related parallel activities of the maritime sector, more technically labeled the interoceanic conglomerate or what we call the new Panama hub of the Americas, grew even faster, more than doubling to reach over a quarter of national output. Reflecting this strong growth even in 2011, the *Economist* reported that Panama's maritime powerhouse was becoming a Singapore for the Western Hemisphere.[37]

[37] "Panama's Economy: A Singapore for Central America," *The Economist*, July 14, 2011.

8

The Martinelli Administration: Trouble in Boom Times

This is not a government of politicians but one that is managed with a business vision, something never before seen in the history of Panama ... nor in Latin American nor world history.

Ricardo Martinelli[1]

A "FAST AND FURIOUS" PRESIDENT TOOK THE REINS

No single description of Ricardo Martinelli's first 100 days in office seems keener than "fast and furious," voiced by one observer.[2] Meanwhile, a powerful earthquake (Richter 6.0) centered in Colon province rocked the capital sixty kilometers away, just four days into his administration, such a rare event that some regarded it as a harbinger of what might come. Not to disappoint the 60 percent of voters who had cast ballots for him, he roared into office announcing an avalanche of what he called "decisive" measures which stirred up controversy yet boosted his approval ratings to 67 and then 77 percent during the first few months.

[1] Statement quoted in Felipe Aldunate, "La revolución de Martinelli," *América Económica,* Nov. 21, 2010.

[2] To describe the pace of activity, veteran PRD analyst Mario Rognoni used the Spanish word *vertiginoso* (dizzying), as quoted in the Associated Press article, "Martinelli tras 100 dias de gobierno con estilo propio," *La Nación* (Costa Rica), Oct. 7, 2009. See also the Notimex report, "Cumple Martinelli 100 dias con promesas cumplidas," *Vanguardia* (Mexico), Oct. 8, 2009; Juan José Rodríguez (AFP), "Martinelli cumple 100 dias como presidente de Panamá con alta popularidad," *La Prensa Gráfica* (El Salvador), Oct. 8, 2009; and "Los primeros 100 dias de Martinelli," *La Estrella de Panamá,* Oct. 19, 2009.

The long and heated 2009 campaign revealed Martinelli's personal style of blunt or plain speaking, known in Spanish as *hablar sin pelos en la lengua*. Once in office, other aspects of his governing personality appeared, when he added vigor and grandeur to his words, pointing out how unprecedented his vision for the country was. His early actions, ranging from handouts to the needy and increased taxes on the rich, reflected decisiveness on behalf of the poor while punishing villains. A self-aggrandizing dimension of his personalist approach, spelling out the significance of his acts, also became more obvious. Finally, observers noted a penchant for "playing hardball" and imposing his will, often described in Spanish *as gobernar a la brava* (acting carelessly or recklessly without regard to others). He clearly resembled other autocratic populists in the Latin American tradition.[3]

Martinelli reaped early approval with programs like "100 at 70" (persons of seventy or older not already on pensions received payments of $100 a month), a 30 percent pay increase for policemen, an unprecedented hike in the minimum wage, and a sharp cut in electric bills for everyone. Meanwhile, on the punitive side of the ledger, he raised taxes on dividends for Colon Free Zone businessmen (who sell mainly to foreigners), bankers, lawyers, and other professionals.

The new president gained more positive attention from early travel abroad, completing five junkets in his first 100 days.[4] During his first trip to the United States, he could not arrange a meeting with President Obama, but while there he met briefly with Secretary of State Hillary Clinton on the margins of his primetime UN speech. He also scored two publicity victories in New York: throwing out the first pitch in a Yankee Stadium baseball game to Panamanian superstar Mariano Rivera and ringing the opening bell on the New York Stock Exchange.

Martinelli's second trip, to Rome, proved even more fruitful. Prime Minister Silvio Berlusconi personally received his forty-person entourage, arranged for a Papal audience, and assembled a big meeting with businessmen and industrialists. His press people touted the economic benefits that

[3] On the general phenomenon, based on comparative case studies, see Michael L. Conniff, ed., *Populism in Latin America*, 2nd ed. (Tuscaloosa: University of Alabama Press, 2012), esp. the theoretical introduction and the Robinson chapter on Panama.

[4] He would go on to make ninety-six foreign trips in his five-year presidency: José González Pinilla, "Los casi cien viajes del presidente Ricardo Martinelli," *La Prensa*, June 27, 2014. Martinelli had called his predecessor the "vagabond boy" for his overseas travel, but the younger leader made eighty-nine, and they tended to be of shorter duration. In comparison, Endara took twenty-three, Pérez Balladares forty-nine, and Moscoso forty.

FIGURE 8.1 President Ricardo Martinelli, his wife María Linares de Martinelli, and President Barack Obama and his wife Michelle Obama, in White House reception. 506 collection/Alamy

Panama would reap from increased trade, investment, business, and a new security partnership with Italy.

First Lady Marta Linares de Martinelli played a prominent role during the early days of the administration and during travels. Martinelli's personalist style extended to her, hoping that her active calendar would rival the good will created by her predecessor, Vivian Torrijos. Marta Linares's visits to charities and community centers, her advocacy for restoration of Parque Omar, her leadership on early childhood education, and her support for school gardens complemented the President's announced dedication to the less fortunate. In classic populist style, she re-enforced and spread the message of helping the needy.

Martinelli's pose as a friend of the poor backfired sometimes. For example, even though he bragged that by turning over his salary for worthy causes helped them, he stumbled during a state visit by the president of Brazil, Luiz Inácio "Lula" da Silva. Responding to Lula's offers to help finance and build Panama's promised new infrastructure, Martinelli impulsively ordered a fancy new Embraer presidential airplane. Newspaper critics noted the hypocrisy of his actions after his attacks on his predecessor's international travel and his reneging on a promise not to buy the new airplane.

In the policy arena, the new president emphasized boosting Panama's economic competitiveness by overhauling regulations and bottlenecks. He proposed an energy market arrangement, higher taxes, government investments, and public works projects that included expansion of the already popular Cinta Costera Highway, new hospitals, and health centers. Far and away his most dramatic announcement of the first 100 days was an underground subway for Panama City and its suburbs, to be called the Metro. To make good on this campaign promise, he created a new subcabinet secretary of the Metro under the ministry of the presidency, appointing one of the country's most respected engineers, Roberto Roy, to do the job.[5]

Early on, Martinelli displayed a style of heavy-handed action. For example, when his presidential honeymoon was interrupted by a transportation strike, a challenge given Panama's size and skewed density, he forced the parties to settle. Other instances of autocratic style included confiscating the Figali Convention Center, a controversial project run by Colombian bon vivant and suspected money launderer Jean Figali. A perfect foil for the new style of leadership, the president simply had the entire project confiscated. Similarly, he authorized awarding an estimated $150 million in no-bid contracts for public works projects to avoid delays.

Opposition leaders found President Martinelli hard to deal with, and he kept them off balance with unexpected moves. For example, he opened a forum on consumer protection with an eloquent speech on the subject, one never previously broached by a Panamanian president.[6] His actions led one critic to say that Martinelli could not be easily categorized. Despite his being a businessman, he appeared to act against business interests to raise money for social programs. In an interview with the Spanish news agency EFE, he described the corruption of incumbent politicians in pejorative terms:

> the people here [in the government] were doing what they wanted. They were collecting bribes just about everywhere; there was laxity in paying taxes; people were taking concessions without paying for them; there were the visas for the Chinese; the Colon Free Zone and the ports are swindling us.[7]

PRD stalwart and television commentator Mario Rognoni, while admiring Martinelli's energy, noted that few members of his new cabinet

[5] Roy had formed part of the 1990s Blue Ribbon Commission to modernize the Canal; see Chapter 4.

[6] "Decisivo apoyo a todos los consumidores," *La Estrella de Panamá*, Oct. 19, 2010.

[7] "Martinelli cambia estilo de gobernar," *La Prensa*, Dec. 9, 2009.

were able to keep up with him. Other critics rated most ministers, except minister of the presidency Papadimitriu, as failing to match the president's pace during his frenetic first 100 days.[8] Observers also called Martinelli's approach a "toxic style of leadership" because of the vitriol he directed at rivals. Most criticized his massive dismissal of government employees, far beyond political appointees, without consulting outgoing officials about their qualifications.

A DIFFERENT KIND OF LEADERSHIP?

Martinelli asserted, and many people believed, that his business approach, rather than personalistic style, best defined his new abrupt pace of governing. He had, to be sure, amassed a fortune with his supermarket chain and other businesses, and eighteen of his thirty cabinet members were also businessmen.[9] Observers nicknamed them the "INCAE cabinet," since so many had attended the Harvard-affiliated graduate school of business in Managua and San José, where Martinelli was one of the earliest Panamanian students. Notwithstanding, fourteen of the thirty also had noteworthy political pedigrees. Nine had served as ministers, vice ministers, or major agency heads, making the cabinet one of the most politically experienced in recent history.

Although Martinelli categorized himself as an entrepreneur, he had held high public office for almost eight years, started a political party, and spent part of the previous decade running twice for president. Vice president Juan Carlos Varela, also one of the country's wealthiest businessmen, had not held public office but served as secretary general of his party, and had run for president. Both seemed to be at least as devoted to politics as to business.

The new minister of economics and finance, Alberto Vallarino, was a banker who had also held public positions. He gained attention for

[8] "Los primeros 100 dias de Martinelli," *La Estrella de Panamá,* Oct. 19, 2009. The article also provides some advice in response to what at first seemed unusual activism by the minister of the presidency: "the minister might proceed with a little more caution over the high profile that he has created and dedicate himself more to executing and coordinating rather than running the show."

[9] A complete list of the cabinet as of June 2011 identified nineteen of thirty as business people (empresarios), see http://oye-pty.blogspot.com/2011/06/lista-de-ministros-y-vice ministros-del.html. With a broader historical perspective, Marco A. Gandásegui hijo observed that Martinelli's "business style" had not been seen in Panama since the 1950s: "Panamá 2009: Elecciones, crisis mundial y movimientos sociales," *Revista de Ciéncia Política* (Chile) 30, no. 2 (2010): 419–27.

selling local bank Banistmo to HSBC for $1.77 billion dollars in 2006. He too had run twice for president, held other cabinet posts, and helped create the Patriotic Union coalition. José Raúl Mulino, the new minister of government and justice, brought considerable experience to Marinelli's team: a distinguished lawyer, he had helped lead the civic crusade against Noriega in the 1980s, participated in party leadership, and served as foreign minister in the Endara government. Minister of commerce Roberto Henríquez had been in and out of politics and the family firm, served as vice minister in the Moscoso government, and became the vice president of Cambio Democrático and was Martinelli's running mate in 2004.

Martinelli's right-hand man, however, raised eyebrows. His minister of the presidency, Jimmy Papadimitriu, cited business experience in the family firm, but his record showed much more devotion to politics. He spent nearly a decade climbing the ladder in politics in Washington, DC, before returning to Panama for a stint in the family business. From the time Martinelli first ran for president in 2004, he devoted himself to his new boss, ran his electoral campaigns, and lobbied for him before the US Congress and with Republican-leaning political consultants with whom he had worked.

Other cabinet designates also blended private experience with politics and public visibility. Minister of education Lucy Moliar, for example, excelled as a television anchor, as had the new minister of social development Guillermo Ferrufino. Finally, minister of Canal affairs Rómulo Roux, small business director Giselle Burillo de Calcagno, and vice minister of commerce José Domingo Arias, had all dabbled in politics beyond their private sector jobs but vied for bigger roles in the CD party during the campaign and once in office.

Regardless of its self-image as a business-like administration, Martinelli's differed substantially from its predecessors and often elicited criticism for it. Papadimitriu turned his role into a virtual co-presidency. Urban transportation came to overshadow most other government programs in the early days. The president's authoritarian style undermined his public support. And corruption spread so widely across the government that, in many ways, it swamped his otherwise positive economic legacy.

The symbiotic relationship between Martinelli and his youthful campaign manager, Papadimitriu, was one of the first features that startled even insiders when it became more fully visible. Ambassador to the United States Jaime Alemán Healy, for example, related that Martinelli told him and two other powerful men presumably close to him, Juan Carlos Varela and Alberto Vallarino, that Papadimitriu would be the only person authorized to speak on his behalf and therefore become a veritable co-president.[10] Although widely referred to as a "super-minister," the degree of investiture was apparently unperceived by many outsiders. Varela himself held the titles of vice president and foreign minister. Two years later, however, Martinelli justified firing Varela as foreign minister because he was not doing his job. Yet evidence of the new power bestowed on the minister of the presidency became rapidly visible, probably painfully so to Varela.

In earlier administrations, ministers of the presidency had limited roles in government, handling scheduling, and coordinating partisan and personal affairs for the president. They managed liaison with the Assembly and oversaw housekeeping in the presidency, coordinating with but not subordinating politically powerful individuals running the national security staff, the urban transportation authority, the press office, and the first lady's staff. Papadimitriu, however, suddenly became a decisive figure in unusual situations: he proposed a law to boost communications security, settled a bus strike, coordinated the visit of president Lula of Brazil, proposed changes in the penal code to crack down on youth crime, and presented the government's budget to the Assembly. This represented a sharp break with past practice.

More instances arose. During Martinelli's first official trip to the UN, Papadimitriu went to Washington, DC, to visit his former boss, Republican minority leader John Boehner, and others. Back home, he negotiated a change in bus speed limits to reduce commute times. He joined the ministers of economics and commerce to welcome delegates to Panama to attend the World Economic Forum regional meeting on increasing competitiveness. Curiously, the *Memorias* of his ministry for 2010 and 2011 are filled with photos of Papadimitriu prominently centered among other government officials, unlike in previous administrations.[11] He executed lobbying contracts in the United States and purchased campaign-style advertising about Martinelli's achievements in the national media long after the campaign was over. Papadimitriu worked vigorously on a whole new urban bus system,

[10] Alemán's detailed and anecdote-filled autobiography is entitled *La honestidad no tiene precio* (Panama: Carvajal Soluciones de Comunicación, 2014).

[11] These observations are based primarily on the annual reports (*Memorias)* of the presidency for 2010 and 2011, when Papadimitriu was minister, in comparison with both earlier and later years, and on author Bigler's personal experience with the Panamanian government over the years.

something Martinelli predecessors had promised yet never found possible to deliver on. The minister of the presidency also publicly announced the creation of the MiBus company, issued contracts to purchase thousands of vehicles, established training for drivers, and visited Colombia to learn about its bus system innovations.

Guided by Papadimitriu, the administration took credit for dismantling the traditional *diablo rojo* private bus system and replacing it with modern and efficient service.[12] Papadimitriu took on another new program, as promised during the election campaign, to establish cold storage centers to move agricultural produce from farms to supermarkets at lower cost to consumers. He, rather than the minister of agriculture, launched this work. In addition, Papadimitriu instituted universal scholarships for high school students and attempted to create a free national Wifi network. Finally, he served as troubleshooter to mediate indigenous protests over mining companies in Bocas del Toro and to settle a garbage collectors' strike in urban neighborhoods.

Several other top Martinelli officials enjoyed close ties, as Papadimitriu obviously did. Gioconda Torres de Bianchini, for example, won Assembly approval to be comptroller general with the president's help and soon exercised her gatekeeper and watchdog budget role in a manner even more sympathetic to the president than customary. Her chief professional experience had been as the auditor of Ricamar, the financial holding company in the Martinelli business empire. In other words, she was Martinelli's private accountant, never showed any modicum of the independence expected of comptrollers, and, for that reason, was staunchly criticized by civil society and good government organizations.

Two other major appointees backed by Martinelli had close personal ties to him, raising considerable resistance from the opposition and legal firms. Supreme court nominations were already controversial due to questionable actions by both Moscoso and Torrijos. Therefore, some civil society organizations and the bar association prepared a list of seventy-one judicially qualified candidates for the office. With his popularity riding high in December 2009, Martinelli simply ignored the list. Almost defiantly, he nominated as justices first his secretary of presidential

[12] Randal C. Archibold, "In Panama City, Colorful Red Devil Buses Yielding to Paler, Safer Kind," *New York Times*, Dec. 29, 2011; and Peter Szok, "Swaggering through Hell: The Rise and Decline of Panama's Red Devil Buses," *Folk Art Messenger* 22, no. 1 (2010): 16–20. In June 2010 Martinelli reduced Papadimitriu's role by appointing former government vice minister Jorge Ricardo Fábrega to head the urban transportation authority.

FIGURE 8.2 Traditional Diablo Rojo bus, now mostly gone from the capital streets. Painted by Rafael Erazo, 2008. Photograph courtesy of Peter A. Szok.

security, José Abel Almengor, whose only experience was a few years as an anti-drug prosecutor. Then he named Alejandro Moncada Luna, the former director of the technical judicial police (Panama's FBI), who he had known during the Pérez Balladares administration and who had joined the CD.[13]

When it came to the massive Metro project, however, Martinelli avoided appointing a personal associate and chose instead the highly regarded engineer Roberto Roy, who he had known during his 1990s stint as minister of the Canal for Moscoso. Roy served as secretary and later director general and brought into his team a veteran of the ACP expansion project, Agustín Arias, and other noted professionals, secured international funding, and built public support for the subway system.[14] In two months, the Metro contracted for planning the first line, sixteen kilometers from Albrook Mall to the edge of San Miguelito. They adopted

[13] "Martinelli nombra sus dos magistrados," *La Estrella de Panamá,* Dec. 17, 2009.

[14] The origins of Martinelli's empowerment of Metro boss Roberto Roy are not clear, although his high performance record seems to have created a political firewall similar to that of the ACP.

the approach the ACP used for expansion of the Canal: pre-qualifying consortia for the major construction elements, while getting the system design done separately. This enabled them to hold bidding for line 1 in about a year and to award the $1.5 billion contract to a consortium of Odebrecht of Brazil, FCC of Spain, and Alstom of the UK in November 2011. As promised, and exceeding most expectations, Martinelli inaugurated line 1 in April 2014, just a few weeks before the election.

Observers sensed rather than fully observed the third and fourth features of the Martinelli administration, its authoritarian style and corruption. Comments began to surface about the divisiveness of his leadership style and his unwillingness to listen to and respect other perspectives. Some of this may have been based more on his behavior in the Pérez Balladares and Moscoso cabinets and the 2009 campaign. Early signs of authoritarianism were his seizure of the Figali property on the Amador Causeway, his role in the abrupt removal of civil society favorite Ana Matilde Gómez as solicitor general by the supreme court, the punitive nature of the penal code revisions related to juveniles, and his widespread dismissal of civil servants. Regarding perceived corruption, his cronyism, nepotism, contracting without competitive bidding, and other abrupt real estate transactions were all at first justified as expedients to produce results quickly rather than signs of corruption. The public needed a longer experience with him to measure the full implications of his actions.[15]

DOING BUSINESS IN A TOUGH NEIGHBORHOOD

The Martinelli team sought to restore the rapid economic growth achieved under his predecessor. His election campaign promised to revive the flow of foreign investment that had shrunk in the 2008 Great Recession and to jack up domestic demand with increased infrastructure spending. How to get it done was the issue. As with planning and launching the Metro, the new government took a business-like yet controversial approach by

[15] The sudden transfer of US ambassador Barbara Stephenson in May 2010, during a year of cool bilateral relations, was not recognized as a clash with Martinelli until months later, due to revelations from Wikileaks cables: see www.radiopanama.com.pa/noticias/actualidad/preocupa-en-panama-informacion-sobre-martinelli-de-wwwelpaiscr/20100510/nota/1268014.aspx. Similarly, the purpose of the communications security law reform to facilitate his wiretapping request that bothered Stephenson so much was not clear until much later.

bringing in the international consulting firm McKinsey to develop a strategic plan for the country. Minister of economy Vallarino said contracting McKinsey was just the kind of thing he had done as president of Banistmo bank.[16]

The resulting *Strategic Plan for Government, 2010–2014*, was a market economy version of the oft-derided five-year plans adopted in command economies. It promised economic growth concentrated in four areas: logistics, tourism, agriculture, and financial services. Following Ardito Barletta's vision, it advocated that Panama become "the hub of the Americas" to exploit the strategic advantages provided by the Panama Canal. About one third of the plan focused on economic strategy. Another third detailed how to achieve social development, and the rest covered financial and investment plans. It also called for reducing the unequal distribution of income and wealth, perhaps to fend off charges that the government wanted to institute predatory capitalism. The claim that the strategic plan (p. 54) "constitutes a singular achievement in the annals of the economic history of the country that will now institutionalize this type of document" typifies the hyperbole of public affairs posturing, along with blanket TV advertising, that continued to the end of the government.[17]

Martinelli's people pushed the economic growth agenda especially hard. During their first months, in office they signed a free trade agreement with Canada; held economic talks with prime minister Berlusconi of Italy and president Lula of Brazil; and won financial and other commitments from major firms in the two countries. Meanwhile, they announced steps in cooperation with the OECD to be removed from the latter's gray list of tax havens. Finally, due to tax and other reforms, major rating agencies raised Panama's credit and forecast it would reach investment grade soon.

Panama pursued several other avenues to promote the flow of foreign funds. First, it facilitated foreign investment with a new office, PROINVEX, directed by an up-and-coming star in the administration, commerce vice minister José Domingo Arias. Second, it joined in the global competitiveness movement and promised to host an international conference, one of more than a hundred similar ones during the Martinelli years.[18] Finally, it eased visa and other requirements for foreign investors

[16] Marianela Palacios, "Vallarino defiende contratación de McKinsey," *La Prensa*, Aug. 8, 2009.

[17] www.mef.gob.pa/es/transparencia/Documents/Plan%20Estrategico%20de%20Gobierno%202011%20-%202014.pdf.

[18] A fascinating series of activities took place in Panama during this period, including the World Surfing Championship and the Baseball World Cup.

and workers, through the Friendly Country program, that grew to encompass more than fifty nations.

Yet economic growth, restrained by the Great Recession, did not come as quickly as hoped, so, in June 2010, the government proposed a more aggressive approach in Law 30, perhaps misleadingly labeled as addressing civil aviation to avoid notice. Yet its main provisions created an investor-friendly environment and included promotion of privatization and foreign investment in utilities, restrictions on labor unions and worker rights, and lifting of requirements for environmental impact studies. Although the deceptive bill, soon to be called the "sausage law," passed without much debate or modification, it rapidly unleashed a storm of protest.

On another front, Martinelli faced security challenges on the borders and in cities across the country. The number of criminal gangs operating in the country jumped from thirty to eighty-five in 2009 and kept climbing under Martinelli to 200 by 2013. The homicide rate also rose steadily to an historic high of 22.6 per 100,000 in 2009, almost triple the rate in 2001. Both growth and security were on Martinelli's mind when he made his first foreign trip, to Costa Rica, shortly after his inauguration. He managed to bring home a draft free trade agreement and a plan for joint promotion of ecotourism. He also observed his neighbor's more efficient delivery of health care. He monitored president Oscar Arias's efforts to settle the crisis that erupted in neighboring Honduras when its supreme court replaced president Zelaya with the head of the legislature.[19] Finally, Martinelli's consultations with Costa Rica gave him a chance to participate in the Mérida Plan for counter-narcotics actions in Mexico and Central America. Started by the United States late in 2007, it extended financial and military support to cooperating nations who fought narcotics trafficking, in coordination with the decade-old Plan Colombia.

The crisis in Honduras, a symptom of instability and violence in the region, was exacerbated in part by drug trafficking and by regional rivalries provoked by ALBA, Hugo Chávez's anti-American leftist alliance. Accordingly, Martinelli decided to use this moment to align his country squarely against ALBA, a departure from the more balanced approach of the Torrijos administration.[20] Panamanian ambassador to the OAS Guillermo "Willy" Cochez became a vocal advocate for the

[19] "Presidente panameño quiere hacer de Costa Rica un socio 'muy estrecho,'" *La Prensa Gráfica* (El Salvador), July 15, 2009.

[20] "Martinelli desafia al ALBA," *La Prensa Gráfica,* July 1, 2009.

Honduran constitutional process that eventually led to the election of Porfirio Lobo as president. The Panamanian position, generally supportive of the US stand, also put the country into direct opposition to ALBA. This led to a gradual distancing from leftist regimes throughout the region and cancellation of the medical cooperation program Torrijos had started with Cuba.[21] Critics claimed these actions violated traditional Panamanian neutrality and were linked to US security cooperation and militarization of the National Police. Chávez struck back at Martinelli by having Venezuelan diplomatic personnel in the country give seminars on the virtues of *chavismo* until minister of government and security Raúl Mulino put a stop to them after observing one during a visit to Los Santos.[22]

National Police reforms had become a sensitive issue under minister Mulino, who, in early 2010, proposed Law 111 to hive off the policing and security functions to a new ministry of public security. This would leave judicial, immigration, customs, border control, and support for provincial and local affairs in the ministry of government. The Assembly passed the law in April. In June, Martinelli appointed the recently selected vice mayor of Panama City Roxana Méndez, whom he nicknamed "the iron lady," to head the ministry of government.

Then Mulino, as head of the new ministry, took charge of establishing some nine naval-air bases to buttress territorial surveillance, regional security, and counter-narcotics cooperation with the United States. The United States increased support for the new naval-air bases, mostly in the Colombian border region of Darien. Mulino and the US embassy curried public support by carrying out the humanitarian New Horizons deployment for 2010 in Metetí, at the gateway to the region. In this training mission with Panamanian counterparts, about 250 US national guardsmen conducted medical, dental, and veterinary clinics and built schools, roads, and community centers during a twelve-week period.[23]

[21] "Martinelli, presidente de Panamá: 'el anti-Chávez soy yo,'" *Tercera Información* (Spain), Oct. 15, 2009, and Percy Alvarado, "El verdadero trasfondo de la decisión de Martinelli de cesar la ayuda médica a Panamá," *Cuba Debate* (Cuba), Feb. 6, 2010.

[22] Isidro Rodríguez, "Panama y Venezuela–se calienta pugna diplomática," http://diloyah.forosactivos.net/t381-panama-y-venezuela-se-calienta-pugna-diplomatica.

[23] Mark P. Sullivan, "Panama: Political and Economic Conditions and U.S. Relations," Washington, DC, Congressional Research Service Report 7–5700, RL-30981, provided details of the shrinking realm of cooperation centered on law enforcement and regional security between the United States and Panama.

The Martinelli administration's increased security effort soon nearly doubled spending, including a proportional increase in police salaries, more bases, and extensive equipment acquisitions. Security outlays reached about 7 percent of GDP, more than double that of Costa Rica, which likewise had no army. Comparable gains in security outcomes, however, were mixed. By 2014, homicide rates declined just 20 percent from the historically high level of 2009. Police broke records in the volume of drugs they seized in 2009 and 2010, but little further progress occurred in that regard. Despite the 2010 reforms, the country soon experienced a big jump in crime and violence, as well as a corresponding increase in incarceration. Under Moscoso, the prison population rate rose from 280 to 342 per 100,000 and then dropped steadily under Torrijos to 270 in 2008. Martinelli's more punitive approach boosted the rate to 386 by 2014.[24] Understandably, Panama's rating on the Global Peace Index slipped from 48th in 2008 (about the same as Costa Rica) to 59th in 2009. By 2014, Panama improved only slightly to a ranking of 57. So despite Martinelli's efforts, public security did not improve appreciably.[25]

THE ADMINISTRATION TOOK A HARD RIGHT TURN

After its highly popular start, the Martinelli administration's approval ratings began to sink after a year and a half in office, when patterns of action like the security crackdown and economic initiatives had been well established.[26] After starting out with so many gestures in favor of the poor, the regime seemed to shift ideologically to the right. Punitive new law-and-order measures were matched by economic policies embracing private and foreign investment and business interests in a way that bordered on predatory capitalism. Martinelli's alignment against international socialism also became starker. Finally, both the Martinelli administration and CD party politics became increasingly authoritarian.

[24] Institute for Criminal Policy Research, World Prison Brief, Panama, www.prisonstudies.org/country/panama.

[25] David Gagne, "Panamá gastó 7% del PIB en seguridad: dan las cuentas?" *InSightCrime* (UK), Dec. 17, 2014. Global Peace Index rankings were accessed separately for individual years.

[26] "Cae popularidad del presidente Martinelli," *La Estrella de Panamá,* Feb. 2, 2011. The article reported the first drop in the President's popularity from 80 to 68.5 percent, but also that 56 percent thought that Martinelli, rather than the supreme court, was mainly responsible for the removal of Gómez.

They manipulated institutions and the civil service to strengthen their political power. Officeholder purges and hierarchical discipline, assaults on the opposition, verbal attacks on the independent media and civil society, and political hardball became commonplace.

By July 2010, the administration's reforms of the penal code entered into force, bringing changes to the structure of government, plans for prison expansion, a law enforcement crackdown, and military base expansion. These measures, accompanied by major new expenditures, soon produced a 40 percent increase in incarcerations. Not surprisingly, no other major policy or legislative initiatives had such a measurable impact during the administration's remaining years.

Perhaps sensing his own vulnerability to corruption charges, Martinelli early on set out to assert control over the prosecutor general. In January 2010, the supreme court abruptly suspended the independent and widely respected incumbent, Ana Matilde Gómez, eventually finding her guilty of unauthorized wiretaps in a criminal investigation. Her replacement, Giuseppe Bonissi, resigned nine months later, after being accused of improperly releasing drug traffickers. In December 2010, Martinelli nominated José Ayú Prado to replace him, who, despite a record of zealous persecution of PRD leaders, was duly confirmed by the Assembly. Two years later, Martinelli nominated Ayú Prado for a seat on the supreme court and proposed replacing him with Ana Belfon, former secretary for judicial affairs under the ministry of the presidency. Many civil society and legal groups criticized these nominations and other Martinelli judicial appointments as blatantly partisan.[27]

The questionable credentials of Martinelli appointees soon came back to haunt him. The first case resulted when the legal community criticized the removal of Ana Matilde Gómez. His later nomination of José Almengor to the supreme court led to accusations that he might have participated in Gómez's dismissal before his appointment. In fact, deputy Zulay Rodríguez denounced the questionable part Almengor had played in removing Gómez. This revelation and other judicial improprieties led to protests by the Catholic Church and other civic and legal organizations and eventually Almengor's resignation from the court in April 2011.[28]

[27] "Alianza Ciudadana critica nombramientos de Ayú Prado y Ana Belfon," *La Estrella de Panamá*, Dec. 19, 2012.

[28] "Pulsean por renuncia de José Almengor," *La Estrella de Panamá*, Mar. 29, 2011; "Exigen la renuncia de Almengor," *Panamá América*, Apr. 4, 2011; and "Anuncian renuncia de magistrado panameño desata polémica," *La Prensa Gráfica* (El Salvador), Apr. 15, 2011.

Other cases that resulted from corruption investigations will be discussed later.

As if the CD majority on the court were not already dominant, its new president, Alejandro Moncada Luna, proposed that Martinelli name three new judges to activate the so-called Fifth Chamber, to increase their overall efficiency.[29] His proposal elicited a polemical response from civil society, yet the government promptly announced the names of three nominees with apparent popular appeal: former vice president Arturo Vallarino, judge Liria Herrera, and judge Anabelle Padilla. Neither the arguments for efficiency nor the appeal of the candidates did much good, and a few weeks later Martinelli withdrew the nominations and asked the Assembly to abolish the project. The public sense of outrage, however, lingered for months.

Martinelli's efforts to influence the Electoral Tribunal (TE) proved subtler but also menacing to its magistrates. Judge Gerardo Solís denounced the use of government resources in regional elections in 2012. Then the TE annulled a special election in El Bebedero, and, the following month, Solís warned a meeting of the national association of executives (APEDE) that, for the first time since the restoration of democracy, widespread electoral fraud might threaten national elections.[30] As we shall see, the Solís warning correctly anticipated the unprecedented level of misspending of government resources in the 2014 election.

In many respects, the administration's most damaging political ploys sought to spur party switching by legislators and to subvert the independence of the media. First, the CD gave financial and other incentives to induce opposition deputies to switch to the government majority. Next, it conducted recruitment campaigns targeting members of the other four parties in the coalition and their deputies. This helped break up the coalition and provoked the departure of the Panameñista Party and most of its senior members. In the face of CD's actions, other parties struggled to impose discipline and preserve party loyalty, especially

[29] As seen in Chapter 4, Pérez Balladares first proposed adding the fifth chamber, a move soon eliminated by his successor Moscoso. In 2011, the supreme court found the latter action unconstitutional, thus reinstating the proposal by Pérez Balladares. See "Magistrados defienden propósito de la Sala Quinta de la Corte," *Panamá América,* June 13, 2012.

[30] Conferencia del Magistrado Gerardo Solís en la reunión mensual de APEDE, realizada el martes 25 de septiembre de 2012. Just over a year later, APEDE warned the country against the danger to democratic institutions caused by the interference of the supreme court in the TE: "Institucionalidad, en peligro," *La Prensa,* Nov. 8, 2013.

among officeholders. Yet their relative weakness, the now-booming economy, and alternative opportunities prevented them from fighting back effectively. CD's discipline and access to government resources allowed it to project an image of hard work and dedication to the public, so it lost only a few members. This enabled Martinelli to exert control over the nomination process, requiring members of his government to resign from the cabinet before becoming candidates in primary elections. For example, Martinelli headed off the electoral ambitions of minister of economics Frank de Lima and minister of government Jorge Ricardo Fábrega and kept them in the cabinet instead.

Finally, the government sought to undermine the authority and independence of the media and to utilize them to increase its popularity. Even before the election, Martinelli had taken control of a large chunk of television and radio broadcasting, as well as *El Panamá América* newspaper. Foreign journalists seemed to be especially vulnerable to influence, and those who resisted found their visas withdrawn. Intimidation of *La Prensa*, just as it was under Pérez Balladares, stood high on the CD priorities list. At one point, the administration induced trucking companies with government contracts to blockade the paper and prevent deliveries of printing supplies.[31]

The government's pro-business economic policies featured efforts to favor foreign investors and businessmen to spur growth, actions often characterized as predatory or crony capitalism by opponents and critics. For example, the CD rammed a revised mining law through the Assembly that allowed Canada's First Quantum and a South Korean partner to create the largest new copper mine in the world, Minera Panamá, a $6.2 billion project, getting ready to come on line in 2019. The owners expected to make Panama the leading mining exporter in Central America and eventually to contribute about half what the Canal did in taxes. This flow of new foreign and domestic investment matched and at times surpassed the historic levels of the Torrijos years and reinforced the country's breakneck economic growth. The economic boom of 2010 erased the contraction of the Great Recession and continued for the rest of the Martinelli administration.

[31] In a display of reconciliation a day after the strike started, Martinelli asked the strikers to leave: "Martinelli pide retirar camiones que bloquean accesos a 'La Prensa,'" *La Prensa*, Aug. 3, 2012; and Randal C. Archibold, "Panama President Ends Blockade at Newspaper," *New York Times*, Aug. 3, 2012.

THE PEOPLE PUSHED BACK, AGAIN AND AGAIN

Public reaction against the right turn by the Martinelli administration was strongest against economic policies and came in three waves that never fully subsided. The government's approval ratings, high at first, eventually fell and then recovered partially before receding fairly consistently, as the public increasingly rejected Martinelli's high-handed style. A sea change in attitudes developed gradually. First, many groups on the left, including labor organizations, teachers, students, and intellectuals, that had been united behind FREDANESSO a few years earlier, rallied in opposition as they had to Torrijos, this time against the anti-labor "sausage law." Then the mining code proposal and abrogation of environmental protections spurred indigenous communities, environmentalists, and their allies to join in opposition. Finally, the weakening of judicial and other institutions, attacks on the media, and attempts to privatize traditional public services like electricity, communications, and the Colon Free Zone, led the Church and its followers, many lawyers, journalists, civil society organizations, and a segment of the business community to unite in opposition to Martinelli.

The first opposition wave occurred in mid 2010 over attempts to ram six major laws and changes in three legal codes through the Assembly. The losers included environmental protections and worker rights buried in the "sausage law." The opposition epicenter, in Changuinola and Bocas del Toro on the northwestern Caribbean coast, erupted in virulent protests that took the Martinelli government by surprise. Protesters, likewise caught off guard by the violence of police reactions, escalated their actions. Organized labor and sympathizers across the country joined the protests. The traditionally activist banana workers of the region (led by SITRAIBANA), who had been losing jobs and income for decades, spearheaded the general strike called by FRENADESSO. Banana workers in Changuinola clashed with government forces, which used birdshot against them. The tragic consequence was six people killed, dozens with damaged or lost eyesight, and over a hundred wounded.[32] A few days later, more than 5000 people joined in the funeral procession for the workers, and sympathetic rallies erupted across the country. Negotiations between the strikers and minister Papadimitriu gradually restored order, and the government agreed to annul Law 30 and make reparations to affected workers

[32] Defensoría del Pueblo, "Informe de sucesos de violación a Derechos Humanos de julio en Panama," *Burica Press*, Panamá por Dentro, July 18, 2010.

and their families. Panama now commemorates the Changuinola Massacre each July 13th.[33]

After these disturbances, the government finally got back to normal with events like a world surfing contest on Pacific beaches, the 2011 Baseball World Cup, and celebration of the one millionth transit of the Panama Canal by a Chinese vessel. Vice president Varela, an alumnus of the Georgia Institute of Technology, presided over the school's inauguration of its pathbreaking Center for Logistics Innovation and Research in the capital's banking district. Mother Nature, however, brought more tragedy in severe storms that left over 9,000 homeless on the mainland and caused unprecedented floods on most of the Guna Yala islands. Commentators used these events to remind the public of the nation's vulnerability to climate change and of the plight of the indigenous population.

Opposition again arose when the government proposed Law 8 in 2011, a complete revision of the mining code, including provisions affecting indigenous lands, simplifying environmental impact rules, and opening another door for foreign ownership of natural resources. This time, suspicions that the Martinelli family had a financial stake in the Petaquilla gold mine added to the controversy. As in the case of the "sausage law," public reaction was quick, harsh, and vociferous. Concern for the flooding of Guna Yala communities likely added to demonstrations, led this time by the Ngäbe Buglé people, environmentalists, and their allies across the country.[34]

By this time, the Catholic Church had become increasingly outspoken about the decline in social justice in Panama, and European environmentalists rallied to support the affected communities. Marches, road closures, and peaceful protests convinced the administration it had again gone too far. The resultant San Felix agreement included compromises by both sides and led to major revisions of Law 8. Authorities nonetheless expelled two Spanish journalists who were filming a potentially embarrassing documentary, a harbinger of future restrictions on the media.[35]

Although the San Felix settlement temporarily ended debate over hydroelectric projects, a new controversy arose when the Ngäbe Buglé

[33] Paco Gómez, "5000 personas acompañan los mártires de Bocas del Toro," *Burica Press*, Panamá por Dentro, July 18, 2010.

[34] Ruxana Guidi and Robert Guerra, "Climate Change Threatens a Caribbean Tribe's Home," *The Atlantic*, Jan. 14, 2011.

[35] "Panamá fuerza la salida del pais de un periodista español, crítico con el Presidente Martinelli," *RTVE*, Mar. 1, 2011.

objected to the Barro Colorado dam in nearby Chiriqui Province that would affect their lands, proposed in Law 415. This time, the government sent its new border forces, SENAFRONT, to break up roadblocks and demonstrations, resulting in one death, dozens of wounded, and 119 arrests. After more than 200 hours of demonstrations followed by two days of negotiations, Chiriqui Bishop José Luis Lacunza midwifed the San Lorenzo Pact. Again, Papadimitriu led the government side, accompanied by the minister of government and the governor of Chiriqui. Ngäbe Buglé general chief Silvia Carrera led a delegation of a score of her people.[36]

Although protests over foreign investment in electricity and dam construction, plus supreme court expansion, had all arisen separately and had calmed during the first half of 2011, the government's June proposal of Law 486 revived and helped unite nearly all the earlier protesters. The idea of privatizing the remnants of the electricity and communications sectors, especially the burgeoning cell phone networks, also brought out middle class and white-collar citizens more than ever before. Critics began to compare the levels of protest to those against Noriega, with some observers proclaiming that the country was on fire.[37] At this point, the major parties of the opposition and many civic organizations organized the Front for Democracy to oppose the measures.[38] With its approval down to half what it had been in 2009, the government ruled out harsh repressive measures. Instead, Martinelli announced cancellation of the privatisation plans and court expansion.

During 2012, the country remained relatively calm, a respite punctuated by the appointment of Jorge Quijano to succeed Alberto Alemán as administrator of the Panama Canal Authority, described in Chapter 7. The calm broke soon, however, when the administration introduced Law 529 to reform the Colon Free Zone concession and allow for the sale of its lands. Panama's second city erupted into mayhem, and demonstrations quickly spread to the capital. On October 20, a boy was tragically killed in Colon and more than thirty others wounded when the police showed a lot less restraint in using force against the largely Afro-Caribbean people than they had with middle-class activists in Panama City. The government quickly withdrew the proposal, which angered some investors who

[36] Elizabeth Garrido, "Pacto de San Lorenzo plantea nuevo scenario tras 200 horas de protestas," *La Prensa*, Feb. 7, 2012.

[37] Elena Jiménez, "Panamá está que arde," *CRHoy.com*, June 18, 2012.

[38] Harry Brown Araúz and Clara Inés Luna Vásquez, "Panamá: El Crecimiento Económico a Expensas de la Política," *Revista de Ciencia Política* (Chile), v. 33, n. 1 (2013): 291.

would have benefited from it. Remarkably, the pushback from the people came so rapidly and stridently that the economic logic of the crony capitalism behind the bill seems to be the one thing they understood about the proposal, while the propaganda about modernization and economic efficiency fell flat.[39]

Although public outrage was reanimated several more times after 2012, especially over corruption scandals, political energy shifted toward partisan and electoral politics, as the Martinelli administration wound down.

RIVALRIES AND AMBITIONS SHOOK UP THE GOVERNMENT

The mysterious resignation of ambassador to the United States Jaime Alemán Healy, like the sudden departure of US ambassador Barbara Stephenson so early in the Martinelli era, should have alerted the public to the turmoil roiling the administration. Still, on the surface things seemed stable. Other personality clashes involved mostly second-level personnel, and course corrections after the "sausage law" debacle and the Changuinola massacre occurred more readily.[40] By early 2011, however, government approval fell steadily, with one radio report calling it in free fall.[41] Yet this erosion of public support did not end the government's attempts to convert – some would say poach – deputies to the CD nor dampen its frequently denied desire to give Martinelli a second term via a constitutional amendment. A major CD drive during the first half of 2011 succeeded in quadrupling its membership to more than 400,000, second only to the PRD. Coalition partners objected to CD raiding their ranks, but before any of them acted, Martinelli preempted friend and foe alike by tweeting that vice president Varela should resign as foreign minister. The country needed a full-time chancellor, he explained, stating that Varela spent too much time in his roles as vice president and

[39] "Sucesos sin responsables; las protestas de 2010, 2011 y 2012," *La Prensa,* Nov. 3, 2012.

[40] Ambassador Alemán resigned after Papadimitriu organized a Martinelli visit to Washington, DC, for a speech at the US Chamber of Commerce, without his knowledge. Despite that setback, his brother, Álvaro Alemán Healy, a veteran Panameñista leader, accepted chancellor Varela's offer just a few months later to become deputy foreign minister.

[41] Erick Simpson Aguilera, Panama Blog, Jan. 27, 2012, shared UNIMER data showing the steady decline from 86 percent in October 2009, to below 70 percent after June 2010, then dropping steadily from 64 percent in June 2011 to 51 percent in January 2012. https://ericksimpsonaguilera.com/2012/01/27/popularidad-del-presidente-martinelli-en-caida-libre/.

leader of the Panameñista Party (PPa). He denied that the action meant an end to the government coalition.[42]

Doubly humiliated by his dismissal via a tweet, Varela had no recourse but to resign and lead his fellow Panameñistas into the opposition: economics minister Vallarino and housing minister Duboy, nine vice ministers, and twenty deputies in the Assembly, and many local officials across the country at least nominally followed the Varela move. Both sides asserted, disingenuously, that the break had nothing to do with a rumored 2009 agreement for Varela to run for president in 2014.

With the government coalition dropping from a majority of fifty-three to a minority of thirty-three of the seventy-one seats in the Assembly, Martinelli's logic puzzled observers. His action suddenly handed a majority to the opposition. Perhaps Martinelli expected his longtime business partner Vallarino and some PPa deputies to stay with the coalition, especially since Vallarino seems to have hesitated before resigning. Martinelli also may have hoped to convert more opposition deputies to those who had already joined the CD. Unofficial spokesperson Giselle Burillo, the minister of small business, explained a bit more expansively that the break was caused by wiretaps showing Varela's disloyalty to the president.[43]

Martinelli moved to consolidate his base almost immediately, while taking his time filling other vacancies. On September 4, he told an electrified political rally that he intended to fulfill the goals of his coalition and assured his CD followers that their party would win the 2014 election. His early cabinet shuffle moved his minister of commerce, Roberto Henríquez, to the foreign minister position. He soon appointed José Domingo Arias as minister of housing and Ricardo Quijano as minister of industry and commerce. Others would follow.

The clash between the government and the PPa, now in opposition, escalated when Martinelli apparently pressured the Panameñista mayor of

[42] "Ricardo Martinelli destituye a ministro de RR.EE. en medio de crisis de gobierno," *América Económica,* Aug. 31, 2011; "Martinelli pidió la renuncia de su vicepresidente y desató una crisis política," *Infobae América*, Aug. 31, 2011, www.infobae.com/2011/08/30/1032506-martinelli-pidio-la-renuncia-su-vicepresidente-y-desato-una-crisis-politica/.

[43] Burillo stated during a TV interview that Martinelli had recordings of Varela that reflected disloyalty to the government and that it had taken him a long time to believe what he heard before acting: "Martinelli tuvo prueba de audio para destituir a Varela de Cancillería," *La Estrella de Panamá,* Sept. 4, 2011. Her statement also reflected the fact that the regime was relying increasingly on personal family links, like hers to the president: see "Panamá, el reino del nepotismo," *La Estrella de Panamá,* July 15, 2012.

Panama City, Bosco Vallarino, to resign. Vallarino had won the 2009 election decisively, but his status as a Panamanian-American dual national posed constitutional issues until Martinelli came to his support. After the breakup of the coalition, local CD leaders began criticizing Vallarino actions, and observers speculated that Martinelli wanted the post for one of his favorites, Roxana Méndez, who had started the period as vice mayor. Vice president Varela came to Vallarino's defense and accused Martinelli of authoritarian threats, but a few days later the mayor announced that he was resigning for health reasons.[44] That same day, Méndez resigned her cabinet post to assume the office of mayor.

The government and the Panameñistas also clashed in the assembly. Two scholars at the Universidad Interamericana demonstrated that under Martinelli the practice of party switching (*transfugismo* in Spanish) reached unprecedented levels. By the 2012 legislative season, the list of twenty-two deputies elected as candidates of the PPa had shrunk to just ten and the PRD dropped from twenty-six to seventeen. Meanwhile, the CD bench, which started with thirteen deputies, had swelled to a thrity-seven-seat majority of the seventy-one-member body, even without its remaining minor coalition partners.[45]

Meanwhile, super-minister Papadimitriu found himself distanced from the president, signaled by a government decree confiscating fifty-six hectares of beachfront property owned by Papadimitriu's parents in Juan Hambrón, near the surfing championship site, without compensation. Papadimitriu promptly resigned. The same day Martinelli denied any change in the government. A few days later his press office announced that chancellor Henríquez would replace Papadimitriu as minister of the presidency and vice chancellor Álvarez De Soto would be acting foreign minister.[46] Although Henríquez, a longtime Martinelli confidante and his vice-presidential running mate in 2004, was later also called a super-minister, in most respects he behaved more like earlier incumbents.

44 "El vicepresidente de Panamá acusa a Martinelli de amenazar a un alcalde para que renunciara," *CRHoy* (Costa Rica), Jan. 12, 2012; and "El alcalde de la capital panameña renuncia por 'motivos de salud,'" *Panamá América,* Jan. 12, 2012.

45 Brown and Luna, "Panamá: El crecimiento," 297–98. The CD later arranged several more defections to increase its majority.

46 Melquisedec Quintero, "Martinelli aceptó la renuncia de Papadimitriu," *Panamá América*, July 16, 2012; "Renuncia de Papadimitriu sorprende a gobierno panameño," Radio LaPrimerisíma, www.radiolaprimerisima.com/noticias/123725/renuncia-de-papa dimitriu-sorprende-a-gobierno-panameno.

Public commentary by key participants on the reasons for the sudden change in the inner circle of the government was limited, but Panamanian media published a good deal of speculation about the break.[47] Much of the interpretation hinged on wiretap evidence, like the ones Burillo revealed about Varela's alleged disloyalty or the Wikileaks cables depicting Papadimitriu's disparaging remarks about the administration to US officials.[48] By then, the public mostly disregarded Martinelli's denials of espionage against both friends and foes. Another explanation saw a dispute between Martinelli loyalists, including Alberto Vallarino, and the Papadimitriu family over the beach property or the president's desire to avoid a corruption scandal. Papadimitriu sympathizers speculate that he left due to the president's chaotic administration.

Public approval of Martinelli fell under 50 percent for the first time in the wake of the Papadimitriu resignation. The president then reorganized his cabinet, appointing Roberto Roy minister of canal affairs (without giving up leadership of the Metro project) and moving Rómulo Roux to head the foreign ministry. He rounded out this shuffle with a new minister of health, asserting that his administration would improve health care and deliver new medical facilities.

Martinelli gamely shrugged off controversies with the media, over the Free Zone and electoral fraud, and adopted a new strategy for his remaining years in office. As long as his people did their jobs, avoided controversy, and seemed to make headway, the president allowed them to develop their own fiefdoms. Henríquez provided an excellent early example in commerce, as did Lucy Molinar in education, Alma Cortez in labor, Salo Shamah in tourism, and Guillermo Ferrufino in social development. They gave the president opportunities to shine in ceremonial inaugurations and to receive the plaudits of grateful citizens. In exchange, they ruled supremely in their separate realms with unusual cabinet longevity.

Yet as ambitions for the 2014 elections blossomed, Martinelli made clear that he would remain firmly in control of the CD. If he could not be

47 "Panamá: ¿Por qué renuncíó Papadimitriu?" http://solidaridadpanama.blogspot.com/2012/07/panama-por-que-renuncio-papadimitriu.html; "Vocero de Martinelli confesó que gobierno intentaba retener a Papadimitriu," *La Estrella de Panamá,* July 17, 2012; Eliana Morales Gil, "El 'tsunami' tras la renuncia de Papadimitriu," *La Prensa,* July 17, 2012; and Gil Moreno, "La renuncia de Papadimitriu," *La Prensa,* July 25, 2012.

48 Tim Johnson's article for the McClatchy newspapers about Obama's long-delayed first meeting with Martinelli drew on these revelations and provided examples of the kind of reports that got constant playback in the Panamanian media: "Wikileaks: Dim View of Panamanian President Obama Will Meet," Apr. 26, 2011, www.mcclatchydc.com/news/special-reports/article24626320.html.

the candidate, because of constitutional prohibition or due to plummeting popularity (eventually below 40 percent), he would manage the succession personally. With at least six ministers actively jockeying for public support as pre-candidates in March 2013, the president abruptly announced that any official who wanted the nomination for president or any other office would be required to resign from their jobs. About half the field, ministers Roux, Arias, and Burillo accepted their boss's control of the process and resigned.[49] Their degree of acceptance of the president's discipline would also be confirmed by actions in later years. Meanwhile, in the face of political opposition and resistance, riding the economic boom became even more appealing for Martinelli.

LOPSIDED ECONOMIC GROWTH CONTINUED

Despite political commotion and failures of many of Martinelli's programs, Panama's GDP growth after 2009 never fell below 6 percent and reached almost 11 percent in 2011 and 2012, a phenomenal streak. Statistically, and in lots of capital city neighborhoods and in the rapidly spreading suburbs of Panama City, prosperity showed in lavish buildings, resorts, shopping centers, and new cars crowding the streets.[50] Even in the countryside and provincial centers, building booms produced multistory high-rises, strip malls, new tourist facilities, improved regional airports, health facilities, and new or rebuilt schools. A report in the country's leading newspaper proclaimed the economic optimism of the era in February of 2013: "Panama is in the best moment of its history to consolidate the sustainable growth of its economy and human development during the next 20 years."[51]

Yet for many Panamanians and outside observers, the unevenness of the boom also glared in the background, just as it had under Torrijos. City buses were even more crowded on longer commutes, *diablos rojos* still careened up congested streets evading control, windshield washers and street vendors hassled drivers at traffic stops, surges in homelessness accompanied the destruction of marginal housing with each major

49 "Martinelli pide a Burillo renunciar; otros ministros prefieron no seguir," *La Estrella de Panamá*, Mar. 13, 2013. New economics minister Frank de Lima and Ferrufino and Molinar cut back on their politicking.

50 The government's pride in the country's economy was clearly reflected in a March 2013 PowerPoint briefing prepared for a regional forum by vice minister of finance Mahesh C. Khemlani, "Economic Performance: Panama and Latin America," in author's files.

51 Nicolás Ardito Barletta, "La economía en Panamá (2000–2013)," *La Prensa*, Feb. 17, 2013.

storm, people mobilized in protests, and the prison populations grew relentlessly as cost-of-living increases squeezed the poor. In many respects, economic development followed the path laid out in Martinelli's strategic plan. As hoped, foreign direct investment blossomed. A 33 percent jump in 2010 nearly matched pre-recession levels, then bounced up to a new record level in 2011 (equivalent to almost 13 percent of GDP), and averaged about 10 percent during Martinelli's final years. Surveying the scene from the tower headquarters of the American Chamber of Commerce, Maurice Belanger commented: "There is still some banana left in the republic, but it is changing fast."[52]

The powerful stimulus of foreign direct investment worked right where it was intended: in the business and logistics hub that Panama had long sought.[53] Canal expansion attracted a cluster of other enterprises that included relocation of transportation firms and the support networks needed for them to thrive. The ranks of regional offices for multinational corporations swelled, shipping firms relocated to Panama, and work began on a billion-dollar petroterminal. Growth in logistics support services boosted attendance at the Panama Maritime conferences and at other trade, business, and economic congresses. A report on the country's economic progress from 2000 to 2013 emphasized that the activity in the hub zone had grown to 81 percent of the national economy.[54]

On the 500th anniversary of Balboa's European encounter with the Pacific Ocean in 2013, Panama hosted the International Academic Congress on the Pacific in the City of Knowledge. The meeting attracted a distinguished audience to hear such recognized experts as Felipe Fernández-Armesto of Spain, Hugh Thomas of England, and its own experts Alberto Alemán and Omar Jaén Suárez, who had just published his history of the Pacific Ocean Basin.[55] About this time, the US National Public Radio vividly described Panama's boom environment:

52 Interview with Maurice Belanger, Dec. 1, 2014.

53 "Latinoamérica crece como destino empresarial," *Capital Madrid*, Dec. 27, 2012; and Aristides Hernández, "Inversión extranjera sostiene crecimiento económico de Panamá," *La Estrella de Panamá*, Sept. 22, 2014.

54 Ardito Barletta, "La economía en Panamá," *La Prensa*, Feb. 17, 2013. The interior region of the country provided 16 percent and native lands the remaining three percent.

55 *Hacia una historia global: 500 años de la cuenca del Pacífico* (Panama: ACP/Ediciones Balboa, 2014). Also see Victoria Isabel Cardiel C., "Omar Jaén Suárez y el Pacífico," *La Prensa*, Dec. 6, 2016.

These days Panama City is a giant excavation site. Roads are being torn up. Excavators are digging out tunnels, while cranes above put the finishing touches on new high-rise condominiums, office towers, banks and hotels.[56]

Yet within this bustling hub of prosperity, Colon sank further into poverty from its glory days at the end of WWII.[57] In 2013, as the city erupted in violence over the proposed Free Zone reforms, some Hollywood film makers decided to use it to portray the wretchedness and chaos of Haiti. Hearing this, *New York Times* reporter Randall C. Archibold took a closer look at the city where the Panama Railroad began in the 1850s. He found:

Panama can lay claim to some of the starkest disparities of wealth in Latin America, ... the persistent poverty in Colon, an hour's drive from the symbols of wealth in Panama City, remains a glaring, festering example.[58]

Archibold hypothesized that the city's downward spiral had been exacerbated by the closing of US military bases upon which its community had been more dependent than the rest of Panama. Additionally, while the Free Zone had grown into the second largest bonded trade center in the world, after Hong Kong, few of its more than 30,000 middle-class employees lived there – most commuted from suburbs or outlying towns. Similarly, few of the thousands of workers on Canal expansion or those building the new Colon-Panama highway came from the largely Afro-Caribbean urban population.

Brown and Luna emphasized that in Colon, when official unemployment in Panama dropped to 4 percent, major public works projects still provided few permanent jobs or lifted workers into the formal economy.[59] Other paths existed: for example, the port of MIT developed a locally

[56] Jason Beaubien, "Panama Booms While Poor Watch from Afar," *National Public Radio*, Apr. 16, 2012, www.npr.org/2012/04/16/150727218/panama-booms-while-poor-watch-from-afar.

[57] Duality is the key feature of other sources for this narrative, including Randall C. Archibold, "Bursts of Economic Growth in Panama Have Yet to Vanquish Old Ghosts," *New York Times*, Dec. 12, 2011; Brown and Luna, "Panamá: El crecimiento"; and Tim Padgett, "Panama's Canal Divides a Country into Haves and Have Nots," *National Public Radio*, June 1, 2014, www.npr.org/sections/parallels/2014/05/30/317394468/panamas-canal-divides-a-country-into-haves-and-have-nots.

[58] Randall C. Archibold, "A Once Vibrant City Struggles as Panama Races Ahead on a Wave of Prosperity," *New York Times*, Mar. 23, 2013.

[59] Brown and Luna, "Panamá: El Crecimiento," 292–94. More broadly, the authors show that the Martinelli administration, in general, prioritized economic goals, especially growth, over political considerations, such as who would be the primary beneficiaries of the growth.

based efficient labor force with a long-term training program. Yet neither the government nor any other major employer in the area provided such training. And although the government had undertaken many projects to benefit the region, public distrust had reached a high level before the Free Zone reform was even attempted.

Besides the growth of the economy, some structural shifts also occurred, especially in the primary sector. Despite the controversies surrounding it, the mining industry expanded more rapidly and promised to become a larger contributor to the economy. The expected increase in export income and government revenue, however, did not produce a proportional increase in employment in rural regions of the country. Most of the new jobs were skilled and well-paid urban ones.

In contrast, agriculture continued its downward spiral. Agricultural exports dropped further, and the reorientation of production for the domestic market, despite relatively strong demand, exacerbated the decline. Increasing construction in provincial capitals and tourist areas absorbed some of the lost jobs in farming but not all. The rural work force suffered further by even more abrupt losses in fishing. The prohibition of long line fishing in 2010, ostensibly to benefit the tourism industry, idled hundreds of boats and put several thousand fishermen and supporting workers out of jobs in rural areas. It also undermined the national contribution to food supply. Despite some gains in the countryside, then, the overall situation continued to be discouraging.

On the national scene, Martinelli took pride from his many achievements. For example, on the World Bank's Ease of Doing Business index Panama jumped to 55th in 2013, almost reaching the level of Mexico (53rd) and behind Colombia (43rd) and Peru (42nd). (Chile and Costa Rica still led the region.)[60] Even better, the government's drive for competitiveness raised the country from 58th (nearly tied with Mexico and Costa Rica) in 2008–09 to 40th and not far below Latin American leader Chile (34th) in 2013–2014 on the World Economic Forum's Global Competitiveness Index.

On the more multidimensional Index of Economic Freedom, prepared by the *Wall Street Journal* and the Heritage Foundation, Panama registered a marked decline in performance, falling from 55th in 2009 (between Mexico and Peru, but well below the top countries of Latin America) to 71st in 2014 (and far below Mexico and Peru, who stayed about the same). Mixed results at best.

[60] Ministry of the Presidency, *Memoria 2013*: 78–79.

Panama scored some gains on other international indices. The UN's Index of Human Development showed that the incremental improvement during the Moscoso and Torrijos administrations continued. The reports for 2010 and 2015, covering the years from 2009 to 2014, showed:

- Life expectancy at birth increased from 76.8 to 77.8 years.
- The potential for learning, the number of years of schooling that a five-year-old could expect, improved from 12.6 to 13.3 years, but the average number of years of education by adults above twenty-five remained the same, 9.3 years.
- Per capita income (in 2011 dollars) increased 16 percent, from $15,656 to $18,182.
- Panama's overall ranking among 188 countries fell from 54th to 60th.

This apparent contradiction between incremental improvement on three of four measures and a fall in rankings was explained by the influence of inequality. Compared with Costa Rica and Uruguay, two geographically and demographically small middle-income countries, Panama dropped in rankings because its coefficient of inequality was much larger than the other two countries. In a way, gini struck back![61]

The UN report also revealed important gender disparities. On this dimension, Panama scored much lower, 96th out of 155 countries, gauged on maternal mortality, adolescent birth rates, male/female labor force participation, and representation in the national legislature. The biggest disparities occurred in the labor force (half compared to men), and only one in five legislators were women. Other low scores resulted from high maternal mortality and high adolescent birth rates, due partly to generalized poverty and isolation of the indigenous on reservations.

CORRUPTION UNDERMINED THE PLANS

With the benefit of hindsight, we know that Martinelli's government stood among the most corrupt in Latin America in the 2010s, but full

[61] The Human Development Index score fell on the basis of the inequality measured by the Gini coefficient and the combined effect of differences in life expectancy at birth, educational attainment, and personal income at birth. The HDI score for Panama dropped from 0.780 to 0.604, while smaller drops for Uruguay, from 0.793 to 0.678, and for Costa Rica, from 0.766 to 0.613, were because of their lower inequality. United Nations Human Development Report for Panama, 2015, see http://hdr.undp.org/sites/all/themes/hdr_theme/country-notes/PAN.pdf.

revelations only came later. Still, officials and informed citizens knew, from the drumbeat of press stories, that things were amiss. His successor would unleash investigations and prosecutions after the 2014 election, to be covered in the next Chapter. For now, we will focus on increasing cognizance of wrongdoing and perceptions of corruption during the Martinelli years.

During most of the Martinelli administration, corruption appeared largely as background noise, noticeable and bothersome but not clearly identifiable. Concern arose over irregular personnel appointments, such as former Martinelli employees taking high positions, and many departures or removals of key figures, including the solicitor general, supreme court magistrates, and the mayor of Panama City. In this milieu, the 2014 nomination of his wife for vice president on the CD ticket seemed normal. Business connections of families linked to the president also drew adverse attention, like the Papadimitriu family's sudden monopoly on the supply of sand for construction projects and the global wheeling and dealing of the Martinelli sons.

Specific revelations, especially about property ownership, were another source of intermittent alarm. In 2011, for example, *La Prensa* ran a barely noticed report about members of the Papadimitriu family getting title to some beach property in Juan Hambrón. It was only after the confiscation of this property the following year, triggering the departure of the superminister from the government, that disputes over titles to lands, as in the Free Zone controversy, became an area for constant vigilance. Major events also provided reminders about corruption. When former dictator Noriega was returned to Panama from France in December 2011 to complete a long jail term at home, the media were full of stories about the ghosts of the past, corruption, and drug trafficking.[62]

Sometimes the hint of corruption was vague and ill-defined, such as the rumors about why Barack Obama kept so distant from Martinelli, put off the latter's White House visit for almost two years, and never reciprocated. This situation likely reflected the embarrassing news of the incarceration of Martinelli's brother Ramón in Mexico for money laundering.[63] In other cases, the Martinelli administration found itself wrapped in what one newspaper called "the long tentacles of scandal." For example, questions about the high cost of radars purchased from Italy in a sweetheart deal between Martinelli and his Italian mentor, Silvio

[62] Archibold, "Bursts of Economic Growth."

[63] "Martinelli oficializó el fascismo: Mauro Zúñiga Araúz," *La Prensa*, Sept. 2, 2011.

Berlusconi, prompted more leaks about other irregular connections and problems with Italian suppliers.[64] Before the end of the term, occasional suspicions about the purchase of supplies for government welfare and school programs, infrastructure projects for the cold storage system and health facilities multiplied into widespread reporting about the sudden enrichment of officials and speculation about key culprits. Gradually, corruption investigations overseas, especially regarding the Berlusconi deals in Italy and the Odebrecht ones in Brazil, also draped some of these tentacles directly over Martinelli and other high officials just in time for the 2014 election.

Corruption indirectly swelled government debt by channeling graft to public officials overseeing new public expenditures. The complicity of officials with contractors allowed for underperformance and waste, a cost that may never be accounted for fully. Finally, the loss of public trust in the face of widespread fraud left a legacy of demoralization that we cannot calculate. These debts, costs, and citizen cynicism must be charged to Martinelli's administration in future historical accountings. Still, some numbers were clear by the end of his term. Martinelli added over $10 billion to the national debt of Panama, compared to just over $1.6 billion by Torrijos and just under $1.5 by Moscoso. By 2014, Panama's debt surpassed $21.2 billion, or 45 percent of GDP, a troubling level for a developing country.[65]

A World Economic Forum analysis showed that by the end of Martinelli's term Panama's global competitiveness ranking fell from 40th to 48th, perhaps due to perceptions of government corruption.[66] At the same time, during the Martinelli years, the Corruption Perceptions Index calculated by Transparency International registered a significant rise, from 83rd to 102nd out of 177 countries.

Corruption also undermined citizens' confidence in their country and its institutions. During the 2014 election campaign, about a quarter of respondents to a poll believed corruption to be the third most important

[64] "Lavitola, el vínculo entre los milliones y Finmeccanica," *La Estrella de Panamá*, Nov. 7, 2011. Another lingering scandal involved suspicions that Martinelli profited from the new mining ventures in Panama through investments his sons managed at Financial Pacific: see "El sistema financiero de Panamá, en peligro tras escándalo presidencial," *El Mundo* (Spain), Dec. 27, 2012.

[65] Roberto González Jiménez, "Ricardo Martinelli aumentó la deuda publica en B/.10,440 milliones," *La Prensa*, Dec. 11, 2014.

[66] "Corrupción causa que Panamá caiga en índice de competividad global," *La Prensa*, Sept. 2, 2014.

problem facing their country, just behind the transportation crisis and the economy.[67] Such anxiety over corruption also risked public shifts in mood that may favor authoritarianism, as happened recently in Venezuela and elsewhere.[68]

Orlando J. Pérez studied the relationship of public opinion about corruption with support for democracy in the middle of Martinelli's term.[69] A national survey (n=1620) during the first quarter of 2012 found that the perception of corruption (noticing or hearing about the corruption of public officials) in Panama was among the highest among the twenty-six countries he studied. Using a scale in which 100 represented widespread perception of corruption and 0 very little, Panama scored 78.4, close to those of Colombia, Argentina, the Dominican Republic, Peru, Honduras, and Mexico. Panama's result came in higher than in earlier years: 73.5 in 2004, 73.7 in 2006, 70.2 in 2008, and 76.2 in 2010. Pérez also discovered that Panamanians reported less victimization due to corruption, like being asked for a bribe at work or to obtain public services. Only 8.8 percent of Panamanians reported such experience during the last year (a little more than the lowest countries), compared with 40 percent or more in Ecuador, Bolivia, and Haiti. Likewise, the data suggested that hearing about major cases of corruption had more impact than personal experience with it.

Finally, Pérez found that citizens expressed confidence that their institutions could withstand government pressures. Over two thirds responded that the Catholic and Protestant churches, the media, and the ACP represented the public interest, while only a third said the presidency, the Assembly, or political parties did so. The supreme court even fared somewhat better than might have been expected. Pérez's findings suggest that most Panamanians believe in democracy as the best form of government.

Martinelli's business approach to governing may not have led directly to corruption and high-handed policies, but two astute observers saw a connection: his 62 percent victory in 2009 seems to have convinced

67 "La corrupción, el tercer problema de los panameños," *La Estrella de Panamá,* Mar. 27, 2014.

68 Olmedo Beluche, "La corrupción y el sistema político panameño," Kaosenlared.net/la-corrupcion-y-el-sistema-politico-panameño, Feb. 3, 2015.

69 "Cultura política de la democracia en Panamá; Evidencia desde el Barómetro de las Américas, June 2013," www.vanderbilt.edu/lapop/panama/Panama_Country_Report_2012_W.pdf.

him that he controlled 62 percent of the "shares" of the country, thereby enabling him to do whatever he wanted.[70]

THE 2014 ELECTION: VOTERS INSISTED ON ALTERNATION

The 2014 elections replayed established traditions and debuted intriguing innovations. Alternation in the presidency, to prevent domination by a single strong force, seemed to be the most important outcome for Panamanians, because they did it for a sixth consecutive time.[71] The 2014 election shaped up early, after the rupture of the CD-PPa coalition led Varela into tacit opposition to Martinelli. Varela and his followers moved closer to the PRD and increasingly active elements on the left. The final three years of Martinelli's term proved the most politically convulsed period since the fall of Noriega.[72]

The 2014 election turned into a three-way race, between Varela for the PPa, Juan Carlos Navarro for the PRD, and José Domingo Arias for the CD. Martinelli had failed to get a constitutional amendment to permit him a second term, as had Pérez Balladares in 1998, so he allowed three novice followers to compete in the primary to head the ticket, evidently planning to control the winner, who turned out to be Arias. Later, he put up his wife, Marta Linares de Martinelli, for vice president, thinking that she could be his agent inside a new CD administration. Late in the campaign, the CD seemed on track to win.

At the time of the government split with Varela, Martinelli had already begun expanding his personal control over the multimedia empire NEX,

[70] Observation by retired US diplomat John Maisto, cited by Panamanian diplomat Guillermo "Willy" Cochez. See the op ed by Cochez, "Panamá y la lucha contra la corrupción," *El Pais* (Madrid), Mar. 10, 2015.

[71] The quality and depth of commentary on Panamanian elections was reflected in these studies: Mélanie Barragán and Stefanie Ruh," Elecciones Panamá 2014: una conflictiva continuidad en el cambio," *Revista Panameña de Política* 18 (Jul.–Dec. 2014), http://es.rfi.fr/americas/20140408-recta-final-de-la-renida-campana-electoral-panamena; and FES (Friedrich Ebert Stiftung), "Panamá, Balance de las elecciones 2014 y desafíos de las fuerzas progresistas," *Análisis*, no. 1 (2014). The website of Panama's TE is an invaluable source for authoritative information, much of it conveniently summarized in Lilian González, "Balance–Elecciones Panamá 2014, FES America Central, mayo 2014," www.fesamericacentral.org/files/fes-america-central/actividades/panama/Actividades_pan/140512_Balance_Elecciones_Panama/Balance%20-%20Elecciones%202014%20Panama_final.pdf.

[72] Centro Gilberto Bosques, "Elecciones presidenciales en Panamá: Análisis del Triunfo de Varela y Desafíos para el Nuevo Gobierno," Mexico, Senado de la República, May 9, 2014: 4.

FIGURE 8.3 CD presidential candidate José Domingo Arias addressing foreign observers at the Superior Electoral Tribunal, prior to May 2014 election. Orlando Sierra/AFP/Getty Images

likely violating a constitutional prohibition on simultaneous ownership of a major newspaper (EPASA's *Panamá América)*, TV, radio, and other media. Meanwhile, other media took up forthright opposition to the government, such as *La Prensa*, or formed alliances with opposing parties, such as Medcom with the PRD. The resulting partisanship of the media made them part of everyday politics.

The administration's media purchasing power, plus Martinelli's ownership of a large segment of the media, gave the CD an edge in the 2014 campaign. A study conducted by the Peace and Justice Commission showed that CD candidate Arias got 32 percent of media coverage, the PRD 24 percent and the PPa 22 percent. The limited ideological differences between the three major contenders facilitated an image-based competition. The two more leftist contenders, Juan Jované and Genaro López, had little media coverage and accused their rivals of simply arguing over the details of neoliberal programs.[73]

[73] Clara Inés Luna, "Las elecciones vistas desde la comunicación de los medios," in FES Panamá, *Balance:* 14–17.

With little of substance for candidates to debate, campaigns fought to define their images as early as possible. In March 2013, the PRD and PPa held presidential primaries, resulting in the candidacies of Juan Carlos Varela and Juan Carlos Navarro. Both received over 90 percent support. Not long afterward, the CD, still a young party, saw a vigorous competition among its three rivals, cabinet members Rómulo Roux, Giselle Burillo, and José Domingo Arias. The leftist Broad Democratic Front (FAD) produced the one big surprise of the primaries, when just 8 percent of its members voted to make veteran SUNTRACS union leader, Genaro López, their candidate.[74]

Once faces became associated with parties, the contenders got to work on defining their programs. The PRD held the most traditional exercise, in which over a hundred professionals contributed to the elaborate "Plan for Everyone." Varela concentrated more on building his People First alliance with the former Torrijos ally, the Popular Party (PP), in August of 2013, and rejected the potential for a unified opposition that would include the PRD.[75] The resulting partisan divisions boiled down to core positions outlined by Ebrahim Asvat:

- Varela stressed the importance of controlling prices for staple items in Panama's Family Basket, promised to call a constituent assembly for a new constitution, offered all Panamanians access to world-class bilingual education, pledged to build a fourth bridge over the Canal, and vowed to increase pensions.
- Juan Carlos Navarro emphasized cutting the cost of the Family Basket by 10 percent, replacing heavy handed law enforcement with tolerance to make people more secure, stationing more police in poor neighborhoods, increasing the autonomy of the judiciary, and developing a nutrition program to combat hunger.
- The Arias program pledged to build on all the Martinelli achievements by adding more lines to the Metro, creating an international university hub and a site for women's services, expanding agricultural

[74] Barragán and Ruh, "Elecciones Panamá," 16–18, provide details on the primaries.

[75] Mélany Barragán Manjón, "Elecciones Panamá 2014: Poder, corrupción y guerra sucia," argues that Varela rejected an alliance with Navarro because PRD supporters were financing advertising against him, while PRD supporters rejected working with Varela because his companies did not pay minimum wage and he had opposed Canal expansion. In *Elecciones y cambio de élites en América Latina, 2014 y 2015*, eds. Manuel Alcántara Sáez and María Laura Tagina (Salamanca: Ediciones Universidad de Salamanca, 2016), 71–94, www.jstor.org/stable/j.ctt1gr7f66.

credits, and adding medicine to the popular "100 at 70" program that Varela had originally invented for Martinelli.
- The independent candidates, especially Jované, expressed more originality, rejecting the free trade deals and logistics hub endorsed by the big three and called for more radical reforms.[76]

Analysts dubbed the 2014 contest the "dirty campaign version 2.0" to emphasize its similarity to the 2009 election. Magaly Castillo cited abuses by the Martinelli administration, confirmed by observers from the Organization of American States, the Carter Center, and the International Republican Institute.[77] And although the Catholic Church had gotten all candidates to sign an electoral pact in 2014, unlike 2009, it failed to achieve the restraints of earlier experiences.

Outside observers listed numerous election infractions, mostly by candidates who used government resources. As a result, the Electoral Tribunal annulled a record fifty-four elections, including fourteen of the seventy-one contests for deputies to the Assembly, mostly for using public funds.[78] Analyst José Ángel Garrido Pérez explained, a bit sarcastically, that almost the whole country had become a *bebedero* (watering trough), alluding as well to a well-known make up election in Tonosí a couple of years earlier that the TE annulled for the same reason. Garrido also illustrated the way the practice worked, describing how PRD candidate for mayor of Panama City José Luis Fábrega had adopted the nickname "the tank of gas candidate" so his constituents would know why they should vote for him.[79] Government agents tried to interfere in TE actions, misused tax law to intimidate rivals and their supporters, wiretapped opponents, and turned blind eyes to diversion of funds and abuse of office. Finally, polls showed that the public resented the breach of constitutional prohibitions against nepotism when Martinelli chose his wife to be candidate for vice president.

Late stages of the campaign turned ugly. The US embassy denied rumors on social media that it had cancelled candidate Varela's visa, but this seemed to have little impact on the election. Instead, Arias's shrinking lead in the polls seemed more newsworthy, as were defections from him by major figures, such as former presidential candidate, entertainer, and

[76] Centro Gilberto Bosques, *Elecciones*, 3–5.
[77] "Elecciones y retos de la democracia panameña," in FES Panamá, *Balance*: 3–7.
[78] Barragán and Ruh, "Elecciones Panamá," 34.
[79] "El pueblo de Panamá estrena nueva conciencia electoral," in FES Panamá, *Balance*: 9–11.

tourism minister Rubén Blades.[80] Gandásegui referred to this tendency as the "punishment" vote, directed at both the Martinelli government and the PRD. He noted that while Varela's party had only about 200,000 registered members, he got over a half-million votes. In contrast, both Navarro and Arias received fewer votes than the registered memberships of their parties. Luna reinforced the importance of the rejection factor, pointing out that Quantix polls showed that just 10 percent of prospective voters rejected Varela, versus 30 percent each opposed to Arias and Navarro.[81]

What may have been the turning point of the election, although not noticed at the time, was the April 4th televised debate, the first in Panama's history with all the candidates on the same stage. Observers generally agree that Jované won the debate on substance but that Varela's calm, presidential presence won the war.

Election polling proved confusing. Barragán and Ruh explained that various polls showed a clear break in preference trends late in the campaign.[82] Lilian González Guevara emphasized a variety of factors, including some positive forces that led to Varela's unexpected victory. For instance, he attracted both young voters and new supporters. She also noted a trend toward split-ticket voting, the declining dominance of the PRD and PPa, and the rejection of *continuismo*.[83]

Beyond the presidential race, other results of the 2014 elections foretold change. Varela's People First alliance won only thirteen of the seventy-one seats in the Assembly, providing a weak platform for governing. The CD's United for Change coalition captured thirty-three seats versus the PRD's twenty-five, causing a realignment of forces with the potential for either conflict or collaboration. The outcomes of the seventy-seven mayoral races across the country reflected a problem for the PRD, because, although it retained control of most mayoralties, its poor results at the national level could undermine future contests. Finally, unprecedented levels of abuses during the 2014 elections emphasized the need for major electoral reforms, as called for by election observers and implied by Varela's call for a constitutional convention.

* * * *

80 Randal C. Archibold, "Incumbent's Party Loses Presidency in Panama," *New York Times*, May 4, 2014.

81 Marco A. Gandásegui, hijo, "La hegemonía burguesa y la izquierda," in FES Panamá, *Balance:* 6–8; and Luna, "Las elecciones vistas," 14–17.

82 "Elecciones Panamá," 23–28.

83 "Factores de influencia y desafíos," in FES Panamá, *Balance:* 11–14.

President Martinelli produced the economic boom that he pledged, but his "business" approach did not distinguish his administration much from those of his predecessors. The blast of measures and the strategic economic plan of the "fast and furious" first 100 days promised supporters the results they wanted and at first even expanded his base of support to an unprecedented level. Achievements included replacing red devil buses and beginning a modern mass transportation system. Meanwhile, minimum wage checks got fattened and electric bills trimmed. Yet gradually Martinelli's personalistic style and the emphasis on expanding the administration's power base became the most characteristic features of his government. Filling the cabinet with appointees known for their business experience did not start an era of transactional politics either. Instead, Martinelli's toxic style of authoritarian leadership became the more identifying trait, and the former businessmen behaved just like politicians once they got into office. Still, personal connections to the president became the linchpin of the administration. First, he elevated campaign manager Jimmy Papadimitriu into a sort of co-president and fixer. For other key jobs, including comptroller general and supreme court magistrates, the only credentials that mattered seemed to be working closely with him in business and political campaigns. Many sensitive roles were reserved for first lady Marta Linares.

The security challenges of the era associated with instability and criminal activity in the Central American region and the rising crime rate within Panama exacerbated the regime's authoritarian tendency. The government's criminal code revision, new ministry of public security, new naval-air bases across the country, acquisition of sophisticated security equipment, and alignment against the Latin American left implied a militaristic and punitive approach to the nation's problems. Yet rather than improve people's sense of security, these measures simply expanded an already high rate of incarceration. Such measures and overlapping political machinations were early signs of Martinelli's increasingly rightist policies during his first year in power. Replacing a potentially hostile solicitor general and appointing cronies to the comptroller general's office and to the supreme court raised political alarms. These were followed by economic measures that favored foreign investment and the interests of regime confederates, more characteristic of crony capitalism.

Martinelli's repeated efforts to alter mining laws, undermine worker's rights, privatize utilities, reduce environmental protections, intrude on reservation rights, and even adjust property rights in the Free Zone reflected an unexpectedly harsh approach to the government's promise of economic progress. On a half-dozen occasions, in response to what were viewed as draconian policy initiatives, the people pushed back with public demonstrations against the regime. A leftist coalition that carried over from the fight against social security reform under Torrijos, FRENADESSO, mobilized students, intellectuals, and the union movement behind the banana workers to protest the infamous "sausage law." After scores of workers were gunned down with birdshot on the streets of Bocas del Toro, the victims of the "Changuinola massacre" created a new martyrdom for popular rights and showed that the regime's policy excesses could be opposed.

The government's effort to extend privatization in the communications field and almost simultaneous maneuvers to subvert the supreme court aroused a second wave of public repudiation. This time the middle class, business community, and civic society leadership that had first mobilized against Noriega joined in the demonstrations and blocked Martinelli's initiatives. Not surprisingly, these defeats plunged the government's approval rating to far below those of the troubled Torrijos years. Yet despite the government's downward spiral, its attention turned to presidential succession. Failing to gain approval for reelection, Martinelli abruptly fired Varela from his second job in the administration, foreign minister. This action embarrassed the leader of the coalition's junior partners in the Panameñista Party, and they abandoned the coalition, apparently along with the chance to be next in line for president. Then, after even super-minister Papadimitriu could not overcome the policy reversals and his family's property corruption scandals, he too bailed.

With key rivals out of the way, Martinelli orchestrated a contest for the CD nomination among three loyal cabinet ministers, inserted his wife Marta Linares de Martinelli as candidate for vice president, and prepared to continue in control from behind the scenes of his chosen successor, José Domingo Arias. With the regime's popular standing severely damaged, two former rivals for the 2009 election returned to the contest. Juan Carlos Navarro forged a new coalition between his PRD and the Popular Party. Varela, on the other hand, at first campaigned alone but later drew support from defectors from the Martinelli coalition and a growing segment of opposition figures.

The successive policy clashes of the Martinelli years might have set the stage for a campaign focused heavily on economic issues. The government had revived the Torrijos boom and launched the development of Panama as a logistics and business hub for the Americas. The Panama City Metro and MiBus system and conclusion of the Cinta Costera highway at last provided real progress for the capital city. Yet the continuing concentration of benefits for the wealthy and already modernized segments of society allowed scant improvement in the lives of most people, with few exceptions.

Rumors and glimpses of corruption that had remained in the background for years soon flowered into scandals. Word spread about the poor quality of public works projects, crumbling school roofs, radars that could not detect smugglers, health centers not ready for use, and the cold storage system that barely functioned in a few remote sites. Likewise, news about the sudden fortunes of regime figures and the prosecution of foreign officials for corruption involving Panama added plausibility to the charges. Perhaps most compelling of all were stories about alleged crimes, indictment, and conviction of Berlusconi in Italy, a businessman/politician even richer, more media dominating, and personalistic than Martinelli. Suddenly, calling the Panamanian leader "Berlusconian" took on new meaning.

Despite efforts by the Catholic Church and civic leaders to restore civility to the 2014 election, it rapidly turned into what was dubbed "dirty war, version 2.0." It could not be salvaged by principled leftist policy advocates nor a televised presidential debate. The early CD lead that Martinelli's media dominance and use of government resources provided, however, soon began to wither. As more independents and youths turned to Varela, the Panamanian public's inchoate rejection of the incumbents carried the once rudely sidelined vice president to victory.

9

The Varela Administration: Toward a More Humane Society

[T]here is a clear, definitive, and ineluctable ethical imperative to act.
Pope Francis

INAUGURATION OF CANAL EXPANSION, JUNE 2016

On June 26, 2016, Panama proudly inaugurated the new expanded locks at both ends of its Canal. The *COSCO Panama*, one of many enormous neo-Panamax vessels built in recent years ahead of the locks opening, had been chosen for making the passage in a lottery among dozens of ships nominated by their respective owners. Ceremonies began in the morning at the Agua Clara locks on the Atlantic side, with huge crowds packed into the visitors' center and live streaming video of the event on the ACP website. Thousands of national and global elites watched from luxury yachts at strategic points along the way, while average Panamanians flocked to other vantage points across the Isthmus.

Brand new tractor tugs, with powerful 360-degree propulsion, preceded and followed the ship into the locks to maneuver it into position for tying off to the wall. The ship's movement through the three locks, controlled with sliding gates the size of 11-story office buildings, proceeded as planned, and an hour later the *COSCO Panama*, now eighty-five feet above sea level, glided into Lake Gatun for its six-hour passage across the center of the Isthmus.

Just a few hundred yards away and clearly visible to many observers, the pair of 102-year-old locks stood poised to resume their work after the ceremony, with the original technology of locomotives, line handlers, and cantilever gates still suited for the smaller ships for which the Canal was originally built.[1]

The inaugural events concluded at dusk beside the Cocolí locks on the Pacific side, with great fanfare, speechmaking, and jubilation. Hundreds of special guests, all the men dressed in formal white guayaberas, sat beneath awnings and heard celebratory remarks by President Juan Carlos Varela, canal administrator Jorge Quijano, and minister of the canal Roberto Roy. The latter's words, assembled at the last minute, proved poetic and inspirational. As he gestured toward the great vessel slowly passing by, he spoke deliberately:

> This ship, the one that you see here, in my mind it's not going anywhere. . . .
> It doesn't even travel on the seas.
> This ship knows its course and only travels in time, into the future! . . .
> It's not carrying containers, merchandise, or iPads.
> This ship carries the hopes and dreams of all Panamanian children of today.
> That's why it can never get lost!

Roy, an engineer associated with the Canal and more recently head of the Metro construction project under presidents Martinelli and Varela, spoke on behalf of all the dedicated Panamanians who had altered the nation's course in the 1990s and thrived in the years since 2000.

Gracefully choreographed dance performances wrapped up the evening, in what had become traditional artistic complements to public ceremonies in Panama. As the sun set, the *COSCO Panama* slipped under the Bridge of the Americas and steamed into the Pacific. A century after the opening of the Canal, Panamanians could take pride in having not only taken possession successfully but matched, with the new locks, the prowess, enterprise, boldness, and grandeur of the original American builders.[2]

VARELA TURNED THE TABLES ON HIS PREDECESSOR

The surprise victory of Juan Carlos Varela in the May 4, 2014, presidential election defied the pundits and caused consternation among political elites. Until that day, polls showed him trailing the other two candidates,

[1] A more detailed comparison of the original and the expanded channels is provided in Chapter 7.

[2] Special thanks to Roberto Roy for his speech, which has been edited for space and English syntax.

José Domingo ("Mimito") Arias of the CD and Juan Carlos Navarro of the PRD. Now Varela, as sole chief of the Panameñista Party (PPa), faced major questions regarding the next five years.[3] Because the PRD had won the biggest share of seats in the Assembly, should he forge an alliance with his party's traditional antagonists? That could help to overcome his party's weak third place position, far behind both the PRD and the CD pluralities in the legislature. Should he prosecute the outrageous allegations of corruption under Martinelli and antagonize his CD loyalists? Should he launch new programs to create a public image distinct from that of his predecessor, under whom he had served two years as vice president and foreign minister before being abruptly relieved of his foreign affairs post and cabinet authority? What did the upset in the polls tell him about the directions his administration should take? Because of these issues, Varela adopted a cautious, deliberate, and low-key leadership style, consonant with the even-tempered manner he had shown throughout the tumultuous Martinelli years.

In answer to the question of an alliance with the PRD to gain a majority in the Assembly, he proceeded to make the deal, helped by the disqualification of five CD legislators by the Electoral Tribunal. That left the PRD delegation strengthened by one seat and open to cooperation when the issues warranted. During the next three years, the parties cooperated when both their interests were served. Regarding corruption in the Martinelli administration, Varela authorized judicial officials to follow their investigatory leads with few restraints. As time went on, they unleashed a wave of prosecutions of former officials that helped to define the first years of public discourse. With respect to new signature programs and projects, he preferred to hold back and oversee completion of unfinished works (e.g., Canal widening, bridge over the north end of the Canal, second Metro line, City of Health, and numerous smaller ones). He took his time deciding which additional projects to undertake and finding ways to humanize the economic boom then underway.

Finally, to gauge his mandate from the electoral victory, he analyzed the polls leading up to the vote. Varela's own opinion data apparently showed him on course to win with a comfortable margin, as in fact

[3] Endara died shortly after the 2009 election, and Mireya Moscoso withheld her support for Varela until August: Edilsa González Roca, "Mireya Moscoso: Presidente Varela puede contar conmigo," *La Estrella*, Aug. 10, 2014. Much of this chapter draws on the excellent article by Carlos Guevara Mann, "Luces y sombras en torno a la institucionalidad democrática," *Revista de Ciencia Política* 36, no. 1 (2016): 259–85.

occurred, so he did not waste resources on unnecessary research. In contrast, Martinelli, managing the campaign for his stand-in candidate Arias and that of his wife, Marta Linares de Martinelli, for vice president, spent lavishly on polls and demanded positive results from his storied Brazilian consultant João Santana, contributing, perhaps, to erroneous projections of victory. In the PRD, the polling usually just added to the growing sense of dismay – it faced an unprecedented second lost election, and internal dissention dogged the party even before the vote.

In hindsight, several factors seemed to have swayed voters. Behind the scenes, the Catholic Church certainly helped Varela, a devout follower of Opus Dei, the conservative society that emphasizes combining personal sanctity with secular leadership. Varela promised to continue pensions for seniors not covered by social security and later lowered the eligibility age from seventy to sixty-five. Young voters surprisingly also rallied to his side, but without clear policy preferences. Finally, the CD campaign inherited ill-advised disputes between Martinelli and an array of powerful figures, some like Bobby Eisenmann and Stanley Motta with whom he had feuded for years and others who switched to Varela or Navarro to punish the exiting president. The public, regardless of the polls, in the end rejected the idea of "Martinellismo without Martinelli" and elected his dark horse rival, Varela.[4]

Varela's cabinet included members with eclectic backgrounds, advanced education, scant government experience, and fresh faces. Beginning with his vice president and foreign minister Isabel de Saint Malo, nine of the twenty declared independent party affiliation, and, together with members of other parties, they created a non-Panameñista majority. Most, regardless of affiliation, could be called technocrats, like engineer Roberto Roy, minister of the Canal. Only four were women, a slight increase over Martinelli's cabinets. Most held graduate degrees, usually from US universities. Minister of government Milton Henríquez, also head of the Partido Popular (PP), was one of the few with an established public persona from his television show and political leadership dating back to the now-defunct Christian Democrats. The ministers' average age of 52 matched that of the president. Only two ministers had

[4] The phrase by Orlando Pérez is quoted in Randal C. Archibold, "Incumbent's Party Loses Presidency in Panama," *New York Times*, May 4, 2014. The Martinelli-employed campaign guru Santana bragged that he had never lost an election. This was his first loss, and he and his wife later went to jail for his role in Brazil's Lava Jato corruption case, which showed that his fees in Panama were paid by money the Odebrecht company extracted from its construction contracts with the government.

FIGURE 9.1 President Juan Carlos Varela, vice president Isabel de St. Malo, and president Barack Obama. https://obamawhitehouse.archives.gov/realitycheck/blog/2015/04/13/photos-president-s-trip-jamaica-and-panama.

previously been elected to public office, a troubling fact since the president himself had also been elected for the first time.[5]

Minister of the presidency, Álvaro Alemán Healy, stood out from other cabinet members because of his close relationship to the president. Alemán became a sort of low key, behind-the-scenes super-minister, in contrast to the in-your-face super-minister of the Martinelli cabinet, Jimmy Papadimitriu. Trained in law, Alemán first became a loyal lieutenant to Varela as vice minister of foreign relations in 2010. He spoke for and stood in for the president on many occasions and issues, more than a mere presidential spokesman.[6] A lifelong Arnulfista and a scion of one of

[5] Guevara Mann, "Luces y sombras," 273–78.

[6] Álvaro Alemán's unusual authority included the "logistics cabinet," the decentralization program, reform of the pension system and the electoral law, national security policy, price controls, and societal consultations about a constitutional convention. See Aminta Bustamante,

Panama's leading families, Alemán entered politics in the Endara administration. The fourth son of Roberto Alemán Zubieta, jurist and former ambassador to the United States, Álvaro is a brother of former foreign minister José Miguel and of former ambassador to the United States, Jaime. Between public jobs, Álvaro took over management of his father's IGRA law firm, one of the largest and most respected in the country.

During his first year, Varela kept a low profile yet unleashed prosecutors on wrongdoers in the preceding administration. Among the most damning cases were purchases of coastal radars, spy equipment, and helicopters from Italian firms, including such giants as Finmeccanica, that gave kickbacks to Panamanian officials; bogus payments for school supplies distributed by the ministry of education, producing more kickbacks; fake purchases of dehydrated food for distribution in schools and welfare centers; kickbacks on major construction contracts executed by the Brazilian construction giant Odebrecht; and many lesser schemes ("a tsunami of complaints," said a Transparency International director) that tarnished the Martinelli administration. As of March 2016, nearly 300 persons had been indicted for illegal acts involving almost $700 million. Authorities suspected that much more had been stolen or spent illegally, while Martinelli bragged about having become a billionaire himself. The accusations and revelations formed a drumbeat in news media for years to come. The former president, meanwhile, traveled abroad before the end of the year to escape likely prosecution, living in self-exile in Italy and later Miami.[7]

Varela scored an important victory in late 2014 when he received a $2 billion loan from the Andean Development Bank (CAF) to carry out programs that emphasized social inclusion and equity for Panama's citizens. A latecomer to CAF membership in 2008, Panama quickly drew on its credits there to help the Canal expansion, the Metro, and the cleanup of Panama

"Álvaro Alemán: gobierno analiza sus decisiones," *La Prensa*, July 1, 2016. A special supplement of *La Estrella* on June 12, 2017, "El Polígrafo de la Estrella," contains an interview and accompanying article, "En la Linea Dos del Metro no hubo coimas." Bustamante stated that Alemán assured the public they should respect Roberto Roy and the Metro contracts, as well as the revival of Del Monte banana exports from Chiriqui.

7 Tim Johnson, "Panama's Ex-President Trots Globe, One Step Ahead of Corruption Probe," *Miami Herald*, Feb. 2, 2015; Guevara Mann, "Luces y sombras," 266. For an exhaustive account of the Finmeccanica case, see Fernando Berguido, *Anatomía de una trampa* (Mexico City: Grijalbo, 2017). Interviews with Alfredo Castillero Calvo, Aug. 17, 2014; Berta Thayer, June 30 and Aug. 16, 2014; Ana Elena Porras, Aug. 19, 2014; Alfredo Castillero Hoyos, Aug. 18, 2014. In fairness to Martinelli, some of the corruption scandals dated back to the Moscoso years, such as the CEMIS case, or the Torrijos administration, which issued some early Odebrecht contracts, as well as deals, including relations with Finmeccanica, that were decided when Varela was foreign minister.

Bay. Varela's request covered many projects, including sanitation of the capital, urban renewal in Colon, expansion of the Metro, an electrical grid connection with Colombia, airport and port expansion, and logistical development. Panama's booming economy vouchsafed the loan, and Varela's emphasis on social development fit well with CAF priorities.[8]

In many other respects, however, the government seemed to be off to a slow start. Other than the immediate implementation of price controls on basic necessities, public sector output downshifted gears. The ceaseless parade of inaugurations of new public works by Martinelli gave way to prolonged silence and media speculation about the list of unfinished works. Health centers, highways, convention centers, and a cold storage system for farm-to-market food handling were far behind schedule and over budget. These had to be evaluated before work could proceed, and they competed with other demands on the budget.

Even nature seemed to slow the pace of life in Panama. The dry season of 2015 produced the most prolonged drought in fifty years and returned with a vengeance in 2016.[9] The conditions driven by another severe El Niño weather pattern dried up rivers, shrank reservoirs, and destroyed crops across almost 70 percent of the country. Some regions experienced power shortages and blackouts for the first time in decades. Carnival had to be cancelled in much of the country due to fire danger. For a second year, the ACP pondered load reductions on vessels and raised serious concerns about the amount of water diverted for human consumption by the country's growing population, more than eighty years after the last reservoir was created. Zica virus outbreaks spread faster than expected, and the 149 cases identified by March 2016 forced emergency mobilization. Tourism, which usually boomed in the dry season, could not fill the room capacity, leading to historically low occupancy rates. As the president celebrated the first anniversary of his election, he must have felt little reassurance from the challenges he confronted.[10]

[8] Press release of Dec. 5, 2014, on the CAF website, www.caf.com. The bank, wholly owned by Latin American and Iberian nations, was chartered in 1970.

[9] Wilfredo Jordan, "Menos lluvia sobre el canal en 50 años," *La Prensa,* June 13, 2015. In February 2016, the ACP announced that the levels of Lakes Gatún and Alajuela were at the lowest level in 103 years.

[10] Still, the world press doted on Panama's progress: see Miguel Forbes, "Panama Achieving Prosperity and Equity at the Crossroads of the World," *Forbes Magazine*, Apr. 28, 2015; and Carrie Kahn, "As Panama's Economy Booms, So Do Concerns over Debt and the Environment," *NPR*, July 1, 2015. Also, the Houston Chamber of Commerce opened a regional office for Latin America in Panama.

Varela's subdued approach to the presidency, called *tortugón* (big turtle) for confrontation avoidance and deliberate pace, contrasted with the vigorous and appealing presence of his wife Lorena Castillo de Varela and that of his vice president and foreign minister, Isabel de Saint Malo.[11] The first lady, after a career as a television announcer, had an out-going, positive demeanor. She fit in naturally with her husband's public affairs team. Saint Malo, a newcomer to politics with diplomatic and management experience, had led the UN development program (UNDP) in Panama for a decade. She also spoke easily to the press and presented the administration's initiatives and its views on current affairs. Both were well-informed, poised, and articulate spokespersons, and the foreign minister often traveled abroad to spread news about the nation. Both women were fluent in English, having been educated in the United States.

THE SEVENTH SUMMIT OF THE AMERICAS AND ADJUSTING GLOBAL ROLES

The Varela administration heartily embraced the opportunity to host the seventh Summit of the Americas, a string of meetings that dated back to Bill Clinton's first in Miami in 1994. In fact, Panama boasted having held the very first such gathering, the 1826 congress convened by Simón Bolívar to promote Latin American unity. Now, Varela could use a hemispheric meeting to showcase the country's spectacular economic growth, the soaring skyline of the capital, its newly expanded airport, and its robust democratic institutions. The foreign ministry quickly ramped up planning to host it in April 2015. They used the main events and many subsidiary meetings to show off the wide array of venues available, from the restored sections of the colonial Casco Antiguo, to the presidential palace, the venerable ATLAPA Center, the controversial Figali convention center, the Biodiversity Museum, the patio of the Foreign Ministry building, Panama Viejo, and the capital's many upscale hotels. It would be a huge undertaking spanning four days.[12]

11 In response to criticism about his indecision and slow pace by the National Council on Private Enterprise (CoNEP), Varela acknowledged that some ministers were acting more slowly: "Varela reconoce que existen ministros lentos en gobierno," *Panamá América,* May 17, 2015.

12 See the lavishly produced *VII^a Cumbre de las Américas* (Panama: Ministerio de Relaciones Exteriores, 2015). A decade earlier, Panama had offered to host the headquarters for the Free Trade Area of the Americas, an effort that collapsed shortly afterward.

Invitations went out to the heads of thirty-five states, including Cuba for the first time in over five decades. Saint Malo traveled to La Havana in September 2014 to invite President Raúl Castro, and Varela highlighted Panama's historic role in his maiden speech at the UN General Assembly. The following December, Castro and US president Barack Obama announced an agreement to restore diplomatic relations, which was reflected in the Summit agenda. A photo op of Raúl Castro and Obama during a side meeting, warmly shaking hands, delighted (or disappointed) observers who cared about the issue. The Secretary General of the UN and the incoming and retiring Secretaries General of the OAS also attended. Pope Francis sent a congratulatory message read by a Vatican emissary.

President Varela set the tone of the summit, dedicating it to "prosperity with equity: the challenge for cooperation in the Americas." He stressed that delegates must work together to promote social and economic development for the less privileged, greater equality, and collaborative efforts to reduce crime across borders. He also spoke of the opportunities for expanding business, due to Panama's "privileged geographic position, its interoceanic Canal, ports, and airports, in hopes of continuing to promote investment and to consolidate its role as hub of air connectivity, multimodal center for logistical services, and headquarters for multinational companies in the Americas." He clearly relished the chance to show off Panama's advancement, even if some of the infrastructure was provided by Martinelli.[13]

To broaden the impact of the summit, conveners set up special forums where persons who worked in civil society, social activists, university presidents, youth advocates, and business leaders met for several days preceding the main event. These forums continued during the summit and produced position papers and recommendations for the plenary session. They included hemispheric "mandates for action" regarding health and sanitation improvements; education enhancements, at all levels; affordable and climate-friendly energy development; migration policies supportive of economic development and human rights; cooperation among nations to achieve greater security against threats of terrorism and organized crime; and democratic governability that guaranteed respect for the law, separation of powers, citizen participation, and human rights. As statements of principles, these recommendations were embraced by

[13] *Cumbre de las Américas*, 6–7, 40–45.

the gathered heads of states and were also forwarded to major development institutions around the hemisphere.[14]

In all, an estimated 17,000 persons attended in official capacities, and thousands more observed from the sidelines. Highlights of the business forum included announcements that Panama's major airline, COPA, would purchase sixty-one new Boeing aircraft and that Silicon Valley companies would assist in spreading Internet access to poor people around the globe. Television stations broadcast most of the proceedings throughout the four days.

Varela and Saint Malo could take pride in the successful summit. Looking back, it marked a boost to Panama's international standing. Hosting the Castro-Obama rapprochement certainly caught the world's attention. The beautiful and historic settings for many of the meetings impressed delegates and observers. Panama's top officials behaved with professionalism and efficiency, and they followed up with processing resolutions and a beautiful 219-page coffee-table book chronicling the summit. The event tended to deflect attention from nagging problems that tarnished the nation's image, like high-level corruption, narcotics trade, money laundering, and tax haven charges.

As with all Panama's post-millennial administrations, Varela's handling of the Summit and his approach to inter-American relations showed consistency in their cooperative intent. At the same time, each government's policies had a distinctive cast. Moscoso emphasized security a little more; Torrijos strove to rebuild third-world connections; and Martinelli pushed harder for foreign direct investment. Varela stressed using Panama's foreign ties to influence and shape the country's domestic politics and societal aspirations, especially with the United Nations and the Vatican.

UNFINISHED BUSINESS: HOLDING MARTINELLI & CO. RESPONSIBLE

Justice authorities assembled more evidence of bribes, kickbacks, and bogus contracts by the Martinelli administration, mounting into the billions of dollars. Several convictions and numerous prosecutions of

[14] "Panama Summit to Usher in New Era of Inter-American Relations," *The World Folio*, March 14, 2015; and *Cumbre de las Américas*, 214–15. Despite the idealism and display of rhetorical cooperation, the encounter, much like the ballyhooed Third Way Dialogues of the 1990s, seems to have had little long-term impact.

officials included confessions implicating the former president, such as payments from the Food for the Poor and other programs. In May 2016, the Supreme Court filed charges against the former president for illegal wire-tapping and procurement of eavesdropping equipment and requested that the foreign ministry file extradition papers with the United States, due to his residence in Miami. In June 2017, on the eve of Varela's first meeting with his new US counterpart, Donald J. Trump, the extradition process began, eliciting a phalanx of Martinelli lawyers fighting back. Meanwhile, many more damning charges surfaced involving more than half the cabinet, the first lady, Marinelli's sons, and other family members.[15]

Possible implications of Martinelli's extradition and prosecution loomed large. In the broader region, Varela's efforts paralleled those of the governments of Brazil, Argentina, and Peru to bring to justice officials who had profited from bribes and other crimes. They also complemented efforts by the United States, Switzerland, Spain, and Italy to identify and prosecute overseas corporate corruption. Successful cases could increase trust in regional governments and businesses and boost investment and trade. Powerful and wealthy people stood against these efforts, however, and marshalled forces to thwart them.

Panama faced delicate issues regarding Martinelli and corruption in general. Publicity surrounding a vigorous prosecution could tarnish the image of Panama as a good place to do business. The country already had one former strongman languish and die in prison; could they afford a second? Moreover, the globally modest but profitable International Banking Center, that thrived on secrecy and open flows of money, could suffer from deeper scrutiny of its operations due to the Martinelli revelations.[16] The Panama Papers scandal of 2016 (which will be discussed later in the Chapter) showed its vulnerability to exposure. Finally, if the government were limited to prosecuting Martinelli solely on the bases of the extradition, could he somehow escape judgement on far more serious charges that could emerge? Panama's international standing, and the future of Varela's successor in the 2019 elections, hung in the balance.

[15] *Reuters*, Sept. 27, 2016; *Transparency International*, Sept. 29, 2016. Isabel Saint Malo, interview, Oct. 7, 2016. Noriega's case presented a similar dilemma – extradited to Miami for trial on the light charges of money laundering and drug trafficking, he was later convicted in Panama of murder.

[16] Panama actually ranks highest on the world stage in maritime law, number 12, but that work is inseparable from its other international legal activities. See Menon, "The Leading Maritime Capitals of the World in 2017," Menon publication no. 28/2017.

As Varela's fourth year in office began, he also had to deal with the backlog of uncompleted and poorly executed projects Martinelli had ceremonially inaugurated prematurely during the campaign. To be sure, some succeeded, like first line of the Metro, the Oceanside Cinta Costera, access to the colonial city, and the ACP operations.[17] Yet to be finished were the hospital and clinic networks, the cold storage system, highways and bridges, schools, and the free Wifi system. Time might be running out.[18] And as always, underperformance led to some projects having to be let to new bidders.

With so much infrastructure having to be redone and repaired to be workable, the remarkable thing is that the government kept the public works motor of economic growth humming.[19] Part of the credit goes to getting new funding, such as the CAF financing; to keeping a vigorous flow of foreign direct investment, even after the completion of the Canal expansion; to new projects, such as the rebuilding of Colon, a natural gas shipping facility, low income housing; and finally to the resurrection of Martinelli's unfinished projects. In the president's new year's address on January 2, 2016, he announced the reactivation of some mega projects. The following cases reflect how complicated it was to get the unfinished business of the infrastructure into working order.[20]

One of the most spectacular promises of the Martinelli administration was to provide universal free Internet access within a year.[21] By November 2016, after the 250th InfoPlaza and 850 Wifi transmission points were installed by the Varela administration, the national secretary

[17] An IPSOS poll showed that more than 80 percent of respondents were happy with these projects yet less than half with pubic services and the police. Félix Ruiz Rodríguez, "El Canal, el Metro y la Cinta Costera," *La Estrella*, Sept. 6, 2015. Still, the third stage of the Cinta Costera, aroused controversy.

[18] Media bias muddled assessments of Varela. *Panamá América*, his Martinellii-controlled opponent, reported that slowed execution of projects cost the country billions: "Paralización de obras por el gobierno causa pérdidas," Jan. 25, 2017. *La Prensa* headlines, however, soon proclaimed the nation on the verge of having the highest per capita income in Latin America: "FMI: Panamá tendrá el mayor PIB per cápita de Latinoamérica en 2018," Feb. 22, 2017.

[19] A study by INDESA showed that the share of Panama's GDP generated by the construction sector rose from an already relatively high level of 9.3 percent in 2010 to 16.5 percent in 2016: "La importancia del transporte y las comunicaciones en la economía panameña," *Foro Empresarial INDESA*, May 2017.

[20] "Varela anuncia reactivación de mega proyectos y llama al diálogo nacional," *La Prensa*, Jan. 2, 2016.

[21] Soon after taking office, Varela committed $25.5 million to advance Internet access: "Panamá ofrecerá internet gratis para sus habitantes," Sept. 14, 2009. Cf. www.fayerwayer.com/2009/09/panama-ofrecera-internet-gratis-para-sus-habitantes/.

for innovation, Irving Halman, reported that 57 percent of the national population had achieved Internet access, just ahead of the Latin American average of 56 percent, but well below the 62 percent in Costa Rica. Halman promised an expansion to 1360 broadcast points at 2G speed. That would enable as much as 80 percent of users access by 2019.

Besides, public works were not the only projects that needed adjustment.[22] The $250 million Italian defense equipment scam, one of the first scrutinized by the administration, revealed corrupt Italian officials bragging about ripping off Panama. Drawing on his skills of fighting for transparency, new ambassador to Italy Fernando Berguido renegotiated the contract with Finmeccanica and other firms for replacement of the useless radars, broken ships, unflyable helicopters, and other equipment. As a result, in February 2016, the two countries announced a bilateral agreement that included medical evacuation helicopters, support guarantees for the radars and other equipment, and a savings of nearly $100 million for Panama.[23]

In May 2016, the National Tourism Authority (ATP) revealed how the long-delayed Figali convention center in Amador would be completed. The Martinelli contract had been cancelled in December 2014. The Varela government then revised the design and conducted new bidding for $194 million, won by a consortium of firms led by Gustavo Him and the China State Construction Engineering Corporation. Now called the Panama International Convention Center, it was scheduled to be inaugurated by the end of 2019, and will have been at least a decade in the making.

Making good on the Martinelli hospital program had many moving parts. In May 2016, the ministry of health revised the original plans for regional centers in Colon, Los Santos, Chiriqui, and Darien, supplementing them with a contract to supply equipment and medicine by the time of their opening in 2017. Although the capacity of the centers remained the same, the new price tags were doubled.[24]

[22] Some critics pointed to Martinelli's underwriting unnecessary contracts, like that for airport expansion in Colon, which had less than twenty flights a week: "Obra millionaria sin uso, Aeropuerto de Colón," *La Prensa,* May 10, 2015.

[23] Berguido, *Anatomía de una trampa*, passim; Gustavo A. Aparicio O. and Yolanda Sandoval, "Estado ahorará $100 milliones en acuerdo con Finmeccanica," *La Prensa,* Feb. 24, 2016.

[24] Angel López Guía and Rosalia Simmons, "Gobierno acuerda con IBT Grupo Reanudar construcción de 4 hospitales," *La Prensa,* May 26, 2016.

The Hospital City project for the CSS, renamed the City of Health by the Varela administration, proved the most complex and controversial. The original contract of $517 million, awarded to the Spanish firm FCC in October 2011, called for seventeen buildings on the 32-hectare site, including a national cancer center, with 320 doctors' offices, 1,242 hospital beds, and a hotel. Problems with the remote location, in what used to be the Fort Clayton antenna field, began with its encroaching on the historic Cruces Trail, the colonial-era mule road to Portobelo. Work halted for fifteen months to make design changes but resumed in January 2016. The entire complex should open in phases during 2019 and later, complemented by a transportation center.[25]

Varela also struggled to revive his predecessor's promised cold storage system. Launched in July 2009, it called for linking four strategically located refrigerated agricultural harvest centers with nine urban produce distribution sites. It would sharply reduce wastage of more than 60 percent of farm production and improve the quantity and quality of consumption, especially in low-income communities. Plans quickly fell through. The Merca Panama center in Chivo Chivo sat idle after its inauguration in 2014, and the number of other centers has dropped from nine to five. Those in Chitre and La Chorrera, scheduled for completion in 2019, will provide access to Chivo Chivo and the new Health City. City officials in Colon took over their incomplete center. The integrated system of harvest points and urban outlets only functions in Chiriqui, where Volcan, Cerro Punta, and Dolega supply the market in David.[26]

Despite antagonistic relations with his predecessor, Varela seemed determined to bring these projects to fruition in order to upgrade the nation's overall infrastructure.[27] Some will still fail, and critics claimed that a public-works-centered development approach perpetuated inequality and fostered little progress in human well-being.

[25] María M. Mur, "Obra millionaria de Ciudad Hospitalaria, paralizada por el gobierno de Panamá," *Vanguardia*, Sept. 27, 2015; and Guadalupe León B., "Ciudad de Salud lleva un 46% de avance," *La Estrella*, Mar. 23, 2017.

[26] Aet Elisa Tejera C., "Reducen mercados de la Cadena de Frío," *La Prensa*, June 27, 2017. Even in the operating harvest centers, however, structural problems led the government to collect a $75 million insurance bond: Aet Elisa Tejera C., "Cadena de Frío reclama fianza aseguradora," *La Prensa*, Feb. 9, 2017.

[27] Gustavo A. Aparicio, "Los dos años de Juan Carlos Varela, entre elogios y críticas," *La Prensa*, July 1, 2016.

BUILDING OUT THE CENTERPORT: SPOKES OF THE HUB OF THE AMERICAS

Ever since the 1970s, Panamanian leaders had championed the notion that their economy could be unleashed by going beyond Canal ship transits to offer multiple services around transportation in general – turning the country into an intercontinental hub for business, often called the Centerport.[28] The 1990s and 2000s saw great strides toward this goal, with rehabilitation of the railroad, new toll roads, the highway to Colon, fiber-optic cables across the Isthmus, airport expansion, container ports at both ends of the Canal, the development of intermodal transportation, spin off businesses such as call centers, a wide array of human resource development projects, and businesses to service the ships, planes, trucks, and visitors who came to Panama. A large part of the economic miracle of the last decade reflected the success of the Centerport or more commonly called the Hub.

During the Torrijos, Martinelli, and Varela administrations, these activities flourished due to two institutional prime movers and a variety of projects both large and small. The ACP and the Canal expansion was of course a principal driver, the first spoke of the new hub. The push to more than double the capacity at Tocumen International Airport became the second.[29] As these projects developed, others added momentum, like port expansions at PSA and in Colon, cruise ship terminals, the maritime LNG plant, continued strength of the ship registry, and more sophisticated ship service facilities.[30]

Another proposal, stalled in 2017, would build a new container port at Corozal, on the Pacific side of the Canal. As data from the AMP showed, handling of containers in the ports of Panama rose from just over one million TEU in 2000 to about 6.6 million by 2011, almost as rapid as government revenue growth from the ACP. Since then, the number of containers moved each year in Panama plateaued at around 6.5 million.

[28] We use the terms Centerport and hub of the Americas interchangeably.

[29] The May 2017 INDESA study showed that the ACP contribution to the transportation and communications sector of the economy stood at 45.3 percent in 2000 but declined to 31.5 percent in 2015, due to growth of the ports, railroad, water, and air transportation. Meanwhile, air transport had the biggest change in relative share, increasing from 4.8 percent to 8.5 percent.

[30] In July 2017, Panama celebrated the 100th anniversary of its ship registry, by far the largest, with over 18 percent (223 million tons/8,094 vessels) of the world's tonnage under its flag, "Panama becomes the largest registry of ships," https://Safety4sea.com, Dec. 19, 2017.

This slowdown in growth resulted mostly from limited capacity on the Pacific side, work on Canal expansion, and a dip in global maritime commerce.[31]

The Corozal project, timed to open a few years after the new locks did, would have relieved capacity bottlenecks, more than container-capacity expansion or a Chinese-built port in Colon. More important, a new port on the Pacific under ACP control could reduce the near-monopoly of container handling there by Panama Ports Company (PPC), a subsidiary of Hong Kong-based Hutchison Whampoa, that had won its concessions in the 1990s. The proposal, like the earlier Canal expansion and ship service activities, was meant to expand future business and to diversify ACP's product mix.[32]

The Corozal container port, proposed to open in 2019, represented several departures for Panama and still faced daunting legal hurdles in 2018. The land designated for it, a 120-hectare tract just north of the port of Balboa, lay on the east side of the Pacific entrance to the Canal. The site was put under ACP jurisdiction, unlike the other ports (MIT, CCT, PSA, Balboa, and Cristobal), for potential expansion of the Canal. When the new locks on the Pacific side were re-sited on the west bank, the land became available to the ACP. Its location adjacent to the railroad and highways made it convenient for a new port. It was the first one designed specifically for neo-Panamax vessels and the first in Latin America to incorporate green technology.

ACP executives, drawing on studies and shipping industry recommendations, argued that container traffic on the Pacific side constituted a bottleneck, with only two ports compared with three on the Atlantic side. The two Pacific ones already operated at capacity, forcing some shippers to divert to other ports in the region. With the advent of neo-Panamax ships using the Canal and the demise of an earlier port project at Farfan, the situation could worsen if Corozal were not built. The ACP did not propose to operate the port but rather to give a concession to a global firm with proven expertise in the industry, to design, develop, finance, build, operate, and maintain it. This plan had the virtue of stimulating competition among the existing ports yet also aroused opposition from some of them. Still, after initial wavering, the Assembly approved Corozal,

[31] May 2017 INDESA study, p. 27.

[32] Interview, Manuel Benítez and Oscar Vallarino, Apr. 8, 2015; "Corozal Container Port," ACP website, 2015; *Maritime Executive*, Oct. 10, 2016; *The Bulletin Panama*, Dec. 27, 2016.

and the ACP issued a call in 2015 for interested companies to prequalify for the tender, based on preliminary designs.

The ACP announcement called for Corozal to be built in two phases, the first of which would open in 2019. Located just north of Balboa, the first dock would be 1.3 km long, accommodate three neo-Panamax ships at a time, handle up to 3 million containers per year, and employ some 2,600 workers. By the end of Phase two, Corozal's dock would stretch a full two kilometers, handle over 5 million TEUs per year, and employ 3,800 workers. In addition, it would have the requisite cranes, warehouses, storage yards, offices, and employee amenities. Advanced green technology would minimize transportation, air, and noise pollution and utilize only electric power. The concession would run for twenty years and be subject to a twenty-year renewal.[33]

Opposition arose to authorizing the ACP to even operate a port, since all the others came under the AMP, governed by its own organic law. The Assembly majority, with strong Varela support, eventually broke the deadlock and authorized the bidding to proceed. Those voting in favor believed that the ACP organic law included a mandate for economic exploitation of the waterway, which would include Corozal.[34]

Opposition mounted from PPC. The company sued the ACP in the supreme court, alleging that their concession gave them exclusive rights to provide dock services, just as it had over operating railroad equipment within its terrain. The court disagreed, deciding unanimously that the concession did not grant them a monopoly.[35] These initial setbacks only increased the company's opposition, however, and, in 2015, it decided to

[33] Michelle de la Ossa Prieto, "Panamá enfrenta falta de muelles en el Pacífico," *Capital financiero*, Jan. 23, 2017.

[34] Rodolfo Sabonge has long advocated diversifying the Canal's business activities so as to fulfill its mission to develop the interoceanic passage fully. See Marinaela Palacios Ramsbott, "Canal de Panamá apuesta a nuevos negogios," *El Capital Financiero* (Bogota), July 22, 2013.

[35] Wilfredo Jordan, "Panama Ports pide la nulidad de la licitación del puerto de Corozal," *La Prensa,* June 13, 2016. Jordan explained that, in 2004, the PPC also sought to block development of the port at Farfan. The other Pacific-side port, PSA, lay on the west bank, in former Rodman Naval Base, but never constituted a threat to PPC's control of the container business because of its limited dock space and lack of multimodal transportation access. The ACP position harked back to Pérez Balladares's decision to grant separate concessions for the ports and railroad, which then-bidder Bechtel Corporation wished to operate jointly. See Chapter 4.

make a stronger case by paying the government its first-ever share of corporate dividends.[36]

In May 2016, the ACP released the names of the four pre-qualified bidders for construction of the first phase, two Dutch, one French, and one Singaporean. All were major players in global commerce and maritime port operations. In October, the ACP announced the tender for proposals to be submitted by February, later extended to March 2017. Yet rather than subdue the controversy, the failure of the initial challenges to the Corozal project and the opening of the bidding seemed to spur more opposition.[37] Suddenly, new citizens' committees appeared claiming the potential for environmental damage, neighborhood disturbances, and other negative impacts.[38] Workers groups, even Canal employees, leftist intellectuals, politicians, and legal gadflies also submitted new claims to impede the process.

Many of the arguments against the expansion of the Canal a decade earlier resurfaced, although this time Varela remained on the side of the ACP. Attorneys for Hutchison Whampoa entered more than a score of lawsuits, and many more were filed despite the unbroken string of legal defeats so far.[39] The controversy and legal challenges did not halt the project, but, in March 2017, the ACP declared the bidding closed when none of the pre-qualified companies submitted proposals. ACP officials and other observers explained that the recent downturn in maritime traffic contributed to the unexpected loss of interest by the contractors. Still, they expected that the project would be revived in the future.[40] After all, the bottleneck in Pacific-side port capacity still needed to be broken, and the increase in container traffic during the first years of Canal expansion

[36] Michele Labrut, "Hutchison Panama Ports Aim to Pay Dividends for First Time," *Seatrade*, Mar. 26, 2015. Panama owns 10 percent of the Panama Ports Company, but, despite the latter's achievement of full-capacity operations for several years, it did not post profits and pay dividends until 2015. In 2018, the ministry of economics opened an investigation into the reasons PPC had paid only $3 million to the government of Panama over 20 years after having generated more than $3 billion in revenue, "MEF: 'Panamá Ports pagó solo $3 milliones al Estado,' *Panamá América*, June 22, 2018.

[37] The project continued to generate controversy in 2017: see Adelita Coriat, "Piden declarar inconstitucional resolución de la ACP," *La Estrella*, Jan. 30, 2017.

[38] José Maria Torrijos Legazpi, "Vecinos de la 'Zona' pelean con la ACP por proyecto portuario," Sept. 1, 2015.

[39] Wilfredo Jordán, "Al menos 11 procesos legales intentan frenar puerto de Corozal," *La Prensa*, Sept. 26, 2016. Jordan also reported on the surge in container business, while Panama ports traffic remained stagnant due to the bottleneck in Balboa.

[40] Kelly Garcés, "Jorge Luis Quijano advierte que Panamá afronta competencia de otros puertos, como Buenaventura," *La Prensa*, Mar. 13, 2017.

showed that near- to middle-range growth potential remained strong. Additionally, ACP's record of successes in arbitration cases over expansion costs both during construction and after inauguration of the new locks added further to its reputation. Former ambassador to the United States Jaime Alemán expressed the sentiment of many Panamanians when he declared "it would be absurd to have struggled so hard for the Canal if we now just turned over a monopoly port concession to a single company."[41]

In another area, the AMP built a special T-shaped dock in Amador to receive workboats and other vessels servicing transiting ships. Dock space along the Canal had grown increasingly scarce, with the expansion project, dredging activities, navigation and communications installations, and the size of neo-Panamax ships. The new dock would decongest the busy Canal waters and concentrate support activities in one site: chandlering, bunkering, repairs, and changing crews. Meanwhile, at Perico Island, a little further along the causeway, the AMP began construction of a cruise ship terminal for the Pacific side.[42]

Tocumen International has become the second major spoke of the logistics hub. The growth of COPA, the nation's flagship airline, has tracked the growth of the national economy since 2000, and recent governments supported it with improved airport facilities.[43] Built in the late 1940s, Tocumen gained importance as a refueling point for flights throughout the hemisphere. By the 1970s, however, most long-haul flights did not need to refuel, so Panama lost traffic. Some improvements helped to attract business, but major development only came after the government granted it autonomy and stimulated expansion after 2000.

Tocumen received a major boost in 2003 when the Assembly transformed it into Tocumen S.A., a private corporation wholly owned by the government yet still answerable to the Civil Aeronautical Authority. In that capacity, it could raise money on its own and through public debt issues. With this new flexibility, its directors commissioned a Master Plan for

41 MarEx, "Arbitrators Dismiss $200 Million Claim for Panama Canal Costs," *Maritime Executive*, Aug. 1, 2017; and "PPC financia campaña contra Corozal, Alemán," *La Estrella*, Feb. 21, 2017.

42 The Spanish government Office of Exports and Investment, ICEX, in conjunction with the Spanish Embassy in Panama, prepared a remarkably comprehensive fifty-nine-page overview of Panama's logistics infrastructure as a guide for potential Spanish investors: "Obra pública y logística, Panamá, 2016," esp. Nota Sectorial Obra Pública y Logística Panamá 2016–ICEX, pdf.

43 The Copa website has used the concept "aviation hub of the Americas" for several years: see www.copaair.com/web/ca/hub-of-the-americas.

expansion and improvement that was been revised and updated several times. The Plan launched phase one, 2004–08, in which it upgraded Terminal 1, both domestic and international concourses. Management added 21,000 square meters of new floor space, twenty-two new jetways, and elevators, escalators, luggage carrousels, flight monitors, and new air conditioning capacity. By the end of phase one, Tocumen operated twenty-eight gates.

Phase two of Tocumen expansion focused on improvements in the existing terminals, with outlying pods to accommodate up to forty gates. Between 2008 and 2012, they installed major new duty-free shopping and restaurant areas, moving sidewalks, and more efficient baggage handling. Meanwhile, road access and parking were added to handle passenger traffic that had nearly tripled, from 2.4 to 7 million. Cargo tonnage also rose, from 96,000 metric tons a year to over 116,000.[44] During this phase, president Martinelli authorized construction of an all-new Terminal 2, south of the existing one, that could potentially double airport capacity again. Some visionaries proposed building out the airport into a commercial city, Panatrópolis, entirely separate from the capital and devoted to air logistics, aviation support, international headquarters, and business travelers.

Phase three studies for Terminal 2, to be completed in 2019, projected a modernistic building with three stories totaling 116,000 square feet, twenty more gates, its own road access, parking, infrastructure, control tower, and venues for business and entertainment. More land had to be acquired and a nearby river rerouted. The toll roads Corredor Norte and Sur already connected downtown to Tocumen, and soon the Metro's Linea 2 would also. With the expansion of COPA and the attraction of more international carriers, passenger traffic ballooned further, with the rapid growth of in-transit passengers. Planners believed 20 million travelers could arrive by 2020, a tenfold increase in fifteen years. This would qualify Tocumen as an airport in the global middle leagues, far bigger than any other in Central America and among the top five in Latin America.[45]

[44] Jéssica Tasón, "Copa busca convertir a Panamá en 'hub' de carga," *La Estrella*, Apr. 25, 2015.

[45] The highest passenger volume among world airports in 2015 was Atlanta with over 100 million. Miami's 44.6 million ranked 30th in the world, and Mexico City topped those of Latin America with 41.7 million and 44th place globally. Tocumen was not listed among even the top ten in Latin America until 2014, when it suddenly jumped ahead of Caracas and San Juan with a 64 percent increase, to 12.8 million. In 2016, Panama

The airport's march to prominence did not evade criticism. Many of its tenders and contracts were canceled, and allegations of graft swirled for years, especially during the Martinelli administration. Varela's new master builder, Joseph Fidanque III, rescinded more than fifteen contracts after replacing the former first lady's cousin, Juan Carlos Pino Linares, as administrator in 2014.[46] Continued lax oversight of Tocumen S.A.'s finances raised serious doubts about its probity, however, and Varela replaced Fidanque with businessman Carlos Duboy in April 2017. Finally, much of the Terminal 2 work has been done by Odebrecht, which recently admitted to bribing hundreds of officials around the world to secure contracts. These charges will cast shadows and complicate matters in coming years. At the same time, the international reputation of Tocumen is still improving, based on the recent recognition from Skytrax as the best airport and for the best passenger service in Central America and the Caribbean. The continued addition of major European and Asian Airline connections should support the increasingly ambitious expansion plans.[47]

The third major component of the logistics hub constitutes the government's efforts to forge cooperation between private and public sectors to harmonize the economy in general. The Martinelli government had charged the ministry of commerce with the task, and then Varela created a logistics cabinet under the auspices of his minister of the presidency. Panama's progress in logistics is shown by its rise in the World Bank's rankings of the logistical performance of nations. In the initial 2007 study, based on six traits, Panama earned 54th place on the list, fourth in Latin America, and well below Chile and Argentina. By 2014 Panama rose to 45th, second only to Chile, and by 2016, Panama was rated 40th with the highest score in the region.[48]

Yet deficiencies in the development of human resources and slow decision-making on the coordination of crucial elements of the hub may be the nation's most serious impediment. For instance, when will the Albrook air terminal be integrated into the Panamá Pacífico center,

remained tenth largest in Latin America with 14.7 million passengers: see www.wikiwand.com/en/List_of_the_busiest_airports_in_Latin_America.

46 Lina Vega Abad, "Tocumen, negocio que crece," *La Prensa,* July 15, 2012; and Alex E. Hernández V., "Tocumen rescinde contratos," Feb. 15, 2015.

47 EFE, "Panama Airport Wins Regional Award for Its Passenger Service," *Panama Today,* Mar. 21, 2018.

48 Roberto González Jiménez, "Panamá mejora desempeño logístico," *La Prensa,* June 30, 2016. For the World Bank data, see http://lpi.worldbank.org/international/global/2016.

where it will have room to operate? How will air cargo expansion, not just passenger traffic, be integrated into the growth of Tocumen and be linked to the country's multimodal transportation networks? How can Panama's public administration raise the operational level of its customs, maritime management, fleet registry, and other crucial services beyond the level of traditional bureaucratic kleptocracy? And perhaps most important, how can the country get the Corozal project back on track and resume broadening the ACP mission? Former vice president and AMP administrator Rubén Arosemena compared Panama's logistical integration to that achieved by Egypt with respect to the Suez Canal and recommended creating a cabinet-level authority for logistical integration.[49] Leading experts in Panama and abroad, with the support of important private sector organizations, such as APEDE and the Maritime Chamber of Commerce, have long argued that the country needs such an official at the cabinet secretary level, dedicated exclusively to logistics coordination.[50]

While Varela has resisted the national integration path to becoming a logistics hub, he has taken two steps in that direction. First, the foreign ministry adjusted its geopolitical vision to match geostrategic realities, by abandoning its diplomatic preference for Taiwan over China. The ACP and much of Panama's business community had long recognized that the place of honor given to Taiwan needed to be passed to China.[51] The recent issuance of contracts to Chinese construction companies for public housing and a new neo-Panamax port in Colon suggested that change was under way.[52] In March 2017, the ACP board held its joint meeting with its

[49] Rubén Arosemena Valdés, "Nuevo enfoque del Canal," *La Prensa*, Oct. 13, 2015.

[50] The Midwestern Association of Latin American Studies (MALAS) included three panels on Panama's logistics hub organized by author Bigler in its meeting of Nov. 20–22, 2014, in conjunction with the Panama Association of Executives, APEDE. Experts Rodolfo Sabonge, CEPAL transportation planner Ricardo J. Sánchez, former president Nicolás Ardito Barletta, and others argued that the national decision-making structure was the greatest impediment to logistics progress. In its April 2015 Annual Conference of Executives, CADE arrived at the same conclusion: "CADE impulsará creación de una Secretaría Nacional de Logística," *La Estrella*, Apr. 7, 2015.

[51] APEDE's 2010 conference theme stressed closer relations with the BRIC nations. In late 2014, Eddie Tapiero and other observers argued for shifting the country's diplomatic relations to China: "Establecer relaciones con China," *La Prensa/Opinion*, July 9, 2014.

[52] Closer ties to China seem to offer economic benefits as compared with Taiwan. The latter's most recent donations included forty-four ambulances, thirty-three garbage trucks, and three hundred scholarships for Panamanian students. China has promised to provide equivalent scholarships, while its companies have nearly $2 billion in investment projects already under way in Panama.

international advisory board in Shanghai and scheduled a visit to the headquarters of the COSCO shipping firm, the fifth largest user of the Canal. Thus, foreign minister Saint Malo's visit to China, full recognition of China, and a subsequent presidential trip with the inauguration of embassies in both countries in 2018 culminated a quiet transition that is now booming into large scale investments and the negotiation of a free trade agreement and expanded Chinese presence in Panama.[53]

The final spoke for Panama's logistical hub could be provided by linking the national planning system to the logistical and operational needs of the hub.[54] In contrast to the private sector-based approach undertaken by Martinelli, Varela turned to an internationally coordinated system financed by the IDB and oriented by the UNDP, which Saint Malo had led for a decade. In his second new year's address to the nation, Varela announced the launch of a national dialogue that would tie Panama's needs to the seventeen goals of sustainable development identified by the UN. He called it the strategic plan for the year 2030.[55] The crucial issue for moving ahead could be to have enough of the work in place by the end of his period to insure that his successor will continue its implementation.

COLON IN THE SPOTLIGHT AT LAST

The city of Colon, located on a mostly fill island at the northern end of the Canal, had an illustrious history that began during railroad construction in the 1850s, when it was called Aspinwall, after the president of the New York company.[56] Panamanians soon renamed it after Christopher Columbus, who landed near there in 1502. The port served as Panama's window onto the Atlantic world and maintained close ties with Europe, New York, New Orleans, and Caribbean locations. Colon, like Panama

[53] Chris Horton and Steven Lee Meyers, "Panama Establishes Ties with China, Further Isolating Taiwan," *New York Times*, June 13, 2017; and Marlene Testa, "China expone eje de trabajo en Panamá," *La Estrella*, June 20, 2017. Interview with Samuel Lewis Navarro, Nov. 14, 2017.

[54] Priscilla Pérez, "Panama da los primeros pasos para convertirse en centro logístico mundial," *El Capital Financiero* (Bogotá), June 23, 2017.

[55] "Varela anuncia reactivación de mega proyectos y al diálogo nacional," *La Prensa*, Jan. 2, 2016. As more details of the 2030 planning process emerged, its roots in the national conservation process under President Torrijos and the importance of climate change and development of alternative energy sources became increasingly apparent: see Aminta Bustamante, "Nace 'Panamá 2030,'" *La Prensa*, July 14, 2017.

[56] The best early history of the railroad is Aims McGuinness, *Path of Empire: Panama and the California Gold Rush* (Ithaca: Cornell University Press, 2008).

City, prospered and contracted with the railroad business and the two Canal construction projects. During the US Canal era, Colon housed a significant portion of its workforce, both Panamanian and American. Its population was predominantly black, descended from colonial and nineteenth century African arrivals and from Caribbean workers who flowed in seeking work. Until the 1950s, Colon had a vibrant Afro-Panamanian social, business, and cultural life that thrived on the relatively high wages paid by the Canal and on the passenger ships that plied the islands and transited the Canal.[57]

From the mid-twentieth century on, however, Colon settled into a long and painful decline, as well-to-do residents migrated the sixty-six kilometers across the Isthmus to the capital in search of schools, jobs, and business opportunities. The 1952 Canal reorganization and 1955 treaty trimmed employee benefits and ejected most Panamanians from zone housing, so former residents crowded into the deteriorating tenements of Colon, some dating back to the French and US construction eras.

Every president since 1990 promised to revive Colon, yet its doleful streets and impoverished citizens never seemed to do well. Since then, some reverted lands and facilities had received fresh investment and expanded, yet the downtown core remained blighted. Simply razing decrepit and unsafe buildings removed eyesores from view but did not lift up their former residents. A duty-free zone created within the city in 1992 could not get off the ground without tourism, which did not exist. Serious shoppers went instead to the Colon Free Zone (CFZ), created in 1948 on the outskirts of the city, mostly owned and operated by a flock of commuters, reflecting the closer practical links to Panama City.[58]

Varela began putting more resources and political effort into turning Colon around, however, partly with funds from CAF the previous year. He committed a half-billion dollars to the 2015 Colon Renewal Project, a variety of efforts to lift Colon out of its secular slump once and for all. Although he emphasized social goals, economic expansion also underlay his plans. He put together an inter-ministerial task force to bend all branches of government to these goals. In October 2015, he unveiled his

[57] Colon and its people are covered in Melba Lowe de Goodin, *People of African Ancestry in Panama, 1501-2012* (Panama: Imprenta Sibauste, 2014); and Michael L. Conniff, *Black Labor on a White Canal: Panama 1904–1981* (Pittsburgh: University of Pittsburgh Press, 1985). Melba Lowe is also the founding director of the charming West Indian Museum of Panama.

[58] Randal C. Archibold, "A Once-Vibrant City Struggles as Panama Races Ahead on a Wave of Prosperity," *New York Times*, Mar. 23, 2013.

overall plan before big crowds of *colonenses*. First, they began completely rebuilding the city's infrastructure, which dated to the last century. Water systems, storm drainage, sewage treatment, a modern electric grid, street paving and alignment, and public parks went in. Unsafe buildings were demolished.

Second, they set out to build over 5,500 new residences to house the city's poor. Most of these were two- and three-bedroom apartments in multistory buildings, but other smaller clusters filled in vacant spaces. Young people received training to qualify for the new construction jobs. Third, schools, clinics, shops, sports centers, social service agencies, and police and fire stations went in to provide basic urban support for the relocated population. Finally, some classic older buildings underwent restoration to preserve the historic flavor of Colon. The president's staff estimated that 206,000 persons benefited from these works.[59]

To complement these new facilities, the ministry of education earmarked $20 million for a new integrated educational center that promised sixty specialized sites for vocational, technical, and academic instruction in the Los Lagos district of the city.[60]

Varela and the Assembly also updated the 1992 law for duty-free shopping in downtown, enlarging it to sixteen blocks. Now called the Colon Free Port, it opened in August 2016. They expected influxes of tourists by cruise ship, railroad, and bus to breathe life into the district. Owners received special credits to restore and remodel their buildings. Meanwhile authorities modified the law that created the CFZ to make it an autonomous government entity, with lower taxes equal to those paid by the duty-free merchants.[61]

Parallel to these developments, the Panama tourism and ports authorities worked throughout 2015 to attract cruise ships to their passenger terminal, Colon 2000. Ships were encouraged to lay over during their transits of the Canal, and others stopped on tropical routes in the southern Caribbean. The railroad had proved a major attraction for foreign visitors, who could embark at one end of the Canal and disembark at the other. The new observation center for the Canal's Atlantic locks proved popular as well. The Spanish cruise line Pullmantur made regular stops at

[59] Press release, Oct. 12, 2015, on the president's website, www.presidencia.gob.pa/. Cf. *La Prensa*, Oct. 13, 2015.

[60] Angel López Guía, "Gobierno aprueba $20 milliones para construir nueva escuela en Colón," *La Prensa*, Jan. 20, 2017.

[61] *La Prensa*, Apr. 5, 2016.

Colon and planned more. In November 2016, authorities announced that the German cruise line TUI, in a marketing collaboration with Royal Caribbean, planned to have up to sixteen of its ships call at Colon. Passengers would join their ships via Lufthansa flights. Authorities spoke of a larger maritime-port at Colon that could attract up to 300,000 visitors a year.[62]

Meanwhile, on the eve of Panama's decision to shift its relations from Taiwan to China, officials approved two mega projects worth $1.8 billion, to be built by the Shanghai Gorgeous private enterprise group in Colon. The first was a new container terminal, a $900 million neo-Panamax facility on Margarita Island to handle 2.5 million TEUs a year. This will nearly equal the pre-expansion capacity of MIT and be four times the size of the original Taiwanese-owned Evergreen terminal. The second new project, also at a cost of $900 million, is for a natural-gas-fired generation plant capable of producing 350 megawatts of electricity. These two should be completed in 2020 and clearly reflect how private and international contributions help grow Panama's logistics hub.[63]

Whether the Varela administration's full court press could finally revive Colon remained to be seen, but observers ranked it the best effort in over a half century. New businesses, decent homes and schools, tourism, and a functioning urban infrastructure went a long way to improving the quality of life for a half-million *colonenses*.

CORRUPTION DREW UNWANTED ATTENTION

Ever since the creation of the International Banking Center in 1970, Panama attracted financial business that made it a regional player in the global economy. By early 2017 it hosted seventy-nine domestic banks and fifteen foreign branches that held about $120 billion in assets. The sector employed tens of thousands and produced millions in profits. Because it complemented other economic roles Panama wished to develop, the Center represented a major legacy of Nicolás Ardito Barletta's early planning initiatives.[64]

62 Press release, Nov. 12, 2016, president's website, www.presidencia.gob.pa/.

63 "Empresa China invertirá $1,800 milliones en Colón," *Panamá América*, Apr. 7, 2017; and www.inversioninmobiliariacr.com/index.php/noticias/noticias-internacionales/item/866-megaempresa-china-shangai-gorgeous-invertira-us-1-800-millones-en-panama.

64 See Ardito Barletta, *Huellas: Contribuciones públicas nacionales e internacionales, memorias* (Bogota: Panamericana, 2016), ch. 4.1. The center could also be considered a private sector spoke in the Panamanian hub.

In addition to the legitimate enterprises the center attracted, however, it also drew operators who facilitated tax evasion, money laundering, drug transactions, and other illicit activities in the 1980s and 1990s. Laws permitting secret bank accounts generated some criticism, as did rules allowing the formation of new enterprises without identifying their owners/beneficiaries/capital sources. Some foreign nations labeled Panama a tax haven, and international organizations called on its authorities periodically to adopt measures to increase corporate and financial transparency.[65]

A 1998 law creating the Superintendence of Banks established an independent body, supported by fees levied on registered institutions, that took over supervision of the nation's financial sector from the previous government commission. The new entity followed the principles of the Basel Committee, a Swiss-based organization promoting sound financial norms and practices worldwide. Since then, the Superintendence has revised its policies along with those of the Basel Committee. It exercised broad powers to license, audit, restructure, and suspend bank charters. By this time, Panama accounted for only a fraction of the assets managed by the big New York, Swiss, and London banks, which escaped regulations that Panama's bankers could only dream of.[66] But the sector's importance to Panama's developing hub remained huge.

Efforts made by the banking regulators to enact best practices and protect the integrity of the center largely succeeded, and the Superintendence won the respect of banking authorities abroad. It also took some contentious responsibilities off the shoulders of elected officials. Every year a certain number of banks closed due to irregularities and insolvency, yet the system as a whole prospered. Two huge challenges to these efforts surfaced in the new century, however, money-laundering and government corruption, which by association tainted the banking sector as well. These crimes had always been present and likely always will be. Their scope and severity, however, grew alarming and brought unwanted attention to the entire business community.

The biggest shock came in April 2016, with the release of the so-called Panama Papers. These constituted the largest leak of banking client information in history, 11.5 million files, from the database of Panama's

[65] Guevara Mann, "Luces y sombras," 263–65; interview, Ebrahim Asvat and Brett Patton, Apr. 8, 2015. Gabriel Zucman, *The Hidden Wealth of Nations: The Scourge of Tax Havens* (Chicago and London: The University of Chicago Press, 2015) provides an overview of the global tax haven phenomenon.

[66] See its website at www.superbancos.gob.pa.

fourth largest offshore law firm, Mossack Fonseca. It specialized in incorporations for clients around the world, whose identities were kept secret. Unknown agents delivered these stolen files to a German newspaper that shared them with a consortium of investigative reporters in Europe. The latter processed and passed them on to some leading newspapers. A huge scandal erupted when the files revealed that prominent politicians from many countries and scores of their family members and associates had hidden billions in assets in tax shelters created by Mossack Fonseca, mostly in other countries. To Varela's chagrin, the episode became known as the "Panama Papers," even though Panamanians and local banks were only marginally involved and much of the global business community showed sympathy for the country's position.[67] Yet the alliterative tag sounded good on the evening news.

President Varela immediately sought to get out ahead of the scandal, pledging to empanel a special commission of experts to study what had happened and what measures should be taken to avoid future events like this. A few days later, he published an op-ed letter in the *New York Times* to explain his actions and put the episode into global perspective. He noted the miniscule participation of Panama in what was a trillion-dollar industry and lamented that his nation should be saddled with the label of tax haven facilitator.

> Panama does not deserve to be singled out on an issue that plagues many countries ... The world must tackle this problem collectively and with urgency, and Panama stands ready to lead the way.

He noted that the foreign ministry was launching further efforts to cooperate with international watchdog groups and that his commission would make recommendations in six months. His piece evinced a strong law-and-order tone.[68]

Positive attention focused on the independent experts' commission, whose report was published in November.[69] It surveyed Panama's place

[67] See Luke Harding's article in *The Guardian*, one of the newspapers that received leaked files, "Panama Papers? The Real Panama Story," Apr. 5, 2016; and the strong statement of support by Steve Forbes in "Panama Papers? Here's the Real Panama Story," *Forbes*, May 10, 2016: "Panama is no sleazy money laundering backwater. Quite the opposite. Panama City is becoming the financial center of Latin America,"

[68] Editorial, "Financial Secrecy in Panama and Beyond," *New York Times*, Apr. 8, 2016; Juan Carlos Varela, "Don't Blame Panama. Tax Evasion Is a Global Problem," *New York Times*, Apr. 11, 2016. See also Saint Malo's talk before the Washington DC Council on Foreign Relations on May 5, 2016.

[69] Comité de Expertos Independientes, *Informe final*, November 2016.

in the global economy and the important role the banking center played. It also catalogued the multiple attempts Panama made to monitor and account for capital flows, especially those for illicit or terrorist purposes. Panama had aligned itself with most of these efforts in years past and had generally improved its reputation for transparency. The commission listed many recommendations that, when adopted, would further improve Panama's compliance with financial rules, without jeopardizing its legitimate business interests. The report left the strong impression that the country was on the right track to overcome the impact of the Panama Papers.

Saint Malo continued on the offensive, promising that Panama would be a leader in avoiding money laundering and complying with international standards, especially through adherence to various agreements to share information among governments. She signed the OECD's Convention on Mutual Administrative Assistance in Tax Matters and committed Panama to adopt the highest international standards to combat money laundering, the financing of terrorism, and related activities. She worked closely with the National Authority for Transparency and Information (ANTAI) to host the 17th International Anti-Corruption Conference in early December. Some 1,600 persons from 130 nations attended and crafted a statement against graft in government. Varela and Saint Malo both made strong supportive statements at the meeting.[70]

The government continued to use international connections for reform. First, it joined with the national chamber of commerce to focus the nation's annual business conference, Expocomer XXXV, on the fight against corruption. Former Uruguayan president Mario Sanguinetti followed Varela to the podium and explained how populism and corruption feed on one another and result in tragedies like the one Venezuela was suffering.[71] Meanwhile, Saint Malo pushed to meet the recommendations of the experts' commission, leading to an OECD announcement that Panama was "largely compliant" in exchange of tax and economic information and would no longer be included in the list of tax havens.[72]

[70] Victoria Isabel Cardial C., "Canciller comparte escenario con la OCDE," *La Prensa*, Jan. 13, 2017; Bertrand Marotte, "Tax-Evasion Crackdowns Promised over 'Panama Papers' Revelations," *Globe and Mail*, Jan. 5, 2017. José González Pinilla and Aminta Bustamante, "Concluye foro anti-corrupción; gobierno promete transparencia," *La Prensa*, Dec. 4, 2016; Carlos Guevara Mann, "Conferencia anticorrupción, una gran farsa," *La Prensa*, Nov. 30, 2016.

[71] www.correodelosviernes.com.uy/Sanguinetti-en-la-Expocomer-en-Panama.asp.

[72] "Panamá ya no podrá ser incluida en lista de paraisos fiscales," *La Estrella*, June 29, 2017.

By the end of 2016, *La Prensa* columnist Rolando Rodríguez lamented that the nation had been tarnished by three international scandals that year, the Panama Papers, Nidal Waked's inclusion on the "Clinton List" of financial crimes and extradition to the United States for prosecution, and the revelations that Brazilian construction giant Odebrecht had given nearly $60 million in bribes to Panamanian officials to win contracts since 2007. Historian and corruption analyst Carlos Guevara Mann soon responded that the nation needed a genuine "new year's resolution" to combat what he considered a disease. Although the Varela administration was pursuing many Martinelli officials in court, its deliberate pace and the independence of corruption prosecutors dragged out proceedings and suggested that it might be waiting, as past governments had done, until the scandals faded from the headlines.[73] Moreover, the continuous advent of scandals in new places, such as the September 2017 arrest of twenty-nine officials of the Fourth Penal Court for collusion with criminals, seemed to threaten the prosecution efforts.[74]

Economy minister Dulcidio de la Guardia told a US news channel in early 2017 that while the Panama Papers scandal had damaged the nation's reputation, it had not diminished foreign direct investment in the country. Moreover, he said, law firms and related businesses constituted only about 1 percent of Panama's GDP, although the steep decline in offshore corporate services in 2016 was certainly felt in the legal sector.[75] Foreign minister Saint Malo delivered much the same message to the World Economic Forum in Davos, Switzerland. The head of an organization of economists, however, speculated that some companies might be reluctant to relocate to Panama, potentially hurting the business sector.[76] Only time will tell.

[73] "2016: un año de escándalos," *La Prensa*, Dec. 31, 2016; "Metas colectivas," *La Prensa*, Jan. 11, 2017. The Nidal Waked case implicated the owner of Colon Free Zone companies in money laundering, landing him on a US State Department "wanted list" of suspected criminals and leading to his extradition for trial. The case became even more sensitive when Waked's ownership of *La Estrella de Panamá* newspaper, the oldest in continuous publication, threatened it with shutting down due to US sanctions.

[74] Marlene Testa, "Fiscalía pide juicio para 29 personas por corrupción en la corte," *La Estrella*, Sept. 28, 2017.

[75] The number of tax-paying offshore corporate accounts managed by Panamanian law firms dropped from 26,865 in 2015 to 18,593 in 2016: "La merma de las sociedades anónimas," *La Estrella*, Mar. 30, 2017, and the Mossack Fonseca firm which launched the scandal was shuttered even before both name partners went to jail.

[76] *Panamá América*, Jan. 19, 2017; Davos Panel "Taxation without Borders," Jan. 20, 2017, on the foreign ministry website.

THE CHALLENGES OF ACHIEVING SOCIAL PROGRESS

The Varela administration quickly instituted social programs to improve the lives of ordinary Panamanians. In his campaign, the president had promised to expand the k–12 scholarship program *beca universal* and to raise the value of pensions to persons over sixty-five years of age to $120 a month. Vice presidential candidate Saint Malo was closely identified with UNDP measurement of standards of living in the country, with the intent of improving them.

The introduction to the president's report to the nation in January 2016 continued to emphasize social actions that would

> positively impact citizens' quality of life; for that, all government actions should be guided by social criteria that address the needs of the poorest citizens, offering them opportunities and conditions necessary for the decent development of their families, to educate themselves, and to achieve the personal goals they choose.[77]

This statement contrasted sharply with those of Varela's predecessor, who emphasized economic growth and infrastructure.

Two and a half years into his administration, the president's webpage flashed news of his accomplishments:

- seventeen new model schools, 2,300 new classrooms, 89,600 students benefitted
- 8,000 new homes delivered to low-income persons, 87,000 more underway, in the programs *techos de esperanza* (roofs of hope) and accompanying infrastructure
- Decentralization, $156 million invested in 1400 community development projects
- Zero poverty promoted by the program *pais de todos* (country of everyone)
- Renovation of Colon, thirty-two percent finished
- 1013 km of new highways, costing $930 million
- 101,000 persons covered in the *censo de salud preventiva* (preventive health census)
- Basic sanitation works costing $302 million and benefitting 89,000 persons.

President Varela clearly hoped to touch every citizen's life in positive ways.[78]

[77] Panama, www.presidencia.gob.pa/, *Informe 2015*, "Introduction," accessed 2016.
[78] Panama, www.presidencia.gob.pa/, accessed January 2017.

The president also pursued another initiative designed to give local officials more authority and funding to achieve their own goals. In January 2015, the Assembly passed Law 66 to decentralize many government programs and to channel property tax and local improvement funds to municipalities. The law went into effect in January 2016 and in the first year raised $231 million. Not all was expended, due to inexperience and new procedures, but the president's office boasted that they made possible construction of children's parks, water systems, public markets, roads, and school lunch facilities. The following year, Álvaro Alemán proposed that the Assembly incorporate the program into the constitution due to its success and popularity.[79]

Varela advanced a vision of progress based on solidarity among all elements of society, so that economic growth and human development could proceed together. His emphasis on solidarity extended to the logistics hub and a sustainable environment. He also hoped to reach out to indigenous peoples and the chronically poor. Specific targets included reforestation of a million hectares, universal bilingual education, maternal and child health for the indigenous, modernization of the power grid, universal Internet access, making available locally grown organic food, elimination of plastic bags, restructuring the national pension system, and improved health care delivery. It was a heady agenda indeed![80]

A UNDP report on poverty showed that Panama had reduced poverty from 36.8 percent of the population to 26.2 percent by 2013 and surpassed the other countries of Central America on the Human Development Index.[81] Yet the report warned about the high potential for a resurgence of poverty with any decline in the economic growth rate, and observers noted that, according to the Comptroller's office, some 40 percent of the employed labored in the informal sector despite generally low unemployment.[82]

To ramp up employment in the northwest, Panama agreed to the return of US-based Del Monte to revive the banana industry, where small

79 *Panama Today*, Jan. 11, 2017.

80 A variety of commentaries and contemporary accounts are reflected here. A summary and overview is provided by Álvaro Alvarado, "Detallan el Plan Estratégico Nacional 'Panamá 2030,'" *Telemetro*, Feb. 22, 2017.

81 PNUD, *Progreso multidimensional: bienestar más allá del ingreso (Informe Regional para Latino América y el Caribe, 2016:* www.cl.undp.org/content/dam/rblac/docs/Research%20and%20Publications/IDH/UNDP_RBLAC_IDH2016Final.pdf.

82 Aleida Samaniego C., "Pobreza, un riesgo para Panamá, *La Prensa*, July 4, 2016.

growers and coops had languished in poverty for over a decade.[83] Analysts expected this to add several thousand jobs and that new investment in the plantations would produce secondary jobs as well.

Three areas of social action proved especially troublesome. In education, officials provided frank revelations about the failure of universal scholarships and other expensive programs to reduce dropout rates or show quality improvements. Except for longer days in an increasing number of schools, other reform measures, such as increasing teacher accountability, got sidetracked in a prolonged national debate over sex education and collective bargaining.[84]

With respect to the old problem of inequality, a report by the INCAE Center for Competitiveness and Sustainable Development in 2016 showed that gaps in the delivery of such basic services as potable water and sewage, nutrition, basic health service, and quality education were not declining. Yet the study emphasized that Panama continued to show progress in access to individual opportunity and inclusiveness.[85]

Varela and Saint Malo tried to address the grievances of indigenous peoples through community visits, new scholarship programs, and recognition of individual achievements. In 2017, these leaders still insisted that the Assembly's failure to ratify ILO Convention 169 prevented their communities from managing government resources for the benefit of their people.[86]

Hoping to capitalize on his poverty reduction efforts, Varela reiterated in his 2017 New Year's message that Panama should be "the country of everybody – zero poverty."[87] He turned its execution over to Saint Malo, who chaired the social wing of his cabinet, to assign responsibilities in individual areas.[88] These included the "roofs of hope" housing program, "the $120 at 65" pensions, and universal scholarships. His message

[83] www.casasolution.com/blog/100-million-for-chriqui-bocas-del-toro-bananas-economic-boon-for-the-region/.

[84] "Aumentan fracasos escolares," *La Estrella*, Dec. 16, 2016; Francisco Rodríguez Morán; "Deserción escolar aumenta a pesar de la Beca Universal," *La Estrella*, Oct. 29, 2016; Urania Cecilia Molina, "Aumenta cifra de escuelas en jornada única," *La Prensa*, February 21, 2017.

[85] Roberto González Jiménez, "Producto interno bruto alto, pero bajo progreso social," *La Prensa*, July 5, 2016.

[86] www.nodal.am/2017/06/panama-la-coordinadora-nacional-pueblos-indigenas-reclamaran-al-gobierno-promesas-no-cumplidas/.

[87] www.presidencia.gob.pa/Presidente-Juan-Carlos-Varela-Rodriguez/Gobierno-prepara-el-Plan-Panama-el-pais-de-todos-cero-pobreza.

[88] www.mides.gob.pa/gabinete-social-adopta-plan-panama-el-pais-de-todos/.

stressed that if the government committed to such giveaway programs, the ministers should insure that they get results.

The evolving leadership must also face new facets of some continuing issues that it has so far handled well. The prospects of a new interoceanic canal in Nicaragua now appear quite unlikely, but the potential for major changes in the competitive environment, whether the development of Arctic Ocean shipping, increases in vessel size and technology, changes in Suez Canal practices and policies, or changes in global demand for shipping services, remain concerns. While the feasibility of a Nicaragua canal appears remote, some of the arguments made about the need for a still larger waterway by 2030 remain valid. Further adjustment of the ACP's range of services, increasing its water supply, and the development of the national personnel needed to meet these changing circumstances are other challenges that must be met.[89]

POLITICAL DISARRAY ON THE ROAD TO THE 2019 ELECTIONS

Despite the non-combative approach of the Varela administration, the country's prosperity and the increased public sector role in society raised the stakes in politics and escalated conflict long before the 2019 election season. Government employment rose 11 percent in less than four years under Varela, surpassing 228,000. Payrolls accelerated more rapidly, from \$203 million a month to \$321 million (up 58 percent). In the Assembly, where staff primarily serve to advance the interests of deputies, 437 employees were added to rolls of 1,601, up 27 percent.[90] Meanwhile, government subsidy programs ballooned, reaching 6 percent of public spending. The total value of the old age payments, scholarships, electricity and fuel subsidies, and others surpassed the revenue provided by the Canal.[91]

With so much largess at stake, efforts to deal with crucial national issues stalled – like reducing costs and eliminating blackouts of the electrical grid, completing the Colon project, averting floods in the Juan Díaz

89 AFP, "Nicaragua's US\$50b rival to Panama Canal 'going ahead slowly' as funding evaporates and China investor keeps a low profile," Feb. 22, 2018.

90 *Vamaganews, Resumen de noticias*, May 11, 2018, data cited are from MEF reports. See also Wilfredo Jordan, "Planilla estatal suma \$321 milliones cada mes," *La Prensa*, May 11, 2018.

91 Wilfredo Jordan y Roberto González, "Presupuesto destina 6 porciento para subsidios," *La Prensa*, Aug. 4, 2017.

River delta and other zones, overcoming traffic stalemates, dealing with the water needs of the Canal and urban consumers, creating a new port in Corozal, and trimming pension system overspending. Meanwhile, contract disputes, labor strife, nationwide strikes, judicial obstructionism, citizen protests, political rivalry, partisan conflicts, and inter-institutional disputes escalated noticeably in 2017 and 2018. In mid 2018, for example, a construction workers strike threatened to reduce GDP growth rate a full percentage point.[92]

The Varela administration's earlier pact with the PRD in the Assembly had enabled a lot to be done. Electoral and property tax reforms and other pieces of legislation were approved. Funding was allotted for increasing government subsidies and infrastructure investments. Multiple investigations of corruption and prosecutions occurred. Panama's business was moving ahead, if deliberately. Unexpectedly, however, an upheaval within the ranks of the PRD rearranged the country's political landscape. Deputy Pedro Miguel González won election as secretary general of the party in October 2016, and he and his confederates decided to shift their strategy to confrontation with the government. The old rivalry between the PRD and the latest generation of Arnulfistas in the PPa returned to stage center. Although the Varela administration patched together a new pact with the CD to maintain a working majority in the Assembly, putting it in motion dragged on for months. During 2017 and 2018, legislative action slowed, and it often seemed that Varela was vetoing as much legislation as he was approving.[93]

By early 2018, PRD efforts to convince Assembly president Yanibel Ábrego, a CD deputy, and her supporters to join them in opposition to the administration had tied the body in knots and left work on some fifty bills at a standstill.[94] Abrupt shifts in committee assignments left legislative allies of the government unable to advance judicial appointments. Although former president Pérez Balladares expressed concern about the

[92] Giovanna Ferullo, "El dólar, el combustible y la construcción arrastran a la baja el PIB de Panamá," EFE, June 2, 2018.

[93] Andrea Gallo, "Varela objeta tres proyectos de ley 'por incovenientes,'" *La Prensa*, Apr. 18, 2018.

[94] On May 1, 2017, *Panamá América* reported that the Assembly had just completed one of the most unproductive periods in history. On Oct. 23, 2017, the headline of a *La Prensa* story said the Assembly had completed its session without discussing any major subjects. Then, on Feb. 7, 2018, an article by Andrea Gallo, "Pugnas frenan el debate legislativo," *La Prensa,* detailed how productive work on more than fifty legislative projects had been paralyzed since the vote in late January in which CD and PRD deputies had joined forces to defeat Varela's nomination of two magistrates for the supreme court.

rising clientelism and graft in the CD-controlled Assembly, little action took place.[95]

After the abrupt shift in Assembly leadership, Varela went on the offensive. Comptroller Federico Humbert put in high gear an investigation into Assembly contracting and payrolls, dispatching a phalanx of government auditors to the legislature. After just a few days of work and several rounds of embarrassing revelations about Assembly largess, Ábrego ordered security personnel to remove the auditors. At that point, the Comptroller retaliated by refusing to authorize any salary payments to the staff of the Assembly. With the pay of more than 3,000 Assembly employees blocked, Ábrego appealed to the courts to regain access to its funds, in anticipation of its coming legislative session.

The Supreme Court had its own problems to solve: its president had resigned and been replaced on an interim basis. The newly politicized Assembly refused to ratify two new magistrates nominated by Varela, while several other seats were filled by alternates. In a number of cases, the majority of the magistrates voting, even on Constitutional matters, were alternates.

Lower courts also experienced turmoil. A new penal system proposed for over a decade could not be implemented due to rules disputes. Judicial misconduct led various judges to be suspended, along with some investigators, prosecutors, and twenty-nine others for colluding with drug traffickers. The government even appealed to the United Nations for outside assistance in dealing with these crises. Meanwhile, civic, professional, and business organizations denounced the judiciary for what they termed a crisis of trust.[96]

Despite the gravity of these problems, some brave members of the judiciary made progress toward enforcing the law. First, charges against former president Martinelli and other high-profile corruption targets advanced despite obstructionism and defensive maneuvering. After his extradition to Panama, Martinelli found himself incarcerated in the same cell that once held General Noriega. Other convictions included the mayor of Arraijan and several cabinet officials. Martinelli's sons and others also faced charges. Second, the 2005 Pact of State for Justice was resurrected to achieve a merit-based appointment system for Supreme Court justices, a strong sign of societal support for judicial reform. Under this new

[95] José Arcia, "El clientelismo se instaló en la Asamblea," *La Estrella*, Dec. 18, 2017.

[96] Adelita Corlatt, "Piden visita del Relator Especial de la ONU," *La Estrella*, Mar. 7, 2017; and Ismael Gordón Guerrel, "CNA abandona por 'inoperante' el Pacto de Estado por la Justicia," *La Estrella*, June 26, 2017. The 2005 crisis is discussed in Chapter 6.

approach, Varela agreed to select his next two nominees from a list of qualified candidates. The selection committee started with 153 names, which it reduced to twenty it considered the most professionally qualified. Finalists were thoroughly vetted, interviewed, and even subjected to testing and psychological examination.[97] Optimists hope that these and other innovations can ensure the integrity of Panama's judiciary.

Panama's electoral system rests on the Tribunal Electoral, a quasi-judicial institution that is implementing recent reforms and a new set of rules for the May 2019 elections. It has been an institutional pillar for coping with intense political rivalries. The following guidelines will be in effect during the next election:

- Presidential candidates are limited to spending $10 million; deputy candidates $300,000, and mayoral candidates $150,000.
- Campaign activities will be confined to the forty-five days before primary elections and sixty days before the general elections.
- Government advertising will be prohibited for ninety days before general elections, and candidates for public office may not inaugurate public works in the year preceding elections.
- Campaign contributions, none larger than 3 percent of the total allowable for the office, must be made public.
- Third parties and media organizations are prohibited from making campaign donations.
- Presidential advertising expenditures must be limited to public funds.
- Political parties that choose to hold primaries to select candidates must do so between August and November of 2018, on dates approved by and according to procedures dictated by the TE.

With primaries for as many as seven political parties and over thirteen independents seeking qualification for the ballot, Panamanian voters will eventually have over forty names of presidential candidates to consider in primaries and the general election.[98] For a time, it appeared that women would be prominent candidates for president in 2019. Vice president Saint

[97] The selection committee pressed its merit approach by reducing the candidates to three names for each of the openings, but Varela rejected this limitation: Getzalette Reyes, "Presidente Varela: 'Yo no pedí ternas, el que decide soy yo,'" *La Prensa,* June 29, 2018.

[98] Twenty-six candidates had enrolled as independents with the TE by May of 2018.

Malo, current first lady Lorena Castillo de Varela, and former first lady Marta Linares de Martinelli topped the list. Also included were several prominent legislators, like Ábrego, PRD firebrand Zulay Rodríguez, and independent crusader Ana Matilde Gómez. Former ministers and party leaders, such as Alma Cortes of the CD, private sector activists like scholar and social reformer Ana Elena Porras, and civil society leaders Magaly Castillo, Annette Planels, and Úrsula Kiener were all mentioned as part of the feminine contribution to politics in Panama.

Irrespective of gender, Panama has never lacked candidates for office. Recent developments suggest an upsurge of interest in running for office, with so much at stake in the control of the government, not to mention the prerogatives of deputies and mayors.[99] The Varela cabinet had been one of the most stable in recent Panamanian history, but several administration figures announced their resignations ahead of deadlines for registering candidacies. Rumors also circulated that as many as half the cabinet may be leaving to pursue electoral prospects in one way or another. A Martinelli appointee to the board of the ACP, Marco Ameglio, also resigned, to run for office. The candidate ranks in other political parties, also appear just as abundant as they are among independents:

- In the PRD, and notwithstanding the revolution in its leadership, old stalwarts like former president Pérez Balladares, two-time candidate Juan Carlos Navarro, and former agriculture minister Laurentino "Nito" Cortizo have all expressed interest in competing against a long list of young turks.
- For the CD, where former foreign minister Rómulo Roux won nominal control of the party from ex-president Martinelli and his allies, at least five Martinelli supporters remain in contention with Roux for the presidential nomination.
- Varela's Panameñista Party remains the hardest to predict but may have the most wannabe candidates. Besides the crop of party leaders in the government and Panama City mayor José Isabel Blandón, the party might also turn to one of the administration's loyal independents, such as vice president Saint Malo or Assembly stalwarts led by the president's brother and party leader José Luis "Popi" Varela.

[99] Ismael Gordón Guerrel, "Presidenciables se abren paso rumbo a elecciones del 2019," *La Estrella*, May 31, 2017.

- Five other recognized but small political parties may also enter the presidential sweepstakes, either with their own candidates or as members of coalitions.

As suggested by the earlier enumeration of neglected national challenges, the issue horizon for the 2019 election campaign may be as varied and unpredictable as the candidates. Yet every election campaign since the restoration of democracy has shown that the winning formula has centered on opposition to the incumbent regime.

* * * *

As of this writing, Varela continued to deal with entrenched opponents and to muster support for his party as it prepares for general elections in 2019, in which he cannot be a candidate for president. Chapter 10 extracts our overall conclusions about Panama's history during the past nearly four and in so doing tentatively assesses the closing years of the Varela administration.

10

Conclusions

How beautiful it would be if the Isthmus of Panama became for us (in the Americas) what Corinth was for the ancient Greeks!

Simón Bolívar

A FOURTEEN-DAY TOUR OF PANAMA

Before turning to our conclusions, we invite the reader to an imaginary tour of the country to illustrate its large and growing complexity. About the size of Austria or South Carolina, Panama impresses with rapid economic growth, global engagement, and socio-political change since 1980. It also has astonishing human and biodiversity due to its location astride the crossroads between oceans and continents.[1] To provide a sense of the variegated landscape and the pace of change, we scheduled a hypothetical two-week itinerary ranging from ocean to ocean and Central America to Colombia. The Panama Canal still provides a centerpiece for the experience, but the tour shows how much country lies beyond the waterway.

The map numbers below identify the suggested daily locations for the fourteen-day trip.

[1] Even historically, Panama's linkages have varied. During the early colonial period, it was associated with the Caribbean. It then became part of the viceroyalty of New Granada and was a province of Colombia when it became independent. Since World War II, it has been more associated with the countries of Central America, although for a time it also belonged to the Andean Pact.

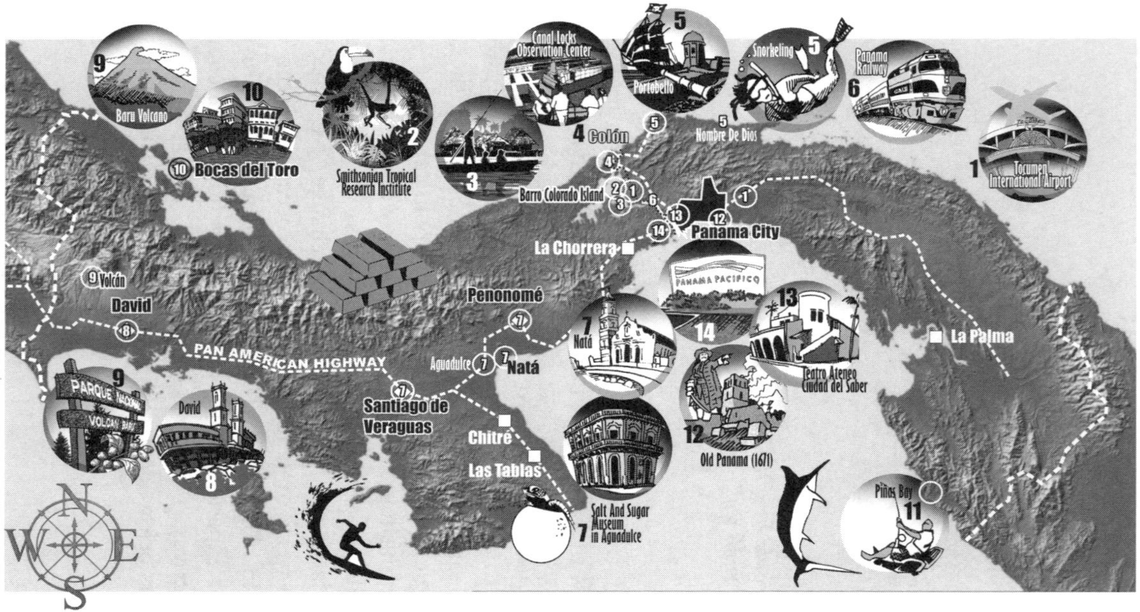

FIGURE 10.1 Map showing popular tourist sites. Courtesy of Roberto Radrigan.

1 Arrive at Tocumen International Airport – tourist bus to Gamboa Rainforest Resort on Gatun Lake. Afternoon/evening – aerial tram tour of forest canopy, visit ecological exhibits, or game fishing on the lake before dinner.
2 Tour the Smithsonian Tropical Research Institute's biological preserve on Barro Colorado Island. Return to Gamboa or move to other hotel for the night.
3 Take dugout canoe trip to rainforest village and spend the day learning about the jungle, playing in the rapids of a tropical river, and learning about local life from residents of the indigenous community.
4 Tour the City of Colon, including its ports, Free Zone, new low-income housing complexes, and the new Canal Atlantic locks observation center. Spend the night in the Sol Meliá Hotel (former US Army School of the Americas).
5 Visit the UNESCO World Heritage historical sites of Portobello and Nombre de Dios (near where the pirate Sir Francis Drake was buried at sea) and go snorkeling for Spanish doubloons at the Bananas Village resort. Return to Sol Meliá or choose another hotel for the night.
6 Take Panama Railway to Panama City – spend the day visiting the Cathedral, Palacio Bolívar, Colegio Javier, the Canal Museum, strolling by the Presidential Palace, Las Garzas, and other sites in the UNESCO World Heritage Historic District of the Casco Antiguo.
7 Start road trip on Pan American Highway to western Panama, with a stop at the Orchid Farm in the Valle de Anton, the historic capital at Natá, the agricultural center in Penonome, and the salt and sugar museum in Aguadulce. Spend the night there or further along in Santiago de Veraguas.
8 Continue road trip with lunch and car tour of the Chiriqui regional capital at David, Panama's cowboy country. Arrive at the Bambito Hotel/resort in Cerro Punta at 6,500 feet above sea level.
9 Explore the Volcan region, tour a coffee plantation, try trout fishing in the Alpine forest, and visit immigrant retirement villages in the Chiriqui highlands.
10 Rough it with backpackers (or not) at Bocas Town Hotel and enjoy the Caribbean oasis on Colon Island in Bocas del Toro. Next morning, fly east across the entire country to Darien province.

11 Try your hand at big game fishing at the Tropic Star Lodge in Piñas Bay, at the edge of the dense Darien jungle dividing Panama from Colombia.
12 Return to modern Panama City and tour the ruins of old Panama (the city destroyed by Henry Morgan the pirate in 1671) and later check into a high-rise or boutique hotel near the banking center or casino and entertainment district.
13 Visit the Miraflores Locks visitors' center on the Panama Canal, tour the nearby City of Knowledge (formerly Fort Clayton), take windshield tour of the Port of Balboa, and visit the chamber of commerce, the maritime chamber or other business, civic, or professional organization.
14 Visit Panamá Pacífico International Center and the growing logistics hub (at the former Howard Air Force Base) and complete the day on the Amador Causeway, with a tour of the Frank Gehry-designed Museum of Biodiversity and an evening at the marinas and tourist facilities adjacent to the Pacific entrance of the Canal.

LOOKING BACK, 1980–2018

Those of us who lived through the years covered in this book could be excused for marveling at the national changes Panamanians have carried out in little over a generation. Their numbers grew by over a third, to four million inhabitants. They suffered through a dictatorship, resisted it, and endured its overthrow by the third-largest US military operation since the Vietnam war. They resurrected democratic government, created a fair elections system, peacefully transferred the presidency to opponents five times, restored human and civil rights, and replaced the army with a National Police. They learned how the Panama Canal operated, oversaw improvements, and took over its management in 1999. Their success, including a major construction project to expand its capacity, earned praise from around the world. They integrated the Canal into the national economy in ways that broadened the nation's maritime vocation and turned Panama into the "Hub of the Americas," partly using new revenue from the Canal. For the past fifteen years or so, the nation has enjoyed some of the fastest economic growth rates in the hemisphere.

Today Panama stands out for its stable government, expanded crossroads for international shipping and travelers, and comfortable standards of living. Its leaders were able to shrug off the "Panama Papers" scandal in 2016, attesting to the nation's resiliency. These successes won widespread respect abroad and greater roles in international affairs, especially multilateral agencies dealing with governance and commerce and more recently the environment. The fact that several foreign ministers also served as vice president meant higher visibility and access to power. Multinational firms paid close attention to opportunities in Panama, investing and locating 147 regional offices there, while tens of thousands of individuals and families immigrated to enjoy mild weather and low real estate prices and taxes.[2] Purchases of beach properties especially boomed after 2000, as did tourism. Economic growth drew tens of thousands of migrants from nearby countries, especially Venezuela and Colombia, where jobs and opportunities had become scarce, but ties to the United States, several European countries, China, and East Asia generally also grew. Many of these immigrants brought capital to invest. Panama's government and people generally welcomed newcomers, as they had in previous times.

RESTORING DEMOCRACY AND HUMAN RIGHTS, DISMANTLING THE ARMY

Freedom House, an NGO that studies the quality of governance and civil liberties around the world, ranks Panama as the fourth oldest democracy in Latin America, behind Costa Rica, Uruguay, and Chile. Political scientist Carlos Guevara Mann noted that the current era of constitutional government (twenty-three years) exceeded that of the previous dictatorship (twenty-one years).[3] Multiple parties took part in elections during that time, and, in each case, voters chose presidents from opposition parties. The Assembly experienced somewhat less rotation in leadership. All elections rated high for efficiency and honesty, in the views of international observers, although recent years saw growing infusions of money of doubtful provenance in excessively long campaigns. Panama enjoyed respectable levels of press freedom, human rights, and individual liberties.

The abolition of the military and its replacement with the National Police and several other agencies in the early 1990s, firmly supervised by a cabinet-level civilian official, represented a major step toward

[2] The last three MNC regional offices in the corporate parade started by President Martín Torrijos in 2005 are JCB, an English international law firm, Isuzu Motors of Japan, and the China Railway International Group; "Panamá sede de tres nuevas multinacionales," *La Estrella*, June 7, 2018.

[3] He counts the years since the 1994 election: "Luces y sombras en torno a la institucionalidad democrática," *Revista de Ciencia Política*, 36, no. 1 (2016): 279–80; https://freedomhouse.org/report/freedom-world/2016/panama.

reinforcing democracy. Panama joined Costa Rica as the only other Latin American nation without an army. Some citizens criticized the fact that many new rank and file policemen had served previously in the military and that most upper-level army officers received criminal pardons in subsequent years. Others decried closer cooperation with US defense authorities and expanded roles in drug traffic suppression and border protection, which they termed "remilitarization." Still, most agreed that the nation was better off by far without the potential meddling of a rival power center.

Public opinion surveys in 2012 showed that Panamanians reported low levels of crime in their lives, compared with most other Latin American nations. Persons living in the biggest cities had higher perceptions of criminality than those in rural areas. They also expressed strong support for the rule of law in combating crime. These overall findings suggest that the management of police services since the 1990s has been largely successful, but concerns for excessive incarceration rates, inconsistent use of merit criteria in judicial appointments, and implementation of procedural reforms in the criminal justice system remain intense.[4]

As the Varela administration drew to a close, political attention increasingly focused on four major issues. First, citizens wanted higher-quality government services like urban transportation, environmental protection, blackout-free electricity, public health, and pensions. Second, pundits noted growing clientelism and dysfunction among political parties and their inability to work together in the National Assembly, much less to achieve legislative and executive collaboration to advance citizen interests. Third, experts deplored the judiciary's inability to cope with generalized corruption and to achieve autonomy and modernization. Fourth, although the Panama Canal expansion has met and exceeded expectations, the ACP now faces growing potential for water shortages, controversy over the development of ancillary services, such as the port of Corozal, and its most serious challenge in leadership succession.

Ironically, the convening of a national constitutional convention that Varela promised during his election campaign to address such problems may be left up to the voters to decide in the 2019 election, which will mark his departure from office.

[4] Orlando J. Pérez, *Cultura política de la democracia en Panamá: Evidencia desde el Barómetro de las Américas* (Vanderbilt Centro para Iniciativas Democráticas, 2013), 30–39.

MANAGING THE CANAL AND ITS EXPANSION

The early chapters of this book showed that Panamanians, who had little engagement with Canal operations before the 1977 Treaty, gradually developed the expertise to take on the complex job of administering it. Zonian Canal executives impeded their progress until 1994, when a strong-willed figure from Washington, Joe Reeder, pushed hard for full compliance with the treaty in time for the 1999 transfer. That innovation finally opened the door for Panamanian leadership.

During the next five years, Panamanians came to occupy almost all top positions in the Canal. The US government cooperated to make sure the Canal ran at peak performance, and the Pentagon belatedly removed its bases and other facilities from the country. Panama, meanwhile, established a new agency, the Panama Canal Authority (ACP), to take over operations in 1999, after a long apprenticeship under US officials. It was duly separated from the rest of government to protect it from political meddling, given budget autonomy and independent cabinet-level supervision, and skillfully interconnected with the international shipping and maritime community. The turnover ceremonies of December 1999 ended nearly a century of US physical presence in Panama. Symbolically, these events marked the end of a colonialist enclave that dated back to 1903. Luckily, dozens of determined Panamanians had learned to plan for, reorganize, and operate the Canal so that it served the nation's interests.

The new Canal managers undertook two initiatives: putting the Canal on a path to corporate operations and designing additional locks to accommodate shippers' needs for larger vessels in the future, called neo-Panamax. Chapter 7 showed the complexity of these tasks, which culminated in the June 2016 opening of the third locks. The ACP scrapped the existing single toll system for one using multiple rates, to take into account classes and values of goods transported and to maximize revenues without scaring off business.

The expansion plan, fully researched and disseminated to the public, won approval in a 2006 referendum and soon went to bid. A consortium of companies, mostly European, won the design-to-inauguration contract and carried out the massive work, estimated to cost $5.2 billion.[5] In the end, it took longer and cost more than budgeted, but once open, it

[5] The final cost of the expansion will not be known until all the pending disputes with the contractors are settled, which could take years. So far, the ACP has won most of the cases brought to arbitration.

successfully accommodated hundreds of super-sized ships and won back business that had temporarily rerouted through the Suez Canal or Cape of Good Hope. In just over a decade, ACP's annual financial contribution to the government of Panama went from $200 million to a plateau at just over a billion dollars. Now, less than two years after completion of the expansion, revenues have jumped to a higher level and are growing toward the $2 billion range as global commerce expands.

The ACP also took on a new challenge, broadening the range of support offered to world shipping to augment its traditional business of moving vessels between two oceans. In cooperation with the Panama Maritime Authority (AMP) and other agencies, the passage through Panama expanded and added chandlering, maintenance and repair, bunkering, insurance, fiber-optic communications, registry, admiralty law, container marshalling and other port services, intermodal transportation, and other services to ships, enhancing Panama's value to global trade. Its latest innovations involve adding natural gas refueling facilities and further expanding and modernizing port capacity, although questions remain about how new facilities, such as the port of Corozal, will be built and controlled. These mostly new services multiplied the economic impact of the Canal and hence its contribution to Panama's GDP even beyond its increasing contribution to the Treasury. After a century of operation, the Canal finally began to fulfill Panamanian dreams about how a ship passage between the seas could serve as the motor of national growth.

Finally, the ACP and other agencies eased the flow of people, goods, and vehicles around the Isthmus by providing two new bridges over the Canal. The existing Bridge of the Americas and Centennial Bridge will soon be joined by the Atlantic Bridge between Colon and the northwest coast, and by a projected fourth crossing north of the Bridge of the Americas. The latter, in the bidding stage in 2018, will add six traffic lanes plus two more for the Metro's third line into the populous Arraijan-Chorrera district and the beach resorts west of the capital city, at an estimated cost of $1.2 billion.[6]

In February 2019, Ricaurte Vásquez was appointed as the new administrator and Ilya Espino de Marotta as his deputy to continue in September the stellar work of Alberto Alemán and Jorge Luis Quijano in managing

[6] The Bridge of the Americas was not opened until 1962. The Centennial Bridge was inaugurated in 2004. The Atlantic Bridge is expected to be dedicated in spring 2019 and the fourth bridge to ease the crossing bottlenecks in 2021 or 2022.

the canal. Quijano has emphasized the importance of a new generation of leadership in the ACP as he completes forty-four years of service. Outside observers emphasize the need for imaginative leadership and dedication to the Canal's historic mission, as it confronts ongoing controversies and even some conflicts of interests among its board members.[7]

GROWING THE ECONOMY TOWARD THE HUB, BOOSTING STANDARDS OF LIVING

In addition to ACP and AMP initiatives to broaden their range of services to maritime customers, the government has undertaken other activities to complement the economy's traditional orientation. Taken together, these new enterprises seek to convert Panama into the Hub of the Americas, the way Singapore has become for Southeast Asia and Dubai for the Middle East.

Air transport, focused on Tocumen International Airport, forms one booming area that is turning the wetlands east of the capital into

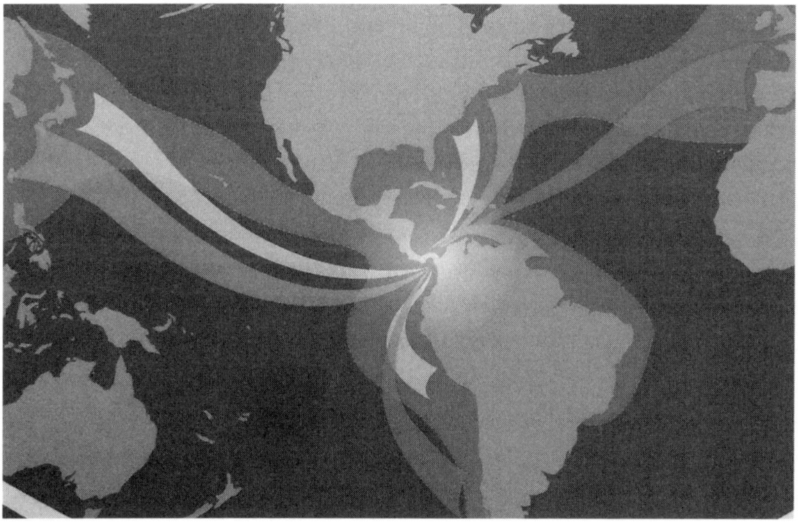

FIGURE 10.2 Diagram illustrating connecting elements of the Crossroads of the Americas. Autoridad del Canal de Panamá.

[7] For instance, two members of the ACP Board are under investigation for corruption, while another member resigned to run for election. Marlene Testa, "El gran desafío para el Canal de Panamá," *La Estrella,* June 21, 2018.

a secondary city in its own right, with two main terminals and their respective towers and runway complexes. Complementary housing at Tocumen ranges from five-star hotels to vast expanses of low-cost homes for workers and service personnel. Airplane maintenance facilities have captured a growing share of that important business in the hemisphere. The Tocumen hub also anchors a network of secondary airports, from nearby Albrook and Panamá Pacífico to regional ones at Santiago, Colon, and David, and including the restored Rio Hato airstrip serving the beach resorts west of the capital. The value of the air transport sector to the economy grew almost twice as fast as the rest of the transportation and communications sector of the economy, over 600 percent from 2000 to 2015.[8]

Other sectors complement the maritime and air hubs. For example, the banking center expanded into a $120 billion industry. Construction, weighing in at nearly a sixth of the economy, attracted big investments and boosted employment while also providing offices for businesses and housing for their employees. Finally, Panama became a popular site for international conferences because of its many venues, easy travel connections, and relaxed visa rules. The several events a month held there also stimulate tourism.[9] With its physical expansion, multiplication of connections, changes in aircraft, and global travel patterns, Tocumen has been resurrected as a transfer center. Steady passenger growth over a decade suddenly boomed, and the airport of the least populous country in Latin America jumped into the ranks of the top airports in the region.

Overall statistics on the economy have been impressive for over a decade.[10] In many years, growth rates reached double digits and usually stood at twice those for the rest of Latin America. In 2017, estimated GDP was 99.48 billion (PPP). During these years, the service sector expanded to nearly four fifths of GDP, at the expense of anemic primary and secondary production. On the other hand, the opening of copper exports from the gigantic First Quantum mines in 2019 will restore some structural balance.

[8] INDESA, "La importancia del transporte y las comunicaciones en la economía panameña," May 2017, 8–9.

[9] Tocumen was not among the twenty busiest airports by passenger traffic in Latin America listed by Wikipedia in 2011, but it jumped to the top ten in 2014 and appears to be on the verge of jumping higher despite the recent expansion of regional airports around the country.

[10] Guevara Mann, "Sombras y luces," 261–63, with some data updated from the World Bank website, http://data.worldbank.org/.

The highly touted Colon Free Zone, however, which combined manufacturing and exports, plateaued in 2015 at $24 billion as it struggles to develop new markets to replace its traditional largest customers, Venezuela and Colombia. Overall, economic expansion was financed largely from profits from the Canal, international bank credits, and foreign direct investment.

What has Panama's phenomenal growth meant for ordinary citizens? Has it translated into higher standards of living? Per capital income has risen steadily with the GDP and was estimated at $24,300 (PPP) in 2017, ranking it in the top 60 in the world (out of 230) and just about even with Chile as the highest in Hispanic America. Forecasts predict that Panama will reach the top of the list by 2019 or sooner. Costa Rica, which ranked above Panama for decades, has now fallen behind, despite its own steady growth, and ranked 81st in the world at $17,200.[11]

Income distribution in Panama skewed decidedly toward the wealthy. People in the bottom socioeconomic ranks earned comparatively less than the well-to-do. Panama's Gini index of 50.7 showed a high concentration of income, compared with a somewhat more equal one of 45.0 in the United States. Most Latin American countries also had more equal distributions than Panama.[12] On the other hand, the percentage of people living in poverty, as measured by the World Bank, shrank from 33 to 23 percent between 2009 and 2015, a healthy improvement for the employed population. Still, some 40 percent of the employed worked in the informal sector, with little stability or safety-net benefits. The huge recent expansion of clientelistic government giveaways, whether universal student or old age payments, also raised doubts about the continuing potential for building self-reliance and economic productivity.

The UN Human Development Index provided other measures of social well-being, ranking Panama 60th out of 188 nations worldwide. Its score of 0.779 rose 9 percent since 2000 and 19 percent since 1990. This was bolstered by rising life expectancy, more years of schooling, and higher

[11] According to the *CIA World Factbook*, the 2017 estimate for US per capita income (PPP) is $59,500, and it ranks 20th in the world: www.cia.gov/library/publications/the-world-factbook/rankorder/2004rank.html.

[12] Carlos Guevara Mann, "Luces y sombras en torno a la institucionalidad democrática." *Revista de Ciencia Política* 36, no. 1 (2016): 260–61. In Latin America, Guatemala, Colombia, Honduras, Paraguay, and Haiti have higher (less equal) Gini indices than Panama; *CIA World Factbook*, country comparisons.

per capita income. Among the Latin American nations (excluding the Caribbean) just Uruguay, Argentina, and Chile ranked higher.[13]

Varela's resumption of a nonpartisan approach to economic planning and decision making in the 2030 plan offered hope for greater social progress. He linked the plan to achieving the UN sustainable development goals. Reviving an approach originated by President Martín Torrijos, the plan seemed to increase the prospects for consensus on climate change and for extending broad access to electricity, potable water, and social services.

Only Panamanians, of course, could judge whether they shared enough in the nation's recent prosperity and whether the new plan would propel the country toward more equitable social progress. The UN study also assessed perception of well-being and overall life satisfaction. Panama ranked high, with a score of 6.6 on a scale of 0 to 10. This score was dragged down, however, by citizens' dissatisfaction with their government and judiciary. Among Latin American nations, Costa Rica, Brazil, Mexico, Argentina, and Chile had higher scores for perception of well-being.[14]

Varela administration progress in alleviating housing problems in Colon was matched by a nationwide effort to create new housing opportunities through a highly progressive property tax reform passed in October 2017.[15] Yet the concerns over the steep rise in the overall expenditure and clientelistic nature of government subsidies, ranging from universal scholarships to "$120 at 65" benefits, has raised questions about the efficacy of Panama's approach to the poor. Supporters warn that a future crisis in government revenue or even slowing economic growth could have a devastating impact on the country's most vulnerable population.[16]

FORGING BROADER INTERNATIONAL ROLES, ATTRACTING FOREIGNERS

During the years of the 1977 Treaty implementation, Panama projected a modest foreign relations position, overshadowed as it was by the United

[13] United Nations Development Program, *U.N. Human Development Report for 2015* (New York: United Nations, 2015), 208–27. Some figures differ from World Bank ones, due to varying definitions and measures. Panama dropped 20 ranks when inequality was factored in.

[14] UNDP, *Human Development Report for 2018*, 266–69.

[15] "Presidente de Panamá sanciona ley que rebaja impuesto de inmuebles," Oct. 17, 2017, www.efe.com.

[16] Aleida Samaniego C., "Pobreza, un riesgo para Panamá," *La Prensa*, July 4, 2016; and "APEDE: Los subsidios tienen que ser temporales y focalizados," *Panamá América*, Nov. 29, 2017.

States and preoccupied with restoring democratic government, preparing for the Canal takeover, and seeking economic stability. The Moscoso years brought a transition from US-centric relations to a broader engagement with the world, though at first mainly in the shipping and international maritime community. The September 11, 2001, attacks on the United States pulled Panama back into the US orbit, emphasizing security cooperation for the Canal. Some of these initiatives expanded, like its role in maritime security, international shipping organizations, and bilateral cooperation with neighboring nations. Torrijos backed his very active foreign minister and won election to a nonpermanent seat on the UN Security Council, engaged more with Central and South American nations, cooperated with the Socialist International, and promoted multilateral agreements on maritime, energy, and environmental matters. Martinelli brought the government's focus back to domestic matters, bullied the US ambassador into an early departure, and then fired his first foreign minister, who likewise had shown limited enthusiasm for international matters.

Finally, Varela, although besieged by his predecessor's scandals, gave his foreign minister greater latitude to expand relations with the outside world, hosting the seventh summit of the Americas and establishing a strong presence in capitals like Washington and the Vatican. At first criticized for the perceived trend toward militarization of security operations in response to increasing border violence, international criminal activity, and migration challenges, Varela fell back on reliance on the United States. His personal connections, visits to the United States, and acceptance of responsibility after the Panama Papers revelations raised bilateral cooperation to a new level. The United States even agreed to clean up some sites contaminated by chemical weapons tests during World War II.[17]

With US relations on such a sound footing, Varela finally launched the restructuring of relations with China and Taiwan. China had already made major inroads in Panama, having displaced Japan as the second largest user of the Canal and in investment projects. The exchanges of high

[17] www.scmp.com/news/world/americas/article/2102750/us-destroy-chemical-weapons-world-war-two-it-left-behind-panama. On the other hand, despite the Varela government's outreach to President Trump, the latter expressed displeasure over his business reversal there, Vice President Pence cut short his 2018 visit, and there has been no movement on replacing Ambassador John Feeley, who announced his resignation at the end of 2017; Eliana Morales Gil y Olmedo Rodríguez, "Organización Trump presiona a Varela," *La Prensa*, Apr. 9, 2018.

level visits, opening of embassies and consulates between the countries in 2017–18, and the launching of free trade negotiations, along with outreach to India and the Middle East, raised Panama's profile of independent international activism to a new level.

Thus, Panama's international relations since 2000 seemed like a pendulum, alternating between active engagements and turning inward. Despite this on-again-off-again pattern, over the past twenty years Panama has developed a stronger presence in international organizations and growing expertise in using that presence to further the nation's interests. In the perennial matter of tax havens/money laundering, for example, the Pérez Balladares and Moscoso administrations reacted defensively without diminishing world opinion that Panama constituted a fiscal paradise. A professional bureaucracy in the foreign ministry, however, learned to parry the frequent accusations and to take more forthright actions in conjunction with the OECD, the UN, the World Bank, and the International Monetary Fund.[18] Through active engagement in these organizations and the media, the foreign ministry coordinated a positive response that impressed foreign observers. Annual ministerial *Informes* reinforced the impression of expert leadership in foreign affairs.[19]

During much of the post-2000 boom, Panama received large numbers of immigrants, mostly from neighboring countries but also from distant lands. Immigration rules, considered lax by international standards, generally encourage arrivals, short-term or permanent, with an array of triggers for residency.[20] The "Racial Melting Pot" initiative of the Martinelli administration codified these rules, which continued in force under Varela. Most of the immigrants, including tens of thousands from Venezuela and Colombia, came in search of jobs and business opportunities. Many US and European retirees settled in Panama, taking advantage of perquisites for property owners. Although some Panamanians complained of an attendant rise in crime and prices due to immigration, the Chamber of Commerce and Assembly favored the open door policy as good for business. A 2015 report by the business think tank APEDE estimated that the country would need 232,000 technical workers that it could not produce internally during the next five years.[21]

[18] See Comité de Expertos Independientes, *Informe final*, Nov. 2016.

[19] See, for example, www.mire.gob.pa/sites/default/files/documentos/memoria-2014–2015.pdf.

[20] See, for example, the UNHCR webpage, www.refworld.org/docid/55ffa6304.html.

[21] Yolanda Sandoval, "Panamá requiere de migración ordenada," *La Prensa*, July 25, 2018.

These developments signaled Panama's coming of age in the international community, after centuries of taking the back seat to Spain, Colombia, and the United States. The nation remains small in territory, population, and GDP but has found seats of increasing significance at the tables of multilateral bodies. Its leadership of the fifty-two-nation Tropical Forest Alliance made a crucial contribution to the achievement of the Paris Accords on Climate Change, just as its role in the International Maritime Organization was fundamental for the development of the new international shipping and port security (ISPS) code after the 9/11 terrorist attacks.[22] Like most countries, Panama wishes to project an image of stability, tolerance, productivity, and compassion. Panama will probably never be a financial dynamo, military power, or diplomatic broker, but its influence will likely continue to grow in coming years.

Panama's vigorous preparations to host the Pope's World Youth Day, January 22–27, 2019, reflect its growing role as a host of international forums. Planning for this culminating effort of the Varela administration held special significance for Catholics and the country's Opus Dei leader. Yet after Panama's repeated successes in hosting more than a score of major international conclaves since the 2003 Miss Universe Pageant, the Youth Day celebrations will also establish Panama as a venue for events of global significance.

VOUCHSAFING NATIONHOOD

Given their varied colonial histories, Panamanians have spent more effort than might be expected debating their national identity and place in the world. Chapter 1 devoted a section to Ana Elena Porras's studies of Panamanianism over the centuries. Today's generation of intellectuals, journalists, entrepreneurs, politicians, and historians, finally freed of US tutelage, has instead devoted attention to questions of nationhood. They emphasized its peacefulness (without an army), maritime vocation, democratic tradition, embrace of diverse peoples and cultures from around the world, and devotion to advancing the arts and sciences. And they enjoy parties, good times, and their world-famous Carnival, as the happiness index cited suggests.

[22] See the Ministry of the Environment Press Release, www.embassyofpanamainjapan.org/en/wp-content/uploads/2015/11/Press-Release-COP2125-nov.pdf; and Chapters 6 and 7 discussions of international maritime cooperation.

Previous sections discussed Panama's post-military society, economic trajectory, and openness to foreigners. In addition, Panamanians value music, literature, the environment, and the exuberance of their flora and fauna. Annual fairs celebrate jazz, books, automobiles, food, families, tourism, interior design, ecology, fashion, beauty, artisan products, health, agriculture, weddings, and much more. Many provincial capitals host their own fairs that feature local attractions. Now that working and middle-class families have cars and the Canal no longer restricts travel, Panamanians have become avid tourists in their own nation, exploring the beaches, new museums, the Amador Causeway, the Canal, ecological sites, and myriad other destinations. No wonder their gasoline consumption more than tripled in the past twenty-five years.

As for science, since the 1977 Treaty, Panama has embraced the Smithsonian Tropical Research Institute's many installations, sponsored multi-faceted investigations during excavation for the Canal expansion, promoted environmental awareness, supported the 2016 Paris climate change agreement, converted a former military base into the City of Knowledge to host universities and research institutions, created the Technological University of Panama, launched the International Maritime University of Panama and put in place the cabinet-level National Secretariat of Science and Technology (SENACYT) to advance education and excellence in these fields. The breadth of these commitments signaled leaders' desires for Panama to have a scientifically up-dodate citizenry. In short, Panamanians show pride in their nationality, which now definitively includes the Canal and its associated businesses, and willingness to protect and support it.

The economic outlook for Panama remains positive, but the increasing seriousness of some challenges demand concerted attention. The Canal expansion is on course to continue delivering a higher revenue stream and focus for growth on the Centerport unless trade wars or some other issues arise to halt the commercial recovery of recent years. New exports from the First Quantum mines and restoration of an economic base on the Atlantic side of Panama should further expand the country's productive base, but then the trends tend to raise as many concerns as confidence. With less on the horizon to spur foreign investment besides Chinese interests, Panama's international debt load could become troublesome. Pessimistic forecasts about the funding of social security pensions and rising health costs raise the potential for a crisis there, and the growth of the government's spending may even outstrip the growth of Canal revenue. Although some recent progress in bilingual education promises an improvement in the supply of the more sophisticated human resources the country needs, recent strikes, labor conflicts, and escalating business disputes augur for economic turmoil and slower growth than any time since the first years of the century.

The future of politics in Panama also seems a bit cloudier at this juncture, but no outcome would be more improbable than the deliberate pace of the Varela government after the frenetic Martinelli years. Major electoral reforms and a huge field of presidential hopefuls will certainly maintain a high level of attention, even with drastically reduced campaign periods and uncertainty leading up to the May 2019 elections. In the country's second formal round of presidential debates, the topics abound: unfinished and lackadaisical prosecution of corruption cases, haphazard judicial reform, long-delayed supreme court appointments, the decline of traditional parties, increasing civic activism, unbridled clientelism, legislative neglect in the national assembly, and the struggle over the role of the ACP. The sixth presidential election since the restoration of democracy may even determine whether the country will finally take on the constitutional reform issue postponed since the 1980s.[23]

* * * *

This conclusion has taken an optimistic tone, reflecting the authors' upbeat views, yet much remains in doubt about the future. Being a crossroads and hub opened the nation up to the vicissitudes of global affairs, which can be unpredictable and even destructive. It also required an outward-looking orientation that drew attention away from important domestic matters. World opinion impinged more forcefully on the hub and affected local life, often with little justification. The very fluidity of life in a crossroads led to surprises both beneficent and unpleasant. All this counseled observers to be guarded in predicting Panama's future. The swirl of accusations about corruption at high levels and in the ranks of politicians warranted caution in reaching conclusions.

We may be positive, however, in writing that Panama has undergone extraordinary changes during the past 38 years, as outlined in this conclusion, and we risk stating that coming years will be filled with new challenges for this remarkable nation. We urge readers who have gotten this far to stay tuned to events in coming decades. We certainly will!

[23] As this book went to press, authorities had still not decided whether to propose the election of a constitutional assembly on the May 2019 ballot.

Interviews by Authors

Panama: Nicolás Ardito Barletta, Eloy Alfaro, Mauricio Belanger, Eddie Tapiero, Oscar Vallarino, Roberto Tom Ford, Roberto Díaz Herrera, Manuel Benítez, Alfredo Castillero Calvo, Angie Ramos Baquero, Carlos A. Mendoza, Rubén Carles, Guilllermo Endara, Berta Thayer, Mireya Moscoso, Stanley Heckadon, Marco Gandãsegui Hijo, Alfredo Castillero Hoyos, Ana Elena Porras, Samuel Lewis Navarro, Fernando Berguido, Miguel Antonio Bernal, Fernando Manfredo, Juan Antonio Tack, Guillermo Cochez, Ebrahim Asvat, Guillermo Saint Malo, Omar Jaén Suárez, Isabel de Saint Malo, Rodolfo Sabonge, Miguel Verzbolovskis, Carlos Guevara Mann, Rosario Arias de Galindo, Octavio Fábrega, Diógenes de la Rosa, Carlos A. López Guevara, Onésimo Sánchez, Roberto Roy, Ricardo López Arias, Melva Lowe Goodin, Yolanda Marco Serra, Ángel Ricardo Martínez, Brett Patton, Dick Koster, Guillermo Márquez Amado, Adolfo Ahumada, Alberto Alemán Zubieta, Orlando Allard, Dagmar de Álvarez, Etty Arjona, Anselmo Alvarado, Alfredo Arias, Adán Arnulfo Arjona, Laurence D. Berger, Guillermo Castro, Guillermo Chapman, Aram Cisneros, Daniel Delgado Diamante, Manuel Domínguez, Marco A. Fernández, Mario Galindo, Ernesto González de la Lastra, Milton Henríquez, Enrique Illueca, Alejandrino Jiménez, Walter Lafitte, Ilya Marotta, Fenán Molinos, Eduardo Morgan, Juan David Morgan, Patricia Martín, Vicente Pascual, Demetrio Papadimitriu, Alexander Psychoyos, Robert Raymer, Jorge Ritter, Aristides Royo, Marcel Salamín, Jerry Salazar, Ana María San Felippo, Paul Smith, Rita Spadafora, Euclides Tapia Campos, Carlos Urriola, Eduardo Vallarino, Ricuarte Vásquez, Ángel Castro.

United States: Gary Adams, Wayne Bray, John Elac, Brittmarie Janson Pérez, Sherman Henson, Raymond Laverty, Richard Wainio, D. P. McAuliffe, Willie Friar, Michael Rhode Jr., Ronald Seeley, Jack Vaughn, Joseph Wood, James Ferrara, Orlando Perez, Joseph R. Reeder, Kenneth Kujawa, Kristen Stewart, Ambler Moss, Paul Smith, Clyde Stephens, Joseph Sullivan, Linda Watt, Margaret Scranton, Michael Donoghue, Carol Stokes, Frederick Becker, Eric Farnsworth, John Fishel, Daniel N. Fisk, William T. Furlong, Peter Hakim, Michael G. Kozak, John Maisto, Margaret Myers, Christopher McMullen, Riordan Roett, Michael Shifter.

Unpublished Documentary Sources

Becker, Frederick A., "Interview with Frederick A. Becker," Library of Congress Manuscripts Division, 2004.

Bushnell, John A., "Interview with John A. Bushnell," Library of Congress Manuscripts Division, 1997.

Comité de Expertos Independientes, *Informe final*, November 2016.

Davis, Arthur H., Jr., "Interview with Arthur H. Davis, Jr.," Library of Congress Manuscripts Division, 1991.

Janson Pérez, Brittmarie, "The Process of Political Protest in Panama, 1968–1989," PhD dissertation, University of Texas, 1993.

Martínez Benoit, Ángel Ricardo, "Demonizing Arabs and Latin Americans: A Comparison of Manuel Noriega and Saddam Hussein in the U.S. Press," MA thesis, Swansea University, 2011.

Moss, Ambler, "Interview with Ambler H. Moss Jr.," Library of Congress Manuscripts Division, 1988.

Nathan Associates Inc., "Programa de Dimensión del Impacto del Canal de Panamá Sobre la Economiía del Pais. Executive Summary," May 5, 2012.

Panama Canal Authority, "The Economic Impact of the Panama Canal on the Republic of Panama. Executive Summary," May 2006.

Robinson, William Francis, "The Arias Madrid Brothers: Nationalist Politics in Panama," PhD dissertation, Auburn University, 1999.

Scranton, Margaret E., "Knowing When to Fold a Bad Hand: Saying No to Bases in Panama," LASA Conference, March 2000.

"Possible Threats to Panama's Democratization in the Early 1990s," American Historical Association meeting, Washington, DC, January 4, 2014.

Stokes, Carol, "History of the Implementation of the Panama Canal Treaties," unpublished typescript in the National Archives, RG185, A1-173, rec. 292563, ca. 1984.

Sullivan, Joseph G., "Interview with Joseph G. Sullivan," Library of Congress Manuscript Division, 2011.

Van de Putten, Frans-Paul, and Minke Meijnders, "China, Europe and the Maritime Silk Road," Glingendael Netherlands Institute of International Relations, 2015.

Bibliography

Alemán Healy, Jaime. *La honestidad no tiene precio*. Panama: Carvajal Soluciones de Comunicaciones, 2014.

Alfaro, Ricardo J. *Medio siglo de relaciones entre Panamá y los Estados Unidos*. Panama: Imprenta Nacional de Panama, 1959.

Ardito Barletta, Nicolás. "The Political and Economic Transition of Panama, 1978–1991." In *Democratic Transitions in Central America*, edited by Jorge Dominguez and Marc Lindenberg, 32–66. Gainesville: University of Florida, Press, 1997.

Estrategia para el Desarrollo Nacional: Visión, realización, actualización. Panama: Editorial Excedra, 2012.

Huellas: Contribuciones públicas nacionales e internacionales, memorias. Bogota: Panamericana, 2016.

Arjona, Nadhji. *Una misión histórica: Gilberto Guardia Fábrega*. Panama: Ed. Libertad Ciudadana, 2003.

Asvat, Ebrahim. *Bitácora del presidente*. Panama: El Nuevo Siglo, 2010.

Bacevich, Andrew J. *The New American Militarism: How Americans Are Seduced by War*. New York: Oxford University Press, 2005.

Baker, James A., III, with Thomas M. Defrank. *The Politics of Diplomacy: Revolution, War, and Peace, 1989–1992*. New York: G. P. Putnam's Sons, 1995.

Barragán, Melanie, and Stefanie Ruh, "Elecciones Panamá 2014: conflictiva continuidad en el cambio," *Revista Panameña de Política*, no. 18, July–December (2014): 9–40. http://cidempanama.org/wp-content/uploads/2015/02/Elecciones-Panam%C3%A1-2014.pdf.

Barragán Manjón, Melany, "Elecciones Panamá 2014: Poder, corrupción y guerra sucia." In *Elecciones y cambio de élites en América Latina, 2014 y 2015*, edited by Manuel Alcántara Sáez and María Laura Tagina, 71–94. Salamanca: Ediciones Universidad de Salamanca, 2016. www.jstor.org/stable/j.ctt1gr7f66.

Berguido, Fernando. *Una vida póstuma*. Panama: Círculo Editorial y de Lectura, 2013.

Anatomía de una trampa. Mexico City: Grijalbo, 2017.

Bernal, Miguel Antonio. "Evolución constitucional desde la separación de Panamá." In *Historia general de Panamá*, edited by Alfredo Castillero Calvo, III:I, 42–44. Panama: Consejo Nacional del Centenario, 2004.

Biesanz, John, and Mavis Biesanz. *The People of Panama*. New York: Greenwood Press, 1955.

Brooks, Charles Morris. *Guarding the Crossroads: Security and Defense of the Panama Canal*. Panama: P & P Group, 2003.

Brown Araúz, Harry, and Clara Inés Luna Vasquez, "Panama: El Crecimiento Económico a Expensas de la Política," *Revista de Ciencia Política* (Chile), 33, no. 1 (2013): 287–301.

Brown, Jonathan C. *Cuba's Revolutionary World*. Cambridge, MA: Harvard University Press, 2017.

Buckley, Kevin. *Panama: The Whole Story*. New York: Simon & Schulster, 1991.

Camargo, Marcela. "La historia rural del siglo XX." In *Historia general de Panamá*, edited by Alfredo Castillero Calvo, III:I, 110–129. Panama: Consejo Nacional del Centenario, 2004.

Caro, Robert A. *The Power Broker: Robert Moses and the Fall of New York*. New York: Knopf, 1974.

Castillero Calvo, Alfredo. "Transitismo y dependencia: el caso del istmo de Panamá." *Lotería*, no. 210, July 1973.

ed. *Historia general de Panamá*, 5 vols. Panama: Consejo Nacional del Centenario, 2004.

Los metales preciosos y la primera globalización. Panama: Editora Novo Arte, 2008.

El descubrimiento del Pacífico y los orígenes de la globalización. Panama: Comisión Nacional para la Conmemoración del Quinto Centenario del Descubrimiento del Océano Pacífico, 2013.

ed. *Panamá: historia contemporánea*. Madrid: Fundación MAPFRE, 2014.

Caumartin, Corinne. "'Depoliticization' in the Reform of the Panamanian Security Apparatus." *Journal of Latin American Studies* 39, no. 1 (2007): 107–132.

Cochez F., Guillermo A. *Las montañas sí se mueven*. Panama: Freedom Publications, 2008.

Imprudencias de un diplomático inconveniente. Panama: By author, 2017.

Conniff, Michael L. *Black Labor on a White Canal: Panama 1904–1981*. Pittsburgh: University of Pittsburgh Press, 1985.

"Panama Since 1903." In *The Cambridge History of Latin America*, edited by Leslie Bethell, 7, 603–642. Cambridge: Cambridge University Press, 1990.

Panama and the United States: The End of the Alliance, 3rd ed. Athens: University of Georgia Press, 2012.

ed. *Populism in Latin America*. Tuscaloosa: University of Alabama Press, 2012.

"Promoting Global Trade: The Panama-Pacific Exposition." In *Panamá cosmopolita: la Exposición de 1916 y su legado*, edited by Adrienne Samos, 18–77. Panama: Biblioteca 500/Municipio de Panamá, 2017.

"Turning Point: Anglo-American Assessments of Panama in 1929–1932." In *Historia y globalización: Ensayos en homenaje a Alfredo Castillero Calvo*, edited by Ángeles Ramos Baquero, 199–212. Panama: Editora Novo Arte, 2017.
Cruz, Barbara C. *Rubén Blades: Salsa Singer and Social Activist*. Springfield, NJ: Enslow Publishers, 1997.
de la Guardia de Corró, María Mercedes. *Hasta la última gota: Gabriel Lewis Galindo*. Cali, Colombia: Cargraphics S.A., 2009.
Delgado, Daniel. *A 25 años de la invasión de Estados Unidos a Panamá: La resistencia armada y sus consequencias*. Panama: University of Panama, 2014.
Díaz Herrera, Roberto. *Estrellas Clandestinas*. Panama: Kinko's Impresores S.A.C., 2009.
La Explosión de Panamá. Panama: Impresos Modernos S.A., 2011.
Omar: De Cuerpo Entero (Anecdotarío biográfico). Panama: Editora Sibauste, S.A., 2013.
Dinges, John. *Our Man in Panama*. New York: Random House, 1990, 1991.
Donoghue, Michael E. *Borderland on the Isthmus: Race, Culture, and the Struggle for the Canal Zone*. Durham, NC: Duke University Press, 2014.
Downes, Richard. "Panama's Historic Transition Brings High Hopes, Uncertainties." *North-South Center Focus* 6, no. 1 (1997).
Elton, Charlotte. "Environmental Aspects of Canal Transition." In *Post-Invasion Panama: The Challenges of Democratization in the New World Order*, edited by Orlando J. Pérez, 57–68. Lanham, MD: Lexington Books, 2000.
Falcoff, Mark. *Panama's Canal: What Happens When the United States Gives a Small Country What It Wants*. Washington, DC: AEI Press, 1998.
Fishel, John T. *The Fog of Peace: Planning and Executing the Restoration of Panama*. Carlisle Barracks, PA: Strategic Studies Institute, 1992.
"The Interagency in Panama, 1986–1990." In *The U.S. Army and the Interagency Process: Historical Perspectives*, edited by Kendall D. Gott and Michael G. Brooks, 65–76. Fort Leavenworth, KS: Combat Studies Institutes Press, 2008.
Ford Boyd, Guillermo. *Valió La Pena*. Panama: Imprenta Universal Books, 2004.
Franck, Harry A. *Zone Policeman 88*, 2nd ed. New York: Arno, 1970.
Furlong, William L. "The Difficult Transition towards Democracy." *Journal of Interamerican Studies and World Affairs* 35, no. 3 (1993): 19–64.
Gandásegui, hijo, Marco A., compiler. *Las clases sociales en Panamá: Grupos humanos, clases medias, élites y oligarquía*, 3rd ed. Panama: CELA, 2008.
"Panamá 2009: Elecciones, crisis mundial y movimientos sociales," *Revista de Ciéncia Política* (Chile) 30, no. 2 (2010): 419–427.
"Población y sociedad en el siglo xx" In *Panamá: historia contemporánea*, edited by Alfredo Castillero Calvo, 505–62. Madrid: Fundación MAPFRE, 2014.
et al. *Antología del pensamiento crítico panameño contemporáneo*. Buenos Aires: Consejo Latinoamericano de Ciencias Sociales, 2018.

Grandin, Greg. "The War to Start All Wars." *Truth-Out*. December 22, 2014. www.truth-out.org/opinion/item/28138-the-war-to-start-all-wars-the-25th anniversary-of-the-forgotten-invasion-of-panama.
Greene, Graham. *Getting to Know the General: The Story of an Involvement*. New York: Simon and Schuster, 1984.
Guardia Fábrega, Gilberto. *El Canal de Panamá: transición y perspectiva, 1990–1996: presentaciones y conferencias*. Panama: Editorial Libertad Ciudadana, 2003.
Guevara Mann, Carlos. *Panamanian Militarism: A Historical Interpretation*. Athens: Ohio University Center for International Studies, 1996.
Political Careers, Corruption, and Impunity: Panama's Assembly, 1984–2009. Notre Dame, IN: University of Notre Dame Press, 2011.
"La Vida Política en el siglo XX." In *Panamá: historia contemporánea*, edited by Alfredo Castillero Calvo, 163–248. Madrid: Fundación MAPFRE, 2014.
"Luces y sombras en torno a la institucionalidad democrática." *Revista de Ciencia Política* (Chile) 36, no. 1 (2016): 259–285.
Gurdián Guerra, Raymundo. "Los Tratados del Canal y su Transferencia, 1967–1999." In *Historia general de Panamá*, edited by Alfredo Castillero Calvo, III:II, 271–72. Panama: Consejo Nacional del Centenario, 2004.
Harding II, Robert C. *Military Foundations of Panamanian Politics*. New Brunswick, NJ: Transactions Publishers, 2001.
The History of Panama. Westport, CN: Greenwood Press, 2006.
Heckadon-Moreno, Stanley, Roberto Ibáñez D., and Richard Condit, eds. *La cuenca del Canal: Deforestación, urbanización y contaminación*. Panama: Smithsonian Tropical Research Institute, 1999.
Hinton, Deane Roesch. *Economics and Diplomacy: A Life in the Foreign Service of the United States*. Washington: New Academia/ Vellum, 2015.
Jaén Suárez, Omar. *Las negociaciones sobre el Canal de Panamá, 1964–1970*. Bogota: Editorial Norma, 2002.
Las negociaciones de los Tratados Torrijos-Carter, 1970–1979, 2 vols. Panama: Autoridad del Canal de Panamá, 2005.
Diez años de administración panameña del Canal de Panamá, 2000–2010. Panama: Autoridad del Canal de Panamá, 2011.
La población del Istmo de Panamá, 4th ed. Panama: Editorial Universitaria, 2013.
Hacia una historia global: 500 años de la cuenca del Pacífico. Panama: ACP/ Ediciones Balboa, 2014.
Kempe, Frederick. *Divorcing the Dictator: America's Bungled Affair with Noriega*. New York: G.P. Putnam's Sons, 1990.
Kissinger, Henry, ed. *Report of the President's National Bipartisan Commission on Central America*. New York: Macmillan, 1984.
Knapp, Herbert, and Mary Knapp. *Red, White, and Blue Paradise: The American Canal Zone in Panama*. San Diego: Harcourt, Brace, Jovanovich, 1984.
Koster, Richard M., and Guillermo Sánchez Borbón. *In the Time of the Tyrants. Panama: 1968–1990*. New York: W. W. Norton & Co., 1990.
Leonard, Thomas M. *Historical Dictionary of Panama*. New York: Rowman and Littlefield, 2015.

Lindsay-Poland, John. *Emperors in the Jungle: The Hidden History of the U.S. in Panama*. Durham: Duke University Press, 2003.

Lowe de Goodin, Melba. *People of African Ancestry in Panama, 1501–2012*. Panama: Imprenta Sibauste, 2014.

Major, John. "The Panama Canal Zone, 1904–1979." *Cambridge History of Latin America*, edited by Leslie Bethell, 7, 643–70. Cambridge, UK: Cambridge University Press, 1990.

Prize Possession: The United States and the Panama Canal, 1903–1979. Cambridge: Cambridge University Press, 1990.

Manfredo, Fernando. *La transición del Canal a Panamá 1979–1990: Memorias*. Mexico: By author, 2014.

Marco, Yolanda, and Ángela Alvarado. *Mujeres que cambiaron nuestra historia*. Panama: UNICEF/Universidad de Panamá/Fondo Canadá-Panamá, 1997.

Martínez García, Fernando. "El Poder de los Medios." In *¿Por qué nos odian tanto? Estado y medios de comunicación en América Latina*, edited by Omar Rincón, 123–48. Bogota: Centro de Competencia en Comunicación para América Latina, 2010.

Maurer, Noel, and Carlos Yu. *The Big Ditch: How America Took, Built, Ran, and Ultimately Gave Away the Panama Canal*. Princeton: Princeton University Press, 2011.

McCann, Thomas. *An American Company: The Tragedy of United Fruit*. New York: Crown Publishers, 1976.

McGuinness, Aims. *Path of Empire: Panama and the California Gold Rush*. Ithaca: Cornell University Press, 2008.

McKay, Alberto. "El Canal, los puertos, movimientos e industrias marítimas." In *Historia general de Panamá*, edited by Alfredo Castillero Calvo, III:II, 93–114. Panama: Consejo Nacional del Centenario, 2004.

McPherson, Alan. "Courts of World Opinion: Trying the Panama Flag Riots of 1964." *Diplomatic History* 28, no. 1 (2004): 83–112.

Meditz, Sandra W., and Dennis Michael Hanratty, eds. *Panama: A Country Study*. Washington, DC: Federal Research Division, Library of Congress, 1989.

Metz, Allan. "Manuel Noriega and the 'Panama Crisis': An Annotated Bibliography." *Reference Services Review* (Fall 1991): 7–44.

Millett, Richard L. "The Failure of Panama's Internal Opposition, 1987–1989." In *Conflict Resolution and Democratization in Panama: Implications for U.S. Policy*, edited by Eva Loser, 21–38. Washington, DC: Center for Strategic and International Studies, 1992.

"Panama's Paradoxical Progress." *North-South: The Magazine of the Americas* 4, no. 1 (1994): 21–25.

Moreno Lobón, Juan. "El proceso económico en el siglo XX." In *Panamá: historia contemporánea*, edited by Alfredo Castillero Calvo, 379–455. Madrid: Fundación MAPFRE, 2014.

Morgan Jr., Eduardo. *Memoria de una embajada*. Panama: Editora Sibauste, 1998.

Morgan, Juan David. *The Golden Horse*. Minneapolis: Two Harbors Press, 2014.

Oppenheimer, Andrés. "Panama's Troubled Resuscitation as a Nation-State." In *Conflict Resolution and Democratization in Panama: Implications for U.S. Policy*, edited by Eva Loser, 39–54. Washington, DC: Center for Strategic and International Studies, 1992.

Panama. Ministerio de Relaciones Exteriores. *VII[a] Cumbre de las Américas*. Panama: Ministerio de Relaciones Exteriores, 2015.

Pearcy, Thomas L. *We Answer Only to God: Politics and the Military in Panama, 1903–1947*. Albuquerque: University of New Mexico Press, 1998.

Pedreschi, Carlos Bolívar. *De la protección del Canal a la militarización del pais*. San José, Costa Rica: Litografía LIL, 1987.

Suelas de mis zapatos: Autobiografía. Panamá: By author, 2015.

Pérez, Orlando J., ed. *Post-Invasion Panama: The Challenges of Democratization in the New World Order*. Lanham, MD: Lexington Books, 2000.

Political Culture in Panama: Democracy after Invasion. New York: Palgrave Macmillan, 2011.

Cultura política de la democracia en Panamá: Evidencia desde el Barómetro de las Américas. Nashville: Vanderbilt Centro para Iniciativas Democráticas, 2013.

Pérez, Orlando A., Marco A. Gandásegui, and Mitchell Seligson. "La cultura política de la democracia en Panamá, 2004." Vanderbilt University, Proyecto de Opinión Pública en América Latina, Sept. 2004.

"The Political Culture of Democracy in Panama: Public Perceptions about the Political System," Latin American Public Opinion Project, March 2004. www.vanderbilt.edu/lapop/panama/2004-politicalculture.pdf.

Phillipps Collazos, Sharon. *Labor and Politics in Panama: The Torrijos Years*. Boulder, CO: Westview, 1991.

Piazza, Ada, and Nicolás Flaño Calderón. *Diálogo social en América Latina*. Washington, DC: Inter-American Development Bank, 2006.

Pippin, Larry LaRae. *The Remón Era: An Analysis of a Decade of Events in Panama, 1947–1957*. Stanford: Institute of Hispanic American and Luso-Brazilian Studies, 1964.

Pizzurno Gelos, Patricia, and Celestino Andrés Araúz. *Estudios sobre el Panamá republicano: 1903–1989*. Panama: Manfer, 1996.

Porras, Ana Elena, ed. *Historias Canaleras: Doce testimonios de la transición*. Panama: Instituto de Estudios Nacionales, Universidad de Panamá, 2007.

Cultura de la interoceanidad, 2nd ed. Panama: Universidad de Panamá, 2009.

"Imaginarios académicos del populismo en Panamá." *Cátedra* 14 (2017): 66–91.

Proceedings of the Universal Congress of the Interoceanic Canal, edited by Melva A. Raven and Gloria Manfredo. Brussels: European Commission, 1998.

Quijano, Jorge. "Intrigas en el Canal durante la transición," in *Historias Canaleras: Doce testimonios de la transición*, edited by Ana Elena Porras, 64–79. Panamá: Instituto de Estudios Nacionales, Universidad de Panamá, 2007.

Robinson, William Francis. "Panama for the Panamanians: The Populism of Arnulfo Arias Madrid." In *Populism in Latin America*, edited by Michael L. Conniff, 184–200. Tuscaloosa: University of Alabama Press, 2012.

Ropp, Steve C. *Panamanian Politics: from Guarded Nation to National Guard*. New York: Praeger/Stanford: Hoover Institution, 1982.

"Things Fall Apart: Panama after Noriega." *Current History* 92, no. 572 (1999): 102–105.

Salamín Cárdenas, Marcel. *Pancho Arias y su Época: Ensayo crítico para una biografía patria*. Caracas: Epsilon Libros, 2005.

Sánchez González, Salvador. "La transición a la democracia en Panamá." In *Historia general de Panamá*, edited by Alfredo Castillero Calvo, III:II, 283–301. Panama: Consejo Nacional del Centenario, 2004.

Scoullar, William T., compiler and ed. *El Libro Azul de Panamá/The Blue Book of Panama*. Panamá: Imprenta Nacional, 1916–17.

Scranton, Margaret E. *The Noriega Years: U.S.-Panamanian Relations, 1981–1990*. Boulder, CO: Lynne Rienner, 1991.

"Panama's Democratic Transition." *The Midsouth Political Science Journal* 13 (Spring 1992): 107–128.

"Panama's First Post-Transition Election." *Journal of Interamerican Studies & World Affairs* 37 (Spring 1995): 69–99.

"Electoral Reform and the Institutionalization of the Electoral Tribunal in Post-Invasion Panama." In *Post-Invasion Panama: The Challenges of Democratization in the New World Order*, edited by Orlando J. Pérez, 101–124. Lanham, MD: Lexington Books, 2000.

Shultz, Richard H. *In the Aftermath of War: U.S. Support for Reconstruction and Nation-Building in Panama Following JUST CAUSE*. Maxwell Air Force Base, AL: Air University Press, 1993.

Szok, Peter A. *La Última Gaviota: Liberalism and Nostalgia in Early Twentieth-Century Panamá*. Westport, CN: Greenwood, 2001.

"Rey sin corona: Belisario Porras y la formación del estado nacional, 1903–1931." In *Historia general de Panamá*, edited by Alfredo Castillero Calvo, III:I, ch. 4. Panama: Consejo Nacional del Centenario, 2004.

"Swaggering through Hell: The Rise and Decline of Panama's Red Devil Buses." *Folk Art Messenger* 22, no. 1 (2010).

Wolf Tracks: Popular Art and Re-Africanization in Twentieth-Century Panama. Jackson: University of Mississippi Press, 2012.

V-Dem Institute. "Democracy for All? V-Dem Annual Report." Gothenburg: University of Gothenburg, 2018. www.v-dem.net/media/filer_public/3f/19/3f19efc9-e25f-4356-b159-b5c0ec894115/v-dem_democracy_report_2018.pdf.

Valle, Amir. *Hugo Spadafora, bajo la piel del hombre*. Panama: Aguilar, Prisa Ediciones, 2013.

Weeks, John, and Phil Gunson. *Panama: Made in the USA*. London: Latin American Bureau, 1991.

Yates, Lawrence A. *The U.S. Military Intervention in Panama: Operation Just Cause*, 2 vols. Washington, DC: US Army Center for Military History, 2008, 2014.

Zimbalist, Andrew S. and John Weeks. *Panama at the Crossroads: Economic Development and Political Change in the Twentieth Century*. Berkeley & Los Angeles: University of California Press, 1991.

Zucman, Gabriel. *The Hidden Wealth of Nations: The Scourge of Tax Havens*. Chicago and London: University of Chicago Press, 2015.

Index

Note: italic refers to figures, bold to maps

Abrams, Elliot, 47
Ábrego, Yanibel, 306
Acción Comunal, 5
Afú, Carlos, 165
Ahumada, Adolfo, 115
Albright, Madeline, 134
Albrook, 105
Alemán Healy, Álvaro, 276, 303
Alemán Healy, Jaime, 237, 252, 290
Alemán Zubieta, Alberto, 116, 117, 121, 130, 203, 220, 318
Alemán, Alfredo, 105
Alemán, Héctor, 174
Alemán, José Miguel, 167, 168, 172
Alfaro, Ricardo, 6
Allard, Orlando, 65
Alleyne, Camilo, 174
Alliance of Bolivarian Nations, 180–183, 186, 243–44
Almengor, José Abel, 240
Alvarado, Carlos, 65
Amador Causeway, 107, 109, 151, 158
Anayansi, 22
Ardito Barletta, Nicolás, 15, 16, 35, 37, 39, 41, 42, 56, 102, 107, 156, 157, 242
  Estrategia para el desarrollo nacional, 41, 107
Arias Calderón, Ricardo, 50–51, 71–77, 119, 135
Arias, Agustín, 240
Arias, Alfredo, 138
Arias, Arnulfo, 5, 7, 12, 13, 14, 31, 33, 43
Arias, Harmodio, 5, 6, 33
Arias, José Domingo, 237, 242, 264–266, 274
Arias, Oscar, 243
Arjona, Adán Arnulfo, 164, 166
Arnulfista. *See* Panameñista Party
Arosemena de Alemán, Pilar, 109
Arosemena de Troitiño, Esmeralda, 175
Arosemena, Jorge, 110
Arosemena, Rubén, 173, 189, 293
Arrocha, Meliton, 144
Assembly of Representatives of Municipalities, 15, 35
Asvat, Ebrahim, 34, 76, 174, 266
Asylum cases, 144–46
Autoridad de la Región Interoceánica, 107 *see* Interoceanic Regional Authority
Autoridad del Canal de Panamá (ACP). *See* Panama Canal Authority (ACP), 1997
Autoridad Marítima de Panamá. *See* Panama Maritime Authority
Autoridad Portuaria Nacional. *See* Panama Maritime Authority
Ayu Pardo, José, 246

Balboa, 22, 257
Banana War, 18, 152
Barés, Carlos, 150
Batista, Fulgencio, 11
Bauman, Robert, 54

Bazán, Dominador, 109, 139, 167
Bechtel Corporation, 103, 226
Becker, Frederick, 147
Belanger, Maurice, 257
Belis, Anel, 65
Benaim, Abner, 54
Benítez, Manuel, 65
Berguido, Fernando, 284
Berlusconi, Silvio, 233, 262, 271
Bernal, Juan Bosco, 174
Bernal, Miguel Antonio, 49, 114
Blades, Rubén, 134, 173
Blandón, José Isabel, 309
Bolívar's Letter from Jamaica, 24, 156
Bolton, John R., 150
Boyd, Aquilino, 19
Burillo de Calcagno, Giselle, 237, 253, 255–56
Bush, George H. W., 29, 40, 52, 77, 80, 82
Bush, George W., *172*, 184
Bushnell, John, 72–75, 79

Caldera, Louis, 121, 133
Calderón, Felipe, 184
Cambio Democrático, 130, 141, 194–95, 245–48, 252–55, 264–67, 270–75, 306–09
Canada, 242
canaleros, 115, 116, 117, 121
Caribbean Common Market, 181
Carles, Rubén, 87
Carter, Jimmy, 1, 2, 20, *135*
Castillo de León, Moisés, 141
Castillo de Varela, Lorena, 279
Castillo, Magaly, 267
Castro, Fidel, 146, 171
Castro, Guillermo, 110
Castro, Raúl, 280
Catholic Church, 250, 275
CEMIS, 151, 165
Census 1911, 4
Centennial Bridge, 153, *163*, 177, 318
Centerport, 44, 68, 286
Chamber of Commerce, 35
Changuinola Massacre, 250
Chapman, Guillermo, 102, 107
Chávez, Hugo, 146, 171, 183, 185
Chiari, Roberto F., 12, 34
China, 187, 216, 293, 323
Chiquilani, Ana María de, 206
Chiquita Banana. *See* United Fruit
Christian Democratic Party, 50, 74, 76, 81, 83, 119, 125, 142, 173, 275
Cigarruista, Alberto, 165, 168
City of Health, 285
City of Knowledge, 110, 113, 138, 154, 183, 257, 314, 326
Climate Change, 216, 325
Clinton, Bill, 30, 134
Cochez, Guillermo, 243
Cold Storage System, 239, 285
Colombian refugees, 139
Colon, 258
  Development, 294–97
Colon Free Zone, 8, 18, 235, 251
Constitution
  1904, 4
  1941, 7
  1972, 18, 35
  2004 amendments, 171
Contadora Island, 36, 93
Container Logistics, 16, 68, 103, 158, 216
Contraloria, 44, 87, 127, 239, 269, 307
COPA Airlines, 281, 290, 291
Cornelison, Joe, 115, 122
Corozal Port, 108, 114, 229, 286–89, 293, 306, 316–18
Corruption. *See* specific presidents
Costa Rica, 243
Crossroads, *319*
Cuban refugees, 100

Dawson, John, 96
de la Espriella, Ricardo, 35, 43
de la Guardia, Dulcidio, 301
de la Guardia, Ricardo Adolfo, 7
de la Madrid, Miguel, 46
Decentralization, 303
Delgado, Daniel, 58, 187, 192
Delgado, Norberto, 162
Delvalle, Eric Arturo, 37, 47
Department of Defense. *See* Pentagon
Department of Defense Dependent Schools System, 62
Diablos Rojos, 152, *240*, 256
Díaz Herrera, Roberto, 38, 45, 47, 49
Díaz, Juan Héctor, 214
Dignity Battalions, 51
Duboy, Carlos, 292
Duque, Carlos, 34, 50

Eaton, Bill, 185
Economic Plan
1970s, 16–17, 45–46
1994, 101
2000s, 151, 157
2010–14, 242
Economy, 8
1980s, 37, 68–70
1990s, 85
2000s, 144
2002–2004, 154
2004–09, 176
2009–13, 256
2014–19, 320
2019–, 326
Ecotourism, 109, 214, 243
Eisenhower, Dwight D., 9
Eisenmann, Roberto, 33, 109, 135, 159, 275
Eisenmann, Rodrigo, 109
El Niño, 160, 228, 278
Election
1932, 5
1940, 7
1968, 13
1984, 41
1989, 50–51
1991, 81
1992 Referendum, 83, 86
1994, 87, *88*
1998 Referendum, 106
1999, 125
2004, 166
2006 Referendum, 220
2009, 194, 233
2014, 255, 264, 273
2019, 305, 327
Electoral Tribunal, 30, 51, 81, 85, 247, 265, 267
1993 Reforms, 87
Ethical Code, 87
Rules for 2019, 308
Eleta, Fernando, 110
Endara, Guillermo, 29, 72, 74, 78, 80, 96, 168, 172, 178, 195
Environmental Protection, 61, 122, 213
Escalona, Arnulfo, 164
Espino de Marotta, Ilya, 225
Executive Directorate for Canal Matters (DIPAT), 57
Falcoff, Mark, xiii
Ferrara, James, 91
Ferrer, Alejandro, 173
Ferro, Simon, 124, 133, 134
Ferrufino, Guillermo, 237
Fiber Optic Cable, 114, 159
Fidanque III, Joseph, 292
Figali Convention Center, 151, 165, 235, 284
Fishel, John, 77
Flag Riots, *11*, 12
Day of the Martyrs, 149
Flores Aguilar, Florencio, 36
Florida State University, 113, 138
Fong, Elizabeth, 162
Ford, Gerald, 20
Ford, Guillermo, 50–51, 71–75, 90, 195
Francis, Pope, 131, 280
Free Trade of the Americas Agreement, 155
FRENADESSO, 194, 249
Fujimori, Alberto, 144

Galindo, Mario, 142
Gallego, Héctor, 146
Gandásegui, Marcos, hijo, 268
Garrido Pérez, José Ángel, 267
GATT. *See* World Trade Organization
Gaviria, César, 145
Gehry, Frank, 109
Gianelli, William, 56, 64
Gold and Silver Rolls, 26
Gómez, Ana Matilde, 178, 241, 246
González, Pedro Miguel, 101, 188, 306
Grandin, Greg, 53
Great Depression, 5
Great Recession, 196, 209, 241, 243
Greenpeace, 139
Guardia, Gilberto, 90–96, 114–16
Guevara Mann, Carlos, 38, 44, 301, 315
Gutiérrez, Carlos, 188
Gutiérrez, Lucio, 183

Haitian refugees, 100
Halman, Irving, 284
Helms, Jesse, 21, 90
Henríquez, Milton, 275
Henríquez, Roberto, 237
Herrera Hassán, Eduardo, 76
Herrera, Balbina, 165, 174, 190, 195
Hinton, Deane, 76

Honduras, 243
Hull, Cordell, 6
Humbert, Federico, 307

Ibero-American Summit, 146
Illueca, Jorge, 37, 43
Immigration, 324
Indigenous communities, 23, 149, 250, 304
Insulza, José Miguel, 181
Inter-American Development Bank, 102, 160
International Banking Center, 8, 16, 69, 282, 297
International Comparisons, 259–60, 262, 292
International Maritime Organization, 65, 149, 191
Internet, 284
Interoceanic Regional Authority, 83, 93, 107–14, 119, 138, 141, 154
Iran-Contra, 40

Japan, 68, 139, 157, 222
Jiménez, Roberto, 182
Johnson, Lyndon B., 12
Jordan, Hamilton, 42
Jované, Juan, 265
Juliao, Víctor, 143
Just Cause. *See* United States: Christmas Invasion
Justice Reform, 192

Kissinger Commission, 40
Kissinger, Henry, 20

La Prensa, 49, 50, 119
Laboa, José Sebastián, 71
Labor Code 1972, 15
Lakas, Demetrio, 15, 18, 19
Langman, María Luisa, 92
Laverty, Ray, 90
Legislative Assembly, 38, 43
Lewis Galindo, Gabriel, 57, 110
Lewis Galindo, Samuel, 87
Lewis Navarro, Samuel, 173, 174, 188
Liberal Party, 142, 225
Linares de Martinelli, Marta, 234, 264, 270, 275
Lindenberg, Marc, 44
Logistics Hub, 292–94
López Portillo, José, 36
López, Genaro, 265

Manfredo, Fernando, 15, 18, 29, 39, 55, 58, 60, 67, 71, 90, 120, 222
Maritime Tribunal, 165
Márquez Amado, Guillermo, 87
Martinelli, Ricardo, 33, 130, 194, 196, 233, 234, 277
  Assessment, 269
  Bus System, 239
  Cabinet, 236, 253, 255
  Corruption, 246, 260, 274
  Extradition, 307
  Infrastructure, 235
  Judicial System Missteps, 246
  Privatization, 251, 270
  Security Crackdown, 245
Martínez, Boris, 14
McAuliffe, Dennis, 55, 56
McTagger, Tilsia, 65
Medicine, Tainted, 187
Méndez, Roxana, 244
Mercier, George, 65
Metro, 130, 197, 217, 235, 240, 266, 283, 318
Molinar, Lucy, 237
MOLIRENA, 50, 125, 141, 196
Moncada Luna, Alejandro, 240, 247
Mondale, Walter, 36
Montesinos, Vladimiro, 144, 145
MORENA, 141
Morgan, Juan David, 110
Moscoso, Mireya, 30, 81, 87, 125, 134, *135*, 140, 146
  Cabinet, 141, 143, 151
  Corruption, 162, 168
  Nepotism, 141
  Pardons, 171
Moses, Robert, 126
Moss, Ambler, 2, 58, 92
Motta, Stanley, 107, 109, 275
Mulino, José Raúl, 237, 244
Murphy Law. *See* Panama Canal Act
Murphy, John, 54
Muschett, Stanley, 84
Museo del Canal Interoceánico, xvi, 215
Museum of Biodiversity, 109, 152

National Assembly, 9, 13, 43–46, 81, 118–19, 131, 141, 148, 152, 168–69, 171–74, 178–79, 192, 238–39, 254, 267–68, 303–06, 316
National Civic Crusade, 49

National Debt, 262
National Guard, 13, 36, 38, 57
Created 1953, 13
National Maritime Service, 138
National Opposition Front, 36
National Security Council, 148
National Truth Commission, 146, 161, 169
Navarro, Juan Carlos, 155, 176, 196, 264, 266, 270, 274, 309
News media, 33–34, 264
Nixon, Richard, 14, 19
Noli, Luis, 65
Noriega, Manuel Antonio, 14, 37, 38, 47, 50, 51–53, 60, 80, 188

O'Neill, William A., 204
Obama, Barack, 234, 276, 280
Operation Miracle, 182
Orfila, Alejandro, 2
Organization for Economic Cooperation and Development, 140, 153, 155, 242, 300
Organization of American States, 15, 19, 53, 145, 181–84, 243

Padilla Véliz, Jaime, 34
Page, Robert, 64
Panama, xv
Democracy in, xiv, 32, 198, 315
Foreign Relations, 322
Happiness index, xiv
Independence, xvii, 3
Militarism, 13
National Identity, xvi, 21–25
Transitismo, 156
Revenue from Canal, 66, 95, 231
Panama Canal, xiii, 205, 224
Canal Zone, 7, 10
Capacity Project, 217
Corporate Social Responsibility, 214
Expansion, 186, 200, 219, 317
Improvements, 67, 92, 210
Interoceanic Canal Commission, 4
Neo-Panamax, 201, 208, 229, 287, 317
Organic Law (1997), 93, 118, 204, 214
Overhaul 1950s, 13
Panama Canal Commission (PCC), 29, 39, 55, 57–64, 114–20, 168–71, 209
Blue Ribbon Commission, 116
Board of Directors, 55–56, 58
Milestone Plan, 116, 122
Panama Canal Employment System, 64
Personnel, 62–65
Referendum, 222
Reversion, 59, 83–84
Segmented Tolls, 207
Tolls, 117, 120, 202, 207–9, 222
Transfer, xvi, 121, 129, 133, 137, 202
Universal Congress of the Interoceanic Canal, 120
Universal Measurement System, 120
Zonians, 25–28, 52, 95, 115, 212
Panama Canal Act, 21, 54
Panama Canal Authority (ACP), 1978, 57
Panama Canal Authority (ACP), 1997, 115–19, 129–30, 143, 287–89, 293, 317–18
International Advisory Board, 122, 204
Panama Canal Museum. *See* Museo del Canal Interoceánico
Panama Defense Forces, 39–40, 47, 52, 74–76, 79–82, 105
Panama International Convention Center, 284
Panama International Maritime University. *See* Universidad Marítima Internacional de Panamá
Panama Maritime Authority, 111, 119, 157, 191, 290, 318
Ship Registry, 8, 119, 190
Panama Maritime Conferences, 191
Panama Papers, 131, 298, 301, 314, 323
Panama Ports, 103, 287
Panama Railroad, 23, 59, 129, 153
Panamanian Public Force, 76, 82, 105, 193, 244, 315
Panamá-Pacífico, 113, 138, 159
Panameñista Party, 13, 30, 141, 195, 247, 253–54, 264–66, 274, 306
Papá Egoró, 87
Papadimitriu, Demetrio, 195, 236, 237, 239, 249, 254
Paredes, Rubén Darío, 37
Parque Camino de Cruces, 61
Parque Metropolitano, 44, 61
Parque Soberanía, 61
Partido Revolucionario Democrático, 30, 33, 39–43, 87–88, 99, 101, 105, 125, 129, 137, 141, 153, 165–66, 170–71, 179–80, 184, 188, 195–98, 252–54, 264–68, 274–75, 306, 309
Frente Empresarial del PRD, 35

PCC Annual Report, 91
Pentagon, 9, 20, 60, 77, 84, 92, 111, 123, 138, 147, 317
Pereira Burgos, César, 175
Pérez Balladares, Ernesto, 30, 41, 87, *100*, 119, 123, 124, 136, 137, 196, 309
  Infrastructure, 104
  Pardons, 101
  Privatization, 103
Pérez, Orlando, 193, 263
Popular Party, 266, 270, 275
Porras, Ana Elena, 22, 156, 309, 325
  Cultura de la interoceanidad, 22
  Los canaleros, 64
Porras, Belisario, 5
Port Authority, 57, 59
Posada Carriles, Luis, 146
Powell, Colin, 167, 170
Public Defender, 126
Public Opinion, 167, 268, 316

Quijano, Jorge, 65, 115, 130, 223, 251, 318

Reagan, Ronald, 20
Real, Ubaldino, 174
Reeder, Joe R., 114–22, 204, 317
Regional Plans, 112
Remón, José Antonio, 9
Rhode, Jr., Michael, 55
Rice, Condoleezza, 186
Ritter, Jorge, 119
Rivera, Reynaldo, 174
Robles, Marco Aurelio, 12
Robles, Winston, 33
Rodríguez, Francisco, 51
Rodríguez, Rolando, 301
Rognoni, Mario, 235
Roosevelt, Franklin D., 5, 6
Roosevelt, Theodore, 227, 229
Roux, Rómulo, 237, 309
Roy, Roberto, 217, 235, 240, 255, 273
Royo, Aristides, 35, 36, 37
Ruiz, Jaime, 193
Rumsfeld, Donald, 175

Sabonge, Rodolfo, 65, 115, 206, 222
Saint Malo, Isabel de, 131, 275, 276, 279, 294, 300, 304
Salas, Aníbal, 147, 172
Salazar, Jerry, 157
Samudio, David, 13, 41
Sánchez Borbón, Guillermo, 49
Sanchez, Nestor, 47
Sánchez, Onésimo, 65
Sanguinetti, Mario, 300
Santa María la Antigua University (USMA), 84
Santana, João, 275
School of the Americas, 13, 59
Schultz, George, 43, 104
Science Policy, 326
Security Agreements, 169
  Border Protection, 150
  Livestock, 150
  Maritime and Border, 149
  Plan Colombia, 193
  Salas-Becker Agreement, 147
SENACYT, 113, 215
Shah of Iran, 36
Silva, Luiz Inácio da, 185, 234
SINAPROC, 138, 193
Singapore, 44, 131, 138, 231, 319
Smithsonian Tropical Research Institute, 44, 78, 158, 326
Society, 23, 321
  Antipoverty Programs, 159, 190, 277, 302
Solidarity Party, 87, 168, 195
Solórzano, Fernando, 191
Somoza García, Anastasio, 144
Spadafora, Hugo, 46
Spadafora, Winston, 165
Stephenson, Barbara, 252
Stone, M. P. W., 91
Suez Canal, 10, 228
Summit of the Americas, *136*, 185, 279–81
Superintendence of Banks, 298
Supreme Court, 137, 143, 164, 171, 172, 175, 239, 307

Tack, Juan Antonio, 19
Tack-Kissinger Principles, 20
Taiwan, 163, 178, 216, 293, 323
Third Locks Project, 7, 68
Thurman, Maxwell, 52, 73, 77, 79
Tocumen International Airport, 140, 286, 290–93, 313, 319–320
Torres de Bianchini, Gioconda, 239
Torrijos, Hugo, 102
Torrijos, Martín, 125, 130, 166, 168, 172, *181*, 182

Torrijos, Martín (cont.)
Assessment, 198
Cabinet, 173, 194
Corruption, 178–79
Disabled Rights, 189
Fiscal Reform, 177–78
Social Security Reform, 179–80
Torrijos, Omar, 1, 2, 14, 17, 99
and Fidel Castro, 17
Funeral of, 31
in power, 15–16
Torrijos, Vivian, 189
Tourism, 109, 114, 153, 154, 284, 311, 312
Transparency International, 164, 262
Treaties
1903, 3
1936, 6
1947, 9
1955, 9
1960s, 13
1970s, 21, 28
1977, xiii, 1
Climate Change, 184
Permanent Neutrality, 40
Tribunal Electoral
1983 Reforms, 38
Tripartite Canal Alternatives, 45, 68, 94
Trump, Donald B., 282

US House of Representatives, 21
US Rate/Local Rate Rolls, 26
US Senate, 7, 21
Unexploded Ordinance, 92, 111, 138, 146, 201
United Fruit, 18
United Nations
Development Program, 84, 112, 155, 161, 183, 279, 302
High Commissioner for Refugees, 150
Human Development, 162, 260
Security Council, 19, 182, 323
World Heritage site, 155
United States
Agency for International Development, 164
Army Corps of Engineers, 116, 130, 218, 223, 226
Christmas Invasion, 53, 71
Coast Guard, 204
Mérida Plan for Counternarcotics, 243
Military Assistance, 175, 244
Military Bases, 3, 113, 137
Status of Forces Agreement, 21, 124
Multinational Counter-Narcotics Center, 123
Panama Review Committee, 57
Reconstruction Aid, 77, 80, 86
Southern Command, 39
Universidad Marítima Internacional de Panamá, 65
State Department, 6, 19, 40, 46, 50–52, 71, 77, 99, 124, 146

Vallarino, Alberto, 125, 195, 236, 253
Vallarino, Bolívar, 14
Vallarino, Carlos, 173
Vallarino, J. J., 93
Van Hoorde, René, 65
Varela, Juan Carlos, 130, 195, 236, 238, 252, 264, 273, 276, 280, 299, 306
Cabinet, 275
Infrastructure, 277, 283
Prosecution of Corruption, 277, 281
Varela, Ricardo, 65
Vasco Nùñez de Balboa. *See* Balboa
Vásquez, Numan, 65
Vásquez, Ricaurte, 173, 177, 219
Vatican, 163, 323
Vaughn, Jack, 12
Velasco Alvarado, Juan, 15
Vessey, John, 46

Wainio, Richard, 91, 96
Waked, Abdul, 34
Waked, Nidal, 301
War of a Thousand Days, xvi
Watershed Management Plan, 61
Watt, Linda, 167, 185
Weekes, Erick, 148
West Indians, 4, 65
West, Togo, 119, 121
Whitman, Merryl, 55
Woerner, Fred, 52, 79
Women Candidates in 2019, 308
Women's suffrage, 7
Wood, Joseph, 65, 91
World Bank, 46, 70
World Trade Organization, 99, 102, 143
World Youth Day, 325

Yates, Lawrence A., 96
Young, Ivonne, 166, 167